Normative Theory in International Relations

Normative theory in International Relations, as it is discussed at present in the framework of the cosmopolitan/communitarian debate, is at a standsill. Cosmopolitan and communitarian positions are generally assumed to be irreconcilable, with no means available for reaching conclusions on ethical questions in world politics. This book pursues three lines of inquiry. First, it aims to examine the nature and the extent of the impasse within this debate. Secondly, it re-evaluates whether the cosmopolitan/communitarian dichotomy offers a complete picture of the most pressing issues at stake within normative international relations theory. The book suggests that a more refined focus on epistemology and questions of foundationalism and antifoundationalism is necessary. Thirdly, it constructs an argument for a new normative approach to international ethics which draws from the tradition of American pragmatism and is attentive to the wider picture of concerns raised in the course of the book.

MOLLY COCHRAN is an Assistant Professor in the Sam Nunn School of International Affairs at the Georgia Institute of Technology. She previously taught at the University of Bristol. She is author of several journal articles, and winner of the 1997 thesis prize of the British International Studies Association.

D1569343

CAMBRIDGE STUDIES IN INTERNATIONAL RELATIONS: 68

Normative Theory in International Relations

CAMBRIDGE STUDIES IN INTERNATIONAL RELATIONS

68   *Molly Cochran*
      Normative theory in international relations
      A pragmatic approach

67   *Alexander Wendt*
      Social theory of international politics

66   *Thomas Risse, Stephen C. Ropp and Kathryn Sikkink (eds.)*
      The power of human rights
      International norms and domestic change

65   *Daniel W. Drezner*
      The sanctions paradox
      Economic statecraft and international relations

64   *Viva Ona Bartkus*
      The dynamic of secession

63   *John A. Vasquez*
      The power of power politics
      From classical realism to neotraditionalism

62   *Emanuel Adler and Michael Barnett (eds.)*
      Security communities

61   *Charles Jones*
      E. H. Carr and international relations
      A duty to lie

60   *Jeffrey W. Knopf*
      Domestic society and international cooperation
      The impact of protest on US arms control policy

59   *Nicholas Greenwood Onuf*
      The republican legacy in international thought

58   *Daniel S. Geller and J. David Singer*
      Nations at war
      A scientific study of international conflict

57   *Randall D. Germain*
      The international organization of credit
      States and global finance in the world economy

      Series list continues after index

Normative Theory in International Relations
A Pragmatic Approach

Molly Cochran

CAMBRIDGE
UNIVERSITY PRESS

PUBLISHED BY THE PRESS SYNDICATE OF THE UNIVERSITY OF CAMBRIDGE
The Pitt Building, Trumpington Street, Cambridge, CB2 1RP United Kingdom

CAMBRIDGE UNIVERSITY PRESS
The Edinburgh Building, Cambridge, CB2 2RU, UK
http://www.cup.cam.ac.uk
40 West 20th Street, New York, NY 10011–11, USA   http://www.cup.org
10 Stamford Road, Oakleigh, Melbourne 3166, Australia

First published 1999

Printed in the United Kingdom at the University Press, Cambridge

Typeset in 10/12pt Palatino   [CE]

A catalogue record for this book is available from the British Library

ISBN 0 521 63050 9 hardback
ISBN 0 521 63965 4 paperback

It is Virginia!
And for her Mom, Mimi and Pop

Contents

Acknowledgements   *page* xi
Abbreviations   xiv
Preface   xv

Introduction   1

Part I: Evaluating the impasse

1   Cosmopolitanism: Rawlsian approaches to international   21
    distributive justice

2   Communitarianism: Michael Walzer and international   52
    justice

3   Beyond the impasse? Hegelian method in the   78
    cosmopolitanism of Andrew Linklater and the
    communitarianism of Mervyn Frost

Part II: Confronting the impasse

4   Poststructuralist antifoundationalism, ethics, and   121
    normative IR theory

5   Neo-pragmatist antifoundationalism, ethics, and   144
    normative IR theory

Part III: International ethics as pragmatic critique

6   International ethics as pragmatic critique: a pragmatic   173
    synthesis of the work of John Dewey and Richard Rorty

7   Facilitating moral inclusion: feminism and pragmatic   212
    critique

8   From moral imagination to international public spheres: 246
    the political and institutional implications of pragmatic
    critique

    Conclusion   273

    References   281
    Index   292

Acknowledgements

This book evolved from a PhD thesis submitted to the University of London in 1996. In working towards and completing such a project, one accrues many debts of gratitude and I am no exception.

Chris Brown, Mervyn Frost and Mark Hoffman have been both good friends and mentors to me. When I was a Masters student at the University of Kent in 1990, it was Chris Brown who first introduced me to normative IR theory and to the idea that I did not have to choose between my research interests in political theory and international relations. Since 1992, when he entrusted me with his Normative IR theory course at the University of Natal, Mervyn Frost has been, along with Chris, a wonderful source of encouragement and enthusiasm for this material. Mark Hoffman was a splendid PhD supervisor in all respects, offering excellent guidance both academic and personal over the course of my thesis-writing adventure. In fact, it was Mark who initially suggested that I look further into Rorty's work. Chris, Mervyn and Mark were instrumental in helping me find my way as a graduate student and I am deeply grateful to them.

I have found myself especially fortunate in the institutions at which I have had the opportunity to study, going back to my undergraduate degree at Davidson College in North Carolina, to Trinity College, University of Dublin, to the University of Kent and on to the London School of Economics. There are many to whom I would like to offer my appreciation for thoughtful conversations and teaching which contributed to my thinking and studies along the way, Michael Banks, Stephen Chan, John Charvet, Michael Donelan, A. J. R. Groom, Cornelia Navari, Lou Ortmayer, Anne Phillips, Justin Rosenberg, Brian Shaw, and Peter Wilson. Fellow students at the LSE and those who participated in the Contemporary Research in International Political Theory BISA Workshop were engaging and helpful in their comments on my work. At the LSE, three research seminars, *Concepts and Methods, Modernity and International Relations*, and the *Seminar in International Political Theory*, were excellent fora for working out the ideas that form the basis of this book. I would also like to thank the LSE and the Overseas Research Students Awards Scheme for their generous financial assistance.

In turning the thesis manuscript into a book, I have many people to thank. First, it was Richard Little, who encouraged me to send the manuscript to the CUP/BISA series and I would like to thank him as well as others at the University of Bristol who participated in an International Politics Research Group, Terrell Carver, Ewan Harrison, and Richard Shapcott, and helped me think through necessary revisions. Also, I am especially grateful to Andrew Linklater and Anne Phillips, my thesis examiners, for their rigorous and constructive critique, which led me to reexamine and rethink several points. As they say, the mistakes are all mine, but I am confident that this is a better book for their advice, as well as that of the anonymous referees. Finally, I would like to thank Steve Smith, John Haslam and the Editorial Board of the CUP/BISA Series for their interest in this work and Con Coroncos at CUP for his assistance at the copy-editing stage.

Chapter 4, since revised, was published under the title 'Postmodernism, Ethics and International Political Theory' in *The Review of International Studies* 21:3 (1995), pp. 237–250. An earlier version of chapter 5 was published under the title, 'The Liberal Ironist, Ethics and International Relations Theory', in *Millennium: Journal of International Studies* 25:1 (1996).

I share with a good friend an interest in reading the acknowledgments at the start of books, because as he once said, it says as much about an author as his or her own work. Now, as I am at last writing my own, I realize that I can give an indication of my training and the people who have influenced me greatly, but it is hard to express the true extent of my gratitude towards those named above and my feelings for the people I have left to thank, those who are especially close to me, my future husband, my parents and sister. Eddie Keene is someone who has had an immeasurable impact on both my heart and my work and I look forward to that all we have ahead of us, together. My parents, Dahl and Jo Cochran and my sister Kacey Weir have given me a lifetime of love and encouragement that well exceeds what any daughter or sister might hope to have.

Abbreviations

TNT	M. Frost, *Towards a Normative Theory of International Relations*
EIR	M. Frost, *Ethics and International Relations*
MC	A. Linklater, *Men and Citizens*
TPC	A. Linklater, *The Transformation of Political Community*
'DP'	J. Rawls, 'The Domain of the Political and Overlapping Consensus'
'KC'	J. Rawls, 'Kantian Constructivism in Moral Theory'
'OC'	J. Rawls, 'The Idea of an Overlapping Consensus'
CIS	R. Rorty, *Contingency, Irony and Solidarity*
'HRS'	R. Rorty, 'Human Rights, Rationality and Sentimentality'
JUW	M. Walzer *Just and Unjust Wars*
SJ	M. Walzer *Spheres of Justice*
TT	M. Walzer *Thick and Thin: Moral Argument at Home and Abroad*

Preface

Normative theory in International Relations (IR), as it is discussed at present in the framework of the cosmopolitan/communitarian debate, is at a standstill. Cosmopolitan and communitarian positions are generally assumed to be irreconcilable, with no means available for reaching conclusions. This book pursues three lines of inquiry in relation to this debate. First, it aims to examine the nature and extent of the impasse within the cosmopolitan/communitarian debate. Secondly, it re-evaluates whether the cosmopolitan/communitarian dichotomy offers a complete picture of the most pressing issues at stake within normative IR theory. The book suggests that a shift in focus onto epistemology and questions of foundationalism and anti-foundationalism is necessary. Thirdly, it constructs an argument for a new normative approach to international ethics which draws from the tradition of American pragmatism and is attentive to the wider concerns raised by the book's assessment of the cosmopolitan/communitarian debate. The three parts of the book take each of these lines of inquiry in turn.

In order to illuminate the nature of the debate between cosmopolitans and communitarians and the extent of its impasse, the Introduction proposes a formulation of three central issues as an analytical tool. These issues are: (1) a concept of the person; (2) the moral relevance of states; and (3) the universal versus the particular. The extent of the impasse is gauged by the degree to which accommodations can be reached on any or all of these three issues. Also, an 'anchor analogy' is drawn in the Introduction that is used throughout the book to facilitate discussion of epistemological issues in normative IR theory. This analogy illustrates the foundational claims implicit or explicit in the work of the writers discussed.

Part I of the book critically evaluates the work of authors who contribute to the cosmopolitan/communitarian debate. It traces chronological developments in the positions of the authors discussed as they respond to their critics, and notes that accommodations *are* evident. However, a structural opposition remains. This opposition rests largely in the third issue of the debate, but the opposition, I will suggest, is not what it may at first glance seem. The universal versus the particular is a tension about the scope with which moral claims can be made in international practice, yet several of these authors are interested in bridging the universal versus the particular gap, albeit, unsuccessfully. I will argue that this is because the nature of the impasse does not concern the *scope* of moral claims on the behalf of individuals or states, but *how* in fact they are made. It involves how claims to ethical judgement in IR are grounded or justified: that is, how we choose whether individuals or states should be the subject of justice. My contention is that the cosmopolitan/communitarian debate is principally concerned with ontological questions and leaves untheorized the rival foundational assumptions upon which these ontologies stand. This analysis of the reasons for the impasse in the cosmopolitan/communitarian debate indicates that epistemology needs to be brought to the foreground of concern within normative IR theory.

Would normative IR theory benefit by temporarily shifting the axis of inquiry away from ontological questions regarding cosmopolitan versus communitarian claims, to epistemological questions which center upon the issue of foundationalism versus antifoundationalism? Part II examines antifoundationalist approaches and asks what they might have to offer for ethical theorizing in IR. Part II demonstrates that such approaches open out the parameters of normative IR theory, enabling a better consideration of the interplay within and between the issues of the cosmopolitan/communitarian debate than that which is available to the writers participant in that debate due to their particular foundationalist tendencies. However, it is also clear that a shift in focus onto epistemology cannot and does not abandon ontological questions. In fact, it is evident from the approaches discussed in part II that a turn away from foundationalism actually shifts the burden of an ethics back onto ontology, since it requires an account of the necessities of relationships between individuals and communities in order to offer a criterion for ethical judgement.

So have we simply come full circle? I will suggest that we have not.

The cosmopolitan/communitarian debate has been a useful framework for drawing our attention to a central issue for ethical theory in IR and outlining its contours: how we determine our ontological priorities when moral problems arise in the relations between individuals and states. However, the communitarian/cosmopolitan debate has served its purpose and normative theory must now move on from this narrow oppositional framing, a framing which no longer (if it ever did) accurately represents the movement in the authors' own positions within the debate. Nor, however, can we slip into the same dichotomous thinking with regard to epistemology in focusing upon a foundational/antifoundational divide. New normative approaches must examine how the axes of ontology and epistemology intersect, keeping in mind a notion of a *range* and not an opposition: there is a range of ontological positions on the individual and the community, and of epistemological positions on foundational claims and their strength or degree.

Part III develops an approach to normative IR theory attentive to the interconnection of epistemological and ontological questions. It is an approach to international ethics derived from American pragmatism, which is designed to suggest a promising way of interrogating the epistemological quiet of cosmopolitan and communitarian approaches. It also has something constructive to propose, by offering an understanding of international ethics as pragmatic critique which works towards as thorough-going an antifoundationalism as is possible, yet grapples with the central ontological question of the relationship of the individual to community in international ethics. The result is a new normative approach that is politically engaged, since it professes a concern for expanding moral inclusion and social reconstruction. The capacity of pragmatic critique to facilitate moral inclusion and social reconstruction is illustrated through an engagement with feminist theory and the concept of international 'public spheres' in the concluding chapters. It is an approach that is aware of the ranges in which fall ontological positions on the individual and the community and epistemological positions regarding foundational claims and their strength or degree.

Chapter outline

The chapters in part I of the book fill out the parameters of the cosmopolitan/communitarian debate by examining the three issues of the debate I have identified, and exploring possibilities for accommodation on these issues with respect to cosmopolitan and communitarian writers in normative IR theory. Chapter 1 looks at two cosmopolitan writers, Charles Beitz and Thomas Pogge, each of whom uses a Rawlsian framework in his effort to establish a theory of international distributive justice. Neither Beitz nor Pogge is interested in seeking possible reconciliations with a communitarian position on an idea of international justice. For this reason, I turn to an extended analysis of the relationship of their work to Rawls, who in his later writings has accommodated objections raised by his communitarian critics. Chapter 2 examines a communitarian approach, represented by the work of Michael Walzer. Walzer is clearly frustrated by a similar condition of stasis in the liberal/communitarian debate, and (unlike Beitz and Pogge) seeks reconciliations which overlap with concerns in the cosmopolitan/communitarian debate. Chapter 3 takes a different tack and examines two writers, a cosmopolitan (Andrew Linklater) and a communitarian (Mervyn Frost), in order to compare and contrast their concerted efforts to reconcile the core tension of the debate. Linklater and Frost differ from other writers in part I because their projects *start* from the identification of a problem in the ethical relationship between individuals and states in international practice, and they work to resolve this tension. None the less, part I concludes that there is indeed a significant structural opposition that cannot be bridged, or at least will not be bridged, as long as these writers proceed as if the ethics which results from their weak foundationalist claims has a non-contingent, universal and fixed application.

The chapters in part II of the book inquire into whether antifoundationalism can offer an alternative approach to ethical theory in IR, unencumbered by the dichotomous thinking and impasse of the present normative framework. Here, I discuss two lines of antifoundationalist thinking in political and normative IR theory. The first flows out of the discourse of French poststructuralism and the second out of the tradition of American pragmatism. Chapter 4 examines the work of poststructuralist writers in IR theory and focuses upon the writings of Richard Ashley, R. B. J. Walker, William Connolly, Jim George, and David Campbell. Chapter 5 looks at the neo-pragmatism of Richard Rorty. I continue to use the formulation of the three issues of the debate as an analytical tool to evaluate the relation of their work to the cosmopolitan/communitarian debate and to assess any implications of their work for confronting its epistemological impasse. While I conclude that these approaches open up the parameters of normative theorizing in IR and help us confront the epistemological nature of the cosmopolitan/communitarian impasse, they none the less, in their will to offer an ethics, fail to relinquish recourse to weak foundations or universals which are linked to ontological priorities in justifying their ethical claims. Thus, parts I and II suggest that we cannot entirely divest ourselves of foundationalist or universalist thinking in the effort to offer principles of ethical judgement in international practice. I conclude that if it is the case that these are unavoidable aspects of normative theorizing and ethical critique, then normative IR theory must find a way to proceed that is aware of the weak foundations and universals invoked in its ethical criteria, such that we might work to avoid the normative impasses and possibilities for oppression and moral exclusion which can result from foundationalist and universalizing tendencies.

Finally, the chapters in part III aim to offer a response to the dilemma of normative theorizing identified through the analysis of the ethics that results from both foundationalist and antifoundationalist approaches: that is, how to employ weak foundations and universals in a way that is not absolutizing, yet can still effectively offer an international ethics that would provide for wider moral inclusion and social reconstruction. Chapter 6 develops a notion of international ethics as pragmatic critique, a synthesis of the pragmatism of John Dewey and Richard Rorty, that works to be as thoroughly antifoundationalist as is possible, yet has a will to universalization that seeks the growth of human capacities and the expansion of 'we' feeling. These ambitions are facilitated through its notion of 'fallibilism', which takes the absolutizing edge off its ethical claims, and through its use of 'moral imagination' to project alternatives to problematic ethical/political situations. Chapter 7 introduces a case study that aims to demonstrate how this notion of international ethics as pragmatic critique is adequately political, critical and imaginative to provide for the moral inclusion of feminist ethical/political concerns in IR. Chapter 8 addresses a difficulty in problematizing the authority of the 'we' of community which is raised in pragmatic critique's engagement with feminist concerns in the previous chapter. Here, I provide more detail on the workings of moral imagination and its capacity to think beyond the power of the 'we' and offer both discursive and institutional possibilities in the notion of 'public spheres' for expanding moral inclusion in international practice.

Pragmatic critique cannot supply normative IR theory with lasting solutions to its ethical dilemmas. However, it provides a method and a *weak* ontological vision that works with sympathy and persistence to facilitate better ways to cope with and make meaningful the worlds we live in and the moral situations we face.

Introduction

All theory in International Relations (IR) is normative theory. By this I mean that even those engaged in positivist approaches, who aim to study world politics in a manner that resembles as closely as possible the methods of natural science, cannot avoid normative assumptions in the selection of what data is important, in interpreting that data, and in articulating why such research is significant. There was a time when such a statement would have been highly controversial. For some approaches within IR it is still controversial today. However, powerful criticisms of the positivist bias towards explanation, objectivity and the fact/value separation, have been unleashed in IR that take the radical edge off of this opening statement.[1] I begin in this way to make the point that, while all theorizing in IR has normative concerns that can be brought to the surface for critical examination, not all theory in IR is self-consciously interested in such an exercise, nor finds it to be an important aspect of theorizing in the discipline.

Therefore, for the purposes of this book, we must have available some criteria for determining what defines normative IR theory as a field. For example, a writer such as Hans Morganthau (1954) could be regarded as a normative theorist, since he holds the view that the Stateman has moral responsibilities to his citizens to clarify and pursue the national interest, and responsibilities to other states, even when in pursuit of the national interest, to demonstrate restraint with regard to the infliction of death and suffering in particular

---

[1] A good account of this critique is Hollis and Smith (1991). Two earlier critiques of the positivist bias in IR which also make a call for a more central place in the discipline for normative theory are Frost (1986) and Hoffman (1985). Another, and more recent, argument that IR theory must move away from positivism can be found in Neufeld (1995).

circumstances.[2] However, the criteria that define my understanding of
normative IR theory would not place Morganthau among the group of
writers who will be the focus of concern in this book. Although it is
not the *only* understanding from which one might work, my understanding of normative IR theory takes as its subject matter the criteria
of ethical judgement in world politics and seeks shared principles for
extended moral inclusion and social reconstruction in international
practice. That is, it aims to move beyond the understanding of IR as a
modus vivendi by illustrating reasons for obligation owed in international practice that cannot be attributed to self-interest alone. Thus,
because Morganthau's view of politics and statecraft sees no room for
the possibility of moving beyond such a condition (since human
nature is marred by egoism and the pursuit of self-interest), his work
is not addressed at length here. Nor do I pay particular attention to
authors within the international society tradition. While international
society theorists may have an interest in the mutual respect of
particular moral and cultural traditions within international practice,
and while some of them may regard solidarism as being normatively
desirable, they are generally sceptical of the idea that international
society could in fact be constituted by anything more than the
responsibilities assumed within an ethics of coexistence position.[3] I do
not deny that the ideas of mutual respect and tolerance, which are at
the base of an ethics of coexistence, are indeed constitutive of a
normative position and are evidence of certain obligations among
persons. Rather, it is simply the case that this is not a normative
position that interests me in this book, since I want to pursue
arguments which go beyond establishing responsibilities that might
accrue from our shared interest in self-preservation and the protection
of a heterogeneous society of states. Therefore, I focus upon forms of
normative IR theory which work to cast wider nets of moral obligation

---

[2] See Murray (1996) for a discussion of Morganthau as a moral theorist.
[3] On the meaning of an ethics of coexistence position, see Nardin (1983). On the
meaning of solidarism see Bull (1966). Although there are clear strands in the work of
Bull (1977) and Vincent (1986) that could be read as supporting the view that we could
move beyond the pluralist position of an ethics of coexistence in international society,
it was not the central aim of their projects to argue convincingly for the need for or the
realization of such a possibility. However, Linklater (1998), who follows many of the
inclinations of the international society tradition and attempts a praxeological analysis
of movement towards and beyond the solidarist elements of the Grotianism in this
tradition is a central figure under consideration here.

among persons, obligations beyond an ethics of coexistence, to generate more just interpersonal and intersocietal relations.

As an enterprise, the normative IR theory in which I am interested begins by asking questions about which relationships between individuals and states can be regarded as legitimate, and whether the boundaries or parameters in which those relationships are presently defined are ethically justifiable. However, it does not stop there, because its inquiry is guided by the aim of improving intersocietal relations by encouraging better forms of responsibility among persons. Of course, this aim assumes the possibility of social learning and agent-directed change within international practice. As Andrew Linklater writes, normative IR theory would not be possible unless one was willing to assert that international agents have 'the capacity to overcome the constraints which neo-realism imputes to anarchy' (1998: 19). Linklater, like others discussed in this book, works to build normative arguments from this presupposition.

In particular, Linklater's recent book, *The Transformation of Political Community* (*TPC*), serves as an important critical foil for the position put forward here. The normative projects in which I am interested and the pragmatist position that I will advance hold that improved forms of responsibility between persons require the expansion of moral inclusion, such that we more meaningfully recognize both the universal and particular attachments of individuals while pursuing the material requirements necessary to their inclusion through forms of social reconstruction. This is very similar to the aim of a 'triple transformation' that Linklater advocates in *TPC*: 'to secure greater respect for cultural differences, stronger commitments to the reduction of material inequalities and significant advances in universality' such that we do not attach more moral significance than is justified to difference with those not like 'us' (1998: 2–3).

However, where Linklater finds many different kinds of normative argument – cosmopolitan, communitarian, feminist, and postmodernist – to be more or less agreed on these priorities, I believe that there are significant epistemological differences between these positions, with important ethical/political consequences, that obstruct the links or overlap that may indeed exist between them. This is particularly strongly felt with regard to their different ontological conceptions of the human need for freedom. Consequently, Linklater does not attach the same importance that I do to tracing the nature and extent of disagreements within normative IR theory. This book will examine the debate at the centre of normative theorizing in IR today: the cosmopolitan/communitarian debate. It will illuminate the epistemological difficulties at its centre and put forward an idea of international ethics as pragmatic critique that works to avoid such pitfalls by eschewing the particular kind of foundationalist argument used by Linklater and others participant in this debate. In several places throughout the book, Linklater's project in *TPC* will be used to demonstrate the many number of ways in which we are in agreement about how normative theory must proceed, and it will also re-emerge to point out places where my approach departs from his epistemologically and politically, helping me to define the particular contribution I hope pragmatic critique might make to normative IR theory.

The chapter begins by offering an account of the case that can be made for normative theory in the discipline and what this kind of theorizing entails. This sets the stage for an introduction to the cosmopolitan/communitarian debate. I will identify the debate's core tension and indicate three central issues which follow from this tension. I will also point to a parallel debate between liberals and communitarians in political theory, illustrating points of comparison and contrast across the two debates. Finally, I will sketch the argument to follow in the book as a whole, which evaluates the impasse attributed to the cosmopolitan/communitarian debate and assesses whether this framework usefully represents the most pressing issues we face in normative IR theory.

The case for normative IR theory

The recognition of normative theory as a field within IR is quite a recent phenomenon. I want to examine the case made for normative theory in IR by comparing and contrasting the work of two writers who were central in carving out a role for this kind of theorizing in IR: Mervyn Frost and Linklater. Both writers construct what they regard as a much-needed bridge that links the tradition of normative theorizing in political theory with international theory, in order to think about the relationships of freedom and obligation between individuals and states.

For Frost, IR is infused with normative questions. He writes that acting in the world requires that we think about what we want to achieve and what are legitimate means for reaching those ends. Thus, he finds the lack of normative theorizing in IR puzzling and wants to identify the reasons why it is avoided in the discipline. There are two reasons for its avoidance, according to Frost: first, there is a bias toward objective explanation which stresses the importance of seeking factual knowledge; and secondly, there is a sceptical position which finds moral argument irrelevant against interest and power in the world (1996: 12–13). Frost proceeds to undermine the positivist bias by pointing to the ways in which fact and value cannot be distinguished in the social sciences, how we become entangled in value questions even in deciding which phenomena to study, and how we use normative considerations to come to understandings about those phenomena. Frost offers several arguments against moral scepticism, the strongest of which is that amoralism represents an impossible position as long as people and states make claims for themselves. Frost makes a case for normative theory being central to the discipline, and thereby links one of the central tasks of political philosophy, the critical evaluation of beliefs and values, to IR.[4]

Linklater works to build the same bridge, only he begins construction from the opposite bank. Where Frost begins by opening the study of IR up to a traditional object of political philosophy, Linklater begins by opening political philosophy up to what he sees as a central concern within IR: the normative problem of the state. Political philosophy has traditionally been concerned with offering an account of the good life within domestic polities, with no attention given to the moral relevance of that polity's main institution, the state. Linklater aims to build an international political theory that draws attention to two issues neglected within political philosophy: first, whether humanity's division into sovereign states is indeed legitimate; and secondly, whether obligations to states are prior to obligations to humanity (1990b: 62).

Admittedly, one might question whether the state as a normative problem has indeed been a central concern of IR. For Linklater, the case for international political theory against such a challenge[5] is not to be made in current theories (or the apparent reality) of interdependence, but by reconstructing traditional issues in the history of international thought. Linklater works to remind the contemporary IR consciousness of a central concern in the history of international theory: the moral relationship between men and citizens. Linklater

---

[4] For an examination of the tasks of political philosophy see Raphael (1970).
[5] For an example of such a challenge, see Linklater (1990b: 4–5, 8–11) where he takes issue with Wight's (1966) often-quoted arguments in 'Why is There No International Theory?'

concentrates on this particular concern in the history of international theory because, for him, the ultimate case for international political theory is found in the dichotomy that arises continually in thinking about IR: 'a dichotomy between the sense of obligation to the state and a belief in obligations to humanity' (1990b: 15). Linklater imbues international political theory with a specific project: to address this tension by seeking out what connects insiders and outsiders in order to provide a 'more expansive account of moral and political experience which the existence of universalist categories requires' (Linklater 1990b: 13).

At this stage, we need to draw some contrasts with Frost's idea of normative theory, since Frost does not imbue normative theory with an explicit project as such. Frost stipulates nothing more for normative theory than the task of evaluating the ends and legitimate means participants in international practice have for pursuing what they deem valuable. Thus, he begins by examining the language we use to discuss normative issues. For Frost, most normative issues are discussed within the language of states, citizens, and the community of states (1996: 79). Since this is the discourse we use, it must be taken into account when examining international practice. Thus, Frost locates his idea of normative theory within what he calls the 'modern state domain' of discourse (1996: 79). For this reason, Frost would object to international political theory as envisioned by Linklater, because the latter looks past established, state-based normative structures and language towards an abstract, rational, moral community of mankind.[6]

The core tension of the cosmopolitan/communitarian debate is reflected in the case these writers make for international political theory and its task: whether individuals or states should be the subject of justice. To put it another way, this tension concerns the focal point of ethical consideration and the subject for whom or which ethical criteria are to be evaluated. Both writers share a commitment to extending human freedoms and moral obligations among persons in international practice, but they disagree about the social institutions deemed necessary to that goal. Although Frost does not assign normative theory with a project as such, his simple point that most

[6] I draw this inference from Frost's response to possible objections to his argument regarding a modern state domain of discourse from the natural law/community of mankind approach or any other argument from a wider moral point of view. See Frost (1996: 84–8).

6

normative assertions in IR implicate the state, and that we must therefore begin with the state, suggests a normative commitment. He points us to the tools we have available, the settled norms of the modern state domain, and argues that what we have provides us with a moral home in which we can work. Frost believes that it provides us with a moral home because he has a commitment to the idea of an ethical state where the claims of individuals and states can be reconciled and freedom can be realized. Thus, state practice is not problematic for him, and a normative theory grounded in the modern state domain is wholly acceptable. On the other hand, Linklater argues that state practice is a problem; it cannot be a moral home for us all. It is an incomplete, not fully rational political practice as long as the universalist impulse towards a community of humankind exists. Thus, international political theory for Linklater must pursue the ways in which the state form is being challenged on an empirical and philosophical level; it cannot rest upon a state-centric domain of practice as Frost would have it.

Thus, either explicitly (Linklater) or implicitly (Frost), each imbues normative theory with the goal of extending moral commitments and enhancing human freedoms through wider moral inclusion. However, their different ideas as to the social institutions required in order to reach this goal lead them to set different tasks for international political theory, and ultimately, send them along different methodological paths, which will be discussed in chapter 3. Frost finds that human freedoms are best developed within states and the state system. This is presently understood in the central debate of normative IR theory as a communitarian approach. Linklater finds that these human freedoms can only be fully actualized within post-sovereign institutions. His is a 'community of mankind' approach, which is regarded as cosmopolitan. None the less, both share the notion that the critical evaluation of norms is central to normative IR theory, and that the problem for normative inquiry is to outline the proper nature of ethical relationships in IR between individuals, of individuals to states, of states to individuals, and of states to other states.

The cosmopolitan/communitarian debate in normative IR theory

This core tension identified above is the tension which fuels the cosmopolitan/communitarian debate, as described by Chris Brown

(1992) and Janna Thompson (1992). Brown and Thompson provide a frame of reference for categorizing the ways in which writers like Frost and Linklater characterize the project of normative theorizing in IR. This framework has taken hold, with the idea of a cosmopolitan/communitarian debate having become very influential among students of normative IR theory. It is one of the central aims of this book to interrogate the usefulness of the framework of the cosmopolitan/communitarian debate, asking whether the cosmopolitan/communitarian dichotomy offers a complete picture of the most pressing issues at stake within normative IR theory.

To begin, let us examine how these two positions are characterized. As for the cosmopolitan position, Brown writes that 'what is crucial to a cosmopolitan attitude is the refusal to regard existing political structures as the source of ultimate value' (1992: 24). Thompson defines cosmopolitanism as 'the idea that a social order must be justified in terms of how it affects the entitlements of individuals or their general welfare . . . independently of commitment to any particular social relations' (1992: 21). Both writers regard cosmopolitanism to be universalist and individualist in orientation. Communitarianism, on the other hand, is particularist and oriented to shared community life: 'the root notion of communitarian thought is that value stems from the community, that the individual finds meaning in life by virtue of his or her membership of a political community' (Brown 1992: 55). Similarly, Thompson writes that communitarianism is 'a moral standpoint which is tied to a local discourse, a particular community or historical tradition' and justice is respect for the values communities hold (1992: 19, 22).

Starting from the definitional base that Brown and Thompson provide, I want to continue in the vein of bridge-building between political theory and normative IR theory by drawing out connections between this debate and the debate in political theory between liberals and communitarians. Both Brown and Thompson see the cosmopolitan and communitarian positions as deriving from traditions of political thought that follow from Kant and Hegel, respectively. It is also the case that the contemporary debate between liberals and communitarians is not necessarily new, since the communitarian critique is focused upon a deontological liberalism that resonates with Kant (Rawls 1971 & 1980), and the communitarian critique itself rings of Hegel's critique of Kant's liberal individualism, as well as Marx's critique of liberalism (see Walzer 1990a: 8). This debate in political theory has been a source for how the framework of the cosmopolitan/communitarian debate has been labelled and defined.

A decade prior to the publication of Brown's and Thompson's books, the communitarian critique of liberalism was building steam.[7] This critique was largely in response to what is regarded as *the* statement of the contemporary liberal position, John Rawls's *A Theory of Justice*. Stephen Mulhall and Adam Swift write that, in a preliminary way, one might characterize the liberal position as constituted by 'a commitment to a vague and general value such as the freedom or autonomy of the individual, and to relate this to the substantive political concern that individuals should have freedom of conscience, of expression and of association' (1992: viii). Similarly, of communitarianism, they write that it 'questions the liberal understanding of the relation between the individual and her society or community, and argues that the emphasis on individual freedom and rights that follows from that understanding is misplaced' (Mulhall and Swift 1992: viii).

These preliminary statements are not dissimilar to those Brown and Thompson give, as we saw above. Cosmopolitans, like liberals, value individual autonomy, and this value is prior to any value placed on the associations that compartmentalize humanity. Communitarians in both political and normative IR theory challenge the liberal/cosmopolitan emphasis on individual autonomy for closing off consideration of the value individuals find in communal practices and traditions. However, as Mulhall and Swift write, these preliminary statements of the constitutive elements of the positions are just that, and more needs to be written to develop the complexity of these positions and different authors' relationship to the debate. In the chapters that follow, I intend to provide the kind of extended analysis of the debate in normative IR theory that Mulhall and Swift do for the debate in political theory. Thus, another central aim of this book is to elucidate the nature of the cosmopolitan and communitarian positions by examining the relationships of various authors to these positions and the extent of the impasse between them. However, we will find that these authors are moving targets. That is, we will discover that their positions shift over time as they respond to critics and that often they are difficult to pin down unambiguously as either cosmopolitans or communitarians. One must see these positions as caricatures with

---

[7] The core communitarian works are: Sandel (1982); MacIntyre (1981) and (1988); Walzer (1981), (1983b), and (1984); and Taylor (1985b) and (1990).

which certain writers have a better or worse fit. In order to chart their movement, the extent to which they match one of these caricatures and to facilitate my aim of examining the nature of the debate, in part I of the book I will discuss three issues which follow from the core tension identified above: (1) a concept of the person; (2) the moral relevance of states; and (3) the universal versus the particular.

Given the close relationship between the two debates in political and normative IR theory, I have adapted these three issues from a formulation used by several political theorists in analysing the liberal/communitarian debate (Caney 1992; Bell 1993; Neal and Paris 1990). For example, in order to clarify the issues which divide liberals and communitarians, Simon Caney looks at three aspects of communitarianism: (1) a claim about the nature of persons, (2) a claim about the value of community, and (3) a claim about the status of political principles (Caney 1992: 273–4). The first issue, concerning the nature of persons, is one in which both debates have drawn very similar lines between liberal or cosmopolitan and communitarian understandings of the person. However, it is important to note features which differentiate the two debates, warranting some modification of this political theory framework.

First, the debate in normative IR theory is distinguished by its concern with the question of the moral relevance of states. Respect for state sovereignty is a principal norm of international practice, and one that has only recently begun to be critically interrogated in the study of IR. This is a task of normative IR theory: to inquire into the value invested in this norm and to determine whether it is justifiable. Such a project involves examining the extent of its reach, and considering whether there are circumstances in which it might be contravened. Political theory, for the most part, is not interested in the question of the moral relevance of the state form, and often takes this institution for granted as the forum in which ideas of the good and the good polity are to be worked out. Thus, in the formulation of the three issues of the debate in normative IR theory that I offer, I replace the question of the value of community in the liberal/communitarian debate with the question of the moral relevance of states.

The second distinguishing feature of the IR debate concerns a difference between communitarians in political theory and normative IR theory. This difference has implications for deciding upon the third issue of the debate and why I think it important to identify the epistemological tension of the debate in normative IR as a contest not only of the status of universal versus particular ethical/political claims but also of the possibilities for the reconciliation of such claims. As Caney points out, communitarians in political theory find that moral argument can only be justified by recourse to the shared value practices of community. Thus, they attach status to political principles which are particular. While communitarians in normative IR theory share this predilection, their attachment to the particular is not that straightforward, since they also seek grounds for shared universal principles – as cosmopolitans do – on which moral inclusion in IR can be extended. However, due to their epistemological leanings towards the particular, there are obstacles of monumental proportion in the way. None the less, the will to universalisation is evident, as will be demonstrated in the book. This motivation among communitarians in normative IR theory to find some principle(s) on which we can transcend the particularism of shared goods and justify wider obligations beyond the confines of community is perhaps motivated by an orientation to the international, and the ambition to find something more stable than self-interest upon which to base more peaceful and just world politics. Similarly, we will find that there are cosmopolitans in normative IR theory who are keen to demonstrate that their universalism is sensitive to and can accommodate particularist loyalties. This serves as a preliminary indication of the complexity we will encounter in talking about dichotomies and oppositions between cosmopolitans and communitarians.

Having discussed these differences, I will now introduce what I understand to be at issue in the three aspects of the debate in normative IR theory. Regarding the first aspect, a concept of the person, this concerns the nature of personhood and how the individual is constituted. Cosmopolitans, like liberals, attribute to the individual a capacity to choose one's life, unencumbered by social attachments. The person is born with this capacity which, as cosmopolitans stress, constitutes a right *qua* humankind that is essential to the moral development of individuals; that is, their moral personality. The communitarian takes issue with the cosmopolitan's pre-social concept of the person. Instead, the person is constituted by the social matrix of which one is a member. The moral ends chosen by individuals under a cosmopolitan understanding are empty, since they are not grounded in the shared meanings and commitments of community membership. Thus, the development of moral personality hinges upon the expression and pursuit of goods within a community.

The question of the moral standing of states concerns whether states and the present state system promote or impede the individual's personal development. A stance on this issue follows from the ontological assumptions contained within a concept of the person, because with such a concept comes a notion of the social arrangements required by that understanding. For the political theorist, what would follow is a consideration of how the domestic polity is to be arranged; whereas, an IR theorist is led to ask what intersocietal arrangements are required for this concept of the person. To the cosmopolitan, who regards the person as morally free to choose one's social attachments, the autonomy of states has no normative relevance. For the communitarian, it is in the sovereign state that ethical duties are made possible, where the individual may achieve freedom and self-realization in one's identification with a social totality. Thus, the sovereign state is morally relevant because it is necessary to the development of the individual as a free person.

The universalism versus particularism tension concerns whether there is a standard by which ethical judgements can be made across plural conceptions of the good: cosmopolitans seek a standpoint for judging ends offered by morally equal individuals; whereas, communitarians focus on the ends of morally equal communities, questioning whether those ends can be evaluated by the same measure. Thus, the epistemological question of grounds or foundations for ethical critique in IR is raised. To mark again the point of difference between the debates in political theory and IR theory here, the political theorist interested in this issue would limit such a standpoint to judging the plural ends chosen by morally equal individuals within a domestic arrangement and whether they can hold universally or particularly therein. Whereas, in IR, this quite obviously has a global dimension, even for communitarians. Since the cosmopolitan understands each individual to be capable of forming a conception of the good, establishing such a foundation is a problem *within* and *between* communities because there are no rational means for choosing among the ends of morally equal individuals when they come into political conflict. Thus, the cosmopolitan attempts a solution through the construction of a detached standpoint from which we can transcend the particularism of plural goods. This method clears the way for the universal claims to the entitlements of humankind which cosmopolitans are wont to make. For the communitarian, values, ends, and goods fostered in the state constitute tradition. Social tradition within the state is the framework which founds and enables ethical discourse. Consequently, grounds for ethical critique are not at issue *within* communities, but it is a problem *between* them as the world cannot be conceived as a single community whose tradition shapes or constitutes the individual. This raises, for the communitarian, the problem of how a standpoint for judging among states' plural conceptions of the good can be offered.

It is important to develop such a formulation for clarifying points of division within the cosmopolitan/communitarian debate, in order to inquire into the condition of stasis presently attributed to the debate by those who contributed to its articulation: Brown and Thompson (Brown 1992: 75, 239; Thompson 1992: 188).[8] The positions taken in the debate are seen to be irreconcilable, with no available means for reaching conclusions on an ethical theory of IR. Brown and Thompson suggest two possible responses to this impasse. On the one hand, such an impasse might be seen as a cause for concern, since without resolution, without some ground for deciding upon criteria, how can normative judgements or critique of intersocietal relations be offered? Thus, some form of reconciliation or suggestion for how the debate is misconceived must be identified in order to make progress in suggesting alternatives for a more just world political order. Thompson attempts reconciliation *via* her idea of a 'society of inter-locking communities' (Thompson 1992: 168). On the other hand, another might suggest, as indeed Brown does, that there is little we can do, since there is no reasonable way to choose between what is in effect a choice between '"gut" feelings' (Brown 1992: 75). However, the fact that there is no means for coming to conclusive decisions regarding the oppositions within the debate is not cause for despair according to Brown. He writes that the idea that we must reach conclusions is a mistaken, 'scientistic notion'. Instead we may be content with 'good conversation' that is resumed as and when required (Brown 1992: 239). Must we be able to reach conclusions in order to offer intersocietal critique? Can we be content with good conversation? This book evaluates the nature and extent of the impasse attributed to the debate by examining possibilities for

---

[8] It is interesting to note that this represents another point of comparison between the debates in political and normative IR theory. The dichotomies within the liberal/ communitarian debate are also presented as if they are unbridgeable, although challenges to this have emerged. For example, see Caney (1992) and Mulhall and Swift (1992).

accommodations on any or all of the three issues of the debate I have identified.

A sketch of the argument

It is the argument of this book that there is indeed a substantive impasse in the cosmopolitan/communitarian debate. While Linklater and I agree on what some may regard as a controversial statement, that communitarians as well as cosmopolitans are interested in the extension of moral inclusion in world politics (1998: 60), we disagree as to whether a significant gap between cosmopolitan and communitarian positions remains which is worthy of acknowledgement. In *TPC*, Linklater offers the notion of a 'thin cosmopolitanism' from which the distance between a communitarian position may not be all that great, since it 'simply argues that existing political communities ought to increase the impact which duties to the rest of humanity have on decision making processes' (1998: 54–5). I agree that there is a shared concern for wider moral commitments, which is my reason for concentrating on cosmopolitan and communitarian positions as forms of normative argument. However, in contrast to Linklater, I see a reason behind the distinction between these positions. Despite possible accommodations being evident, particularly on the first two issues of the debate, there remains a structural opposition regarding the correct or proper foundation for justifying ethical claims in international practice; that is, whether individuals or states should be the subject of justice and moral consideration in normative IR theory. I contend that what appears to be the most intractable issue of the debate, the epistemological tension of the universal (claims for humanity) versus the particular (claims for states on the behalf of their citizens), gives way to a more important underlying question about *how* to ground the ontological positions at work in cosmopolitan and communitarian argument. What is at stake in the impasse of the debate is not the universal or particular *scope* of moral claims, but *the way they are put forward*: that is how one justifies and enforces one's claims.

I will suggest that this debate is embedded in the context of a wider debate in the social sciences about modernist, foundationalist epistemologies. The social sciences have experienced an onslaught of critiques which challenge the search for foundations or grounds for ethical judgement that hold absolutely and universally. With the exception of Linklater, for all intents and purposes, participants in the cosmopolitan/communitarian debate do not seriously acknowledge these critiques or their implications for their own work. Thus, the book suggests in part II that normative IR theory should shift attention to a different set of problems than those upon which cosmopolitans and communitarians now focus. In focusing on how to determine ontological priorities regarding individuals and communities, normative IR theory has left untheorized the epistemological assumptions which ground their ontological priorities, and it is precisely these epistemological assumptions that are the source of the impasse between cosmopolitans and communitarians. Alternatively, I will suggest that we should redirect our attentions to epistemology to interrogate whether, in fact, we should be engaged in foundational thinking when offering ethical positions in IR. Therefore, I examine what antifoundationalist approaches, which are participant in this wider debate in the social sciences, suggest for normative IR theory in comparison to the foundationalism of cosmopolitanism and communitarianism.

In order to make sense of the range of foundationalisms invoked by the writers discussed in the book – foundationalist and antifoundationalist – and the dilemma this presents for normative IR theory being able to move beyond its present impasse, I use what I call an *'anchor analogy'*. This is a metaphor for illustrating the strength or weakness of the foundations invoked and of the ethics that follows from these foundations. To offer an anchor is to employ foundations for justifying ethical positions. It represents an epistemologically centred argument, a claim to moral knowledge. To believe that this anchor rests firmly in solid ground represents *strong* foundational thinking. Examples of what I mean to indicate by *strong* foundations include absolute and universal notions such as Kant's categorical imperative or Hegel's *Geist*. In contemporary political and normative IR theory, few authors are willing to offer such grounds for ethical claims. Instead, they suggest *weak* foundations loosened from prior transcendental or theological underpinnings and grounded only in the moral consensus achievable among humankind. By a *weak* foundation, I want to suggest that the anchor offered is understood to be resting in ground which is liable to shift and cannot be assured of resting secure.

These different foundations have repercussions for the fixity of the ethics which follows from them. Here, I suggest the categories of *contingent* and *non-contingent* ethical claims, which are connected to *weak* and *strong* foundations. An ethics which is *non-contingent* is that which is connected to the *strong* foundationalist claim, as it is believed to hold absolutely and universally across time. An ethics which is *contingent* follows from *weak* foundationalist claims and understands its ethical claims to be only as strong as the grounds invoked. Thus, the historicity of its ethical claims are taken seriously and are understood to be temporary and provisional, and are thus specific to the context of time and place in which they are offered. I argue that the writers participating in the cosmopolitan/communitarian debate invoke *weak* foundations of varying scope in the sense I suggest; however, the epistemological impasse of the debate rests in the fact that they do not fully acknowledge the implications *weak* foundations have for the international ethics they advocate. *They proceed as if their weak foundations yield non-contingent ethical claims.*

This suggests to me why Linklater sees that it is 'unwise to draw a sharp distinction between communitarianism and cosmopolitanism' (1998: 55) and why I find that there is indeed a structural opposition that has to be explored. Building upon Linklater's idea of what distinguishes thick and thin notions of cosmopolitanism – that a thin notion relinquishes an absolute conception of the good (1998: 49) – I am agreeing that we are all the equivalents of thin cosmopolitans when I suggest that all we have left to draw upon today are *weak* foundations for normative theorizing. However, I am going one step further by saying that the way in which we use those *weak* foundations, whether we use them *contingently* or *non-contingently*, is significant. Although Linklater is attentive to anti-foundationalist critique, he contributes to the cosmopolitan/communitarian impasse by not properly acknowledging that the good behind even his thin cosmopolitanism may have to be put up for question (see chapter 3). This is where antifoundationalist approaches represent in one respect an opening in the gridlock of normative theory at present: they understand the ethics that results from an antifoundationalist position to be *contingent*. However, this is not to say that antifoundationalists altogether avoid foundationalist thinking. They do invoke *weak* foundations in their ethics and are rarely self-aware of their investment in them. None the less, in working to eschew grounds for ethical judgement, antifoundationalist approaches create new space for thinking about the interplay between the positions on the issues of the debate.

This recommends a third possible response to how normative theory might proceed: to draw ethical conclusions, but to regard the conclusions found as no more than temporary resting places for ethical critique. I argue that the cosmopolitan/communitarian debate is not the only, nor is it even the best, terrain upon which to construct a normative theory of IR. By this I mean that the kind of conclusions, or non-conclusions, generated by this debate are not the only ones possible for normative IR theory. Instead, *contingent* conclusions – which are understood to be fallible and distanced as much as possible from the foundationalist project in which the cosmopolitan/communitarian debate rests – are an alternative and improved terrain upon which normative IR theory can be constructed, albeit a shifting and unsure terrain.

This book intends more than a ground-clearing exercise *within* the cosmopolitan/communitarian debate. Instead, it suggests something more akin to a grave-digging exercise for the idea that the cosmopolitan/communitarian debate is *the* framework for approaching normative IR theory. The impasse between cosmopolitans and communitarians is a product of the fact that they are locked into a debate about ontological issues which actually rest on prior epistemological claims about *how* to ground attributions of moral significance to individuals or states, but which fails to acknowledge the primacy of this epistemological issue. In pursuing ontological questions – that is, theorizing the moral status of persons and states in relation to the necessities of being – the debate has left virtually untouched the *non-contingent*, epistemological assumptions at the heart of its structural opposition. While the cosmopolitan/communitarian debate has done important work in drawing attention to certain ontological positions and their tensions within normative theorizing in IR, it is incapable of posing these tensions without dichotomizing them because of the unquestioned nature of the underlying epistemological assumptions of participants in the debate. Because of its recourse to foundationalist epistemology, it speaks in terms of *oppositions* rather than a *range* of ontological positions which may or may not shade into one another, yet will always have to be negotiated and renegotiated.

Thus, the third central aim of this book is to construct in part III an argument for a new normative approach to international ethics which is attentive to the ways in which the axes of ontology and epistemology intersect and the consequences of their interaction for conclusions about possibilities for moral inclusion in world politics. What will be proposed is a notion of international ethics as pragmatic critique. This rests on a method of critical intelligence, which is ontologically oriented to an understanding of persons as being both socially and personally constructed in their striving towards improved forms of autonomy. This method values social cooperation and group memberships which range in scope from the local to the international and distances itself as far as possible from epistemologically centred thinking. It follows from this epistemological distancing that attention is thrown back onto ontology, however, with a difference. It does so with the acknowledgement that having no recourse to strong foundations means that our ethics, and our ontologies, can only come to provisional places of rest as solutions, conclusions or answers; they will continually be up for revision. For pragmatic critique, this revision always comes back to this *weak* ontological priority: *growth*, where growth is defined as making better and more meaningful worlds for ourselves.

Part I Evaluating the impasse

1 Cosmopolitanism: Rawlsian approaches to international distributive justice

Introduction

Cosmopolitans seek to interrogate and complicate the value conferred upon sovereign states in the contemporary international system, since cosmopolitans take individuals, not states, to be the starting point for moral consideration. They question the way in which boundaries of state authority serve as the boundaries of obligation owed among individuals in international practice. For example, cosmopolitans would challenge the claim of a particular state that the poor in the moral void outside its boundaries are not its responsibility. They do not accept that, at best, these poor can only hope to be the beneficiaries of charitable aid that flows across boundaries. For cosmopolitans, what is at issue here is the possibility of justice in an international system of states.

For cosmopolitans, to think about justice requires that we look past privileged practices and institutions, relinquish the power invested in these social constructions, and consider the simple question of what kind of relations between individuals can be said to be reasonable or fair. Accordingly, the question that considerations of justice raise for international practice is whether states represent a privileged power practice and whether they, like individuals, should be the subject of an inquiry into justice. In exploring this line of inquiry, I will concentrate upon cosmopolitan approaches which follow out of the work of John Rawls.

By choosing this focus, I do not intend to suggest that all conceptions of justice among cosmopolitans are to be identified with a Rawlsian approach. Clearly, one can point to cosmopolitan approaches of a non-Rawlsian character.[1] However, I choose to concentrate on this perspective as it has been the most influential conception of justice in defining the cosmopolitan position in contemporary normative IR theory. Much of this influence can be attributed to the considerable extent to which the framework of the cosmopolitan/communitarian debate derives from contemporary justice debates in political theory between liberals and communitarians: a debate stimulated by the work of Rawls. Within IR, Charles Beitz (1979) is the writer generally attributed with the first significant contemporary attempt to tackle a cosmopolitan theory for deriving principles of international justice in which he adapts Rawls's domestic formula for establishing principles of justice.[2] Subsequent to the writings of Beitz, Thomas Pogge (1989) has also drawn upon Rawls's work in order to internationalize questions of distributive justice. This chapter aims to critically examine the work of Beitz and Pogge in light of the progression in Rawls's own work on justice in order to assess the cosmopolitan position as it stands within normative IR theory and the possibilities for accommodation in the cosmopolitan/communitarian debate. Interestingly, of all the writers discussed in this book, Beitz and Pogge are closer than any others to being archetypical of the position they represent, and it is only through tracing the developments within Rawls's work that possibilities for narrowing the poles of debate might be found.

In *A Theory of Justice* (*TJ*), Rawls (1971) begins with the problem of how we can develop procedures to arrive at fair principles of justice that can be agreed to by all.[3] Critics point to a fundamental problem in his formulation. The assumptions upon which these procedures are derived are not universal (as Rawls suggests), but instead, are particular to Rawlsian liberalism. Since 1971, Rawls has written numerous articles, recently revised and collected in *Political Liberalism*

---

[1] For a non-Rawlsian, Kantian conception of cosmopolitan justice see O'Neill (1986), (1990), and (1994). Barry (1989) is another cosmopolitan who takes a non-Rawlsian route to international justice, which instead, draws from Thomas Scanlon.

[2] Although not a developed study of international distributive justice, Danielson (1973) offers an earlier critique of Rawls for failing to extend the redistributive principle beyond domestic societies.

[3] It is important to note here that Rawls is not concerned with the question of whether considerations of justice apply to states. His aim is to develop a theory of justice for individuals within the confines of domestic society.

(Rawls 1993b).[4] In his later work, Rawls redirects emphases, and in the opinion not only of his critics, but those sympathetic to his earlier work as well, significantly alters his theory of justice. The first section begins by looking briefly at the early Rawls of *TJ* and then turns to an account of Beitz's efforts to construct a theory of international distributive justice. In the second section, I argue that it is important to explore the movement of Rawls's work since 1971 as this movement is reflected in the studies of international distributive justice by Beitz and Pogge. I use Chandran Kukathas and Philip Pettit's outline of two stages in Rawls's later work (Kukathas and Pettit 1990: chapter 7): first, to characterize Beitz's retreat from his critics as a retreat similar to that of the Rawls of stage one, which leans upon more expressly Kantian lines; and secondly, to examine Pogge's interest in international applications of Rawls's domestic conception of overlapping consensus in the second stage of his work. In the third section, I examine the implications of the development in Rawls's thought and its reflection in the work of these international theorists for the cosmopolitan position and the debate in normative IR theory as a whole. The extended exegesis of changes in Rawls's work and its influence on these writers makes the format of this chapter different from others in part I of the book. However, this exceptional treatment is warranted in order to indicate that while Beitz and Pogge are not specifically concerned to locate points of accommodation within the cosmopolitan/communitarian debate, the movement in Rawls's thinking suggests the possibility.

Early Rawls, Beitz and an international theory of justice

What follows is a simple exposition of a complex and important book. It is a thumbnail sketch of those points relevant to the concerns outlined above: themes Beitz draws upon, and themes redirected in Rawls's later writings that are picked up by Pogge. To begin, the basic

---

[4] In this chapter I will refer to the original articles rather than their revised equivalents in Rawls (1993b). Granted, Rawls maintains that there is new thinking in these pieces collected in the book. However, the main points that I am extracting from them – his historical contextualism, his understanding of the self as being socially constructed as well, and his claim that moral personality can differ within varied social contexts – remain largely unchanged.

structure of society is the fundamental subject of justice for Rawls. He defines society as 'a cooperative venture for mutual advantage', and the role of justice as the provision of a set of principles by which participants in society can 'define the appropriate distribution of the benefits and burdens of social cooperation' (Rawls 1971: 4). Thus, Rawls's theory of justice is a theory of distributive justice, and therefore implies wider forms of moral inclusion.

Individuals cooperate because they recognize that life within society offers more beneficial returns than life on one's own. None the less, they do have divergent interests. Prior to entering societal arrangements, individuals have their own projects and desires, which are not always compatible. Rawls insists on the separateness of persons: they are not the means to societal ends. That individuals are free and equal in virtue of their capacity to have a sense of justice and to form and revise a conception of the good, is something Rawls takes as given and that cannot be overridden by any good of society. Thus, principles of justice must be publicly agreed to by all. Rawls revitalizes the contractarian tradition from its nineteenth-century slumber, to propose a formula by which principles appropriate to the justice of basic social institutions may be chosen by those participant in a cooperative social scheme for mutual advantage.

Rawls asks the reader to consider a hypothetical 'original position' in which individuals come together under a 'veil of ignorance'; that is, they know nothing of their own situation, talents, profession, or status. Thus, they do not possess the kind of knowledge which might bias or inhibit a fair choice of principles. Rawls argues that from such an original position, the agreements reached epitomize justice as fairness because they 'evaluate principles solely on the basis of general considerations' (1971: 137). In addition to understanding individuals to be free and equal, the concept of justice as fairness also holds that individuals are rational and mutually disinterested. In regard to these latter aspects attributed to persons under justice as fairness, Rawls makes two points of clarification. First, disinterestedness in one another's affairs does not mean that individuals are egoists. Disinterestedness only suggests that individuals attempt to procure as many primary social goods (rights and liberties, opportunity and income) as possible (Rawls 1971: 13, 144). Secondly, rationality should be interpreted in terms of economic theory; that is, we select the 'most effective means to given ends' (Rawls 1971: 14, 143). This formula for filtering 'arbitrary contingencies' from a 'desired solution' produces, in a pure procedural fashion, the following principles of justice (Rawls 1971: 302):

1. Each person is to have an equal right to the most extensive total system of liberties compatible with a similar system of liberty for all (the Maximum Equal Liberties Principle).
2. Social and economic inequalities are to be arranged so that they are both: (a) to the greatest benefit of the least advantaged, consistent with the just savings principle, and (b) attached to offices and positions open to all under conditions of fair equality of opportunity (the Difference Principle).

Although Rawls's *TJ* stimulated the development of cosmopolitan positions on international distributive justice, Rawls himself did not see that his principles of societal justice could be extended to the realm of the international for two reasons. First and foremost, as the basic structure of society is the subject of justice for Rawls, and society is defined as a cooperative venture for mutual advantage, the fact that the world is not such a society, according to Rawls, means that his principles of justice do not apply internationally. For Rawls, there is no *global* society as such that can be legitimately regarded as a collaborative scheme of self-sufficient relations. Secondly, as there is no global society, there is no global surplus for which principles of distributive justice need to be found. Rawls writes that he would be satisfied if he could 'formulate a reasonable conception of justice for the basic structure of society conceived for the time being as a closed system isolated from other societies' (1971: 8). One might seize upon the 'for the time being' in the above quote as a hint of an opening. Nevertheless, even in his most recent writings, Rawls offers no signs of changing his stance on the viability of a theory of international distributive justice: although he does argue for the just international distribution of basic liberties, he continues to deny the possibility of a theory covering the fair international distribution of opportunities and resources (1993a).[5]

---

[5] See Rawls (1993b: xxviii–xxix), where he writes that justice between states, among other issues neglected in *TJ*, is provided for generally by 'focusing on a few main and enduring classical problems' in political theory. This recourse to classical political theory, conceived to be centrally concerned with the domestic polity, fails to address a question, the consideration of which distinguishes international political theory, and which is central to the discussion of justice between states in international political theory: the question of the actual moral relevance of states. Thus, possibilities for international distributive justice are not given adequate consideration here. However, in a more recent piece, while he still fails to justify or problematize the value placed

Rawls does consider an international original position, but it yields no more than international norms familiar to us all: the equality of nations, self-determination, a right to non-interference, and that treaties are to be kept (Rawls 1971: chapter 58). Clearly, this in no way represents a radical call for international redistribution. However, Beitz sees the potential for such a call within a Rawlsian framework. According to Beitz, Rawls has the facts wrong, and writes that an otherwise worthy theory of justice stops short of its full potential. Accepting Rawls's two principles of justice, Beitz aims 'to point out some features of this view that require further development in the face of certain facts about the world' (Beitz 1979: 129). There is a sense in which Beitz hedges his position by offering two arguments, which could be regarded as weak and strong,[6] for international distributive justice: one argument takes states to be the subject of justice, and the other argument takes individuals to be the subject of justice. The first, or weak, argument takes on board the usual assumption in IR theory that states are self-sufficient entities in order to make a case for international distributive justice in arguing that there *is* a global surplus that requires distribution: natural resources. His second, or strong, argument challenges self-sufficiency as a fact about states in the light of international interdependence, and he uses this to make a case for a global difference principle.

In assuming the self-sufficiency of nation-states, Beitz turns to

upon sovereign states in international practice, Rawls does offer extended discussion of international justice in regard to human liberties (Rawls 1993a). In order to claim that Rawls maintains in this piece as well that his theory of justice cannot provide sufficiently for the possibility of international distributive justice, I must draw an important distinction. In thinking about international distributive justice, one must differentiate between theories that cover the fair distribution of liberties and those that are concerned not only to cover liberties, but the fair distribution of opportunities and resources as well. In developing the idea which Rawls labels as 'the law of peoples', an extension of his notion of the well-ordered society, Rawls is arguing for the just distribution of basic equal liberties in international practice. However, he is not suggesting that a theory of international distributive justice can cover fair distribution of opportunities and resources in the way his domestic theory of justice does. Thus, he continues to suggest that his theory of domestic justice does not have international application. As will be discussed, Beitz and Pogge demand a theory of international distributive justice that provides for both equality of liberties *and* equality of opportunities and resources. I must thank John Charvet for drawing my attention to the importance of making this distinction explicit.

[6] Here I do not use the terms weak and strong in the same sense that I set out in the Introduction in regard to foundationalist argument. Where I do intend this meaning, the terms will be in italics.

Rawls's international original position to reconsider the development of principles of justice for the law of nations. He writes that Rawls's selection of principles 'seems unexceptionable', but he neglects an important consideration, the question of natural resources (Beitz 1979b: 136–43). Just as participants in the domestic original position would factor out considerations of natural talents due to their morally arbitrary nature, natural resources would be viewed as similarly arbitrary on an international level. Thus, the veil of ignorance over the international original position would compel the parties to examine the distribution of natural resources. Although Rawls's approach to natural talents is vulnerable to several objections, Beitz argues that the distribution of natural resources is a 'purer case' of being morally arbitrary, because 'unlike talents, resources are not naturally attached to persons' (Beitz 1979b: 139–40). Beitz also argues that it is wrong to assume that where there is no social cooperation there is no problem of resource distribution claims. Moral bonds are not limited to those with whom we are involved in a cooperative scheme. Those participant in the international original position would have as part of their general knowledge an awareness of the fact of uneven distribution and scarce resources; and thus, not knowing their own access to resources under the veil of ignorance, they would naturally agree on a resource redistribution principle (Beitz 1979: 140–1). Therefore, Beitz concludes that the 'case for an international resource redistribution principle is consistent with the assumption that states are self-sufficient cooperative schemes' (1979: 143).

His second argument renders the first to be superfluous, because he moves to make a strong case for international redistribution in writing that we all know that the assumption of self-sufficiency is unsustainable. The fact of international interdependence, 'by now part of the conventional wisdom of international relations', undermines the notion of the state as a self-contained, self-sufficient cooperative scheme (Beitz 1979: 149). Thus, we cannot limit Rawls's concept of society to the nation-state, because the network of international interdependent relationships points to a 'global scheme of social cooperation' (Beitz 1979: 144). This being the case, global interdependence means that the difference principle can apply internationally. Beitz sees no reason why the widened scope of a cooperative venture for mutual advantage would necessarily change the principles of justice (1979: 151). An international difference principle works for the globally least advantaged representative *person* in the first instance, but it would also require that intrastate inequalities be addressed as well (Beitz 1979: 153). Despite making individuals the subject of international distributive justice in this strong argument, he goes on to write that as states remain the central players in world politics, they, as a 'second-best solution', are in the best position to follow through on the measures necessary to realize an international difference principle.

Why do states represent a second-best solution? Despite the indecision in Beitz's conclusions on the appropriate subject of justice, states or individuals, his case for international distributive justice denies the empirical and moral relevance of states. He writes that the existence of states is a fact of world politics, but the autonomy of states cannot be maintained in the face of interdependence. Global interdependence infringes upon a state's autonomy. Autonomy is something we confer upon states, a mistake which results from 'reading "states" for "persons"' (Beitz 1979: 76). In addition, Beitz finds that international interdependence constitutes global social cooperation; and thus, statehood becomes morally irrelevant. Moral relations do not begin and end at state boundaries, since social cooperation extends beyond the reaches of the state. Therefore, according to Beitz, international distributive justice applies only derivatively to states and principally to persons in founding principles for the establishment of just social arrangements.

The later Rawls and his influence on cosmopolitan thinking on justice

Having outlined Rawls's *TJ* and Beitz's extension of this work to establish a theory of international distributive justice, I will now trace the movement of Rawls's subsequent work and its reflection in the work of Beitz and Pogge. *TJ* is often attributed with revitalizing political theory, as what has since been labelled the 'communitarian critique' in response to Rawlsian liberalism has generated a debate between liberals and communitarians that has captured the attention of much of contemporary political theory.[7] It is clear in Rawls's later work that he is concerned to address elements of this critique, but the extent to which he has been swayed by the communitarian position is

---

[7] See Sandel (1982); MacIntyre (1981) and (1988); Walzer (1981), (1983), and (1984); and Taylor (1985b) and (1990).

open to debate. None the less, many commentators note that Rawls is today offering a political liberalism with more expressly communitarian concerns than the Rawls of 1971 (Kukathas and Pettit 1990: 110–18; Mulhall and Swift 1992: 198–220; Bellamy 1992: 234–40). Are the changes no more than clarifications or shifts in emphasis; or do they represent a more significant alteration of his theory of justice? First, we must turn briefly to the substance of the critique.

It must be acknowledged that the communitarian critics are not speaking with one voice, but one can generally discuss their principal concerns as follows.[8] These writers point to the inadequacy of liberal abstraction in theorizing about political life, and liberalism's failure to appreciate the value placed by individuals on shared communal understandings and notions of the good. Michael Sandel criticizes deontological liberals such as Rawls for an incoherent conception of the person as prior to her ends, detached from her attributes (Sandel 1982: 19–23). For Charles Taylor, Rawls's theory is a form of atomism, which as a 'basic error' fails to appreciate the ways in which individuals are socially constituted (Taylor 1985b: 309). This conception of the person is reflected in Rawls's claim for the primacy of justice, a well-ordered society being one in which rights act as a constraint upon societal goods that may impinge upon self-defining individuals. For Alasdair MacIntyre, this search for rational, broadly practicable moral foundations represents a Western political culture in decline, because we have turned our backs on the tradition of the virtues, which locate moral life within communities (MacIntyre 1981: chapter 17). Michael Walzer advocates the particular and the plural, the value of communal meanings denied by the universalism of Rawls's original position (Walzer 1981: 388–93).

From the Kantian to the political: movements in the later work of Rawls

With these criticisms in mind, let us turn to what Kukathas and Pettit argue are two movements in Rawls's work since 1971 (Kukathas and

---

[8] Allen (1992) makes a distinction between strong communitarians such as Sandel and MacIntyre versus the moderate communitarianism of Walzer and Taylor. Mulhall and Swift (1992: 155) also separate Walzer and Taylor from the pack, as their communitarian critique does not 'entail a wholesale rejection of liberalism and liberal values'. For a similar interpretation, see Bellamy (1992: 242–43).

Pettit 1990: 120–21).[9] Rawls's writings from 1971 to 1982 represent the first movement, as Rawls concentrates upon elaborating the Kantian underpinnings of his moral philosophy. I will label this first movement, the 'Kantian phase'. From 1982 onwards, the second movement is marked by a move away from his Kantian roots, in which he rewrites his account of liberal justice as political not moral. I refer to this second movement as the 'political leap'. In this section, I will discuss the key texts of the first and second movements respectively, 'Kantian Constructivism in Moral Theory' ('KC') and 'The Idea of an Overlapping Consensus' ('OC'), and assess any significant changes and their relation to the communitarian critique (Rawls 1980; Rawls 1987).[10]

The Kantian phase

Critics of *TJ* maintain that Rawls's conception of the person is unclear. Rawls does discuss two attributes of persons – first, that they are free and equal moral persons, and secondly, that they are rational choosers – yet these critics demand a more precise answer from Rawls to the question: exactly what kind of person is behind the veil of ignorance and participant in the original position? In 'KC', Rawls elaborates the Kantian orientation of his work, in particular, he aims to emphasize the way in which a Kantian understanding of moral personality is at the base of his theory of justice – a move Beitz repeats in response to his critics. Rawls seeks a notion of Kantian autonomy which leaves behind the metaphysics of a noumenal, rational self that is free of moral conflict (Rawls 1980: 516). Alternatively, he appeals to what we can agree to on the basis of common sense. Moral principles are constructed upon a fair procedure that represents ideals we already intuitively accept. Rawls is also more specific on the scope of the 'we' here. His concern is to focus upon a theory of justice which draws upon the latent understandings within liberal democratic societies. Thus, unlike Kant, he suggests that conceptions of moral personality vary from one moral tradition to another (Kukathas and Pettit 1990: 126).[11] It is Rawls's assumption that a fair procedure among those who

---

[9] Kukathas's and Pettit's discussion of these movements is similar to Arneson's (1989) outline of three significant changes in Rawls.

[10] I regard these texts as key, not simply within the body of Rawls's work, but also with respect to the writings of the international theorists concerned.

[11] This conception of variance in moral personhood has interesting repercussions for IR theorists attempting to build upon Rawls. I will discuss this later in the chapter.

share common sense notions about 'how they conceive of their persons and construe the general features of social cooperation among persons so regarded' will yield fair principles of justice (Rawls 1980: 517).

Rawls's strategy for deriving such principles rests on three distinct model conceptions: the moral person, the well-ordered society and the original position (Rawls 1980: 533). The moral person has 'two highest order moral powers': the capacity for a sense of justice and the 'capacity to form, to revise and rationally pursue a conception of the good' (Rawls 1980: 525). It is the moral person's interest to realize and develop these powers as well as to preserve her conception of the good. The well-ordered society is characterized by four features. First, a well-ordered society is 'effectively regulated by a public conception of justice', based upon beliefs which are widely accepted (Rawls 1980: 537). Secondly, citizens of this society recognize themselves and each other as free and equal moral persons. The third and fourth character-istics are that the 'circumstances of justice' – moderate scarcity and a plurality of conflicting goods – will be in place, and finally that the well-ordered society will be stable as concerns its conception of justice (Rawls 1980: 522, 525). As for the original position, it incorporates the model conceptions of the moral person and well-ordered society. It constructs two principles of justice, upon an understanding of our-selves as moral persons and upon ideas of a well-ordered society, by assuming a preference for the primary goods necessary to our moral capacities and by a veil of ignorance which eliminates morally irrelevant factors that could influence decisions and result in unfair outcomes.

The setting of the original position is framed by what Rawls terms the 'Reasonable'. The Reasonable entails mutuality and reciprocity among free and equal moral persons, which is represented in the original position by demands for generality, publicity and universality, and by demands for primary goods and justice in regard to basic political structures. These are to be distinguished from the Rational features of the original position: the assumption that the parties are rational and that they pursue the greatest amount of primary goods possible. The distinction between the Reasonable and the Rational is important, as their relationship is the basis for a Kantian autonomy derived not from a dualistic metaphysical abstraction, but from a conception of rationality grounded in our common sense understand-ing of ourselves as free and equal moral persons. Rawls writes that the Reasonable presupposes as well as subordinates the Rational:

> [t]he Reasonable presupposes the Rational, because, without concep-
> tions of the good that move members of the group, there is no point
> to social cooperation nor to notions of right and justice . . . The
> Reasonable subordinates the Rational because its principles limit,
> and in the Kantian doctrine limit absolutely, the final ends that can
> be pursued. (Rawls 1980: 53)

To assess what has changed with this Kantian phase, I will look at the
'who', the 'whom' and the 'what' represented in 'KC' as compared to
TJ. The 'who', a concept of the person, is much more developed in the
Kantian phase. Rawls addresses the ambiguity which surrounded the
concept of the person depicted in the original position of *TJ* as both a
rational chooser of ends and a free and equal person inclined to follow
justice. The rational autonomy (in an economic theory sense) of the
individual in the original position was no more than a representation
that is not to be confused with the ideal of the autonomous, moral
person of a well-ordered society (Rawls 1980: 533–4). The distinction
between the Rational and the Reasonable assists this clarification by
framing rational autonomy within the purview of the Reasonable,
providing for a fuller realization of autonomy. Not only has the
concept of the person in Rawls been clarified, but it is also more
pronounced, in the sense that the 'who' has taken on a fundamental
role in Rawls's theory of justice. As William Galston writes, '[i]n the
Dewey Lectures ['KC'], the ideal of the person plays a direct rather
than a derivative role' (Galston 1982: 495). In 'KC', Rawls wants to
make a clear distinction between three model conceptions, but as
Galston argues, these three sets of constraints on choosers are not as
independent as they may appear. Aspects of the well-ordered society
(the publicity condition and the assumption of a diversity of ends)
and aspects of the original position (the veil of ignorance and the
account of pure procedural justice) are all grounded upon an assumption of moral personality: that the individual is free and equal in her
moral capacities.

As stated earlier, this substantive moral position regarding a conception of the person is congruous with our shared understandings of
ourselves as free and equal citizens, and the 'our' here represents
those of us participant in liberal democratic societies. Thus, the scope
of the 'whom' to which Rawls's theory of justice applies has narrowed
from its interpretation in *TJ* where it was relevant to any society,
defined as a cooperative venture for mutual advantage. Instead, in his
Kantian phase, Rawls clarifies that he is not attributing universal

applicability to his principles of justice. In fact, the scope in 'KC' has narrowed to the degree that it encompasses not simply those within liberal democratic societies, but those within liberal democratic societies such as the United States. With Rawls's new emphasis upon moral personality, the validity of the principles of justice is now specific to contemporary liberal democracies such as the United States where such a conception of the person can be found within common political understandings.

The principles of justice have not changed in this Kantian phase, nor has the use of the original position to derive those principles. Yet Rawls works in 'KC' to clarify the function of the original position as a device that helps us realize shared ideals latent in our political culture. Here, the 'what' behind the these principles, that which motivates the choice of the two principles of justice, is important. Rawls writes in 'KC' that '[f]ree persons have a regulative and effective desire to be a certain kind of person' (1980: 548). It is this assertion regarding moral personality – that it is our aim to develop our capacities for following justice and forming a conception of the good – which motivates the process of construction leading to Rawls's two principles of justice. But why should we be compelled by this assertion about ourselves? Is it enough that we can identify this concept of the person in liberal democratic culture?

The gap between the communitarians and Rawls is not as wide as originally perceived. Neglected within the communitarian critique are several points clarified in this Kantian phase, works written by Rawls prior to the first publication among the communitarians in 1981: MacIntyre's *After Virtue*. For example, Sandel's charge that Rawls holds an inadequate metaphysical assumption of the individual as unencumbered and pre-social neglects Rawls's assertion that to form and pursue a conception of the good is integral to moral personality. Thus, in no sense would Rawls presume that individuals could be wholly cut off from their ends. Also, there is Rawls's claim in 'KC' that moral personality is embedded in the political culture of liberal democracy. This claim takes the sting out of Walzer's charges against universal starting points and attempts at founding universal principles of distributive justice. In *TJ*, where the notion of primary goods was based upon needs determinable from general knowledge available in an original position, this could be a fair criticism. However Rawls's change of tack in 'KC' links primary goods to the assumption of moral personality and its 'higher order interests' which can be located in liberal democratic practice. None the less, the communitarians do have Rawls on the defensive in this regard: that his theory of justice stands on a metaphysical assumption regarding personhood which constitutes not a thin, but a thick theory of a liberal good. It is to this defence that Rawls turns in the second movement.

The political leap

The difficulty Rawls faces is that the Reasonable, the basis for the original position, is a moral conception. As a moral conception, it cannot apply to everyone unless all accept the Reasonable. Thus, in the face of challenges to this moral conception, there is no ground for the original position. Rawls abandons the foundering position of Kantian moral personality in a leap to the political, stressing the importance of the political in finding consensus on justice in conditions of plurality and diversity.

Although Rawls does not presume that individuals can be wholly cut off from their ends, he does argue in 'KC' that there is a public/private distinction such that a person can put aside the goods she holds privately to pursue agreement on the arrangement of basic social institutions in the public, political sphere. It is upon this public, political sphere that Rawls builds a response to his communitarian critics. In his writings from 1982 to 1989, Rawls differentiates between a political conception of justice and a comprehensive moral doctrine, a distinction he had not made in previous writings. The concern of this political conception of justice is to secure an 'overlapping consensus' within liberal democratic societies, which must contend with the fact of pluralism. Kukathas and Pettit hold that this second movement represents a rejection of the Kantian impulse in his earlier work (1990: 121n, 139). While I appreciate the usefulness of understanding Rawls's work in terms of two phases, I will argue that this idea of a wholesale rejection of Kantian moral philosophy in his move to the political is misleading.

Rawls's article, 'The Idea of an Overlapping Consensus', is the key to understanding this distinction regarding the political, and is also important to Pogge's formulation of a theory of international distributive justice. Here, Rawls suggests that the aim of political philosophy within constitutional democracies is to find a *political* conception of justice, which is publicly justifiable and stable across generations. Rawls outlines three features of a political conception of justice (1987: 3–7). First, a political conception of justice remains a moral conception regarding the basic structure of a constitutional democratic society; that is, how the main political, economic and social institutions fit together in a unified scheme of social cooperation. Secondly, a political conception is *not* a general and comprehensive moral conception with broad application, like perfectionism, utilitarianism or Marxism. Instead, it is concerned only with the basic structure of society, holding no prior commitment to a wider doctrine. Finally, a political conception of justice is formulated in terms of 'certain fundamental intuitive ideas viewed as latent in the public political culture of a democratic society' (Rawls 1987: 6).

What motivates this political conception of justice? It is Rawls's thesis that the historical and sociological conditions of democratic society demand that we look at the justice of its basic institutions in a certain way. The fact of pluralism is the principal one among these conditions. Within modern democratic society there is a diversity of general and comprehensive doctrines, incommensurable ideals of value and the good, which make the need for a political conception of justice a practical matter. Another condition to consider is that the fact of pluralism is not going to dissipate. Rawls sees the fact of pluralism to be a permanent feature of the public culture of constitutional democracies. Also, if any comprehensive doctrine were maintained in such a society, it could only be through the oppressive use of state power (Rawls 1987: 4).[12] These conditions require that a theory of justice must look beyond general and comprehensive conceptions in order to find a publicly acceptable *political* conception of justice which can specify fair terms of social cooperation among free and equal citizens, supported by an overlapping consensus. An overlapping consensus is that which can be supported among those who espouse different comprehensive religious, moral or philosophical doctrines. Although the comprehensive conceptions are conflicting, an overlapping consensus may still exist as different premises may lead to the same conclusion. Rawls writes that 'we simply suppose that the essential elements of the political conception, its principles, standards and ideals, are theorems, as it were, at which the comprehensive doctrines in the consensus intersect or converge' (1987: 9).

In the second part of 'OC', Rawls is concerned to take up four objections against the idea of social unity founded on an overlapping consensus: (1) it is a mere *modus vivendi*; (2) it implies scepticism as to

---

[12] Rawls (1987: 4n) lists four additional social and historical conditions to consider.

whether a political conception is true; (3) a workable political conception must be general and comprehensive; and (4) an over-lapping consensus is utopian. Against the objection that an over-lapping consensus is a mere *modus vivendi*, Rawls writes that the object of consensus is moral. An overlapping consensus is affirmed on moral grounds and it is expressed in public life. These two factors contribute to its stability, something a *modus vivendi* clearly lacks. In response to the second charge of scepticism regarding the truth of political conceptions, Rawls says that he does not appeal to a political conception of justice simply to avoid conflict, but to distinguish between issues that can or cannot be removed from a political agenda in order to find a stable overlapping consensus. The problem is that difficult issues will not be eliminated, and at times, 'in affirming a political conception of justice we may have to assert at least certain aspects of our own comprehensive religious or philosophical doctrine' (Rawls 1987: 14). In this instance, restraint is called for in asserting no more than that which one thinks is compatible with consensus. Thirdly, those critics who argue that an overlapping consensus must be general and comprehensive say this is required in order to prioritise the conflicts of justice that are sure to arise. Rawls responds by saying that 'a political conception is at best a guiding framework of deliberation and reflection which helps us reach political agreement on at least the constitutional essentials', and that in itself is sufficient (1987: 16). Finally, Rawls answers the charge of utopianism, that no basis for overlap exists, by pointing to a way in which an overlapping consensus may emerge. It begins with a *modus vivendi* that changes in time to an overlapping consensus as people recognize the success of political cooperation over time and grow to have more trust in one another.

Now, let us turn back to the 'who', 'whom' and 'what' questions to assess any shifts in this second movement. As for the 'who', the distinction between political and comprehensive conceptions of justice has its implications for Rawls's concept of the person as well. The ideal of moral personality is fashioned into a political conception of the person as citizen, whose 'freedom and equality are to be understood in ways congenial to public political culture and explic-able in terms of the designs and requirements of its basic institutions' (Rawls 1987: 7). This new emphasis upon a political conception of the person is prompted by Rawls's recent attention to what he calls the 'fact of pluralism' and the need to find a publicly justifiable conception of the person as citizen that spans diverse comprehensive goods. It is Rawls's assumption that this is possible because 'the comprehensive doctrines of most people are not fully comprehensive' (Rawls 1987: 22–3). Thus, the individual can separate the comprehensive doctrines one personally holds from ideas which facilitate agreement in the public, political realm. As Stephen Mulhall and Adam Swift write, for those who are not committed to a liberal conception of a public/private split, this will involve 'a greater or lesser degree of schizophrenia', making such a conception of the person undesirable (1992: 209). However, this is more than a question of desirability. It is a question of feasibility: whether an individual can legitimately set herself apart from what she regards as valuable in determining the justice of basic social institutions. Rawls does recognize that he cannot 'avoid comprehensive doctrines entirely', as his concern for public justifiability hinges upon his conception of moral personality as being valuable (Rawls 1987: 8).

The 'whom' has not changed in any real sense in Rawls's move to the political. The scope remains a conception of justice for liberal democratic societies in accordance with shared understandings therein. Only one difference is notable, not in the scope of the 'whom', but in his focus upon the circumstances of the 'whom'. Rawls has an increased awareness of social and historical situations, in particular, the fact of pluralism that clearly affects his turn to the political. The aim of his political philosophy has shifted from a concern in 'KC' to address the deadlock in reconciling freedom and equality in basic social institutions to a more gritty concern with the practical problem of identifying a shared political basis for a stable conception of justice.

Again the principles of justice put forward in *TJ* stand. Yet, the 'what' that motivates those principles has been re-articulated in Rawls's political leap. The Kantian concept of moral personality reflected in the derivation of Rawls's principles of justice is re-articulated as a political conception of the person. This, in turn, is a product of an overriding concern with the fact of pluralism. Kukathas and Pettit claim that Rawls turns his back on Kant as it appears that the condition of pluralism leads Rawls to abandon in 'OC' the comprehensive liberalisms of Kant and Mill. They contend that Rawls is no longer concerned with what would be the most desirable principle of justice, but with what is feasible, what ensures stability (Kukathas and Pettit 1990: 142). However, although Rawls rejects comprehensive moral doctrines as a basis for a conception of justice, he has not abandoned Kant nor has he abandoned a desirable conception of justice. To be sure, Rawls wants to move away from a Kantian moral conception that is universal in scope, but he maintains that within the historical and social circumstances of liberal democratic society, a Kantian idea of moral personality is publicly agreeable. On the other hand, Rawls's very concern for public justifiability is linked to his commitment to a Kantian understanding of moral personality as valuable in itself. As Mulhall and Swift write, if Rawls found himself in a non-liberal society forced to choose between public justifiability and a conception of the person as citizen, he would not yield to whatever was indeed publicly justifiable, but, instead, would work towards a conception of justice compatible with his conception of the person as free and equal (Mulhall and Swift 1992: 213). Rawls is not forswearing Kant, since his political conception of justice turns on an account of moral personality. The problem for Rawls, then, is *how* to maintain that what motivates his theory of justice is a substantive, not comprehensive, moral concep- tion. Is such a matter of degree plausible?

This is an important question because Rawls wants to suggest that a political conception of justice based upon an understanding of persons as free and equal citizens is compatible with diverse compre- hensive doctrines, such that when a comprehensive good clashes with a political good, we accept that the comprehensive good must be constrained in the name of that political good which is better able to win public agreement. Mulhall and Swift point out that Rawls is unclear in his defense of the inviolability of the political good (Mulhall and Swift 1992: 220–6). In 'OC', Rawls uses the example of a religious believer who challenges a public conception of justice that removes the truths of religion from the political agenda to support equal liberty of conscience. In responding to this challenge, Rawls acknowledges that 'we may have to assert at least certain aspects of our own comprehensive (by no means necessarily fully comprehen- sive) religious or philosophical doctrine' (1987: 14). Whether fully or partially comprehensive, the point is that it *is* comprehensive, making it difficult to maintain the political versus comprehensive distinction. In 'The Domain of the Political and Overlapping Consensus' ('DP'), Rawls (1989) offers an alternative defence. He invokes the idea of reasonable disagreement: there will always be unyielding issues of reasonable disagreement that we must bear with tolerance. So again, in response to the religious believer who challenges the inviolability of the political, one can only suggest to him that it would be unreasonable to force his comprehensive religious doctrine upon others, thus avoiding recourse to a 'partially' comprehensive doctrine for a defence.

Mulhall and Swift argue that Rawls has a dilemma on his hands. Either he argues that challenging the domain of the political is wrong, and invokes a comprehensive or universal moral doctrine which in itself compromises the limits of the political, or he argues it is unreasonable, which seems to allow circumstances when violating the limits of the political would be legitimate (Mulhall and Swift 1992: 226). I will label this dilemma as Rawls's 'Kantian conundrum'. The appeal of Kant's practical philosophy is its invocation of a conception of the person as a free and equal moral being, which provides grounds for critical judgement without recourse to assertions of prior moral facts or foundations. The conundrum lies in whether one can indeed invoke a Kantian notion of moral personality without getting caught in universal, absolutist claims and the metaphysical oppositions of noumenal and phenomenal realms.

This is particularly difficult for someone like Rawls. Because he uses such a conception of the person as the basis for his distinctions between, and prioritisation of, the right over the good, the political over the comprehensive, and the public over the private, he must contend with the fact that Kant's own distinction between the right and the good hinges on an appeal to the idea of a transcendental noumenal self. From the above discussion, it is clear that Rawls has not found a satisfactory way of maintaining an argument for the right over the good, a political/comprehensive distinction. Thus, it leads one to question whether such an argument can be maintained *without* turning to foundationalist, metaphysical assumptions. This is reflected in the tension evident in the Reasonable constraining the Rational, so that the political is seen to be inviolable in clashes with comprehensive doctrines; and, thus, is not dissimilar to the strong opposition between the noumenal and phenomenal realms. Also, Rawls's original position, a procedural representation of the categorical imperative, works as an Archimedean point. Yet, this Archimedean point misses the crux of the conundrum. Despite attempts to ground moral personality in liberal democratic culture, to represent it as a political, not fully comprehensive conception, the understanding of the person as a free and equal moral being represents a notion of the good in itself. It does so without offering, nor seeing the need to offer, a satisfactory answer to the question why we should support this conception of the person upon which Rawls's theory of justice is constructed. It is a foundational assumption which justifies, but is itself not up for question.

From the Kantian to the political in international distributive justice

These two movements in Rawls's later writings are evident in the work of Beitz and Pogge. Beitz, in response to critics of his theory of cosmopolitan justice in *Political Theory and International Relations*, falls back on more expressly Kantian lines, as does Rawls of the first movement. Pogge is interested in applying Rawls's domestic conception of overlapping consensus internationally. However, in fashioning a theory of international distributive justice upon Rawlsian lines, there are two difficulties which must be addressed by these writers. First, as discussed in part one, Rawls's theory of distributive justice applies only to the domestic realm and not to the international. Secondly, as the sections above argue, throughout his later writings, Rawls uses the 'good' of moral personality foundationally in his theory of justice and is caught in a Kantian conundrum. I will now examine the writings of these cosmopolitan theorists to see how their work reflects these movements in Rawls's thinking and how, if at all, they address these two difficulties.

Charles Beitz

In 'Cosmopolitan Ideals and National Sentiment', Beitz (1983) turns to 'KC' and the notion of moral personality to respond to his critics. Beitz accepts the argument of Brian Barry which challenges that international interdependence is not at a level that can sustain an argument for a global cooperative venture with the requisite mutuality (Barry 1989: 432–62). Resigned that his original justification 'misses the point', Beitz none the less maintains that the scope of the original position should still be global. Also, his position on the proper subject of justice is made clearer in this article when he writes that the original position represents *individuals* as free and equal moral persons. Since the criterion of membership is a capacity for a sense of justice and a capacity to form, revise and pursue a conception of the good, then membership should be global, because all humans have these capacities no matter if they are part of a cooperative scheme or not (Beitz 1983: 595). He understands that this is worthless without basic institutions for which global principles of justice would apply, but it no longer matters whether international cooperation exists, since he distinguishes between an *existence* and a *feasibility* condition. As long as international cooperation cannot be proven to be unfeasible, a theory of international distributive justice is possible.

Beitz then turns to address a new obstacle thrown in the way by Rawls in 'KC'. In asserting that his principles of justice are limited to liberal democratic societies, Rawls again denies a global application of his theory of justice. Beitz offers two objections (1983: 596). First, he writes that it is empirically questionable whether there is greater agreement in modern democratic societies than other societies as to the conception of the person which frames the original position. This is certainly plausible. Secondly, according to Beitz, this limitation in scope contradicts the nature of the conception itself, even though the basis of the conception of the person may be parochial. Beitz writes that 'we are compelled to take a global view in matters of social justice by features internal to our conception of moral powers' (Beitz 1983: 596). The problem is that this second argument fails to take into account a shift in Rawls's Kantian phase: his conception of moral powers has changed. Beitz's global argument stands on Rawls's original formulation in *TJ* that the concept of the person represents an Archimedean point, the nature of which is universalizable (Rawls 1971: 584). Yet, in his Kantian phase, Rawls distinguishes himself from Kant by suggesting that there is variance in conceptions of moral personality. If conceptions of moral personality vary outside of liberal democratic society, then global principles of justice can no longer be derived from an original position animated by such a conception. In addition, his cosmopolitan position regarding the moral irrelevance of states founders if conceptions of moral personality vary and are intertwined with the political culture of societies. Thus, Beitz is still constrained by a Rawlsian theory of justice that refuses international application. Disregarding this, his theory of distributive justice remains limited. In relying upon Rawls's account of moral personality, he fails to offer us any further justification of why we should support the liberal conception of the person that bolsters his cosmopolitan justice. Here, too, it remains a foundational assumption beyond justification.

Thomas Pogge

In connection with the second movement in Rawls, Pogge is interested in extending the distinction Rawls develops in 'OC' between two models of institutionalized coexistence to international relations (Pogge 1989: 218n) Rawls is concerned in 'OC' that common interest in peaceful relations, a *modus vivendi*, is not enough to guarantee stable, just relations within liberal democratic societies, and he looks to an overlapping consensus, agreement on certain shared values, as something more substantial upon which assurance could rest. It is Pogge's aim to demonstrate why an overlapping consensus is needed in international practice, and how we may come to an overlapping consensus upon a conception of justice, the scope of which is global and the subjects of which are individuals.

To begin, Pogge writes that the central problem of contemporary world order is not the absence of world government. Intergovernmental agreements and international institutions exist. 'The heart of the problem' is that 'statesmen and citizens are left without a *moral* reason for wanting their state to support this order, which is seen as merely the crystallization of the momentary balance of power' (Pogge 1989: 218). Pogge's two hypotheses are that the present world order is a *modus vivendi*, and that international institutions are largely unsuccessful because they lack the shared values integral to well-ordered national societies (Pogge 1989: 222). The actors in a *modus vivendi* are prompted by their self-interest to participate in a scheme that curbs competitive behaviour within terms that remain in the actors' best interests.[13] Association in such a scheme is neither peaceful nor just, as 'each participant cares primarily for its relative position, the terms of a *modus vivendi* will essentially reflect a dynamic bargaining equilibrium . . . largely detached from any values they may have' (Pogge 1989: 221).

Pogge's claim is that we must 'transcend the prevailing *modus vivendi*' and work towards a value-based order (1989: 227). We replace institutions based on bargaining, premissed along the lines of distributions of power, with institutions based upon shared values. A shared value is not a common interest in peace or coexistence; such a shared value would merely be instrumental to the interests of the

---

[13] Pogge assumes the actors to be governments. In other words, this is an intergovernmental *modus vivendi* (Pogge 1989: 222).

parties. Instead, a scheme is value-based when participants share 'some important ultimate values' which are incorporated in their institutions (Pogge 1989: 228). Progress for Pogge begins with even a narrow consensus, as long as it allows for 'institutional fixed points' immune to transitions in power and interests of the participants. The 'foremost prerequisite' for a value-based international order is that 'societies should accept – *morally* rather than only prudentially – the continued existence of one another and the values central to their domestic social contracts' (Pogge 1989: 228). Pogge lists three other necessary conditions: (1) the parties are convinced that there *ought to be* a fair scheme for the distribution of the benefits and burdens among all the parties, (2) that parties can identify and perhaps extend some common values, (3) that each is willing to modify their values to some extent (1989: 229). Like Rawls, Pogge holds that with the experience of trust and cooperation, commitment to a just scheme based on shared values would deepen and widen.

Pogge posits one last condition, a 'decisive condition' of international pluralism: 'the idea that knowledgeable and intelligent persons of good will may reasonably favour different forms of (national) social organization' (Pogge 1989: 230). He writes that there are two reasons for advancing the idea of international pluralism: realism and plausibility. Realism elicits the recognition that international pluralism could rescue us from the fragility of a *modus vivendi*, because the shared moral acceptance of international pluralism would assure the existence of each other's societies and associate values. Secondly, Pogge finds that this condition is plausible, given various and conflicting accounts. He writes that it is certainly more plausible than one who claims to have *the* answer to a just world. Like Rawls, Pogge argues that we cannot establish the truth of any value or end upon which society should be organized, nor can we reasonably advocate just *any* social organization. For the most part, we must understand our disagreements about these issues as 'reasonable disagreements', and we can work from this for a world in which many different reasonable positions can coexist (Pogge 1989: 232).[14]

---

[14] Pogge goes one step further than Rawls, by suggesting ways in which this overlapping value consensus might come about. He proposes an international ethical dialogue between teams of political philosophers and international lawyers to deliberate on ways to identify, codify and extend areas of shared value consensus (Pogge 1989: 235). This is just one of several extraordinary thoughts which

Despite Pogge's distinction, his basis for justice remains instrumental, and not based on something more substantial such as a shared moral understanding. Pogge does not get beyond a shared interest in peace and coexistence, which he himself identifies as an instrumental concern. This is made clear when the question is raised: is it satisfactory to declare that you accept '*morally* rather than prudentially' the existence of others? To convince us, Pogge appeals to our self-interest in keeping our values. 'On the realist argument it is, then, for the sake of our values themselves that we should modify these values in the direction of greater tolerance' (Pogge 1989: 231). This is an instrumental appeal, whether it hinges on the survival of values or lives. Increased tolerance enhances stability, enabling international structures in which plural social forms can thrive.

Pogge's idea of justice based on an overlapping consensus turns on a Hobbesian, practical concern for order. Rawls's political emphasis has been similarly accused of a Hobbesian concern for order and stability (Hampton 1989: 799–802; Kukathas and Pettit 1990: 140–42). There is a difference though. To be sure, Rawls is concerned to accommodate the fact of pluralism, finding a stable, workable conception of justice. None the less, his conception of justice remains tied to the moral ideal of the individual as citizen, free and equal in her moral capacities. Pogge, on the other hand, makes no similar appeal to moral personality. For example in his discussion of why international pluralism is plausible, he invokes Rawls's discussion of 'reasonable disagreements' in 'DP'. Pogge writes that his endorsement of international pluralism allows that one may argue that some forms of social organization are 'not reasonable'. Note that he does not choose Rawls's strong argument against the challenge of publicly-

compromise an otherwise worthy project. Pogge also attributes the world (note that the time of publication is 1989) with a siege mentality when he writes, 'several major societies are committed to the belief that their form of regime is plainly superior . . . and that it would not be wrong in principle to destroy the opponents' domestic institutions' (Pogge 1989, p. 230). It is a struggle to the death in the present *modus vivendi* as 'neither side believes that were it significantly weaker, its values would be allowed to survive' (Pogge 1989, p. 230). The nature of the security dilemma he presents is limited to ideological conflict; that is, whether capitalist and socialist social organizations can see fit to tolerate each other's existence. It is misleading, even with hindsight after 1989, to reduce international conflict to the ideological, and even unnecessary in the context of his aim to point out the need for realism in working towards a value based-order. Other factors, such as potential nuclear catastrophe, environmental destruction, world-wide economic recession, etc., suggest a similar need.

compromising comprehensive doctrines, to draw upon the 'partially' comprehensive good of the political concept of the person, in order to label such an imposition on the citizen as wrong. Thus, Pogge's conception of justice can be seen to be tied less to an ideal of the person (a moral conception) and more to an interest in order (an instrumental, but not moral concern).

If we turn to the second of the two difficulties that arise for IR theorists adapting Rawls's work, it is clear that, in Pogge's recourse to 'reasonable disagreement', he escapes the criticism levelled against Rawls and Beitz for not justifying the concept of the person upon which their liberal/cosmopolitan conceptions of justice rest. However, in avoiding the strong argument, Pogge's case is then vulnerable to circumstances when regard for international pluralism can legitimately be violated by self-interested parties. Thus, his original interest in transcending the present *modus vivendi* that he finds so morally objectionable is potentially compromised. In answering Rawls's own objections to the extension of his theory of justice to the international, Pogge points to the misguided starting point of searching for an idea of justice for closed societies. Rawls and Beitz (in his first, weak argument) consider distributive justice for closed societies, but Pogge argues we can agree that this is an academic exercise, since we all recognise global interdependence. Pogge says that his global interpretation of Rawls is plausible within a Rawlsian framework because he is in line with Rawls's two main reasons for beginning with basic structures as the primary moral subject: to adjust for institutional inequalities, and to assert that the inequalities produced are governed by a maximin criterion (Pogge 1989: 246–49). Whether or not this is the case, Pogge is trying to maintain a global difference principle in the face of objections that Beitz has already accepted (Brown 1992: 190n). International interdependence is not at such a level that mutuality exists in a global cooperative venture; thus, the idea of a global surplus requiring distribution cannot be maintained. It is puzzling that Pogge makes no move to address nor make a redirection of the argument on this point.

A cosmopolitan position on international distributive justice: an assessment

This chapter is written with a sense that understanding these movements in Rawls's work is important to an analysis of cosmopolitan

theories of international distributive justice, and to the cosmopolitan/
communitarian debate as a whole. As discussed in the introduction, at
the centre of the debate are three issues: a concept of the person, the
morality of states, and the question of universalism versus particularism. What follows is an assessment of Beitz's and Pogge's positions
on these issues, an assessment which suggests that the poles of the
debate have narrowed with the incorporation of ideas from the later
work of Rawls into cosmopolitan theorizing in IR.

A concept of the person

The characterization of the cosmopolitan concept of the person draws
heavily from the idea of liberal individualism in political theory, that
each individual has the capacity to choose her life, unencumbered by
social attachments. It is a matter of debate whether this idea of the
pre-social self suggests that individuals possess moral personality –
and the rationality assumed by that notion – outside of society; or
whether this pre-social identity recognizes the social attachments of
persons, yet holds that subjectivity is personally chosen, and is given
independently of one's associations. In my view, Rawls holds the
latter assumption about the pre-sociality of persons in *TJ*, but the later
Rawls accommodates an understanding of persons as being socially
chosen as well. A decidedly Hegelian shift is evident in Rawls's later
work as he turns his attention to an examination of values located in
current social practices (Kukathas and Pettit 1990: 143– 6; Galston
1982: 512–14). Conceptions of moral personality have become candidates for such an examination and are subject to variance within
different social practices, suggesting that moral personality is vulnerable to social construction. This movement in Rawls indicates that he
no longer understands the self to be personally chosen alone. This also
indicates that it is not imperative that a cosmopolitan position hold
steadfastly to an idea of the self as pre-social either, particularly a
cosmopolitanism that draws from a Rawlsian framework.

It is true that Beitz fails to acknowledge the shift in Rawls's
characterization of conceptions of moral personality, and that he
continues to draw from a singular, universal concept of the person. As
for Pogge, he implicitly endorses a conception of the person as free
and equal in using a Rawlsian framework, but he does not mention
moral personality, not even in his discussion of our positive duty to
mutual aid and negative duty not to inflict harm or injustice on others.

Although Pogge does draw from Rawls's later work where recognition of the social construction of persons is evident, we cannot draw any conclusions as to whether Pogge only adheres to a personally chosen self. Clearly, there is little or no sign of a readiness on the part of these cosmopolitans to appreciate the communitarian stance on this issue. However, the shift in Rawls suggests it is a possibility. For cosmopolitans, the assumption of the unencumbered or pre-social self works foundationally as a ground for the claims of individuals against the practice of states and other international actors. To concede degrees in which the individual might be socially as well as personally chosen does not undermine the possibility of grounding such claims; that is, as long as some understanding of the individual having a subjectivity found independently of society is operative. Thus, concessions on this first issue of the debate can be arrived at from a cosmopolitan standpoint.

The moral standing of states

Another defining characteristic of the cosmopolitan position is its challenge to the prevailing assumption within international practice that states are morally relevant. However, here too I find that accommodation within the cosmopolitan position on this issue is possible. While the moral relevance of states is not a question for Rawls, it is central to the debate in international political theory in which cosmopolitans claim that considerations of justice in international practice should begin with individuals not states. Both Beitz and Pogge hold that individuals should be the subject of international distributive justice, yet Beitz is clearly the harder critic of the two on the value conferred upon state sovereignty. He finds that the exalted moral status of the state circumscribes our ability to address questions of international distributive justice. None the less, in *Political Theory and International Relations*, Beitz does make a weak argument for international distributive justice that begins with states, in addition to his second, strong argument, which starts from the consideration of individuals. Also, in 'Cosmopolitan Ideals', Beitz's attack upon the moral inadequacy of states seems to have lost its steam. As discussed above, in response to criticism about the lack of mutuality at the present level of interdependence assumed in his work, he chooses to fall back upon a moral conception of the person instead of reinforcing his arguments about the immorality of states and state-centric practice. Actually, he even compromises his case against prioritizing statehood as he concedes that there are good reasons for supporting patriotic sentiments (Beitz 1983: 599).[15]

On a position regarding the morality of states, Pogge, once again, is unclear. He writes that an international original position should begin with individuals, not states as Rawls suggests. He comes to this conclusion, not through considered arguments regarding the moral inadequacy of states, but from the position that Rawls 'would be begging a crucial question, provided we allow that justice may *fail to require* the states system in its present form' (Pogge 1989: 258). Yet, when discussing the value of international pluralism he writes that its 'widespread acceptance' would allow that 'value clusters with their coordinate national forms of regime, are morally accepted and perma-nently protected' (Pogge 1989: 231). Pogge accuses governments and statesmen of being morally repugnant, not the state form itself. One can infer that Pogge is willing to do no more than suggest that the state system may not be integral to considerations of international distributive justice. An openness to the value of states is evident among these writers. Thus, it is not an improbable suggestion that cosmopolitan writers can concede that states have some moral rele-vance. However, what remains primary for cosmopolitans is that ultimately, individuals are the focus of considerations of justice.

The universal versus the particular

The cosmopolitan position on this third issue is characterized by a will to universalization in making claims for the entitlements of humankind. While Rawls, in his later work, clarifies that his will to universalization on principles of justice is limited to overlapping consensus within 'United States-like' liberal democracies, these inter-national theorists continue to pursue principles for international distributive justice that can be universally shared. Thus, these cosmo-politans seek a detached standpoint from which we can transcend the particularism of plural goods in international practice. Accordingly, foundations are invoked. In Beitz's rearticulation of his position on international distributive justice in 'Cosmopolitan Ideals', he places added emphasis upon a conception of moral personality and its *universal* nature to bolster his global extension of Rawlsian principles.

---

[15] Brown suggests this point (1992: 177).

Despite Rawls's shift in finding that conceptions of moral personality vary according to the social and historical conditions of societies, Beitz continues to use his Kantian conception of moral personality as a fixed point from which a theory of justice can be evaluated. Pogge also posits an Archimedean point. However, his is located not in a concept of the person, but in an overlapping consensus. Such a consensus on values provides 'institutional fixed points that stand above ordinary negotiation . . . immune to shifts in power and interests' (Pogge 1989: 228). For Pogge, an overlapping consensus can work foundationally and universally.

Both Beitz and Pogge are concerned with the problem of how we can reach consensus on a conception of justice in a world of plural societies; and thus, both aim to locate a ground for universal consensus. However, neither is willing to posit *strong* foundations of a Kantian, noumenal kind. None the less, they offer epistemological foundations of a *weaker* kind. The fixed points they locate are not transcendentally loaded, but, instead, have more humble origins as claims which are universally agreed to be shared among all persons. Yet, Beitz's concept of the person and Pogge's overlapping consensus are used in a *strong* foundationalist way to bolster a *non-contingent* ethics, despite the characterization of these grounds as *weak*. Returning to the 'anchor analogy' drawn in the Introduction, I argue that these authors proceed as if these notions are anchored in firm ground, generating an ethical critique of international practice, the criteria of which are stable, absolute and universal in their capacity for judgement. Thereby, workable universal conceptions of international distributive justice are facilitated across particular and plural conceptions of the good in international practice.

For these cosmopolitans, this is an issue on which there is little room for accommodation to a communitarian, particularist perspective. This is evident from Beitz's and Pogge's refusals to accept and move with Rawls's own shift in focus to the particular, despite using his work as a point of departure. The will to universalization is fundamental to the cosmopolitan's central concern of putting individuals first in making ethical claims on the behalf of humankind. Can this will coexist with an appreciation of particularist forms of moral argument? Rawls suggests as much when he attempts to defend the priority of the political – that is, a particular, American liberal democratic vision – over the comprehensive moral doctrine on the basis of a universal conception of moral personality. From Rawls's example, once again, concessions in a cosmopolitan position are conceivable. However, in this instance, it is unclear exactly *how* these concessions might be arrived at, because of Rawls's Kantian conundrum identified above. Rawls's own difficulty in satisfactorily defending why we should prioritize the political over the comprehensive or universal, suggests that the kind of foundation invoked has repercussions for the extent to which universal and particular moral argument can be pursued together. That is, from Rawls's predicament, it is hard to see how a cosmopolitan who begins with a universal conception of moral personality, no matter how weakly conceived, can satisfactorily embrace particular moral argument when that argument is grounded upon an idea of moral personality that is not up for question and held *non-contingently*. Thus, the third issue of the debate appears to be the most intractable.

Concluding remarks

Of Beitz and Pogge, only Beitz calls his theory of justice a cosmopolitan theory. Yet as the discussion above indicates, Pogge's cosmopolitanism is suggested by the concept of the person implied in his Rawlsian framework, the international original position he posits composed of individuals and not pre-formed societies, and his will to universalization in the notion of an international, overlapping consensus. In assessing the cosmopolitan position, and the implications of the movements in Rawls's later writings for this position and for the impasse in the debate as a whole, two points can be made.

First, it appears that the poles of opposition between cosmopolitans and communitarians may not be as rigid as generally suggested in normative IR theory literature, since possibilities for accommodation are evident on the part of cosmopolitans on the first and second issues. As discussed above, there is the possibility of a sea-change among cosmopolitans in regard to the concept of the person. Despite the pre-social starting points of Rawls, Pogge and Beitz, these writers do acknowledge the significance of individuals' social connectedness, and, as the movement in Rawls's work suggests, there is room for an acknowledgement that individuals may be socially constructed as well as personally chosen. Regarding the morality of states question, the cosmopolitans show an openness to the value of states. However, the dispute on the universal versus the particular stands. As discussed above, Rawls's own turn to the consideration of values in particular social practices has not diminished the will to universalization in these cosmopolitans, nor has it offered a viable alternative which indicates how these two forms of moral argument can be pursued together, instead of at the expense of one or the other.

Secondly, what this analysis of a cosmopolitan position indicates is that, while cosmopolitan theories exhibit possibilities for closing the gap between the poles of debate, those poles will not collapse. There is a structural opposition at work. In Beitz's and Pogge's cosmopolitanism, there are assumptions that operate in a *strong* foundationalist way such that there is little or no room for accommodation. Also, the difficulty that a *non-contingent* foundation presents, even when one attempts a distinction between political and comprehensive moral argument, is evident in Rawls's Kantian conundrum. Thus, Rawlsian approaches suggest no clear way out of the cosmopolitan/communitarian impasse. This leads to an insight that will continue throughout the book, that it is on the question of epistemology, manifested in the third issue of the debate and the relative strength of foundational assumptions employed, that headway in normative theory in IR is either advanced or compromised.

2 Communitarianism: Michael Walzer and international justice

Introduction

Communitarians in normative IR theory focus attention upon the value that social attachments have for individuals, and the implications of such attachments for the moral relevance of states in international practice. Communitarians in both political theory and normative IR theory hold that the individual's self-actualization is realized in the expression and pursuit of shared goods within a community. Because communitarians find that it is within the community that ethical relationships between individuals are made possible, they take communities to be the ultimate source of value in moral thinking. Therefore, considerations of justice must begin with community. While communitarians in both fields are rarely explicit about what kind of ties and associations are key to the *construction* of 'community', it can be said that normative IR theorists are fixed upon considerations of what kind of associations *represent* 'community' and, thus, should be accorded value in international practice. Generally, the form of community assumed or identified is the sovereign state or the nation. Thus, in international practice, considerations of justice for communitarians begin with these two forms of community.

This chapter will examine and critically evaluate the state-based communitarian position as it is articulated by Michael Walzer. Walzer is a communitarian whose writing crosses the boundary between the debates of liberals and communitarians in political theory and cosmopolitans and communitarians in normative IR theory. One might also argue that Walzer's work crosses the boundaries of the cosmopolitan/communitarian divide as well. Walzer is a writer who displays some markedly cosmopolitan features in the course of the reconciliations he seeks across the lines of these debates and I will be careful to draw attention to them. As anticipated in the introduction, we will find that Walzer, among others, is a moving target who cannot be categorized without qualification. However, through an analysis of Walzer's work in relation to the three central issues of the debate in normative IR theory, I will illustrate that tensions remain in the reconciliations he attempts, tensions which show Walzer to make more, rather than less, of a good fit with the general caricature of communitarianism.

There are other writers in normative IR theory to whom one might turn to examine the communitarian position: for example, those who focus upon the nation, and not the sovereign state, as the community most valued by individuals (Miller 1988 and 1994; Tamir 1993; Thompson 1992). However, since my focus in this book is upon forms of normative IR theory which are oriented to the possibility of expanding moral inclusion, I am less interested in exploring a communitarianism based upon the nation, because I find that these authors have not satisfactorily addressed the repercussions of the closed nature of the nation for considerations of international justice. Of the communitarians who focus on the state as community, and are committed to thinking about the possibilities for international justice from a communitarian position, two distinct understandings of the moral relevance of states can be identified. First, an instrumentalist understanding finds the state to be morally relevant because of its role in providing a locus for ethical relationships, thus having the character of an ethical conduit or facilitator of such relationships. The second is neo-Hegelian in character and finds the state to be more than a facilitator of ethical relationships, but ethically significant in itself. One reason for choosing to focus on Walzer is to highlight the work of a key proponent of the former understanding of state-based communitarianism.[1] Chapter 3 will highlight the second understanding, which is developed in the work of Mervyn Frost. Also, I choose to focus on Walzer – as I chose to focus on Rawlsian approaches to cosmopolitanism in the previous chapter – because of his close links to the debate in political theory, which has been a seed-bed for the debate in normative IR theory and its characterization.

The relevance of Walzer's book *Just and Unjust Wars* (*JUW*) to IR is

---

[1] There is another writer who shares this instrumentalist understanding of a state based communitarianism, Charvet (1998). Charvet's idea of a 'contractarian communitarianism' is being developed in a forthcoming book.

not in question. Its arguments are familiar to many IR specialists. Yet, Walzer's book *Spheres of Justice (SJ)*, for which he is best known in the field of political theory, is seldom cited in the IR literature. This is hardly surprising since the book is a theory of justice which is not intended to apply internationally. To be sure, issues with international repercussions are discussed in *SJ*, such as territory and rights to control membership within a territory. Also, in this book Walzer shares with the writers discussed in the last chapter a focus upon questions of *distributive* justice in particular. However, in contrast to Charles Beitz and Thomas Pogge, Walzer finds that distributive justice cannot have international reach because distributive justice, according to him, can only arise from the shared meanings within political communities. Thus, by Walzer's theory of distributive justice, there can be no *international* distributive justice because it cannot take as its focus the 'common life of citizens but the more distanced relations of states' (1983b: 30). He writes in *SJ* that to talk about international justice would require 'a different theory, a different book' (1983b: 30).

While Walzer finds that distributive justice cannot extend internationally, it is not the case that he has nothing to say about international justice in *SJ*. For example, Walzer sees that distributive justice within domestic communities is not insignificant as a starting point for problems of justice globally. More significantly, as Joseph Carens writes, there is an aspect to *SJ* that concerns universal principles of justice which apply, in at least some minimal way, to all states (1995: 58). Carens points to two examples: Walzer's discussions of the rights of alien people already within a territory, and of the rights of 'guest workers' invited to a country. In these cases, and to a more limited extent in the case of his discussion of refugees, Walzer defends the rights of these individuals against the interests of communities. This argument suggests to Carens that it is 'based on general, even abstract, liberal democratic principles' (1995: 50), and to me that it resembles cosmopolitan principles of justice in normative IR theory. Therefore, Walzer's work is complex on at least two levels: (1) the way in which his thoughts on domestic justice and international justice link together; and (2) the way in which he resorts to a universal, cosmopolitan argument to fill in remaining justice concerns that his communitarianism cannot address. This chapter will also attempt to elucidate the ways in which these two levels of complexity impact upon each other and the debate in normative IR theory.

In order to develop these points, my analysis will draw heavily from Walzer's book *Thick and Thin: Moral Argument at Home and Abroad (TT)*. Here, Walzer's central aim is to reconcile the particularist methodology he elaborates in *SJ* with the universal commitments explicit in *JUW* and implicit in *SJ* and other works, such as *Interpretation and Social Criticism* or his piece 'Objectivity and Social Meaning. *TT* concerns not only this, the third issue of the debate, but also touches upon the other issues of the debate – the concept of the person and the issue of the moral relevance of states – and seeks reconciliations regarding these issues. In the first section of this chapter, I will trace the development of each of the three core issues of the cosmopolitan/communitarian debate throughout Walzer's writing and his efforts to address the tensions within them. I will outline the responses he offers in his earlier work, highlight some difficulties there, and follow this with a discussion of the ways in which *TT* is an effort to address particular tensions that remain in regard to these three issues. Although Walzer does not say so, *TT* could be construed as that 'different book', or more likely, a lead-up to that book, which offers a theory of international justice. Therefore, the second section examines the international ethics that results from Walzer's position in this book: his minimalist morality for international relations. The third section concludes by offering a final assessment of the implications of Walzer's minimalist morality for communitarianism and the debate as a whole.

Walzer and the cosmopolitan/communitarian debate

A concept of the person

In his early work, Walzer sidesteps any direct engagement with a theory of the self. However, there clearly is a concept of the person behind his project. Walzer attributes the rights of life and liberty to individuals in *JUW*, but he does not expound upon those rights except to say that they are simply a part of being human. He writes, '[i]f they are not natural, then we have invented them, but natural or invented, they are a palpable feature of our moral world' (Walzer 1977: 54). This is one example of the way in which Walzer relies at times upon universalist utterances when he can find no other defence. However, one is led to ask, who is the 'we' to whom this moral world belongs? These rights are taken as given and universal, yet there is much at stake within these rights about which he says very little. For example, the rights of states to territorial integrity and political sovereignty 'derive ultimately from the rights of individuals' (Walzer 1977: 53). From this it follows for Walzer that 'individual rights underlie the most important judgements that we make about war' (1977: 54). Further elucidation is needed of how these rights are derived, but it is not provided in *JUW*.

Nor is it explicitly provided in *SJ*, even though there are also arguments there that rely upon the assertion of abstract, individual rights. For example, Walzer writes that '[n]ew states and governments must make their peace with the old inhabitants of the land they rule'; their expulsion by new governments would be unjust, because the state's claim to territory only comes about by virtue of an individual's right to place, and 'it can't be said that the first always or necessarily supersedes the second' (1983b: 42–3). Why, and on what basis, are individual rights in this particular case justified as trumps against collective rights? Unfortunately, we get no more answer from Walzer than, the fact that 'Hobbes made the argument in classical form' (1983b: 42–3). However, I would argue that there is something worthy of note going on when Walzer makes such cosmopolitan gestures: the aspects of personal justice which concern him are not properly located within a theory of justice beginning from the shared meanings of community.

Consequently, Walzer must have an appreciation of the personal, yet in the prologue of *SJ*, Walzer writes that he will not be arguing from the 'idea of the personal'. None the less, and despite his occasional appeal to abstract, individual rights, his idea of justice hinges primarily upon his understanding of how the person is socially constituted. To begin with, he suggests that humans universally share the need for community, and it is through the culture, religion and politics of a community that other socially recognized needs are generated (Walzer 1983b: 65). Further, our identity as individuals is shaped by these historical determinations, the way we 'conceive and create, and then possess and employ social goods' (Walzer 1983b: 8). In fact, according to Walzer, justice takes persons as its starting point; that is, persons who are seen to be socially constituted. Ultimately, the subject of Walzer's theory of distributive justice is the shared understandings of persons about social goods, and the ways in which individuals relate to one another through those goods (Walzer 1983b: 18, 261).

In the conclusion of *SJ*, Walzer finally addresses the idea of the universality of persons: that which constitutes humans as equals. He writes, 'one characteristic above all is central to my argument. We are (all of us) culture-producing creatures; we make and inhabit meaningful worlds' (Walzer 1983b: 314). As we are all equal in this ability to create these worlds, and since there is no way to 'rank and order' such creations, respect for what others create is a matter of justice. For Walzer, this respect for individuals and the numerous worlds humans are wont to make is a moral requirement. To deny such respect is a form of coercion that Walzer's egalitarian politics works to correct.

Clearly, there is a concept of the person at work within Walzer's project: a person who is historically and socially constituted, and whose social integration must be reflected in a theory of distributive justice and in considerations of international justice. This understanding of persons as 'culture-producing creatures' is at the base of the goods for which Walzer argues consistently throughout his work. So, why is he reluctant to elaborate the significance of an idea of the self for his work on justice? Perhaps it is due to the loaded nature of the question. The debates between liberals and communitarians, and cosmopolitans and communitarians, set up an artificial dichotomy: a choice between a concept of the person which is either pre-social or socially constituted. Walzer writes in 'The Communitarian Critique of Liberalism' that neither of these views can be maintained, nor are they necessary to the arguments of liberals or communitarians (1990a: 6–23). Further, he observes that '[c]oncessions from the other side come too easily to count as victories' (Walzer 1990a: 21). A pre-social self is not the liberal's preoccupation. The liberal is simply interested in a self who is capable of critical reflection upon his or her socialization. On the other hand, the communitarian is willing to admit that socialization is not all-encompassing. For Walzer, the main issue 'is not the constitution of the self but the connection of constituted selves, the pattern of social relations' (1990a: 21).

However, while he is primarily concerned with the social relations of persons, Walzer does not manage to leave the issue of the self's constitution alone. In fact, in his recent work, Walzer is more forthcoming about his idea of the person, developing its significance to his project. In *TT*, Walzer's final chapter is titled 'The Divided Self'. Here, he claims that the self is divided in three ways: first, among its interests and roles; second, among its identities; and finally, it is divided among its ideals, principles and values (Walzer 1994b: 85).

These divisions overlap, making the individual, and consequently the social world, highly complex. However, in his final chapter, Walzer focuses on the third of these divisions, since it is this division which makes self-criticism, the vehicle of moral deliberation, possible. Walzer writes, 'my inner world is thickly settled' (1994b: 96). Each of us hears the voices of numerous critics representing different values, none of which is necessarily chosen by any of us, but they *are* us because we are 'socially as well as personally constructed': the self is 'a complex maximalist whole . . . a thickly populated circle' (Walzer 1994b: 98). We draw some critics in closer than others, but the result is that the person is the product of all of these self-critics, 'its embattled center' (Walzer 1994b: 99).

Walzer sees the play among these self-critics as beneficial; the more self-critics interact, the better. Without this play, selves are 'dominated' or 'thin' because they repress other expressions of the self, listening to only one critic (Walzer 1994b: 99). He adds that 'within every thin self, there is a thick self yearning for elaboration, largeness, freedom' (Walzer 1994b: 100). The process of elaborating thick selves is unknown, but what is important is that room for such elaboration is allowed. In Walzer's opinion, this space can only be provided by pluralism. Thus, Walzer offers a concept of the person as 'thick' and historically specific, which supports the pluralism he defends in his project. He writes, 'thick, divided selves are the characteristic products of, and in turn require, a thick, differentiated and pluralist society' (Walzer 1994b: 101). This has repercussions for world politics and considerations of international justice when he goes further to add that, at times, there are mismatches when thick selves are 'not at home' in some societies, and this causes pain which can be relieved by redrawing borders both internal and external (Walzer 1994b: 101–2). With this suggestion, his conception of the 'thick' self feeds another theme in Walzer's projects both domestic and international: the will to a politics free of coercion.

While Walzer's concept of the person relates to the interconnection of selves in a cobweb of social determinants, he is at the same time making a claim regarding the way in which these entanglements constitute the self. Thus, Walzer undermines the distinction he draws between the constitution and connection of the self. He argues that liberals and communitarians can agree that the person is indeed socially constituted, yet is at the same time capable of critical reflection upon that socialization. According to Walzer, liberals and communitarians differ on the relative importance of the ways in which selves are connected. The liberal places little, if any, value upon the social connections of persons, which are important to the communitarian. Therefore, Walzer claims that reconciliation is possible on this issue; the debate can take a step forward, acknowledge agreement on the constitution of the self, and move on to the more significant question of the self's connections. Nevertheless, by developing a conception of the thick, divided self, Walzer employs a specific conception of the self's *constitution* in his effort to support the goods of community, pluralism and a politics free of coercion. To defend his claim regarding the self's connections – that the accommodation of plural communities is necessary – he turns to the self's constitution: an understanding of the person who, in times of crisis, falls back fully on her parochialism. I will argue that this is one of several tensions that linger in the resolutions Walzer attempts within the debate.

The moral standing of states

JUW is criticised by cosmopolitans for wrongly privileging the rights of states over the rights of individuals (Doppelt 1979; Luban 1985; Wasserstrom 1978). In 'The Moral Standing of States', Walzer responds by reiterating his argument in *JUW* that states' rights are founded upon a theory of individual rights. While Walzer regards the critique as a misreading – the likely product of philosophical disagreement on the nature of political life within communities – I am more inclined to regard it as being suggestive of the fact that despite his significant gestures towards individual rights, Walzer does indeed morally privilege the state, since he regards it to be the ultimate form of political community at the base of his considerations of domestic and international justice. In order to demonstrate this, I will examine his work on a theory of distributive justice, where his stance on the nature of political life in communities, and thus, his position on the moral standing of states, is more fully developed.

In *SJ*, Walzer writes that community is perhaps the most important good that there is to be distributed (1983b: 29). What makes community valuable is that its constitution is determined internally, by its members. Were that internal choice to be taken away, the good of community would be undermined. He considers one other possible setting for a theory of distributive justice: humanity. However, this would require a leap of imagination, since no community of humanity exists. As noted above, Walzer dismisses the idea of a community of humankind as the setting for distributive justice. He does so for the reason that, even if some agreement could be reached on just distributive arrangements, that agreement could not be enacted without breaking political arrangements, already established, which happen to constitute states today. Thus, that which is most valuable about communities would be taken away: their decision-making capacities.

This is one among several indicators which imply that the institutional form of political community assumed by Walzer is the state, even though he talks about other forms of community such as the neighborhood, club or family. Another indicator that is particularly suggestive of this assumption appears when he defends the importance of control over membership for the self-determination of communities. For Walzer, it is in the choice of membership that the nature of community is set because the particularity of cultures relies upon closure (1983b: 62). Without closure, the distinctiveness of cultures is in jeopardy (Walzer 1983b: 39).[2] Thus, Walzer is preoccupied with separation, writing of spheres, walls, boundaries and borders, because he understands separation to be the vehicle of group, and thus individual, freedom. However, he is interested in separation at a particular institutional level: the state (see Walzer 1984). Because Walzer sees local mobility to be important to individual choice, modern democracy needs the 'kind of largeness, and also the kind of boundedness, that states provide' (1983b: 39).

The sovereign state is the guarantor of this closure and separation, since the state has at its disposal the authority to preside over crucial membership decisions. The state, as Walzer writes, is the 'agent of separation and the defender, as it were, of the social map' (1984: 327), protecting its collective life from external threats. Territory is a vital part of this collective life which, without the guardianship of the state, loses its effective self-determination. Thus, for Walzer, the state is an ethical requirement, which any theory of justice must accommodate by specifying the rights of its inhabitants as well as its collective rights to self-determination (1983b: 44).

The crux of the instrumental character of Walzer's understanding of the moral relevance of states is the role he believes that the state plays as guardian of the shared life created by its members. Decisions about

---

[2] Walzer does acknowledge there is no evidence to show that culture cannot thrive in cosmopolitan environments (1983b: 38).

the distributions of social goods within their distributive spheres are integral to that shared life. The state ensures justice by working to keep domestic spheres separate, 'protecting churches, universities, families and so on from tyrannical interference' (Walzer 1983b: 44). Thus, the moral value of the state is judged against the way in which it maintains the 'institutional integrity' of those spheres, as well as the 'integrity of the state itself' (Walzer 1984: 327). Yet, Walzer recognizes that the state is coercive by virtue of its authority. He responds to those critics of the state who warn of its potential for violence towards its citizens by writing that its power is effectively mitigated through institutional separation, a principal achievement of liberalism. Such violence at the hands of the state can only be licensed today in authoritarian states. The problems for liberal states are different. Their worry is coercion exercised by those using influence – gained either through corruption or privilege – to trespass across institutions and distributive spheres (Walzer 1984: 329). The good liberal state recognizes the value of its internal associations and bolsters their cooperative efforts (Walzer 1990a: 19–20).

However, since *SJ*, Walzer has put considerable effort into reconsidering forms of political community other than the state. This may be due to a recent preoccupation of his with forces of pluralism, which he sees as articulations of both group and individual difference that are 'unsettling' liberal states. For Walzer, modernity has unleashed forces that are disrupting associative tendencies. He identifies what he calls the 'Four Mobilities': geographic mobility, social mobility, marital mobility and political mobility (Walzer 1990a: 11–13).[3] These mobilities have repercussions within and beyond state boundaries. According to Walzer, they are rupturing communities and demoralizing both groups and individuals.

The issue of alternative political forms is also raised in *TT*, where he writes that there is no 'single best political unit . . . self determination has no absolute subject' (Walzer 1994b: 68–9). He adds that conflict over boundaries of self-determination is a product of the reality that 'bounds need not enclose, in every case, the same sort of space' (Walzer 1994b: 79). In fact, new possibilities for political community are particularly important to his discussion of the needs of the

---

[3] Walzer writes that the difference between liberals and communitarians is that liberals welcome the Four Mobilities as a fulfilment of liberty, whereas the communitarian laments the discontent generated by lost associative ties (1990a).

divided self. The divided self, in large part a product of the forces of pluralism, is 'best accommodated by complex equality in domestic society and by different versions of self-determination in domestic and international society' (Walzer 1994b: 103). By 'different versions' of self-determination, Walzer indicates that he does not mean the *nation*-state alone.

Walzer's position on the moral standing of states offers opportunities to narrow the poles of the cosmopolitan/communitarian debate. Walzer recognizes that, in order to accommodate the forces of pluralism at work today and the needs of thick, divided selves, institutional forms of political community other than the state must be moral possibilities as well. In *TT*, Walzer considers 'cities, nations, federations [and] immigrant societies' as other forms of self-determining political units in world politics (1994b: 69), but he opens these possibilities only to retreat to the cosy confines of the state when faced with the instability this pluralism engenders. This, to my mind, is the primary indicator of his assumption of the state as the ultimate form of political community, and it is why I would argue that Walzer, despite his universalist and cosmopolitan elements, not only fits comfortably within, but actually defines, an instrumentalist understanding of state-based communitarianism. He writes that, in times of crisis, the 'protective shelter that [state] sovereignty alone provides in the modern world seems morally appropriate, perhaps even necessary' (Walzer 1994b: 69). What begins as a promising suggestion about the need to seek out different forms of self-determination concludes with most of the work of differentiating such versions to be done domestically, within sovereign states. In regard to the forces of pluralism and the Four Mobilities, Walzer writes that ultimately the best agent for dealing with the crises thereby generated is the nation-state (1990a: 16). It is out of an instrumentalist concern for being able to deal with crisis that Walzer falls back upon the state and its guardianship. Thus, a tension is generated in Walzer's latest work: a will to encourage new political forms of self-determining communities is held back by a concern that only the state form appears able to handle the crises that communities have to face.

Universalism versus particularism

JUW and *SJ* share the same methodological starting point: shared understandings within a specified sphere or practice. The only difference is the *scope* within which this common starting point is employed in his theory of just war and aggression versus his theory of distributive justice. In *JUW*, Walzer begins from the common, shared understandings about war which constitute its moral reality (1977: xxvii). He begins with the 'present character' of these understandings regarding the moral world, and not with the aim of creating a new moral reality (Walzer 1977: xxviii). Thus, the shared understandings of peoples toward particular goods is Walzer's starting point. However, in this instance, the shared understandings extend globally. Walzer points to the continuity over time and across cultures in beliefs about the problems of war and the language in which it is discussed. Shared understandings about the problems of war reach globally, rather than locally, because goods that are universally shared are at stake: the rights to life and liberty.

The scope of shared understandings in *SJ* is limited to particular social, distributive goods, which serve as Walzer's starting point here. For Walzer, there are rights other than life and liberty which follow not 'from our common humanity; they follow from shared conceptions of social goods . . . local and particular in character' (1983b: xv). This is the realm of distributive justice, where rights to social goods can only be held in the moral worlds created and shared by communities. Thus, 'different social goods ought to be distributed for different reasons', differences which in fact 'derive from different understandings of the social goods themselves – the inevitable product of historical and cultural particularism' (Walzer 1983b: 6). Walzer acknowledges that his argument is 'radically particularist', since he finds that justice is relative to particular communities and, in turn, is particular to distributive spheres within communities. When conflicts arise over distributions, 'the ultimate appeal in these conflicts is not to the particular interests, not even to a public interest conceived as their sum, but to collective values, shared understandings of membership, health, food and shelter, work and leisure' (Walzer 1983b: 82). The problem is that common understandings 'are always subject to dispute' as well as change over time, and, as there is 'no single point of access to this world of distributive arrangements', or no 'single criterion' for distributions, the question of socially recognized needs is 'open-ended' (Walzer 1983b: 4, 82–3, 182). Thus, it is difficult to say whether any such judgements are wrong. Instead, it is a matter of interpretation regarding shared understandings.

Two criticisms of Walzer's method are generally offered (see

Galston 1989; Rosenblum 1984). First, Walzer is charged with relativism. Since common understandings change over time, and because they are always a matter of dispute, Walzer writes that there can be no one criterion for saying when judgements about those shared understandings are wrong; so, the social critic is left with the task of interpretation (1983b: 4, 82–3, 182). Thus, the question of relativism is raised, because there are no foundations for social criticism. The second criticism charges him with inconsistency, because he offers a particularist methodology couched at times in abstract, universal language regarding the nature of humans – that they have rights to life and liberty, and that they are 'culture-producing creatures'.

Walzer responds to the first criticism in two books, *The Company of Critics* and *Interpretation and Social Criticism*, in which he argues that effective social criticism must emanate from the shared moral worlds of particular communities. To begin with, he must defend interpretation as a legitimate moral philosophical approach. In *Interpretation and Social Criticism*, Walzer points to three approaches in moral philosophy: the 'path of discovery' (natural or divine revelation), the 'path of invention' (an invented morality as 'universal corrective' to plural values), and the 'path of interpretation' (morality as practised and understood in our day to day lives). He argues that discovery and invention are diversionary, because 'we already possess what they pretend to provide': an existing moral world which offers us the means to both reflection and criticism (Walzer 1987: 19–21). Moral philosophy is primarily interpretive, since our actually existing moral world is built upon the ways in which we justify ourselves and, when there is disagreement on 'received opinion', all we can do is 'go back to the "text": the values, principles, codes, and conventions that constitute the moral world – and to the readers of the text' (Walzer 1987: 29–30).

Walzer's next move is to discredit the ideal of the disconnected critic. His point is that the tools for criticism are what they are 'because of what a moral world is, because of what we do when we construct it' (Walzer 1987: 46). Try as we might to find an external standpoint, it remains a product of the moral world from which it is proffered. Walzer proceeds in *The Company of Critics* to examine the work of a group of social critics, in order to flesh out the idea that the most forceful social criticism is that which starts within the existing moral world and 'voices common complaints', something which only the 'connected critic' can do (1988: x, 16).

In response to the second criticism – the charge of inconsistency in his method – Walzer argues in 'Nation and Universe' that this age-old dichotomy between universalism and particularism is getting us nowhere. His aim is to stand among those who are seen as the opposition – universalists – to offer a 'nonstandard variety' of universalism which can convey the 'appeal of moral particularism' (Walzer 1990b: 509–13). Walzer labels this nonstandard variety as 'reiterative universalism' (1990b: 509–13).[4] 'Reiterative universalism' can embrace universal claims, but it does so in a way learned through plural experiences, encountering others whose difference breeds a respect for particularity and humility (Walzer 1990b: 515). Walzer anticipates the question whether there is any 'common substance' to reiterated moralities, and his answer is that there is not: 'reiteration makes for difference'. However, we do find an 'overlapping plurality of sets' which resemble each other (Walzer 1990b: 525). For example, we can recognize different principles of justice and interpret ways in which 'their' principles resemble 'ours', but these interpretations can only point to the 'differentiated commonalities' of justice because these features are the products of a historically particular moral world (Walzer 1990b: 525–26). Thus, justice for Walzer is a reiterative moral principle with particular manifestations, yet which is universal in its warrant across plural moral cultures.

In *TT*, Walzer develops the argument begun in 'Nation and Universe', and explores when and how we can make use of these overlapping sets of values. He asks what we can take from them to develop the ideas of 'moral minimalism' and 'moral maximalism': two 'different, but interrelated kinds of moral argument' (Walzer 1994b: xi).[5] They are different in that minimalism is the product of 'mutual recognition' across different moral cultures of principles that are constantly reiterated, readily acknowledged and intensely felt. Maximalism, on the other hand, has a 'thickness' about it. It produces, over a long history, a culture interwoven with distinctive practices and principles that sets it apart as a moral world unto itself. However,

---

[4] He differentiates reiterative universalism from covering-law universalism in that reiterative universalism is 'particularist in focus and its pluralizing tendency' (Walzer 1990b: 513).

[5] Walzer does not employ the idea of 'reiterative universalism' in *TT*, but he does speak of the 'reiteration' of minimalist and maximalist principles. Also, minimalism is clearly developed from the idea of an 'overlapping plurality of sets' of reiterated moralities expressed in 'Nation and Universe'.

moral minimalism and maximalism are interrelated because 'minimalist meanings are embedded in the maximal morality' (Walzer 1994b: 3). We always start moral argument from our particular thick, maximalist conceptions, but in times of personal and social crisis or political confrontation, 'minimalism is liberated from its embeddedness' to seek out features of moral agreement held across thick moral cultures (Walzer 1994b: 3). As long as we recognize that the moral minimum is derived from our own thick morality, we can examine the overlaps to give an account of the moral minimum.

I will postpone analysis of Walzer's account of moral minimal rules until the next section, which develops in detail the implications of his latest work for considerations of international justice. First, however, I will briefly summarize the implications of Walzer's position on these three issues of the cosmopolitan/communitarian debate discussed above. It is clear that, from his communitarian starting point, he works to resolve oppositions in the debate. First of all, he offers a concept of the person that is not only socially constituted, but personally chosen as well. While understanding the state and the role it plays for individuals and groups to be morally significant, Walzer willingly admits that the rise of new institutional forms of community with moral relevance of their own is possible. On the third issue of the debate, Walzer offers a means of reconciling the irreconcilable – universalism and particularism – through offering a universalism that is qualified by its fit with our thick, particularist moral understanding. While he makes some interesting moves in *TT* towards collapsing the poles of the debate, tensions, as discussed above, remain. Are these tensions debilitating to a workable theory of international justice? The test is in its application. Thus, I will now turn to an examination of the moral minimal principles of international politics offered by Walzer.

A minimalist morality for international relations

In *TT*, Walzer discusses three moral minimal principles reiterated in international politics: the principle of self-determination; the principle that aggression anywhere is a criminal act; and what he labels the 'crucial minimalist principle', that tribalism must always be accommodated (1994b: 67, 71, 81–2). The third principle is crucial because the first and second largely follow from the third, and because it rests on what I will argue in this section are natural, covering law-like, assumptions regarding human nature, which under-pin Walzer's project.

Walzer writes that we can recognize the principle of self-determination, the first moral minimal principle, repeated throughout history, even in strange idioms. Today, self-determination is presented in terms of democratic rights, such that membership in a community is associated with rights of consent and self-governance according to the ideas, maximalist in nature, of that community. Although it is a general principle in international politics, self-determination also elicits fear, particularly in multi-national states, because of the potential disorder that might result from one group after another calling for self-determination. As Walzer sees it, we should make room for these groups, since there are many possible ways in which self-determination can be accommodated other than separation or domination, such that we need not be fearful. None the less, Walzer does want to suggest times in which separation is justified.

This is where the second minimal principle is introduced, to explain the case of the 'captive' nation. The example he gives is of the Baltic states, once sovereign nation-states, now wrongly captured: wrongly, because aggression, a criminal act according to the second minimal principle, was used. Thus, the restoration of their independence as sovereign states is required. Separation can also be granted to national minorities that should have been independent, when there is evidence of a core community which perhaps was not conquered, but has suffered under oppression. Walzer draws two sets of distinctions as a general guide to the just treatment of national minorities: between territorially concentrated and dispersed minorities, and between minorities radically different from, and those marginally different from, the majority population (1994b: 73). Dispersed, incorporated minorities can be accommodated by the state through measures such as ensuring equal citizenship, education, expression, *etc*. On the other hand, the claims of highly concentrated, marginal national groups are not as easily accommodated: for example the Albanians in Kosovo. While Walzer suggests three possible solutions, he concludes there is no ideal set of arrangements, and that we can only work 'slowly and experimentally' (1994b: 3). Nevertheless, it is a moral requirement to work at this problem.

It is a moral requirement because of the third, 'crucial' minimalist principle: tribalism must always be accommodated. By 'tribalism', Walzer means 'the commitment of individuals and groups to their own history, culture and identity', a commitment which generates moral thickness (1994b: 8).[6] Walzer attributes a naturalness to this commitment and the moral thickness it creates, writing that they are both a 'permanent feature of human social life' (1994b: 81). Thus, tribalism, or moral thickness, cannot be denied. Our 'crucial commonality' as humans is our particularism. We are not always wholly parochial. Only in times of crisis do we see ourselves fully through our tribal affiliation. Normally, we are divided selves, identities multiplied in the complex societies of modernity.

What is valuable in moral minimalism is 'the encounter it facilitates': moments when the abstractions from thick moral cultures coalesce to provide us with the closest thing we can have to a 'full-blooded morality' (Walzer 1994b: 11, 18). Walzer writes that this minimalism affords a 'critical perspective', which, in the case of the moral minimal principles for international politics, results in a critical 'moral minimal test'. Any nation seeking statehood must accommodate national minorities within its boundaries if it is to receive international recognition, aid and the like. Moral minimalism makes it incumbent on states to uphold this critical principle and to find points of agreement on a number of suitable political arrangements for assisting minorities at risk (Walzer 1994b: 81).[7]

The question arises: does the moral minimum ever sanction the use of force? Walzer writes that some reiterated values such as 'truth' and 'justice' are 'better defended with the moral support of outsiders than with their coercive intervention' (1994b: 16). This is a product of the moral minimal principle of self-determination and its associated rights of self-government and consent. However, if life and liberty are at stake, then force *can* be justified by the moral minimum, because the will for such help or assistance can in no way be confused in such an instance. With justice or truth, moral maximalisms can get caught in the crossfire. It is hard to draw the line where a fight for a reiterated moral minimal principle of justice ends and a fight for 'our' kind of

---

[6] Tribalism is an unfortunate expression for the commitment he wants to identify. Perhaps if it were a genealogical point to retard notions of progress in what we understand by our social commitments, I would be more sympathetic, but I think he uses tribalism in an effort to convey an understanding of naturalness to this commitment.

[7] Just as Walzer's idea of complex equality in domestic society requires a self-active, motivated citizen, similarly his international moral minimalism requires self-active, motivated states within international relations. This kind of requirement leaves his ideas of both domestic and international justice vulnerable to unmotivated actors.

justice begins. Moral maximalisms cannot justify the use of force for Walzer.

So, then, what does Walzer's minimalist morality offer in the way of a theory of international ethics? On the whole, it is simple. Communities are a good needed by persons who are equal in their capacities as culture-producing creatures. Thus, communities must be allowed space to create and maintain their lives as their members see fit. The ultimate ethical requirement is that we learn to engage our maximalist moralities in ways that do not impinge on others with their own maximalist pursuits. This creates a need within inter-national relations to find ways to accommodate the commitment of persons to communities, allowing them self-determination. To block this commitment would be unjust, because it constitutes a form of coercion. Thus, *international justice* is a matter of releasing the constraints on communities, which prohibit them from living the shared lives they desire for themselves. However, Walzer's project *cannot* offer anything towards the question of international *distributive* justice, because just social arrangements are the product of maxim-alist moralities, which can only be worked out by and for the community concerned.

The minimalist/maximalist divide sets up two moral realms for persons: the domestic and the international. The domestic realm is that of maximalist morality, where issues of distributive justice can be played out. It is also the place where the person's inner division is a product of social differentiation; in part determined, in part personally chosen. Here these divided selves are best served, according to Walzer, by distributive arrangements which reflect social differentia-tion: that is, complex equality, the determinations of which can only be worked out in a maximalist way. The realm of the international, on the other hand, is the world of minimalist morality, where persons' commitment to community is to be accommodated. Inner division of the self is a product of cultural differentiation, and so the divided self is best accounted for in the international realm by different forms of self-determination, and not only by the nation-state (Walzer 1994b: 82, 103). Yet, no matter what institutional form of social arrangement is adopted, the shared life of communities must be respected. Thus, justice in the international realm is not a matter of distribution, but a matter of order and non-intervention, so that communities can live in the moral worlds they create for themselves without disturbance or interference.

The separation of these realms is evident in an illustration Walzer offers at the end of chapter 3 in *TT*: 'Maximalism and the Social Critic'. Here he writes that, if he were offered the opportunity to give a seminar on democratic theory in China, all he could do would be to offer his own views on democratic theory and suggest that the Chinese would have to come up with their own. Moral minimalism requires this much: Chinese democracy must be defined by China itself. To the charge that he is neglecting the individual rights of the Chinese, he responds that this would be untrue. The minimal rights to life and liberty are assumed. The difference is in terms of maximal rights, beyond life and liberty, and that is not for him, the outsider, to decide. Other rights of a political or economic nature, which are maximalist in character, must be left to the local critic. This explains why human rights, generally speaking, are not stipulated by Walzer to be a minimalist principle. The role of the social critic in the international realm is limited to a defence of the minimalist rights of life and liberty. It cannot reach to other political and economic aspects of an understanding of human rights, because of the ultimate value Walzer places upon the good of community. Granted, Walzer does not ignore individual rights, but is this position satisfactory for a theory of international justice? In his chosen example, he assumes an atmosphere of democratic institutions and pluralism by suggesting a local critic can have a voice. Having accepted his own role as an outsider, and having made the assumption that the local critic will be able to speak effectively, Walzer fails to acknowledge that there may be a need for outside interference to create the requisite atmosphere for social criticism.

In attempting to reconcile the universal and the particular, Walzer has created an artificial separation of domestic and international realms. For example, when he attributes the division of the self to forces of socialization domestically and of cultural difference internationally, the obverse is readily apparent as well. There can be forces of international socialization through hegemony (Ikenberry and Kupchan 1990), and normative and institutional international structures (Bull and Watson 1984; Gong 1984), as well as cultural difference within domestic societies (Kymlica 1995), which also influence the individual. Walzer's separation of moral worlds (maximalist/domestic, minimalist/international) rests upon three problematic assertions: (1) that a moral community is definitive of an actual political institutional form; (2) that there is a significant level of commitment to community to justify its minimal rights of self-determination and accommodation; and (3) that common understandings are indeed discernible.

First, it cannot be said that particular moral communities will necessarily be contiguous with the legal, political forms of the state.[8] For example, an international social solidarity constitutive of moral community could be attributed to transnational social movements founded on shared values and, ultimately, traditions, which lead to collective social/political action across state boundaries: women's movements, peace movements, environmental movements, etc. (Johnson and Maiguashca 1994). Walzer himself stresses that divided selves listen to numerous other voices than that of nationality, and so no single social arrangement, such as the nation-state, can be *the* institutional form of community. Moral community can reach across state boundaries, thus rendering the domestic/international separation problematic. In fact, Walzer does not manage to keep the two realms neatly apart, especially when he draws upon what he assumes to be a more or less universal community of rights-speakers to defend individual rights to life, liberty and place, as I will demonstrate below. Secondly, since selves are divided, how can we be sure of their connection to community? Walzer writes of the extent to which it is only in times of crisis that we feel our parochialism in full. Normally, we have numerous identifications. Walzer comments on the ways in which the forces of modernity have multiplied personal identifications, making moral communities vulnerable. These kinds of strains must have repercussions for the individual's level of commitment to community. If true, this undermines the moral significance placed upon the good of community, and the domestic/international split more generally. Finally, there is a potential difficulty in the value Walzer's international ethics places upon community: it is not always easy clearly to discern the shared understandings that found the good of community. Recognizing that these understandings change and that they are difficult to judge, Walzer seems unconcerned to offer us a way to identify them beyond the suggestion that they are palpable. I am not asking Walzer to provide something that he himself accepts that he cannot give: a method for judging these understandings. I am, however, suggesting that he needs to offer a method for identifying shared understandings so as to defend their existence. With domestic

---

[8] Galston makes a similar point (1989: 121).

and international forces of socialization at work, how do we unpack them to ensure that these understandings go with this community, thereby constituting its value? He must have a method for determining which shared understandings can be attributed to particular communities, such that their rights to self-determination can be justified.

The separation of domestic and international moral realms is not only compromised by the above practical considerations. It is compromised philosophically, by the naturalist claims Walzer makes in grounding minimalist principles of international ethics. His 'crucial' minimalist principle, that tribalism must always be accommodated, and the associated principle of self-determination, follow from essentialist claims Walzer makes about what is required by humans. Humans need community. Their attachment to community is a natural, and thus permanent, feature of human life; for this reason, community is at the core of Walzer's project. In addition, there is little discussion of how it is that these minimalist principles come to be reiterated and mutually recognized in different times and places, except only to say in a parenthetical aside that 'some naturalistic account seems best' (Walzer 1994b: 17).

It is because of this 'naturalness' that we should recognize as morally legitimate these minimalist principles for international relations. However, is this kind of justification not similar to a covering law, the kind of justification which, as Walzer argues in 'Nation and Universe', enforces singularity? I am not convinced that what Walzer presents as the moral minimum is not some form of a maximalist imposition particular to Walzer's own American, liberal democratic, moral world. Granted, he writes that the moral minimum is expressed out of our own moral thickness, but we should be wary of the ways in which the lines can get blurred; that is, where the minimalist principle ends and our maximalism takes over. I see four instances in Walzer's work which warrant caution in this way.

First, in discussing moral minimal standards to which all societies can be held, Walzer writes that we in the West talk in terms of rights, the language of our moral maximalism. Then, however, he goes on to say that rights are a good way of discussing such principles, and that he will use this language and assume it is translatable (Walzer 1994b: 10). Whether or not this can be considered a transgression may be debatable, but the sense in which lines can be blurred between minimalism and maximalism is also evident in a second point. In his discussion of cultural pluralism as a maximalist idea, Walzer writes that the idea of cultural pluralism is the result of a thick understanding of liberal politics, and that minimalism would require something less (1994b: 17). However, does it? The crucial minimal principle of accommodating tribalism is an expression of respect for plural cultures. It could be said that at the base of Walzer's moral minimalism for international relations are some very thick notions derived from good, old-fashioned, liberal values of tolerance and space for self-determination. Thirdly, Walzer's preoccupation with increasing pluralism of both individuals and groups, the Four Mobilities, etc., is a particularly American preoccupation, generated by the nature of American social and political culture. Is this creeping pluralism really a universal concern for *all* cultural communities? Finally, Walzer is silent regarding the *content* of liberty, which he posits as a universal minimal principle along with life.[9] The rights of life and liberty in tandem ring familiar to American, liberal democratic ears and require little if any qualification, but by Walzer's own reasons it is hard to see why the defence of liberty should not be qualified in the same way as, say, justice or truth. Similarly, it is hard to know whether the embattled community whose liberty we may think to be threatened really wants our help or not. Liberty too, has maximalist understandings which can interfere and complicate the use of force in its defence, and which seem to have clouded Walzer's own objectivity in determining moral minimalist principles of international relations. Thus, tensions also exist in Walzer's attempt to reconcile the universal and the particular through the idea of minimalist and maximalist moralities.

A communitarian position on international justice: an assessment

Walzer's work on both domestic and international justice holds particular significance for the cosmopolitan/communitarian debate as a whole, because it points to ways in which the poles of the debate could be narrowed from a communitarian perspective. Below, I address each of the issues of the debate in turn.

[9] Walzer does defend his stipulation of life as a minimal principle (1994b: 16).

A concept of the person

The characterization of the communitarian position on the concept of the person in normative IR theory largely derives from the communitarian political theorists' understanding of persons as socially embedded. However, in developing the idea of the divided self in *TT*, Walzer accommodates both positions in the debate by arguing that the individual is both personally and socially constituted. He adds that concessions on this issue come easily from both sides in the debate between liberals and communitarians. Although Walzer ends up drawing a distinction between the constitution and the connection of selves that he cannot maintain, this does not have consequences for the probable conclusion that the two positions on the concept of the person are reconcilable. It is clear that, in suggesting that individuals are fully or radically embedded in social practices and are incapable of critical thinking about those practices, communitarians do not want to deny the agency of persons. This is evidenced by Walzer's turn to the social critic in matters of interpretation. None the less, while the communitarian position can recognise that aspects of the individual are personally chosen, it cannot relinquish what it finds to be an empirically valid and morally significant claim: that individuals are socially constituted. This aspect ultimately has moral priority for communitarians.

The moral standing of states

The communitarian position in normative IR theory is generally distinguished by its claim that states are morally significant to international practice. Walzer holds this view, but he is prepared to suggest possibilities for accommodation on this issue as well. Regarding the moral standing of states, he maintains that state sovereignty remains morally important, but that, with the divided nature of the self and its multiple identifications, priority cannot be given to only one form of political or legal community. I think this accommodation within the debate is potentially workable and interesting. He starts down a promising path, but unfortunately, stops in his tracks, paralysed by the theme of crisis which runs through his work. This paralysis leaves him caught in the eternal return to the state when it appears as if all else could fail. Although Walzer does not satisfactorily allow room for the play of alternative forms of social practice, he does demonstrate an openness towards them and recognizes the possibility of a moral role for institutional forms other than the state. However, whatever the form or forms that prevail, it will remain the case that the communities represented by those forms will be the primary subject of justice for communitarians.

The universal versus the particular

The communitarian position in normative IR theory is also characterized by its claim to particularism in the method and scope of moral thinking and ethical judgement. However, since communitarians seek grounds for moral inclusion to facilitate more just international practices, they too have a will to identify possibilities for universal claims in international practice, even though they see more obstacles to those possibilities than cosmopolitans are willing to recognize. This aim to locate a ground for some form of universalization is evident in Walzer's efforts to establish a minimum morality for international practice. Walzer's foundation for this minimalist morality is the good of community, which must be allowed space to engage in its maximalist pursuits as long as it does not impinge on the maximalist pursuits of other communities. His is a *weak* foundationalist claim. It represents a *weak*, rather than a *strong* foundationalist claim, because, as *SJ* makes clear, he understands the good of community to be a good which is particular to the shared life and understandings of a certain community, specific to time and place. To return to the anchor analogy, Walzer's position is one that he sees to be resting not in firm ground, but in the shifting sand of the contingencies of history and social circumstances. However, he proceeds in his articulation of a minimalist morality in *TT* as if this anchor is sunk in something more firm and lasting, since, as we saw earlier, he speaks of the good of community in naturalist terms. For Walzer, community is a *permanent* and *essential* feature of all human life, on which universal consensus regarding its moral significance can be reached. Also, in *SJ*, when aspects of personal justice are left unattended by an idea of distributive justice based on community, Walzer falls back upon a form of natural rights theory to defend the rights of individuals in particular cases like that of the alien or the guest worker. Consequently, his ethics is *non-contingent*, since he employs these grounds as if they provided a *strong* foundation on which we can always rely for ethical critique and judgement. Yet, as discussed above, I have my doubts as to whether Walzer satisfactorily acknowledges the indebtedness of his universalist minimum morality to his particular moral world. Both practically and theoretically, I find Walzer's attempted reconciliation of the universal and the particular problematic. The idea is right that we live with both the universal and particular, and an either/or choice is untenable and unproductive. The difference is that I understand that universal to be *my* universal, more the product of my particular moral world than Walzer appears willing to admit. To fail to recognise this can result in exclusions and oppressions, as part II of the book will show. Thus, with regard to Walzer's communitarian position, I find the most difficult problems for reconciliation in the debate to be on the issue of the universal versus the particular.

Concluding remarks

In assessing the implications of this communitarian position for moving beyond the impasse of normative IR theory, the task is made easier than in the last chapter – where possibilities for reconciliation had to be inferred from movements in Rawls's later work – because Walzer aims to address oppositions of the debates in political theory and normative IR theory, in order to illuminate areas of potential reconciliation. Walzer's work suggests that the poles of opposition have narrowed on the three issues of debate. However, tensions remain on all three issues that are the product of foundational claims to which the communitarian is committed: first, despite his acknowledgement that persons are personally chosen, and although he has what some might call a cosmopolitan eagerness to protect the rights of individuals against the community in certain cases, the social embeddedness of persons remains Walzer's *prior* moral consideration; secondly, and consequently, despite recognizing other forms of morally relevant communities, the state as community remains the subject of justice; and finally, despite his will to make universal claims for more just international practice, the particular remains morally prior for Walzer. Walzer is restricted in terms of what he can present as a theory of international justice. Walzer disables the international social critic by limiting the critic's room for commentary only to the realm of minimal rights. The minimalist/maximalist divide relegates distributive justice to being a matter exclusively for domestic society, and sidelines human rights from minimal moral status in international relations. It leaves order as the only subject for international justice, so that moral communities can live their shared lives peacefully, as they wish. Perhaps this is all that international justice can do, but it runs counter to Walzer's own suggestion that we must balance the claims of both the individual and the collective. He writes that 'we can never be communitarians or liberals simply, but now one, now the other as the balance requires' (Walzer 1994a: 191). As it stands, he still wants to make an either/or choice, the balance requiring more often than not that we prioritize the state as community. It would appear that Walzer's minimum morality requires some ballast, leaving more work for those seeking reconciliations within the framework of the cosmo-politan/communitarian debate.

Beyond the impasse? Hegelian
method in the cosmopolitanism
of Andrew Linklater and the
communitarianism of Mervyn Frost

Introduction

The cosmopolitan/communitarian debate was not explicitly formulated or labelled as a debate in normative IR theory at the time
Andrew Linklater and Mervyn Frost wrote the works which have
since been definitive of cosmopolitan and communitarian positions.
However, the tension of the ethical relationship between individuals
and states in international practice discussed in Linklater's *Men and
Citizens in the Theory of International Relations* (*MC*), and Frost's
Towards a Normative Theory of International Relations (*TNT*)[1] is the core
tension upon which the debate was later constructed and articulated
by Chris Brown and Janna Thompson (Brown 1992; Thompson 1992).
Therefore, neither Linklater nor Frost is writing their respective works
with something called the 'cosmopolitan/communitarian debate' in
mind, but in these books they seek to resolve this core tension in order
to facilitate the extension of moral inclusion and more just intersocietal relations. Thus, for the aim of evaluating the extent of this
impasse and possibilities for accommodation within the debate, it is
important to examine these books in particular and the work that has
since followed from these writers.

I choose to examine the work of Linklater and Frost together for two

---

[1] I refer here to Frost (1986) since this was the original text that was formative of the
debate. However, Frost has rewritten a good portion of this text, published recently
under the title, *Ethics in International Relations: A Constitutive Theory* (*EIR*). Since Frost's
argument for a constitutive theory of the individual – on which I focus – remains
largely the same as in *TNT*, in this chapter I will mostly refer to *EIR* which is the more
readily available text today.

connected reasons.[2] First, it will be useful to examine in tandem a cosmopolitan and a communitarian attempt to reconcile the ethical relationships between individuals and states, in order to compare and contrast areas where accommodations are evident or likely. Linklater and Frost are particularly good for this purpose, since, unlike the cosmopolitan and communitarian writers discussed in the earlier chapters, the projects of these writers *begin* from the identification of this core tension and the will to resolve it, as well as the issues which I argue follow from it.[3] Secondly, it is particularly interesting that both Linklater and Frost employ Hegelian method in the theoretical resolutions they attempt. Can Hegelian method be a source of reconciliation within the cosmopolitan/communitarian debate, and move us beyond what appears at this stage in the argument of the book to be a significant impasse? In the first section of this chapter, I will outline Frost's and then Linklater's positions on each of the three issues of the debate and point to the ways in which their conclusions provide possibilities for accommodation on both sides of the debate. The second section examines Hegelian method and asks whether it can indeed collapse the poles of opposition within the debate. The third section of the chapter evaluates the international ethics that results from both Frost's and Linklater's positions, and offers an assessment of the implications of Frost's and Linklater's international ethics for the debate as a whole. Finally, the chapter closes by drawing conclusions for part I of the book regarding the extent of the impasse in the debate and the possibilities for moving beyond it.

---

[2] It is interesting and surprising that both Frost and Linklater have yet to either comment or refer to the work of the other in their writings, despite clear connections across their projects.

[3] Clearly, Beitz (1979) and Pogge (1989) begin from the problem of the proper ethical relationship between individuals and states in seeking cosmopolitan theories of international distributive justice. However, they are not specifically concerned to resolve tensions within the issues around this core problem which separates cosmopolitans and communitarians. In the main, possibilities for this must be inferred from connections in their work with the later work of John Rawls. Walzer (1994b) on the other hand, does recognize this core tension and seeks avenues of reconciliation on the three issues which stem from it, but his project does not begin with this task as does Linklater's and Frost's. It is a concern, I would argue, that Walzer picked up only later in his work; in part, as a response to his own critics, and in part, in frustration with the stalemate that unfolded between liberals and communitarians in political theory.

Bridging the cosmopolitan/communitarian divide? The international political theory of Frost and Linklater

A concept of the person

In an unpublished conference paper, Frost (1993) discusses the concept of the person that is at issue in the debate between liberals and communitarians in political theory. Here Frost argues that the communitarian critique, which posits a socially constituted self within the context of historical communities, is too simple. To say individuals are enmeshed in communities does not offer a full enough account of how individuals are socially constructed. Frost argues that our experience is better represented by saying that we are embedded in practices rather than communities, because: 'practices together do not form any neat social arrangement which might be accurately described as a community' (1993: 9). According to Frost, practices represent social arrangements which accomplish a good valued by those who are a part of a practice. 'By participating in a practice we, by definition, achieve a good we could not achieve in any other way. Within a practice we gain a constituted identity not achievable in any other way' (Frost 1993: 10). This then raises two questions: first, how is the person constituted by a practice; and secondly, which practices are integral to our self-actualization as persons? Frost's constitutive theory of the individual, drawn from what he calls a 'secular interpretation' of Hegel's political philosophy, suggests answers to both questions (1996: 143).

Constitutive theory is an understanding of individuality as a product of mutual recognition developed within a hierarchy of institutions or practical associations, the most important being the family, civil society, and the state. Following Hegel, Frost writes, it is in the family that one experiences value for the first time, value in being recognised as a family member. Love binds the family and is 'partially constitutive of ourselves and our loving them is also constitutive of ourselves', such that we would be different people without this love (Frost 1996: 143). However, the family alone is not sufficient for the development of the individual for two reasons. Since it is bound by love – a feeling – the development of the person rests on unfirm ground, something that is not fully rational. Secondly, a person's development, or individuality, requires that she leave the family unit in order to realize her own personal needs and interests separate from family interests. It is in the association of civil society that the individual can express her own ends and have them recognized.

Civil society is an association based upon rights to private property, market exchange and first generation rights, which include, for example, the safety of persons, freedom of association and freedom of conscience. In civil society, individuals pursue their wants within a system of law that invests all with holding such rights equally. Recognition of the person having rights in civil society is constitutive of individuality, and offers the person another way of being valued. Yet, like the association of family, civil society is deficient in constituting individuality fully. Yes, the individual is constituted as a rights holder, but so is everyone else. Thus, civil society is an alien realm of rights holders struggling against one another for their ends. In addition, the law feels like a constraint upon one's pursuits. Here in civil society, the individual has set herself apart, discovering, exploring and pursuing her own needs as a person separate from a whole. Thus, the individual and the whole seem at odds with one another. The unity of the person – a synthesis of individuality with the social whole – can only be realized in the ethical state.

In the state, the individual wills that the good rests in her association with the societal whole, because she recognizes that her individuality is 'grounded' in it. As a result, the whole no longer feels external or alien as it did in the market-oriented 'on your own' competition of civil society, and its law no longer feels like a constraint. Society and the individual are reconciled within the state. 'In sum the crucial feature of the state is that in it citizens come to self-conscious appreciation of the way in which they constitute the whole and are constituted by it' (Frost 1996: 149). However, a fully-fledged, free individual is not guaranteed within the state: first she must be a citizen in a good state; and secondly, that state must itself be recognized as having rights within a society of sovereign states in order for individuality to be fully actualized. More about the qualities of this good, ethical state and its recognition within the society of states will appear in the next section on the moral standing of states.

Similarly, Linklater subscribes to a Hegelian concept of the person as socially constituted, but the emphasis is on the development of persons in an hierarchy of associational forms in history rather than in a hierarchy of institutions within the ethical state. Linklater regards the person as 'historical, as a self-developing and self-transforming being' working towards her realization as a free being, and it is on this concept of the person that he founds his international political theory (1990b: xii). Individuals have a capacity for self-determination, and across history have increasingly realized that capacity for freedom in a succession of more rational social institutions. It is from a Marxian account of periodization, derivative of Hegel's philosophy of history, that Linklater models his notion of a philosophical history of inter-societal relations as the general flow of mankind towards freedom over time.[4]

In order to trace humanity's increased capacity for freedom in history, Linklater begins by examining the individual's constitution within and between tribal societies, which represents the first in a scale of societal forms. Within tribal society, relations are based upon kinship and custom. These relations are immediate; that is, the person is undifferentiated from the whole such that tribal society is experienced as an unchangeable 'natural order'. Reliant upon their own ways of life, tribal communities are naturally estranged from one another. This represents a state of unfreedom, since persons are unaware of their capacity to change what is a seemingly unalterable order, and because they are not compelled to address their estrangement from outsiders. The measure of this unfreedom is the fact that persons in tribal societies are not tapping into their unique capacity for self-determination so that they 'exhibit the lowest form of self-consciousness' (Linklater 1990b: 171). Either by conquering communities or by entering into commodity exchange, individuals are cajoled out of tribal social relations because of problems of scarcity due to limitations of scale in kinship relations. Thus, individuals are forced to break out of the immediacy of tribe and custom, entering into relations with outsiders. From the challenge to tribal ways, the person gains for the first time a conception of herself apart from the whole, a consciousness of individuality. As a result, a higher, more open form of societal relations is ushered in. This higher form of intersocietal relations is required for three reasons: first, because of the limited nature of forms of social control; secondly, because of the lack of means to protect the interests of outsiders taken in; and finally, because of the problem of members being harmed by those from other

---

[4] In another piece, Linklater (1996d: 208–9n), he acknowledges the indebtedness of this account ultimately to Hegel's philosophy of history.

societies. Consequently, a higher level of societal institution emerges, the state.

As persons begin to break down the relations of estrangement with outsiders and learn a sense of their own independence, laws and law-making institutions are needed to integrate more variegated forms of social interaction. A wider, more unified social system – the state – is required to centralize institutions and the use of violence. This represents a move to a 'legal, political society', which introduces the idea of citizenship: that each is to be treated equally under the law. With the breakdown of kinship relations and custom, law now serves as the glue which gives these expanded social relations cohesion. Citizenship is now 'the basis of their association together' (Linklater 1990b: 182).[5] This represents a higher stage of freedom for the individual, as relations within states allow for the development of the human capacity for self-determination.

> The state is expressive of a higher stage of self-consciousness . . . one where members wish to preserve values they care for most: their status as individuals capable of engaging in relations of personal independence and abiding by principles which apply to persons equally, regardless of cultural or ethnic identity. (Linklater 1990b: 182)

While Linklater understands the state to be a higher stage in the individual's social construction, the state remains a 'particularistic community conscious of its separateness from the world beyond' (1990b: 182). Thus, relations of estrangement with an outside world remain, and we must look to ways in which relations between states can lead to further developments in human self-determination and freedom. I will reserve for the next section, which concerns the moral standing of states, a consideration of Linklater's account of the further stages necessary to the self-actualization of the individual, but what is important to understand at this point in the argument of the chapter is the way in which the individual, for Linklater, is socially constructed and experiences greater degrees of freedom within higher scales of societal forms.

It follows from the Hegelian line of Frost's and Linklater's work that both writers have problems with contractarian notions of social

---

[5] It is interesting to note the emphasis Linklater places upon the role of law and law-making institutions in his account of a scale of social forms, since this is an emphasis he shares with Hegel in his philosophy of history.

obligation in liberalism, particularly regarding liberal assumptions about a concept of the person (Frost 1996: 141–7; Linklater 1990b: 13–14; Linklater 1992a: 92–3). Contract theory holds that individuals are born with inalienable rights, rights that exist in the state of nature prior to any social arrangements. From this supposition, contractarians argue that, in order to protect these rights, individuals consent to enter into social arrangements and yield to a sovereign authority. Objections to the instrumentality of liberal contract theory and its heuristic use in explaining political obligation are discussed, but a key objection to liberal contract theory for Frost and Linklater is its understanding of the individual as a pre-social rights holder. Rights can only be endowed within social relationships and at no stage are individuals unencumbered by social obligations.[6] While Frost and Linklater are concerned to make a case against a contractarian, pre-social individual and trace the ways in which individuals are socially constructed, they are not at the same time arguing that the individual is not personally constructed as well. Indeed, the individual's own self-interpretation[7] is an essential part of a Hegelian concept of the person.

To say a person is self-interpreting means that she is able to construct an understanding of herself as to who she is and what her goals are. To act is an expression of one's self-interpretation and those actions cumulatively articulate one's self-understanding within social institutions. Thus, an individual's self-interpretation constitutes society as well as the individual in turn being constituted by society. Individual and society are mutually constitutive. For Hegel, there are two fundamental elements to an understanding of the person and her development: (1) that the individual is personally constituted by her own self-understandings and (2) that the person is socially constructed through her participation within communities. These two elements are vitally linked, since, for Hegel, one's self-understanding can only develop within society. This explains Frost's and Linklater's

---

[6] This is an important point which distinguishes Linklater from such cosmopolitans as Beitz and Pogge. For Linklater, since the rights of individuals can only be established within the social arrangements of community, his cosmopolitanism seeks the achievement of a moral community of mankind in which those rights are equally shared. Beitz and Pogge see no need to identify a community in which individual rights are made possible, since they find that these rights are inalienable and pre-social.

[7] I borrow this term from Charles Taylor (1985b) who, in an Hegelian fashion, employs the phrase 'self-interpreting' to illustrate the way in which the individual is personally constructed.

emphasis upon tracing the ways in which particular associations constitute the individual, but this emphasis cannot be construed as willful neglect of how the individual is personally constituted. In fact, both writers look to social institutions because they are primarily concerned with the development of the individual's capacity for self-interpretation and freedom.

Thus, Frost and Linklater share a Hegelian concept of the person which suggests that the divide on this issue in the debate can be bridged. This conception does not recognize an either/or choice between an idea of the person that is personally chosen versus one that is socially constructed. Instead, both are understood to be essential components to an understanding of the individual and her development.

One last point regarding the concept of the person should be stressed, which has implications for a claim about the possibility of accommodation within the debate as a whole to be made later in the chapter. Although Frost and Linklater share a Hegelian concept of the person, they begin at opposite ends of its construction. Linklater sketches the individual's construction *via* participation in a succession of societal forms in history, starting with tribal societies. Whereas, Frost begins at what was for Hegel the end of that evolutionary chain of social institutions – the ethical state – to examine the individual's constitution within it. The choice of where to begin in discussing the constitution of the self reflects the normative commitments of each writer to the social institution of the state.

Frost wants to demonstrate the ways in which the state is funda-mentally ethical, reconciling the tension between individual and society as a whole. Thus, Frost begins at the end of Hegel's philosophy of history: the state, and the individual's constitution within it. Linklater is concerned to trace the history of societal forms, because he finds that the state blocks the extension of moral community to humanity. Thus, Linklater starts at the beginning to make an argument for the idea of increasingly rational or free societal relations unfolding in history: a momentum, which in his view, must take us beyond the state. Their respective normative commitments have obvious impli-cations for the understanding of both writers of the moral standing of states to be discussed below. However, these commitments work foundationally throughout their writings, reflected in the way they discuss a concept of the person, and, ultimately, the way they pursue Hegelian method as well.

The moral standing of states

In contrast to Michael Walzer's instrumentalist understanding of state-based communitarianism, Frost's is an ethical understanding and, as mentioned in chapter 2, represents a second notion of state-based communitarianism. Frost sees the state as a fully rational, ethical institution because it is within the state that individuals come to be recognized, and recognize others as free persons. It is through this recognition that we realize the ways in which the individual and the whole are mutually constitutive; and thus, the person is reconciled with the obligations of societal membership. Frost compares a contractarian notion of the state with his constitutive understanding of the state to underscore its ethical quality.

Frost writes that the contractarian begins with the question, why should I, having rights of personal autonomy, agree to give up that autonomy to the state? Thus, what is being asked is what can the state do for me, giving any response a necessarily instrumental quality. The state then represents a device which serves individual interests rather than having any particular moral character. Frost criticizes instrumental understandings of the state for asking the wrong questions (1996: 141–7; 1994a: 20; 1993: 7–9; 1991: 183–96). Instead, we should begin with the recognition that being a rights holder means we are already involved in practices which are complex relationships of obligation. Thus, we should be asking whether states as a practice contribute to the development of individuals as free, moral beings. For Frost, the answer is yes. According to constitutive theory, the state 'should not be seen as a device which protects individual rights, but as a comprehensive arrangement between people who by mutually recognizing one another in certain specified ways come to constitute one another as free individuals' (Frost 1996: 151).

Free individuality is not assured within states. It is the product of a certain kind of state. That state is one where persons recognize each another as citizens under a body of law that they sanction themselves and that they understand constitutes them as citizens (Frost 1996: 152–3). Thus, a better status – that of a free individual – is offered to those in states where 'citizenship rights are well respected', generally democratic states (Frost 1996: 153; 1993: 15). However, in turn, that free individuality as a citizen of an ethical state can only be conferred if it is recognized as autonomous within a system of sovereign states. The state is 'a whole amongst other wholes . . . an individual *vis-à-vis* other states' (Frost 1996: 151) such that, in order to actualize its free individuality, the state must be recognized by other states. To be recognized as autonomous, a state has to be fully rational or ethical; that is, 'the citizens experience the well-being of the state as fundamental to their own well being' (Frost 1996: 153). Brown has challenged Frost on this point, writing that few states in the system of sovereign states can be considered ethical in this regard. Thus, most states are undeserving of the sovereign status they possess (Brown 1992: 120). In one article, Frost responds to this criticism by writing that the understanding of the ethical state which constitutive theory offers is, granted, not represented in all states recognized as autonomous; but he argues that this is not the point. What is important is that this understanding 'gives us a perspective from which to judge sovereignty claims', so that when states claiming sovereignty 'are not providing the other dimensions needed for freedom within their states, their claims are to that extent diminished', providing a measure for ethical critique within the states system (Frost 1994a: 18). In *EIR*, Frost adds that this is not a once and forever judgement. He writes that a criticism such as Brown's sees recognition as having a 'gate-keeping' function: you deserve recognition or you do not, and most do not (Frost 1996: 153). On the contrary, constitutive theory sees recognition as a 'way of treating a person or group of people in order to establish a certain kind of practice between you and them' (Frost 1996: 154). This suggests that one might initiate a commitment to educating a state to the ways of ethical state practice that ordinarily might not be recognized under a 'gatekeeping' understanding of recognition, and that the state recognizes the initiator as having something to teach them.

Frost is clear that he would not maintain that states will always exist, or that only states can constitute individuals in the ways constitutive theory elaborates (1996: 90). Also, he has no difficulty with the idea of an individual being a citizen of several sovereign bodies at once, since he does not find 'multiple and overlapping citizenships' to be 'ethically objectionable' (Frost 1994b: 24–5). Regarding the possibility of a world state, Frost writes that as long as it is not founded by imperial expansion it would be justifiable. However, it must be the product of the 'action of autonomous *states*' through some federal or confederal procedure; it cannot wipe the global slate clean and begin with a new contract for humanity (Frost 1996: 158). This is important for Frost, because in order to build any new institutions that are to have moral significance we have to work from the institutions we have, acknowledging the ways in which we are presently constituted by them. From this stem Frost's objections to natural law, community-of-mankind or any wider moral point of view in approaching normative issues in IR. They fail to account for the morally significant role states play in our lives, and try to argue from a 'clean slate'.

While Linklater is clearly advocating a cosmopolitan moral community of mankind approach, none the less, he does recognize the moral value of states for the vital role they play in the development of human freedom and self-actualization. For a theorist offering a philosophy of history of increasing self-actualization through a scale of forms, it follows that states, while a 'temporary association' on the way to a moral community of mankind, are none the less, morally significant (Linklater 1990b: 54). That final stage is a product of societal forms gone before and while not fully rational, each prior form has it own degree of reason. Thus, each stage has moral significance for its contribution to the progress of intersocietal life. The state and state system have important moral roles in this progress. Here again, Frost's and Linklater's Hegelian leanings lead to overlap in their accounts of the freedom of individuals being dependent upon the state's recognition by others in a society of states. Linklater writes that:

> freedom requires not merely the existence and preservation of relations of personal independence within a system of law, but . . . the attempt to secure the freedom of the state's members through gaining and granting a certain kind of recognition: the recognition of the freedom and equality, the sovereignty, of separate political associations. (1990b: 191)

What has occurred in this stage is the transformation of a previously necessitous realm of states' interests into a system of international obligation mutually to guarantee each other's rights as sovereign states. This represents a step forward in intersocietal relations for Linklater, because it 'signifies the further extension of the area of common good in a world of separate societies' (1990b: 193).

While a step forward, to recognize state rights of independence is only a first step. According to Linklater, this principle must be built upon to create a range of principles founded on justice, because to work only from an obligation to respect state sovereignty, while an improvement, is in itself deficient. It potentially blocks the formation of new international organizations that can further individual freedoms. Most important, in expanding principles of justice and grounding IR upon those principles, he writes, 'states make a significant move towards regarding the species, albeit still organized in a plurality of sovereign states, as the primary ethical reference group' (Linklater 1990b: 195). This, for Linklater brings about the final stages in the history of a scale of forms, when states operate on the level of making 'moral claims and counter-claims'. States recognize that to make a claim is to assume a system of duties and obligations such that any moral claim has to be referred to international society. Thus, rights within the society of states can only be conferred by that society as a whole. Rights are up for intersocietal negotiation (Linklater 1990b: 195–6). This understanding generates a condition of moral expectation across boundaries which develops our capacity to see 'the whole of organized humanity, not merely the interests of those associated together as the central ethical reference group', and renders the prior division between men and citizens unjustifiable, as 'the importance of sovereignty undergoes a corresponding decline' (Linklater 1990b: 197).

For Linklater, in this final phase, individuals experience a newly found moral connection with humanity, that is, they hold obligations beyond those formerly held for fellow citizens only. Thus, new political arrangements are required. The sovereign state must be replaced with 'a global legal political system which affords protection to all human subjects as moral equals' (Linklater 1990b: 199). This account of a scale of forms highlights a history of rights and duties gradually being extended to all of humanity. In sum, Linklater regards states and the system of states as integral to the process of this extension, but while having moral significance for their part in the development of human freedoms, the state's moral standing is clouded by the fact that it is, as Linklater writes, 'simultaneously standing in its [moral development's] way' (1990c: 147). States sanction a moral particularism towards their own citizens which requires moral justification for Linklater. It requires justification because Linklater finds that trends toward universalism in moral beliefs are evident within states and the system of states (Linklater 1990c: 147). If we examine them, we can see three trends towards moral universals which undermine the moral particularism of state sovereignty prevalent today: (1) an increase in the ideal towards the protection of human rights; (2) recognition of the need for collective action to improve the social and economic situation of the world's poor; and (3) the need to strengthen world community to face the effects of technical-instrumental rationality (Linklater 1990c: 150–1). These trends are a sign that we are moving beyond the men versus citizens moral dichotomy and that now our task is to envision new political forms which can further these developments.

I think it would be fair to infer that Linklater would say Frost fails to recognize the way in which the state form and the moral particularism it fosters inhibits the extension of moral consideration to all individuals. Also, one can infer that Frost would charge Linklater with failing fully to understand the importance of the state and the completeness with which it and its recognition within a system of states can fulfill individual freedoms. At the crux of this argument is the question: are states and the system of states morally inclusive or exclusive? The issue between Frost and Linklater is not whether states are morally significant, but the degree to which they are morally significant, that status being complicated by whether one finds the scope of the state's ethicality to be limited. As noted in the first section, both writers are concerned to extend possibilities of moral inclusion, but they differ over their ideas of the social institutions necessary to promote this aim.

Frost understands the state and the system of states to be morally inclusive. He writes that the practice of sovereign states in IR 'is one which includes all of us as insiders' (1994b: 16). We all participate in multiple practices, practices that are located within the wider practice of states. Yet, what makes the state unique, what constitutes it as the fundamental practice in developing the whole person as free, is that it confers rights of citizenship upon the individual from which we all draw value (Frost 1993: 14–15). Thus, the boundary around the state is, for Frost, 'a moral boundary around a valued institution – the ethical state' (1994b: 21). However, he writes that this boundary is in no way to be construed as drawing a line at which our obligations to outsiders end (Frost 1994b: 21). According to Frost, even to draw this boundary and make a claim that it should be respected actually opens the state up for 'inspection across a whole range of social values' (1994a: 19) Actually, this is a point similar to Linklater's above. For Linklater, when intersocietal relations reach the level of making moral claims those claims have to be referred to international society. As Linklater writes, at this level, a system of obligations is inferred, what Frost labels a body of 'settled norms'. While the preservation of the society of states and state sovereignty are at the top of Frost's list of norms, also included are obligations which expand upon these principles, extending principles of justice, which as Linklater suggests, are necessary for further moral inclusion. For Frost, such principles – 'settled norms' – located in the domain of state practice today include: the rejection of domination as a legitimate goal in IR, the promotion of modernization, democratic institutions, duties to protect citizens and to protect human rights, and interstate economic cooperation (1996: 104–12). Thus, in making any claim, a state lays itself bare to judgement against this body of norms by the system of states, thereby widening the scope of moral expectation.

Clearly, Frost and Linklater share the goal of moral inclusion and even notions of the institutional forms or levels required, but Linklater would argue that Frost's domain of state discourse stops short. Citizenship, while important to the moral development of the individual, has at the same time obstructed wider obligations to humanity. He writes that citizenship and its boundaries, as any alien or refugee can tell you, is 'one of the principal forms of exclusion in social and political life' (Linklater 1992b: 26). So, while the state does confer something of value, at the same time, it confers a right that interferes with our ability to see humanity as our primary ethical reference group, and thereby inhibits the moral inclusion of all. An interest in this kind of exclusion is at the centre of Linklater's turn to discourse ethics in the postscript to *MC*, in later articles, and in his recent book *The Transformation of Political Community* (*TPC*). Because open dialogue about the structure of society and politics is critical for the possibility of discourse ethics, 'discourse ethics cannot be completed by a number of separate experiments in democratic participation within independent sovereign states', since sovereignty 'restricts the capacity of outsiders to participate in discourse to consider issues which concern them' (Linklater 1996a: 294). Linklater therefore argues that the idea of the state as a bounded moral community must be reconstructed.

If the state is to be reconstructed, how far should this reconstruction go, and what would a reconstructed state look like? Until the publication of *TPC*, it was difficult to pin down exactly what Linklater thought the future role of the state might be, leaving one to wonder whether the state could ever be fully rational and thus, ethical. However, this latest study of the nature of political community gives us a much clearer picture. The state can be ethical or fully rational, but not the state as we know it.

In *TPC*, Linklater reiterates the cosmopolitan position elaborated in *MC*, with a new emphasis on the ways in which this universalizing ethic can accommodate concerns about particularity and difference, as well as antifoundationalist critiques which have gained momentum in the last ten years. Here he elaborates his vision of the dialogic community where '[p]articular social bonds remain but they are reconstituted in light of a normative commitment to engage the systematically excluded in dialogue' (Linklater 1998: 107). This orientation to those who may be internally excluded, like subaltern groups within the community, and to those outsiders who may suffer exclusion, means that such communities are well placed to participate in 'wider universalities of discourse' that Linklater sees as engaged in ensuring 'rights of participation for the victims of transnational harm' (1998: 107). These wider universalities take different forms and Linklater's discussion of these forms corresponds with, and elaborates on, the final stages in the scale of forms he considers in *MC*: a pluralist international society of states, a solidarist society of states, and a post-Westphalian society of states. While different, what these frameworks share is that 'each involves progress beyond one type of unjustified exclusion' (Linklater 1998: 168). For Linklater, each stage of progress represents a significant level of reconstruction of the state to the extent that, within the most progressive post-Westphalian framework or discourse, notions of sovereignty, territoriality and national citizenship are no longer immediately linked to the concept of the state (1998: 167–8). In the course of this progress, the state participant in these 'wider universalities of discourse' takes on new political responsibilities until the rational, post-Westphalian state is differentiated by the fact that it rejects totalizing projects and 'encourages the emergence of new forms of political community in which the potential for higher levels of universality and difference is realised' (Linklater 1998: 45).

For Linklater, what Hegel, and by implication Frost, are right about in their analyses of the moral standing of the state is that the state has played, and will continue to play, a significant role in mediating loyalties and advancing human freedom. However, what they have failed to properly acknowledge is that the state, by claiming an exclusive grasp on notions of sovereignty, territoriality and national citizenship, has done so in a way that was oppressive and exclusionary. According to Linklater, the state must re-fashion the ways it takes up its responsibility towards balancing the many loyalties at work today: subnational, national and transnational. Ultimately, the state will be transformed as it recognizes *new* responsibilities in the manner it pursues this mediating role.

As noted above, Frost readily admits that few states live up to the status of ethical states, but he argues that the potential for that status to be realized unfolds once we become aware of the ways in which the rights we enjoy and claim for ourselves are constituted by the wider practice of states of which we are all a part. All the constituent elements are in place for modern states to achieve that status. Yet, as it stands, the state has moral importance for the status of citizenship it presently confers upon individuals. For Linklater too, the moral significance of states is evident in the achievement of securing citizenship rights, but the full potential of those rights to realize human autonomy cannot be fulfilled as long as they are coupled singularly with the bounded, territorial, political entity that is the state as we know it. Thus, the characteristics and roles which define the state at present are not fully rational according to Linklater, and the state will have to be transformed in order to achieve the kind of ethical status that Frost wants to confer on it. It is perhaps through this question of how to best realize what is at the centre of concern within citizenship rights, human autonomy and moral inclusion, that we might understand the normative commitments to institutions that they make: Frost to the ethical state, and Linklater to the moral community of mankind in a post-sovereign world.

To conclude this section, it has been argued that the moral signifi- cance of the state is not at issue for Frost and Linklater. What is at issue between them is the scope of the state's ethicality as the state exists today: whether it limits the extension of moral commitments, and, thus, compromises human freedom. Despite this difference, the moral significance of the state is evident for both writers. This is further suggested by the fact that they see the state form as historical and not necessarily here to stay, yet they find that any new political communities that evolve will have to serve a moral role similar to that which the state plays today: connecting personal loyalties and offering the individual the valued status of citizenship, whatever new scope citizenship might take. Also, both writers appear to be wedded to the idea that we have no choice not only to talk about and use the word *state*, but to imagine its potential to be fully rational or ethical. Frost is quite explicit about why we have to maintain the state domain of discourse. Interestingly, in *TPC*, Linklater still talks about states even though the states we will find in the immanent post-Westphalian order will not be familiar to us. Also, he adds that this post-Westphalian *state* will at last be rational in the sense Hegel intended. Once again, it appears that the poles of the cosmopolitan/communitarian debate on this issue of the moral standing of states are not as rigid as often presented. This point of agreement – that any new social institutions must serve a moral role similar to that of the state – indicates possibilities for accommodation. However, an important tension remains in the positions of the two writers concerning the present scope of the state's ethicality.

The universal versus the particular

It has been argued that while Frost and Linklater share similar normative goals and a recourse to Hegelian method, their different positions on the scope of the ethicality of today's state lead them to separate institutional commitments, which have implications for each of the issues of the debate. In the case of this third issue, which concerns how and with what scope we justify the ethical claims we make, there are two implications to consider. The first concerns the different starting points of the writers in articulating their projects, and the second concerns how each employs Hegelian method to different effect in defending the claims that flow from their respective starting points. However, I will reserve discussion of these two implications for the second section of the chapter where I explore the extent of these differences and their significance in assessing the possibilities within Hegelian method for moving beyond the impasse attributed to the cosmopolitan/communitarian debate. Here, I will concentrate on what both writers share when it comes to this question of the universal versus the particular. Despite using Hegelian method to different effect – as will be explained in the second section – the end result for Frost and Linklater is the same. Both are defending their normative claims for the institutional requirements of human freedom universally and foundationally, in the *weak* sense. Yet, Frost and Linklater do so with the aim of being attentive to, and respectful of, particular ethical principles as well. They seek to reconcile universal and particular moral claims. This is evident in the way each addresses the problem of the value pluralism of particular goods in IR.

Frost's idea of a constitutive theory recognizes the value of particular arrangements founded and agreed to within ethical communities, arrangements that shape these historical communities and set them apart. He sees this as a widely shared belief, instituted by the non-intervention norm settled within international practice, which expresses the value of a 'variety of autonomous states' (Frost 1994b: 26). It is this norm, among others in a body of 'settled norms', that we can use to address the problem of value pluralism in constructing a normative theory of IR. In order for state autonomy to be recognised, and thus, a plurality of states established, a state must agree to abide by the 'settled norms' of the international system. This is in effect what occurs when a state signs on as a member of the United Nations. It has agreed to act in accordance with the United Nations Charter, and in turn expects to be duly recognized as a sovereign state having the rights and privileges associated with that status as a member of the states system. Frost's point is that we are all participants in this international practice and that we are constituted within it by the rights we claim as citizens of sovereign states, and the rights we recognize others as having as well. Thus, value pluralism is not an obstacle to normative IR theory. These norms apply universally, yet maintain the integrity of particular community arrangements in the recognition of state sovereignty. Thus, these norms accommodate universal and particular ethical principles in establishing a universal method for critical, normative analysis of IR.

Linklater writes that international political theory requires universals. He sees Kant's basic moral intuition as right, and wants to defend something like the kingdom of ends which results from Kant's categorical imperative: that all human beings are morally equal as right-bearers and should be treated universally as ends and not means. However, since Linklater takes on board Hegel's critique of Kant, he finds that this way of reasoning must be de-transcendentalized; that is, understood to be located in and circumscribed by our historical and cultural situatedness (1990b: 144). None the less, Linklater sees that international political theory must be able to defend the existence of obligations to humanity which link insiders and outsiders in order to suggest the 'possibility of overcoming relations of inter-societal estrangement' (1990b: 12, 15).[8] For Linklater, the existence of

---

[8] A point of clarification is called for here. It is important to note that, throughout *MC*, Linklater uses the terms universal and particular to refer to types of moral claims. He writes that his project is about morality, not epistemology. In writing about the issue of the universal versus the particular in the cosmopolitan/communitarian debate, I am using the terms to refer to the way in which we justify our value claims epistemologi-

the tension between men and citizens or the existence of the tension as he formulates it in *TPC*, the universal versus the particular, is enough to justify the cosmopolitan international political theory he pursues in these books. However, Linklater is well aware of the difficulties, both theoretical and practical, in supporting this claim to universal obligations among mankind. Thus, justifying a universal claim in the face of value pluralism and the diverse goods held within communal memberships is recognized by Linklater to be a problem. In the postscript of *MC* and to a more developed extent in *TPC*, Linklater addresses the tide of contemporary antifoundationalist thought, which he attributes with having forced a reconsideration of claims to universality along with recent pressures to respect the rights of minority and subaltern groups. The methodological problem of justifying universal claims in theory takes shape within the practice of IR as a problem of unilaterally projecting Western values. Within Western conceptions of the state and international society, Linklater sees a Western moral universalism with exclusionary tendencies that must be contested (1992b: 32).

While Linklater recognizes these obstacles in justifying universal obligations to humanity, he sees that the problem 'is not universalism as such', but a particular kind of universalism which pursues Archimedean points (1998: 48). In *TPC*, Linklater argues that universalism can take guises other than that of the absolutizing variety. This is evident because those who critique the universalism at the base of the cosmopolitan project – postmodernists and feminists – 'implicitly draw from the reservoir of moral universalism' (Linklater 1998: 48). Indeed, in the postscript to *MC* and in work since, Linklater has pursued a critical theory of IR which blends the critical projects of Habermas and Foucault to produce a theory that can bolster universalism, yet at the same time meet the antifoundationalist challenge. Thus, Linklater is of the opinion that the force of these critiques has had the ironic effect of significantly improving the cosmopolitan project by leading it to take on board the idea that 'there are limits to universality just as there ought to be limits to difference' (1990b: 209). Therefore, in *TPC* Linklater articulates the idea of a thin conception of cosmopolitanism as opposed to the thick, Archimedean version which

cally. The sentence referred to here in *MC* demonstrates that Linklater cannot avoid epistemological questions in his idea of international political theory. In fact, in the postscript of *MC* and in *TPC*, he turns to the problem of method in the face of antifoundationalist critiques as a central point of discussion.

excludes by enforcing a singular, typically Western vision of the good. His thin cosmopolitanism seeks to 'support the development of wider communities of discourse which make new articulations of universality and particularity possible' (Linklater 1998: 49). This support takes the form of not privileging either commitments to the individual or the community, but in being focused on the need and capacity to justify any forms of exclusion that may occur (Linklater 1998: 50).

In summary, both Frost and Linklater use Hegelian method to make universal claims about the development of humankind's capacity for freedom. They illustrate the connections between individual freedoms and societal commitments and between universal and particular ethical claims. However, they do so in dissimilar ways to support different institutional commitments. The positions of these authors, as they have just been outlined, suggest a way in which the two opposite poles might be accommodated. Hegelian method may provide for the possibility of reconciling universal and particular justifications of value claims. However, final judgement on this question must be left to the end of the second section.

Bridging the cosmopolitan/communitarian divide? The potential within Hegelian method

In the last section, I suggested that two implications follow from Frost's and Linklater's different positions on the scope of the state's ethicality: first, in the starting points chosen; and secondly, in the way each employs Hegelian method to different effect. To consider the repercussions of these differences for possibilities within Hegelian method to break the impasse of the debate, I will begin by briefly outlining, once again, the dissimilar points at which Frost and Linklater begin their ethical projects.

Frost's starting point is the modern state domain of discourse, an international practice which includes us all. Frost writes that this is a reasonable starting point because it is easy to defend: we all use this discourse (1996: 88). However, it is unproblematic, ultimately for Frost, because he has a normative commitment to the idea of the ethical state and finds it to be realizable in the state form and its practice as we know it. For this reason, Frost draws from Hegel's philosophy of right, or law, to point to the ways in which state and interstate practice are an end goal for human freedom, and provide a moral home for us all.

Linklater on the other hand, takes as his foundation the 'nature of man as an historical subject' (1990b: xii). He begins here because he has a belief in the progress of man's capacity for self-determination, which will ultimately result in a moral community of mankind to realize the fullest human freedom possible. He does not accept the state and state practice as an end goal. Thus, Linklater draws from Hegel's philosophy of history, beginning where Hegel begins, tribal society, to relate a long history of the development of individuals' capacities for freedom in a series of forms of intersocietal relations. As his philosophical history of intersocietal relations aims to show, these forms will take us beyond the state as we know it.

From the second implication, that Frost and Linklater use Hegelian method to different effect, the question arises: how can both writers use Hegelian philosophical method to justify different positions regarding the social institutions required for increased human freedoms? Both Frost and Linklater turn to Hegel's method of tracing the individual's self-actualization through a hierarchy of social forms, institutions realized through a dialectical process which generates more rational social relations; that is, increased freedom for individuals through social and ethical commitments. Yet, while sharing this method, Frost and Linklater use the method to very different effect in terms of the extent of radical institutional change suggested and the way these claims support the goal Frost and Linklater share of extending moral commitments. I argue that this reflects a tension inherent within Hegelian method itself, a tension which resulted in the famous Right/Left split among Hegelians in the nineteenth century. I find this split to be a rich area to explore in illuminating differences in the way Frost and Linklater use Hegelian method, as well as the strengths and weaknesses of such a method for social inquiry.[9] I will not delve deeply into the substantive issues of the split. Instead, I will only highlight its central tension as it is necessary to the

---

[9] The notion of using the Right/Left Hegelian split for comparing the work of Frost and Linklater was first raised for me by a question put to Frost by Chris Brown when Frost (1994b) was presented at the LSE's Ford Foundation Workshop. Brown suggested that Frost is trying to combine the projects of both the Right and Left Hegelians in his constitutive theory. As the following discussion will demonstrate, I do not agree fully with the suggestion. However, I do find the split to be an interesting vehicle for examining the different ways in which Frost and Linklater use Hegelian dialectical method.

argument that this Right/Left tension is manifest in the different ways Frost and Linklater use Hegelian philosophical method.

The split is often attributed to a basic ambiguity regarding Hegel's attempt to link the rational or ideal to the social world that exists, which generates problems of interpretation. The passage in the *Philosophy of Right* from which this ambiguity arises reads, 'what is rational is actual, and what is actual is rational' (Hegel 1967: 26 par. 12). It was Friedrich Engels who originally credited this passage with dividing Hegelians into Right and Left schools by virtue of two possible interpretations following from it. The Right Hegelians read the passage as an endorsement of present institutions, since the very existence of these institutions is evidence of their rationality proven through the historical process of dialectical negation. The actual, what is real, is therefore rational. The Left are distinguished by their interpretation of this passage as a call to make what exists rational. The real has to be made rational, brought closer to the ideal to unleash the momentum of radical change. While Engels's account of this passage has been affirmed by many commentators writing since, caution must be advised in investing this conclusion with too much weight, as it produces misleading categorizations of the Right as *status quo* orientated and the Left as revolutionary. Also, it blurs the meaning of two terms used with precision by Hegel, actuality and existence, and thus, misrepresents what was for Hegel a unity: reality reconciling actuality with the ideal. With this caution, which will be explored further below, what remains is an explanation of how it is possible that Frost and Linklater have come to use Hegelian dialectical method to the bifurcated effect that they do: Frost for moderate internal critique of the institutions we have, and Linklater for radical critique to yield more rational social forms. I will discuss how Frost employs Hegelian method in a manner closer to Hegel's own use and how Linklater takes it along a direction explored by the Marxist and Critical Theory traditions.

As discussed in section one, Frost begins normative analysis by examining the language we commonly use to talk about normative issues, that of citizenship, states and interstate relations, for which the rules are largely considered settled. Thus, his normative theory proceeds by identifying an area of agreement or domain of discourse within international practice from which we can make judgements about actions within that practice. Once this area of agreement or 'domain of discourse' is identified, the normative theorist lists the norms that are settled within the discourse and works to elaborate a background theory that can justify the agreed norms. In this way, you have a theory that represents the character of a practice or institution, and supports the norms of the practice. Thus, a measure is provided against which difficult normative issues,'hard cases', can be held and judged.[10] To hold a hard case up for scrutiny against a background theory makes it possible to find answers 'without getting involved in "deep" discussions about the basic justifications for the institutions within which these issues arise' (Frost 1996: 98). Yet, judgement about hard cases is complicated by the fact that the background theory can at times be out of sync with 'settled norms' of the practice. At this juncture, John Rawls's technique of reflective equilibrium is employed to overcome a 'lack of fit' by looking to both the 'settled norms' and the background theory to find some point of equilibrium from which a judgement on the hard case can be made (Frost 1996: 99–100).

In addition to supplying a measure for making judgements about hard cases, a background theory also affords normative analysis a degree of efficiency. It steers us away from complicating arguments, which rehash justifications of the institution or practice itself every time that a hard case must be decided. Thus, the establishment of a background theory is critical to Frost's idea of a working normative theory. Frost justifies the modern state domain of discourse; that is, he supplies a background theory via a Hegelian dialectical method, which demonstrates how it is that we as individuals are constituted by the practice of states. What is key to this being able to serve as a background theory is that it can reconcile norms in the practice of states that may appear incongruous. For Frost, the task which faces a background theory of the modern state domain of discourse is that of reconciling international norms which value the maintenance of state sovereignty with the protection of human rights. States rights must be squared with the rights of individuals. This is the reason why a constitutive theory of individuality is so fitting as a background theory according to Frost, because an individual's self-actualization and freedom entail social membership. His neo-Hegelian constitutive theory demonstrates how individual rights and states's rights are intertwined with, and indeed require, one another.

---

[10] The method Frost assigns to normative theory is shaped along the lines of Ronald Dworkin's theory of 'hard cases' in law, which Frost sees as having a wider scope of application (Frost 1996: 93).

Hegelian method is particularly suited to Frost's requirements because it is the intention of Hegel's *Rechtsphilosophie* to point to an historical process of the individual's abstraction or separation from social and traditional ties, and her eventual reconciliation with the social world through philosophy. It is the task of philosophy, according to Hegel, to illuminate the ways in which the social world is a 'home' for us. We have before us the elements constitutive of our freedom. The historical transformations that have yielded the institutions of the family, civil society and the state provide us with the content necessary to that freedom. The difficulty is that this content appears alien and hostile, as civil society and the state are large and complex social forms which seem to lack meaning. It is Hegel's aim to reveal the meaning in these forms so that the individual no longer feels estranged in the social world. He exposes what is mere appearance to unveil the rationality inherent in the modern social world, a rationality which shows the individual's self-actualization to be a product of our commitments to the institutions of the family, civil society and the state. Thus, the constituent parts for being 'at home' in society are in place.

Thus, Hegel's philosophy is an affirmative methodological exercise. This does not mean that Hegel is simply mapping the rational onto whatever exists, and nodding to the status quo. He recognizes deficiencies in the social world deserving of social criticism, but he finds that critique can only be conducted from within. As the example of the French Revolution demonstrated for Hegel, social change can only be effective and stable if it draws from existing traditions and institutions yielded through history. Social ideals must be forged within the real to be effectual. While Hegel grants that the institutions in place are in need of reform, what is important to understand is that they are, on the whole, worthy of preservation because they have a rational substance which needs only to be revealed. For this reason, Hegel viewed philosophy's task to be positive, that of pointing to what is valuable in the social world, since critique on the other hand comes rather easily (see Hardimon 1994: 30).

Frost is arguing a similar line. We must begin with what we have. A normative theory of a social world constructed out of the air is no good for us. Normative goals must be instructed by reality, and reality for IR at present is a world of states. Not only must normative theory be instructed by the discourse within which we operate, but when we examine that discourse closely, we must evaluate whether, and if so how, its component parts can be brought into coherence. That is what a background theory does, what Frost's constitutive theory claims to do. It is Frost's aim to show us the ways in which our claims to be individual rights holders of a certain kind are connected to our membership of particular institutions (Hardimon 1994: 165). Frost also wants to illustrate the ways in which we are connected and indeed constituted by a number of institutions within our social world, and argues that within the state domain of discourse we have the tools we need for the realization of human freedoms. Frost's normative theory recognizes the deficiencies of states in the world today, finds that there is room for critique, but maintains that freedom and reason are inherent in the institutions we have. While he admits those institutions may some day take a form different from states, they will perform a similar ethical role, reconciling the rights of individuals and groups. Thus, like Hegel's philosophical method, Frost's constitutive theory is also affirmative.

With the affirmative nature of this methodological stance, working from the social institutions in place, and choosing to illuminate and defend their rationality, one can easily see how it can be interpreted as being conservative and orientated to the *status quo*. It is true that Hegel did not envision the possibility of significant progress beyond the stage of historical development which he knew. Similarly, while Frost considers the possibility of alternate forms of social membership and citizenship, he too sees that we have all we require for our freedom to be in place. Linklater on the other hand, disagrees. Like the Left Hegelians before him, he sees a need for progress beyond our present stage of historical development, an imperative to make the real rational.[11] This imperative is the result of a perception of the Left Hegelians of their world in the 1830s, and of Linklater today, that not all is reconcilable and good with the social world as it exists. For the Left Hegelians, this meant that the liberal impulse had to be placed outside of the established state institution which they found to be fomenting social alienation, and relocated in the social unrest of artisans and peasants (see Toews 1980: 214–16). Internal reform or adjustments of the state apparatus would not suffice. Linklater shares with the Left Hegelians, and the Marxist and Critical Theory tradi-

---

[11] It is interesting that in *TPC*, Linklater actually invokes the critique of the Left Hegelians in his discussion of the weakness of Hegel's position on the state. He refers to the Young Hegelians, the movement which gave expression to the philosophical ideas of the Hegelian Left (Linklater 1998: 159).

tions which follow, the idea that radical institutional change is required to alleviate the individual's alienation from the social world, and to realize human freedom. According to Linklater, the liberal impulse of international political theory also requires that it be relocated from the state into the pull of universalist principles and politics towards more inclusive moral communities. Thus, while employing Hegelian dialectical method, Linklater takes an altogether different starting point from Frost in order to suggest and defend the need to move beyond the state as we know it towards post-sovereign political communities.

As Linklater does not share Frost's normative commitment to the institutions of today's state domain of discourse, he cannot begin from the same methodological starting point. Instead of starting from where we are, a world of states, Linklater's method proceeds by piecing together in *MC* a philosophical history of IR. What a philosophy of history affords is the possibility 'to approach different types of IR with a view to determining their contribution to the process of humanization' (Linklater 1990b: 160) This allows us first, to place a variety of intersocietal relations on a scale of ascending types of social formations; and second, to build a sociology or political economy that explains the empirical processes of transformation from one type of intersocietal form to another (Linklater 1990b: 160–1).[12] The measure for this scale is 'the extent to which each approximates the conditions of realized human freedom', a measure which takes as its foundation a belief in a human capacity for self-determination and the idea of progress in the realization of this capacity over time (Linklater 1990b: xi). Thus, in starting from the beginning, tracing increasing degrees of human freedom realized from tribal society to the present, Linklater constructs a method that can provide a criterion for helping us determine when social forms have outlived their usefulness – something Hegel is accused of never providing – to help us determine which features of the real are rational.[13] For Linklater, the real is not

---

[12] The second task is not explored in this book, but is left to be the subject pursued in Linklater (1990a). As this work concentrates more on the empirical question of how moral community has expanded, rather than upon a theoretical defence of why that should indeed be a goal worthy of pursuit, I focus in this chapter on *MC* and other works which perform the latter task.

[13] Regarding this accusation put to Hegel, see Kolakowski (1978: 78). I would not fully agree with this charge against Hegel. Things in the world, including the state or other institutional forms, are actual or rational to the degree that they live up to their essence.

rational as long as tensions exist that exacerbate feelings of unfreedom and social alienation. Linklater sees a tension within the modern state form that, against the backdrop of an unfolding history of human-kind's increased capacity for freedom, points to the need for a further stage of historical development. That tension is represented in the relationship of men versus citizens, the force of universal com-mitments to humanity that butt against the moral boundaries drawn around states. Thus, his method aims to show how the social formation of states is one last hurdle in the progress of human freedom.

As discussed above, in *TPC* the tension of men and citizens is reformulated as one between universalism and particularism, the existence of which shows that the real is not rational. However, with this recent book's focused attention upon being responsive to anti-foundationalist critiques, Linklater is careful to demonstrate that the balance his praxeological analysis seeks between universality and the difference which concerns these critics is one which does not rely on the kind of philosophical history that sees Reason at the end of history with a capital R. Linklater writes that his discourse ethics has a different kind of confidence in the notion of progress: one that takes its impulse from the German tradition of philosophical history but relinquishes 'its faith in the existence of a continuous, irreversible path of historical development' (1998: 90). With this qualifying statement, he goes on to offer an account of the sociology of forces which could be seen as contributing to wider universalities of discourse, a discussion which proceeds in a not dissimilar way to that of his scale of forms argument in *MC*; that is, by demonstrating how obstacles to human freedom are gradually overcome across time and place. The central paradox that is highlighted through this sociology concerns the modern state: 'on the one hand, it is the site on which radical intensifications of social control have been estab-lished but, on the other hand, it has been the setting for unprece-dented efforts to eradicate the tyranny of unjust exclusion' (Linklater 1998: 146–7). As the method in the scale of forms argument of *MC* aims to suggest and the praxeological analysis which follows Link-later's sociological inquiry in *TPC* anticipates, there is immanent in our pluralist society of states 'the transition to a condition in which sovereignty, territoriality, nationality and citizenship are no longer welded together to define the nature and purpose of political associ-ation' (1998: 44).

To access these different uses of Hegelian method as a problem for reconciling the issue of the universal versus the particular and the impasse of the debate as a whole, it would be helpful at this point to return to Hegel and that infamous passage. To understand Hegel's meaning in writing that the rational is actual and the actual is rational, we must have a clear understanding of two terms used in a precise manner by Hegel: existence and actuality. For Hegel, existing things have an essence or fundamental rational structure. If that thing does not live up to its essence then it merely exists. If a thing does realize its rational structure then it achieves actuality. Thus, not all things which exist are indeed actual for Hegel. Such an understanding of these terms radically alters the way in which this passage is interpreted. Hegel is using the concept of the actual to link the ideal with that which exists. He is not simply suggesting that all that exists is rational, but only those things which have made manifest their essence.[14] Thus, Hegel cannot fairly be accused of being an apologist for the status quo. However, his critics are right to point out that the possibility for radical critique is limited by Hegelian method. As Michael Hardimon writes, the central institutions of the family, civil society and the state have an absolute standing. They can be criticized for not living up to their essences, but 'the underlying rational structure of the family, civil society and state cannot themselves be criticised', meaning that 'in the modern social world legitimate criticism will inevitably be reformist' (Hardimon 1994: 80–1).

What is at issue regarding Hegelian method and the possibility of reconciling universal and particular justifications of ethical claims is the question of where critique is to be located: internally, that is, within present institutional forms; or externally, breaking the forms in place to construct new forms. For both Hegel and Frost, our only option is to begin from the pre-agreed institutional arrangements that we inherit. Like Hegel, Frost's constitutive theory attributes the family, civil society, state, and the system of states with a form of absolute standing.[15] It is true that the state may not realize its essence as an ethical community, but that essence as a standard or ideal is not

---

[14] This account follows closely the interpretations of Hardimon (1994: 52–56) and Sayers (1987: 148–50).

[15] I say a 'form' of absolute standing because Frost is willing to acknowledge that the institutions themselves may change, yet the roles these institutions play in the constitution of the individual, particularly the state as an ethical community, have an absolute standing for Frost.

at issue in Frost's writings. It is a foundational assumption. Like Hegel, Frost understands the only legitimate critique to be internal critique. Thus, change within international practice is a matter of internal institutional reform rather than radical institutional critique.[16] Linklater, and the critical Left tradition he follows, sees this starting point as an unjustifiable limitation on social critique and the level of human emancipation possible. Because Frost considers the state to be fully rational, no criterion for determining its obsolescence is necessary. This is why Linklater pursues a kind of philosophical history and Frost does not, because Linklater wants to build an argument for a historical momentum of progress that takes us beyond the state form in realizing human capacities for freedom: Linklater's non-negotiable ground.

Thus, this methodological question turns on a foundational question concerning what ground should be the locus of critique. Since Hegel was trying through his method to illuminate the rational in this finite world, while at the same time to acknowledge the deficiencies in forms that had not lived up to their essences, one can see how two schools could emerge – one locating critique within rational, actual forms, and the other locating critique outside of those forms to push them toward their underlying rational structure. Neither Frost nor Linklater presumes the possibility of grounding their methods on some abstract, transcendent, Archimedean point, being the good Hegelians that they are. None the less, each constructs a *weak* foundation, from which their method and ultimately their social critique and resulting ethics follow: Frost upon pre-agreed institutional frameworks in place; Linklater upon a belief in the development of the human capacity for freedom. To return to the anchor metaphor, they both suggest that the anchors of their normative commitments rest in shifting sand, since neither regard their respective starting points to be static. Both regard them to be in a dialectical process of change, the motor of which, for Frost, is the lack of fit between norm and background theory, and for Linklater, is the tension of men versus citizens or the universal versus particular. However, despite the *weak* formulation of the foundational assumptions that guide the projects of Frost and Linklater, despite signs of possible accommodations and the best

---

[16] And thus, my reason for not taking on board Brown's suggestion (mentioned in note 9 above) that Frost is trying to have it both ways – Right and Left – since Frost sees reason in present institutions and sees the need for change. Instead, Frost is simply trying to have it Hegel's way, juxtaposing the status quo and reform.

efforts of these writers to resolve the debate's core tension, evidence of these *weak* foundations being used in a *non-contingent* way shows in the structural opposition that remains and is reflected in all three issues of the debate. As I have argued, the fact that both can use Hegelian method to develop their positions is a product of a structural opposition in the way Hegelian method can be interpreted and employed: on the one hand, for the purposes of reform; and on the other, for the purposes of radical or revolutionary critique. Once again – this time in the case of using Hegelian method to bridge the cosmopolitan/ communitarian divide – it appears that the poles of the debate are not likely to collapse. Where Frost sees contradictions within present state-based institutions to be reconcilable via the process of reflective equilibrium, Linklater sees the only possible resolution to be radical institutional change.[17]

The ethic that results from the international political theory of Frost and Linklater: an assessment

As this comparative analysis of the work of Frost and Linklater demonstrates, Hegelian dialectical method provides us with interesting tools for demonstrating at least some level of accommodation within the cosmopolitan/communitarian debate. However, there appears to be a key element missing in its tool kit: a means for determining whether critique internal to institutions is effective critique. This is a problem that results from using a secularized version of Hegelian method. In one respect, all neo-Hegelians are Left Hegelians in their insistence that the history of *Geist*'s self-actualization through the self-realization of humankind must be replaced by a story of the self-actualization of humankind unfolding in history in order to be workable. As a consequence, the incontrovertibleness of his teleology, its *strong* foundation, is removed. Thus, the motor of the dialectic cannot be assured of running. Therefore, Hegel's means for demonstrating that internal critique is indeed effective critique – that the measure of a thing lives up to its rational structure – is compromised by the secularization of his philosophical system. This does not

---

[17] Thus, Linklater's reluctance to accept the state as fully rational may be in part a consequence of the critical, Left Hegelian methodological tradition with which he identifies.

mean that Hegelian dialectical method cannot be constructively appropriated in a secular way. It simply means that there is a new problem for those who make this move, the problem of how one justifies the now qualified ground from which dialectical method and ethical critique must follow, since recourse to the *strong* foundation of *Geist* is at an end. Thus, an examination of what kind of ethic results from the *weak* foundations they construct is necessary.

To evaluate Frost's starting point of the pre-agreed framework of the modern state domain of discourse, I will turn to his analysis of the non-intervention norm in IR (see Frost 1994b). In examining the non-intervention norm, Frost begins by suggesting there is much happening in this post-Cold War world which leads us to ask whether the non-intervention norm should be modified. Frost contends that because constitutive rules are embedded deep with other constitutive rules in any practice, to consider whether or not it should be changed requires that we ask which rules of present international practice are constitutive of the practice, and which are not. To change a constitutive rule is to change the practice as a whole, so this calls for the careful consideration of many far reaching consequences. Frost's next move is to argue that the non-intervention norm is a constitutive rule of IR practice and suggests that the next question we must consider is what would be a good reason for changing this constitutive rule.

The difficulty in answering this question is that we are participants in the practice we are considering as a candidate for transformation. The problem for ethical critique is that there is no outside point from which to make judgements about the need for change. Thus, internal critique is required. Frost writes that the first assumption of internal critique is that for the most part we find the practices in which we participate to be normatively coherent. We may have to adapt those practices as circumstances change, and we may have to think about a background theory when questions are raised by new circumstances, but as long as the theory found can reconcile those questions, there is no call to change the practice. For Frost, the post-Cold War world is a time of changing circumstances, and constitutive theory is the background theory that can reconcile the questions raised, in particular the rights of individuals and the rights of states. Thus, there is no need to change the non-intervention norm, and consequently, international state practice, because we can accommodate change and the new questions raised about intervention within the practice we have.

As in the case of Hegel, we cannot fairly charge Frost of being an apologist for the status quo. However, as this example shows, his starting point within contemporary international practice leaves no space for imagining new institutional possibilities. We are in this practice and, as a consequence, we have to theorize from this practice. The only cause we might have for radically altering international practice would be if constitutive theory or no other background theory could be shown to be capable of reconciling the norms of the present practice. For the time being, Frost thinks constitutive theory has this covered. Frost's problem with Linklater would be that he does not give significant due to the value found in our present institutions, the state in particular. As Frost would argue, Linklater's international political theory is empty, since it does not acknowledge the normative coherence we find within the modern state domain of discourse today. Linklater is aiming for an external standpoint he cannot achieve.

Frost's constitutive theory has an inherent appeal since it is comprehensive and formulaic. If difficult questions arise due to changing circumstances, we examine the justificatory backbone that is constitutive theory, and check its fit with existing norms and the question at hand. Its method is efficient. There is no need to mess with the underlying philosophical assumptions of the practice itself, as long as constitutive theory can reconcile the norms of the practice on its own or with the adjustments of reflective equilibrium. Yet, at the same time, there is also something inherently dissatisfying with its method in the fact that is formulaic. In working procedurally from a background theory that takes as *given* the ethical status of the state, there is not enough room for expressing philosophical doubt about this institution. For example, questions about what the normative structures around this institution might close off – say, limitations or possible impositions on other ethical-political discourses and practices – is not actively encouraged. Frost is willing to acknowledge that the form of the state may change and another or several institutions may assume its role, but he gives this limited, if any attention. Consequently, he offers no inducements or mechanisms for imagining the alternative normative structures that, as he acknowledges, may evolve.

There is also the question of international distributive justice, a justice which covers both liberties and material resources and opportunities. How is the self-actualization of the have-nots and oppressed who are confined within the state boundaries of dictatorships, or broken down, ineffectual governments, to be made manifest within international practice? Frost's approach again rings of Hegel. It is a matter of making us aware of the rationality within the system of states, that international practice is a 'complex constituting structure', meaning my freedom is compromised by the unfreedom of others, and thus, making the idea that we have no duties to foreigners an 'illegitimate position' (Frost 1994a: 21). I believe this idea of such connections and resultant responsibilities to one another across boundaries is right on target, but more needs to be done to illuminate these connections within international practice: how they evolve and how they work to alleviate structural inequalities in world politics.[18]

My difficulty with Frost's normative IR theory is that he is not willing to dig through the philosophical storage areas of international practice. By this I mean that we must ceaselessly inquire into which ethical-political discourses and practices are being excluded when norms of international practice are deemed 'settled'. Constitutive theory cannot stand as Frost would have it, on the merit of its ability to reconcile norms within international practice. For his starting point to be justified, we have to share his confidence that there is indeed widespread agreement today about values regarding the state, state sovereignty, democracy, citizenship and human rights, and that they are normatively absolute. How can we be confident that these norms and their institutions are not an imposition of Western discursive and material power? Frost has a ready answer to this question. Most states have offered their formal agreement to these norms in choosing to belong to the United Nations Organization (Frost 1994a: 13). However, can we be sure that this is not a form of normative homogenization within international practice, conflicting with Frost's own claims to the importance of diversity? The problem here is that although Frost suggests that the ground from which his project proceeds – the modern state domain of discourse – is not a permanent, ahistorical ground, he proceeds as if it is a *strong* foundation that is not up for question or negotiation. His use of this foundation does not reflect its characterization as a *weak* foundation, since it works *non-contingently*, as if anchored in *terra firma*. Therefore, my problems with Frost's position are both epistemological, in how he uses the *weak* foundations

---

[18] This is particularly so for a neo-Hegelian approach on the issue of the equality of material resources and opportunities, since poverty is the one question for which Hegel had the humility to admit that he had no answer.

he holds, and ethical/political, in what kind of injustices are assumed answerable as a consequence of a faith in the rationality of the state domain of discourse.

Linklater, on the other hand, sees that the philosophical presumptions of the international practice of states, and the forms of exclusion it perpetuates, must be justified. He begins by locating his method outside of the discourse of states, grounded in a understanding of the self as having the capacity for self-determination. To evaluate Linklater's methodological starting point, and the ethic that results, I will turn to his recent book, *TPC*, to examine further his idea of the different responsibilities of dialogic communities which participate in the *three wider universalities of discourse* he identifies: a pluralist society of states, a solidarist society of states, and a post-Westphalian society of states.

For Linklater, dialogic communities are defined by sharing the aim of 'striking appropriate balances between universality and difference', whereby the measure of what is 'appropriate' is established through open dialogue with those who may be affected by the balance established (1998: 107–8). This particular kind of attention to the rights of individuals to pursue their legitimate ends and to forms of exclusion which block those pursuits is socially learned through the experience of modernity. According to Linklater, the 'key to understanding the progressive dimensions of modernity' is in the paradox of the state mentioned above: its 'totalising practices provoked a series of political challenges which led to the elaboration of a complex system of citizenship rights' (1998: 164). If we carry out the full logic of those citizenship rights – being witness to the failures of the exclusionary state in balancing the forces of fragmentation and globalization, and in responding to the forms of transnational harm against which individuals have had little recourse – we can see the need for, and find evident, the very real possibility of participating in wider, more advanced universalities of discourse.

I must proceed carefully here in using the phrase 'more advanced' because, in order to be true to Linklater's notions of a thinner idea of progress, and thin as opposed to thick cosmopolitanism, he states quite clearly that there is no sense in which one of these three wider universalities, or societies of states, can be regarded as superior to others. They cannot, because a discourse ethics respectful of difference must acknowledge 'that groups can enjoy the right to a separate existence which exempts them from the duty to cooperate closely with others' (Linklater 1998: 167). Nevertheless, all three frameworks facilitate the establishment of a universal communication community because each in its own way 'widens the boundaries of community to ensure due consideration for the interests of others' (Linklater 1998: 167). For example, today's more or less universal pluralist framework recognizes the rights of outsiders, states to be exact, to recognition as equal members of a society of states. A solidarist framework, evident among liberal states today according to Linklater, extends that recognition by seeing not simply states, but individuals and minority groups as subjects worthy of equal consideration in a society of states. Within the post-Westphalian framework, the logic that is the full extension of citizenship rights can be realized in a society that is composed of states which are no longer linked with the conceptions of sovereignty, territory and nationality that in the past have constricted possibilities for consultative, dialogical processes between individuals affected by transnational actions.

However, I use the term 'more advanced' because I am not convinced that Linklater does not have a thicker conception of progress at work than he is willing to suggest. Through his praxeological analysis, Linklater is anxious to demonstrate that this post-Westphalian order could be an objective reality that arises out of closer cooperation within a solidarist framework. However, one might ask, why should he be so concerned, particularly if one framework is not necessarily superior to another? He is concerned because he places the greatest weight of the burden of responsibility for the realization of a universal communication community on the shoulders of those participant in the dialogic communities which operate in a post-Westphalian order. Essentially, it is the weight of the unfinished project of modernity on their shoulders. As it is the post-Westphalian state or dialogic community which has the capacity to participate in all three frameworks, it can work to ensure that 'each communicative framework makes its appropriate contribution to the progressive transformation of international society', and, in addition, Linklater assigns it with 'special obligations to establish and maintain these diverse communities of discourse and to assist any developmental tendencies which promise to eradicate unjust exclusion within them' (1998: 211). If, as Linklater writes, more 'progressive' states work to end unjustifiable exclusion, and those which do not are not as 'enlightened' because they 'fail to contribute to the unfinished project of modernity', then the cumulative effect of these points leaves me: (a) less convinced that there is not something more 'progressive' going on in a post-Westphalian framework than others; and (b) wondering whether Linklater makes a mistake not dissimilar to that he attributes to Hegel and his view of the state. That is, does Linklater have an unjustified faith in the project of modernity and its capacity to reconcile or balance universality and difference, in the way that Hegel was confident of the modern state's capacity to perform this same balancing act?

While I would not disagree with Linklater's point in *TPC* that many different writers, critical theorists as well as feminists and post-modernists, are converging around the idea that social and political theory must be focused on the new institutional possibilities for achieving higher levels of universality and difference, I would dis-agree that their 'different voices are in harmony' on this. (Linklater 1998: 74). Indeed, I see that postmodernists and certain feminists have a scepticism in regard to modernity that cannot be discounted here by asserting 'harmony' on the above. There is a scepticism similar to that of the Left Hegelians, in that they can find no reason to invest faith in modernity to balance questions of universality and difference. However, where the scepticism of the Left Hegelians was on the whole politically based in regard to the failures of the state, the scepticism of postmodernists and certain feminists is epistemological, albeit most certainly having political implications as well. Their antifoundationalism means that neither the end goal of the project of modernity nor little if anything else can ground or justify claims made on behalf of universality, difference or some balance of the two.

It is not that Linklater does not acknowledge this foundationalist/ antifoundationalist divide among those who share his interest in accommodating universality and difference. He simply goes on to write that he will be putting forward an argument for a foundation-alist project which has confidence in progress towards a universalist rational morality, and which attempts to anchor possibilities for expanding moral inclusion in the community of humankind (Linklater 1998: 76). Indeed, he says that he has only given up for the time being on the possibility of an Archimedean perspective which sees that humanity might one day converge around the good of something akin to Kant's universal kingdom of ends. None the less, it remains the case that the idea that all human beings are morally equal and should be treated universally as ends is not up for question within Linklater's project. This foundational claim is a weaker formulation of the idea of moral personality assumed by Beitz, since Linklater recognizes the social construction of persons. Yet, to return once again to the anchor analogy, even though he does not argue that this is an anchor that rests in firm ground, his writings betray a conviction that it is an anchor that one day must and will find firm ground in which to rest. It is immanent as evidenced by philosophical history and historical sociology. Linklater recognizes that foundations today have to be *weak*, and he is right that *weak* foundations open up possibilities for finding overlap in divergent positions. However, I want to suggest that he is not acknowledging the possibility that a significant obstacle may remain in seeking convergence when one holds a *weak* foundation *non-contingently*. If he recognized this remaining obstacle as a possibility, and anticipated that taking on board *weak* foundations may mean that we have to hold them *contingently* as well, he would be in a better position to suggest that he is in harmony with the 'different voices'. However, as it stands, I think that Linklater does not take seriously enough the epistemological critique of these antifoundation-alists and what it might mean for his project and the reconciliations he attempts.

By holding his *weak* foundation in a *non-contingent* way, I would say that Linklater not only underestimates the gap between himself and others with whom he seeks to find overlapping positions (not only with the antifoundationalists, but also with communitarians, as mentioned in the Introduction), he also creates related difficulties which are methodological and political in character. I will turn to the methodological difficulties first.

To the extent that Linklater acknowledges that his foundation is *weak*, he argues that the only way to demonstrate that an appeal to common humanity can have any transcultural validity is through dialogue (1998: 79). He recognizes that there are very different approaches to discourse ethics. However, he defends the adoption of an approach which builds on the procedures laid out by Jürgen Habermas,[19] albeit one which takes on board the need for a responsiveness to difference much earlier in the process (Linklater 1998: 94–100). Linklater writes that it is the aim of Habermas to define procedures that promote 'authentic' dialogue, such that 'individuals are equally free to express their moral claims' (1998: 92). What is immediately evident here is that Linklater's *weak* foundational claim –

[19] See chapter 8 for a brief discussion of Habermasian discourse ethics.

that humans should universally be treated as ends – is built solidly into the procedures of discourse ethics to generate a 'rational' outcome. What is problematic here is that the rules of discourse, and thus the 'rational' outcome these procedures are set to produce, are not at any stage up for question. Linklater writes that discourse ethics is philosophical history without the determinism of teleology (1998: 90), but the determinism of teleology is in effect replaced by procedures, since the procedural requirements of his discourse ethics are *non-contingent*. Two unfortunate consequences follow from this methodological impulse. First, it is not clear how this process can properly accommodate difference in the way that Linklater would like, other than in the sense of a promise to be attentive to it. Is this sufficient or do the procedural assumptions undermine such an attention to difference from the start? We cannot be sure from the account presented in *TPC*. Where the first concern is fixed upon the possible limitations of the starting point of discourse ethics, the second concern is based on the rule-bound nature of discourse ethics itself and how this could circumscribe the potential play of institutional imaginings. I would argue that the procedural nature of Linklater's approach ultimately limits the parameters of imaginings about new institutions which might balance universality and difference. As a result, Linklater may be narrowing the range of alternative institutional forms that could prove to be workable routes and motivation towards this post-Westphalian polity.

These difficulties are not purely methodological, since they could have political repercussions as well. Because Linklater does not go into much detail as to how the proceduralism of discourse ethics is operationalized within his project, I am less interested in whether the following critical suggestion is indeed evidence of a narrowing of institutional possibilities due to the proceduralism of discourse ethics, than I am in pointing out a political problem that I find results from the way in which Linklater maintains his *weak* foundational claim in a *non- contingent* manner. I do not see how the unfolding experience of modernity and the logic of the full extension of citizenship rights can ensure the progress Linklater envisions, without a *wider* conception of the institutions of international political practice.[20] I say this because I

---

[20] It goes without saying that Linklater wants a wider conception of who is included in political practice. Instead, my point here is that in order for this to be facilitated, he needs a wider conception of international institutional practice beyond states.

am not convinced that the state will sit idly by as the momentum of its central paradox rolls over it, forcing it to take on new responsibilities and make the kind of dialogical transformation that Linklater suggests for the extension of moral inclusion and human freedom. I think Linklater is convinced that this will happen because, despite words about the need to establish the good of the project of modernity dialogically, he holds a firm, *non-contingent* belief in what he reads immanently from past and present intersocietal practice. Again, I cannot help but wonder if Linklater is making a mistake not dissimilar to one made by another of his favourite writers: Karl Marx. As Marx underestimated the resources of the state to absorb and redirect the social tensions generated by industrial capitalism, is Linklater under-estimating the extent to which the state can absorb the spilling-over of boundaries of ideology, moral community, trade and the like, in this increasingly interdependent world?

I share Linklater's aim of a will to expand moral inclusion, however, I argue that we must look beyond both *non-contingently* held foundations and state practice to have any hope of encouraging it. Where Linklater sees that connections or responsibilities between persons are to be historically and sociologically unfolded and illumi-nated as more or less given in a future institutional form, I find that these connections have to be *created*. Whether state boundaries – or any other kind of boundaries – are denoted on world maps or not, we will still face the difficulty of establishing human connections and obligations beyond our immediate associations. Linklater's idea of a commitment to common humanity and dialogue cannot be assured of being the social glue for dialogic communities that he wants of it. Thus, the task of educating ourselves about the ethical connections which link humankind will always be with us, no matter the shape, scope or institutionalization of communities. This means that we cannot count on the paradox of the state to create and mould dialogic communities as forces of the progress of modernity, nor can we count on the state yielding to any such paradox and transforming itself. We need to be imagining institutional possibilities in addition to the post-Westphalian state – other forms of global governance via international organizations, non-governmental organisations, and international public spheres – which may facilitate the creation of these connections, thinking much more broadly about international political practice than normative theory in IR has in the past, having been fixed largely on the relations between individuals and states. Granted, while I see that this process of the creation of and education in wider moral commitments will always be a task for us, Linklater does go a long and admirable way in getting us to think about the transformations which will be central to this task.

To conclude, both Frost and Linklater share the normative goal of moral inclusion and the project of education and development towards its actualization. While I agree that this is a worthy normative goal, I have reservations with the way each pursues it. Frost's methodological appeal is in working from the solid base of institutions in place and checking their fit against an adaptable justificatory formula, a background theory. Nevertheless, the difficulty with Frost and his starting point within constitutive theory is that there is little scope for imagining new normative or institutional possibilities. Linklater's method, on the other hand, opens up the parameters for thinking about new institutional forms, and about what gets excluded in modern state-based forms, but does not think beyond the institutional possibilities of IR as inter-state activity, albeit radically transformed inter-state activity. Thus, in effect we have a trade-off between a method that offers a practical ground for normative analysis, but has limited capacity for suggesting radical change, versus a method capable of envisioning radical change, but with limited capacity to imagine the normative and material conditions of that change.

Regarding the potential of Hegelian method for moving normative IR theory beyond its present impasse, the ways in which Frost and Linklater employ this method suggests a 'reform' versus 'radical' change opposition. This chapter has demonstrated that Hegelian method does provide some measure for accommodations within the debate, yet a significant structural opposition remains. The foundational starting points of the two writers – one, communitarian, beginning from the modern state domain of discourse, and the other, cosmopolitan, focusing upon the individual's capacity for moral autonomy and freedom – cannot be negotiated for these writers, and the way they use Hegelian method to different effect reflects this. This may say less about Hegelian dialectical method and more about arguing from *weak* foundations in *non-contingent* ways. However, despite the best efforts of Frost and Linklater, the core tension of the cosmopolitan/communitarian debate remains.

CONCLUDING REMARKS TO PART I

The cosmopolitan/communitarian debate is indeed at an impasse, and the nature of that impasse is epistemological. Part I has examined the work of cosmopolitans and communitarians regarding the three issues of the debate – a concept of the person, the moral standing of states and the universal versus the particular – to examine the extent of the impasse, and to seek avenues for accommodation within the debate so that normative IR theory might get out of its present rut. However, although possibilities for reconciling tensions within the debate are evident in the work of all of the writers discussed, a fundamental structural opposition remains that distinguishes cosmopolitans from communitarians: their foundational starting points. It is interesting that while all of the writers to varying degrees recognize that theorists today can no longer argue from the position of *strong*, ahistorical grounds in justifying their moral claims, they none the less have a will to proceed as if *weak* foundations can yield *strong* claims for ethical judgement. To put it another way, *weak* foundations for these writers do not necessarily mean that the criteria for ethical judgement which follow from them are just as weak and vulnerable to change or critique. As long as these writers are not prepared to recognize that their *weak* foundations and the judgements which follow from them are *contingent*, up for negotiation, and are possible candidates for revision, then the structural opposition within the debate will remain.

This leads me to ask in part II whether antifoundationalist approaches can unlock the stasis of this debate. There I will examine two lines of antifoundationalism found in political and IR theory, French poststructuralism and American pragmatism.

Part II Confronting the impasse

4 Poststructuralist antifoundationalism, ethics and normative IR theory

Introduction

This chapter examines one line of antifoundationalist thinking in IR literature which flows out of French poststructuralism, in particular, that of Michel Foucault and Jacques Derrida. Once far removed from French poststructuralism, IR has experienced the injection of this antifoundationalist project into the discipline by writers such as Richard Ashley, R. B. J. Walker and William Connolly. Among others, these three theorists challenge what they identify as the regulative functions of contemporary IR discourse.[1] Following the lead of the poststructuralists, these writers critique the foundations of Enlightenment thought – progress, modernist notions of rational humankind, meaning constructed in dichotomous relationships and universalist assumptions in theory and method – to argue that modernity is knowledge seeking and that its practices of knowledge production actually shape social and political reality. In directing this critique to the constructions of contemporary international theory, these writers problematize the dominant understanding of IR as a world of sovereign states which demarcate inside from outside, order from anarchy, and identity from difference. More generally, they challenge the notion of sovereignty as an ahistorical, universal, transcendant concept, be it applied to the sovereign state, the sovereign individual or a sovereign truth. Sovereignty and the dichotomies regulated by its power are

---

[1] This is but a short list of a growing body of IR literature influenced by poststructuralism: see Ashley (1987) and (1988); Ashley and Walker (1990); Campbell (1992) and (1993); Campbell and Dillon (1993); Connolly (1991) and (1995); Der Derian (1987) and (1992); Der Derian and Shapiro (1989); George (1994); Shapiro (1992); Sylvester (1994); Walker (1993); and Weber (1995).

foundationalist mechanisms of domination and closure which limit the play of political practice. It is the aim of these writers to hammer away at these limitations to open space for plural and diverse practices in world politics.

Initially, this chapter concentrates on shared themes in the work of Ashley, Walker and Connolly regarding their analysis of world politics and its theorization. I have limited the larger part of this chapter to the work of these three writers in order to explore the contributions of poststructuralist theory to ethics and IR in more depth than would be possible by consulting the large body of work by those writing in this area. I have selected these three writers in particular, because they reflect a diverse and reasonable sample of this antifoundationalist IR literature influenced by poststructuralism, and because these writers were central to the articulation of a poststructuralist response to mainstream IR literature: one was originally an IR critic of neo-realism (Ashley); one an associate of the World Order Models Project (Walker); and one a Foucauldian political theorist interested in international theory (Connolly). However, later in the chapter, I will address more recent moves in poststructuralist IR theory – in response to critics who charge them of lacking an ethics – to make plain the ethical significance of this literature.

Practices such as genealogy, deconstruction and reading the world textually are strange to mainstream IR theory, yet such practice is the (anti)method that informs the poststructuralist critique of traditional thought in IR.[2] Variations upon these practices lead to their diverse use among a number of writers. Of the three writers discussed here, Connolly is most selective, taking issue with deconstruction and its 'theoretical postponism' (1991: 13–14 and 56). Yet, despite differences regarding how such practices may be used, common themes between these writers can still be discerned. The first section of this chapter will identify shared themes, which include the closed nature of world political imagination, the crisis of modern sovereignties, and a 'politics of resistance'. The second section examines the implications of the poststructuralist critique for the cosmopolitan/communitarian debate and takes each of the three central issues in the debate in turn. Finally, the third section evaluates the ethics that results from this approach and assesses any potential it may have for moving normative IR theory beyond its present impasse.

---

[2] For an introduction to these practices see Der Derian and Shapiro (1989: xiii–22).

Cutting the moorings of international relations theory/practice[3]

Closure in world politics

While rejecting its 'doctrinal elements', Foucault writes that the modern attitude or philosophical ethos of Enlightenment thought may still inform a critique of our epoch:

> [t]he critical ontology of ourselves has to be considered not, certainly, as a theory, a doctrine, nor even a permanent body of knowledge that is accumulating; it has to be conceived as an attitude, an ethos, a philosophical life in which the critique of what we are is at one and the same time the historical analysis of the limits that are imposed on us and an experiment with the possibility of going beyond them. (1984: 50)[4]

Like Foucault, Walker admits 'a certain continuity' between forms of modern critique and poststructuralist perspectives, yet he wants to 'challenge those affirmations of modernity that have degenerated into dogmatisms' (Walker 1993: 18). Thus, we are presented with a critique performed not from outside modernity, but at its margins.

From the 'margins', or 'borderlines', it is the aim of the writers discussed here to undercut the dogmatism central to IR theory/practice: the assumption of the sovereign state as given. Ashley writes that a position at the margins is 'unsettling' as it is 'never precisely drawn', but unceasingly redrawn or rewritten, thus providing a 'non-place' from which to critique the modern search for permanent ground (1989: 272). Connolly too, is concerned with 'multiplying sites' of global politics to counter the ever present longing for a 'politics of place' (1991: 34). To eschew the modern emphasis on territoriality grants entry to the gamut of political and social practice closed off by the contemporary need to fix identity and history in sovereign spaces. Thus, the task of these writers is set in the asking of '*how*' questions

---

[3] I use the notation 'theory/practice' because for Ashley, Walker and Connolly, theory is understood as practice. As Ashley writes, theory 'does not stand outside of modern global life, as if at some Archimedean point'; rather, it is linked to working knowledgeable practices (1988: 228). There is a significant difference, however, between the position represented here and the way in which Ashley writes as if he were speaking outside of modernist confines in 'Living on Borderlines: Man, Poststructuralism and War' (1989).

[4] It is worth mentioning that Foucault offers a more antagonistic representation of the attitude of modernity in his earlier work: see Foucault (1970).

over the *'what'* questions of explanatory IR theory, which seek facts and evidence. Ashley asks, 'how, by way of what practices, are structures of history produced, differentiated, reified and transformed' (1987: 409)? Walker writes that the poststructuralist turn involves 'trying to understand *how* theories of IR . . . have been constituted on the basis of historically specific and increasingly contentious claims' (1993: 18). Connolly is also concerned to demonstrate *how* IR theory is produced, contending that the intertext between old and new worlds is a 'better "model"' than any 'relation between "theory and evidence"' (1991: 38).

Uncertainty is the undercurrent beneath the 'how'. The sovereign constructions of modernity are responses to, and derive their authority from, the fear of contingency, the meaninglessness of the world, and the absence of criteria for judging truth. The collapse of the church and dynastic empire in early modern Europe unleashed a crisis of identity and representation. Connolly recognizes in those lost after the death of God the need for 'secular reassurances', the assumptions of which are based in 'the unconscious phenomenology of life and death in late modernity' (1991: 16). These compensations, which organize, domesticate and tame contingency, act as a 'filter to theorization' (Connolly 1991: 20). Ashley and Walker label this attitude of despair 'religious', and, like Connolly, agree that it fashions theory by turning 'this fear into a desire, a desire to fill the void, to compensate for the lack, to impose a center of universal judgement capable of effecting limitations and fixing a space, a time, an identity beyond question' (1990: 381).

In IR, the centre capable of all those things and more is the sovereign state. The narrative of how this centre is constructed begins with the global condition of anarchy as a foundational truth. The anarchy problematique sets up the sovereign state as an authoritative solution to the problem of order and contingency in world politics (Ashley 1988: 229). That solution is represented in the sovereign state as a site where humankind's struggle with the universal and the particular is resolved (Walker 1993: 78). Walker writes that territorial sovereignty acquires relevance by demarcating space where universal principles such as justice and right are possible, as against an outside realm of mere relations, rather than genuine politics. Secondly, the sovereign state is significant in its affirmation of temporal boundaries, making progress towards universal claims possible, separated from the contingency of the outside (Walker 1993: 62–63). The fixity of these boundaries, and the sovereign entities outlined is maintained through what Ashley terms 'heroic practice'. Heroic practice replicates understanding of the state as 'an unproblematic rational presence . . . the self-sufficient force of international history's meaning' (Ashley 1988: 231).

The idea that the sovereign state is here to stay, a permanent feature of IR, is regarded as unproblematic within IR, and as worthy of little thought. Yet, these writers regard the silence surrounding this constitutive feature of world politics as actually having much to say. As Walker writes, where there is silence in received wisdom, 'power is often most persuasive' (1993: 13). The sovereign state represents an arbitrary political relation imposing order upon that which cannot be ordered. Discipline is imposed through intense organization. As Connolly writes, 'one must now program one's life meticulously to meet a more detailed array of institutional standards of normality and entitlement' (1991: 21). Thus, identity is constructed though modes of domination which instruct thought and conduct. For these writers, the sovereign solution is no solution at all.

The crisis of modern sovereignties

According to these writers, state sovereignty is weakening. It cannot maintain its ordering of social life across the endless play of multiple forces of fragmentation and integration at work in the world today. Nor can it maintain its hold upon history or universal truth, as the acceleration of time erases notions of lasting structures, fixed criteria or assured meanings. These writers are concerned to identify pressures which destabilize the sovereign notions fastened to historical, political representations called states. Walker writes that evidence of change is all around us, yet there is no clear understanding of its effects. If we pursue the implications of the pace of recent change, and inquire into the ways 'temporal acceleration' increasingly characterizes political life, the early modern resolution of space/time constructs in the sovereign state can no longer be taken for granted (Walker 1993: 14). Ashley speaks of a 'global crisis of representation – a crisis in the enframing and fixing of the sovereign grounds of domestic society that the modern state, as a focus of legitimate violence, may be claimed to represent' (1988: 255). In acknowledging the role of non-state actors in IR, the discipline loosens its hold upon claims for the sovereign state. This space for universal assertions is compromised by the inability to express with certainty what is to be included or excluded; boundaries cannot be steadfastly maintained. Thus, the claims to power and authority of the state become ambiguous. Connolly locates the crisis of sovereign states in what he identifies as the 'globalization of contingency' (1991: 24). This condition of late modernity, engendered by global insecurities over the environment, nuclear holocaust, terrorism, etc., resists mastery no matter how hard state-centred discourse may try. However, the irony for Connolly is that the more late modernity seeks mastery, the more 'it creates global contingencies that haunt it with a new fatefulness' (1991: 27).

A point of clarification is required here. Despite the temper of the arguments above, these writers are not challenging the significance of states in IR today. Otherwise, what impetus would there be behind a critique of sovereign statehood in IR? As Walker writes, what is at issue in examining change in world politics 'is not the eternal presence or immanent absence of states', but instead, whether 'the principle of state sovereignty offers a plausible account of contemporary political practices' (1993: 14).[5] There are multiple infringements upon states today; transnational processes of all kinds undermine claims to sovereignty. The task of these writers is not one of denying the existence of states, but one of drawing out the implications of a global politics without recourse to sovereign impositions of identity, unity and permanence. At stake are the foundations upon which states gain significance.

A 'politics of resistance'

One may respond that such a challenge against sovereignty is a fundamental destabilization of statehood as well as the international system, premised upon interaction between sovereign entities. Such a challenge is profoundly disturbing. As Ashley writes, now the anarchy problematique 'really is an *anarchy* problematique' (1988: 253). These writers recognize the fear elicited by facing a fragmented world and having no foundations. Walker comments that 'it remains exceptionally difficult to renounce the security of Cartesian coordinates, not least of all because they still provide our most powerful sense of what it means to look over the horizon' (1993: 162). The

---

[5] This view is also expressed in Walker (1988: 102–3).

attempt at closure, the imposition of these historical constructs called sovereign states, is assumed less dangerous than 'the hell of infinite openness', writes Connolly (1991: 59). None the less, resignation over what would be left without these coordinates is not licence for theoretical concealment. In the opinion of these writers, such imposition actually increases violence.

Connolly explains this increase in violence as a response to the gap between the globalization of contingency and the state's self-suffi-ciency (1991: 24). As the notion of sovereignty attached to states grows 'increasingly anachronistic', the state responds by extending discipline wherever it can, sustaining 'collective identity through theatrical displays of punishment and revenge against those elements that threaten to signify its inefficacy' (Connolly 1991: 206). According to these writers, the violence of suppressing difference, anarchy, and contingency results in more grievous consequences than that of exposing our vulnerabilities. Thus, the politics of Ashley, Walker and Connolly sets out to open what is closed.

As Jim George writes, this activity creates a 'postmodern politics of resistance, be it articulated at the dissenting margins of academic life, or as part of a more direct social movement of change' (1993: 233). There are two aspects to this politics. The first is to oppose those practices which claim authority over subjectivity, objectivity, space, time, inclusion, exclusion, truth and falsehood, etc. This task places a large burden upon poststructuralist method – that is, the efficacy of deconstruction or genealogy – in breaking sovereign notions. The second aspect promotes democratic pluralism to encourage the growth of new political practices in the space cleared by poststructuralist method. Later in the chapter, this poststructuralist politics will be further elaborated.

Similar closure? The cosmopolitan/ communitarian debate

By a poststructuralist account, the cosmopolitan/communitarian debate is a legacy of the modern era. Modernity, marked by the rise of the abstracted individual as subject and the conviction that we as individuals must each establish our own 'goods' for the practice of our lives, generates a number of dichotomies which the cosmopolitan/communitarian debate perpetuates. Where I can only draw inference from the work of Ashley concerning this debate, Walker and

Connolly speak directly to the limitations of this conversation and also its counterpart in political theory: liberalism and communitarianism (see Connolly 1991; Walker 1993 and 1994). I will address the three issues of the debate and related concerns expressed by these writers.

A concept of the person

Regarding a concept of the person, a poststructuralist perspective takes issue with the modern understanding of the individual as subject. The dualism in the liberal or cosmopolitan account of the autonomous subject as separated from the objective world and unencumbered by social attachments, rings for Walker with 'the same modernist dichotomies that have been reified so smoothly within claims about state sovereignty and political realism' (1993: 8). As Ashley writes, 'from a genealogical standpoint, there are no subjects, no fully formed identical egos, having an existence prior to practice . . . . Like fields of practice subjects emerge in history' (1987: 410). With the communitarians, these writers agree that subjectivity is integrally tied to objectivity, meaning that any understanding of the individual as subject is linked to the historical practices of the social matrix and, similarly, the understanding of those practices are reinforced by subjective consciousness.

While communitarians challenge the liberal or cosmopolitan, unencumbered subject, according to the poststructuralists, they too have a conception of the individual as subject and having a capacity for agency, but with a difference. The communitarian version posits a subject who is socially constructed, yet chooses for herself to recognise social practices and institutions in which she is participant. The poststructuralist writers are highly sceptical of the notion of agency attached to modern subjectivity, whether liberal or communitarian. Ashley writes, 'the subject is itself a site of power political contest, and ceaselessly so' (1987: 410). Against the communitarian, then, these writers argue that identification with social tradition is not freely chosen by the individual, but instead, is an imposition of authoritative practices at work within modernity. There are no grounds, however hard modernists of cosmopolitan and communitarian persuasions might try, for this claim to agency. Therefore, a concept of the person is illusive, and its essentialist search, misguided. None the less, as will be developed in the third section of the chapter, there are ontological convictions at work within the poststructuralism of these writers that concern the normative significance of individual autonomy.

The moral standing of states

This notion of agency, that individuals choose for themselves the 'goods' by which they conduct their lives, has implications for the issue of state morality. As Connolly writes, late modernity forces a choice between treating one's life as a project – that is, being 'indebted to the institutions in which one is enclosed' and conforming to territorial norms – or not to treat one's life as a project – that is, choosing one's own way and increasing 'one's susceptibility to one of the categorizations that licence institutional discipline from another direction' (1991: 21). His tone regarding either choice is caustic at best, since together the liberal and communitarian choices 'licence a lot of discipline' for Connolly (1991: 28). Both attempt to mitigate the resentment of social membership for the modern subject either by 'enabling self-reliance' or by elevating 'the experience of connectedness to a larger community', yet only at the cost of discipline by the hand of the market economy or the imposition of universal norms within the community (Connolly 1991: 28).

According to Connolly, this idea of a choice disregards contingency in the social world and works to control it, either through asserting sovereign man's ability to master nature, or through the idea of harmonization or attunement within the sovereign state. Thus, sovereign practices are maintained through this debate. Cosmopolitanism and communitarianism represent two knowledge practices. Such practices, as Ashley understands them, contain 'their own exemplary and replicable strategies and technologies for the disciplining of plural historical practices in the production of historical modes of domination' (1987: 409). Thus, the idea of a choice informing either position's stance regarding the issue of the morality of states is no choice at all for these writers. Once again, modernity generates one more false dichotomy, in this case, a dichotomy of two ethical theories which maintains an opposition between cosmopolitan and communitarian standards.

However, like the cosmopolitans, these poststructuralists contest arguments for the morality of states on two counts. First, the state's moral legitimacy rests in its claim to be the community in which ethical duty is made possible, a forum where universal principles can be recognized. Walker argues that this is a dubious claim as the communitarian fails to acknowledge the problematic character of community in IR: community is assumed to be contiguous with the sovereign state (1993: 51n). Secondly, following from that, the state's claim to power and authority is ambiguous, and sanctions much violence in the effort to maintain one community among plural communities.[6] From this challenge to the efficacy of sovereign statehood, these writers go on to invoke a new, cosmopolitan understanding of democracy as non-territorialized, no longer 'locked behind the bars of the state' (Connolly 1995: 157).

The universal versus the particular

For these writers, another modernist construct in the cosmopolitan/communitarian debate is the dichotomy of universalism and particularism that its foundationalism generates. The assumption that fuels this dichotomy is that ethical principles must have a foundation or a universal basis of truth. The poststructuralist account denies any grounds or foundations for a universalizable ethic, be it located within moral persons or within communities. Thus, the conflict between the two positions over a criterion of ethical judgement across communities is moot. We should not be bothered to play the justificatory game with which good foundationalists entertain themselves. Neither the cosmopolitan attempt to secure a ground for universalist ethics, nor the communitarian presumption of a universal foundation of truth within the particularity of community can establish itself without sovereign assumptions. Thus, as Walker writes, 'universalism, to put it bluntly and heretically, can be understood as the problem, not the solution' (1993: 77). For these writers, a will to universalism and the foundationalism it assumes is a source of exclusion, oppression and violence in world politics. What Walker's statement suggests for normative IR theory is that, as long as its central debate seeks solutions through recourse to foundationalist claims (either by cosmopolitans on behalf of individuals, or by communitarians on behalf of their community of choice), not only will the problem of the impasse remain, but a lot of further violence will be sanctioned as well. Thus, regarding the issue of universalism

---

[6] These arguments are similar to the cosmopolitan position of Luban (1985: 195–217 and 238– 47).

versus particularism, the poststructuralist attitude challenges the attempts of universalists to resolve particularity and difference into sameness; and for the poststructuralists, such universalism errs on the side of both cosmopolitanism and communitarianism. However, as will be discussed below, I find that universals also 'err' on the side of the poststructuralists.

Does giving up on foundationalist thinking not sink us in a mire of ethical relativism? These poststructuralist writers would again castigate such a concern as typically modern. Relativism misleadingly assumes an either/or choice between building upon what we have or embracing a nihilism that denies any criterion of progressive politics (Walker 1993: 16). Walker's preference is for poststructuralist 'celebrations of uncertainty' over the dubious claims of human essences on which modern universalist ethics is founded. Connolly too, writes that the 'relativist worry is untimely', as the more important concern in this time of 'closure and danger, is to open up what is enclosed, to try to . . . stretch and extend fixed patterns of insistence' (1991: 59).

Thus, the poststructuralist turn in IR consigns the cosmopolitan/ communitarian debate into the junk heap of modernity. Yet, while denying its dichotomies, it does follow along lines parallel to the oppositions within it; crucially, while denying a universalizable ethics, it maintains *weak* foundations which inform a poststructuralist 'politics of resentment'. The next section will examine the ethics and consequent politics that result from the grounds, understood as historically *contingent*, proffered by these writers.

Beyond the impasse of the cosmopolitan/ communitarian debate? An antifoundational or non-universalizable poststructuralist international ethics

The ethics that results

Ashley, Walker and Connolly ascribe universal attributes to the closure of world politics: a ubiquitous fear of difference and contingency, and the silent (or sometimes not so silent) violence of sovereign notions of statehood. This comprehensive vision fuels an ethical condemnation which calls for new, alternative political practice. Clearly, a criterion of judgement, however understood, must be at the base of such condemnation. In other words, antifoundationalism does not preclude the will to an international ethics. Yet, have these writers not disclaimed the possibility of grounds or foundations for ethical discrimination? Have they placed the will to a poststructuralist international ethics in a bind of its own making?

These writers understand world politics to be infused with ethics, that the ethical is political and the political is ethical. Walker writes that his chapter 'Ethics, Modernity, Community' is motivated by a sense that work concerned with ethics and IR is important (1993: 50). Yet, poststructuralist interest in ethics and IR starts by developing a critical understanding of the limitations of ethical theory, in particular, its reliance upon modernist foundational assumptions. As Ashley and Walker write, traditional ethical thought relies upon:

> the imposition and observance of limitations that can themselves be unambiguously defined and justified from the standpoint of a sovereign center of judgement that commands a space, authenticates what is valuable and good within, defines alien and dangerous modes of thought and conduct to be excluded, and is itself beyond question. (1990: 390)

Despite their antifoundationalism, these writers do not deny the possibility of ethics, nor do they want to. What is suggested is a thorough re-examination of what we understand by ethics (Walker 1993: 79). An ethics is possible, but it is not ethics as we traditionally conceive of it; a new understanding is required. Alternatively, they invoke a qualified ethics, described by Connolly as a 'second order ethicality' (1991: 12). Such an ethics recognizes the frailty of universal claims, since they are understood to be historical constructs. Unlike the cosmopolitan and communitarian writers discussed in part I of the book, these writers recognize that the acknowledgement of the historical constructedness of one's claims has repercussions for the absoluteness and universality of ethical argument that follow from those claims. Aware of the historicity of value assertions, this qualified ethicality offers no pretence of temporal or spatial roots. It is a *contingent* ethics. Consequently, ethical considerations challenge what it means to talk about world politics today, asking what freedom, democracy and community represent without, as Walker writes, a recourse to a 'sovereign center' (1993: 79). Connolly offers one version of a qualified ethics which he labels as an 'agnostic ethic of care', and Ashley and Walker offer another version, an 'ethics of marginal conduct'.

Connolly looks to Nietzsche and Foucault to articulate a second-order ethicality. 'The primary quest is not for a *command* that answers "why" or a *ground* that establishes "what" but for *ways* to cultivate care for identity and difference in a world already permeated by ethical proclivities and predispositions to identity' (Connolly 1991: 10). This means exposing the paradox of ethics, that identity is formed through the designation of difference, in order to crack the closure of modernist ethical pronouncements of identity, making room for an 'agnostic ethic of care' (Connolly 1991: 14). This agnostic respect is nurtured by genealogy and democratic politics, as both encourage the 'experience of contingency in identity' despite its sovereign accounts. Connolly recognizes that these are dangerous practices, but he writes that it is better to expose the paradox of ethics than suppress it, as the interplay of these dangerous practices may one day reveal a productive counter-ontological possibility (1991: 11–13).[7]

In a special issue of *International Studies Quarterly*, edited by Ashley and Walker, they outline their conception of an 'ethics of marginal conduct'. Marginality represents the 'inability to speak and labor in a register of desire', desire being the will to fix identity, space and time (Ashley and Walker 1990: 388). They celebrate the space of freedom and the possibility of new modes of ethical conduct, liberated through critique of the paradoxical nature of a universal ethical system that requires marginalization and exclusivity to ground judgement. They recognise that this 'celebratory register of freedom' is purely negative, wrecking the possibility of ethical discrimination, but, as they write, at least those at the margins 'do not sit idly awaiting answers that can never come' (Ashley and Walker 1990: 391). This ethics of marginal conduct can in no way be formalized to delineate the good life, but they argue that it does not hinder discussion of how we might 'orient' such an ethics. Its orientation, as they discuss it, does not exclude territorialized ethics nor lead to any form of totalitarianism. It does not reject, but it questions territorialized ethics to widen the scope of an ethics of freedom, and uses democratic practices of listening, questioning and speaking to 'traverse the institutional limits' so that 'where this ethic is rigorously practised, no totalitarian order could be' (Ashley and Walker 1990: 395).

---

[7] This is an example of a line of thought in Connolly's work with which I am particularly sympathetic: Connolly is self-aware of the 'sovereign accounts' and universals within his own work, but he warns against them and carries on with the hope that some counter-ontological possibility may yield. The following chapters will indicate my reasons for this sympathy.

As this outline indicates, clearly, this is not an ethics in any comprehensive or *strong* foundationalist sense, yet it remains questionable whether it represents a non-universalized or a non-foundationalist ethics. Clearly, they prefer to suggest what this ethics is not. They focus their efforts upon critique, critique of foundationalist epistemology in particular, rather than stating what their alternative ethic might affirm. None the less, it does affirm. Connolly writes, 'no affirmative theory can proceed without invoking ontological presumptions; several political theories today conceal their own presumptions' (1991: 67). Similarly, the ontology at work in the writings of these poststructuralists, as well as the grounds they invoke to bolster that ontology, need to be brought to the surface for a closer look.

While Connolly's idea of an ethics holds out hope for a counter-ontology to modernist presumptions, Ashley and Walker refuse to suggest any such hope. Yet, it is clear that two outcomes are desired by all three writers: freedom and democratic plurality. The will to these effects shapes an ontology that locates freedom in the privileging of multiple practices. A transcendent condition, something better than what we know, is a product of opening what is closed. Their 'politics of resistance' reflects this ontology. Walker suggests a progressive politics in writing that 'the most interesting ways forward will be opened up by those who seek to speak to the possibility of new forms of political community while resisting the [prior] resolutions' (1993: 80). By breaking the 'blackmail of heroic practice', Ashley writes that we can free its 'victims' and make possible 'new connections among diverse cultural elements . . . and new ways of thinking and doing global politics' (1988: 254). Connolly dispenses with the nostalgia for a determinate 'politics of place' and suggests 'multiplying sites at which the issues of freedom and unfreedom can be posed in late modern life' (1991: 34).

The poststructuralist turn could itself be accused of a silence similar to that which these writers charge against the theory/practice of sovereign statehood. In affirming that the play of contingency and multiple, conflicting political practices is preferable to our closed world-political imagination, these writers are invoking ontological presumptions, which by their nature are universal. However, they are less sovereign in character than the ontology behind territorialized ethics, since the grounds they invoke are understood to be *contingent*; but, all the same, they are still sovereign, because they do not avoid invoking grounds. I will argue that these writers do not succeed in articulating the new understanding of ethics that they intend: an ethics independent of universal categorizations or foundations.

Poststructuralist international ethics: an assessment

This is not the first time these writers have been charged with asserting truths or contradicting themselves. And when so charged, Connolly emphatically responds, 'the simple answer is yes on all counts. Yes, yes, yes, yes, yes' (1991: 60). To suggest that their work is contradictory or relativist is to maintain a sovereign centre of judgement over their invocation of contingency and paradox (Ashley and Walker 1990: 375). In asserting that their account of ethics is in a bind or self-contradictory, I could be charged with imposing coherence, as a typical modernist would. These writers can insulate themselves from critique by castigating as modernist those who trespass at the margins and question their direction, but this would be unfortunate, since to suggest incommensurability between demands for coherence and an ethics or politics of the margins is itself a knowledge practice that can make its constructions impenetrable. However, it is true that I am asking for a measure of coherence in: (1) suggesting that while these writers reject the modernist framing of the cosmopolitan/communitarian debate – the subjectivities assumed, its foundationalist and universalist thinking – they are not unfettered themselves by these modernist aspects; and (2) asking whether they can still maintain that their will is to locate a non-universalizable ethics if these aspects can be found in their writing. For me, this suggests that perhaps the notion of universalizability, assumed by the idea of an 'ethics', needs to be rethought and critically interrogated.

Poststructuralist IR theory, as represented by these writers and the 'politics of resistance' they promote, aims to articulate an ethics that can 'identify the intolerable'; discriminate among identities, rather than celebrate 'any and every identity'; and destabilize institutions of violence.[8] Thus, it is affirmative. However, there are those good foundationalists or modernists who would argue that the possibility of its affirmation is stymied by a poststructuralist method which refuses secured grounds for ethical judgement and identifies violent power/knowledge practices within the very foundations necessary to

---

[8] For each of these ethical aims see respectively, Walker (1993: 52); Connolly (1991: 14); and Ashley and Walker (1990: 394).

ethical critique. It is the aim of the poststructuralist turn to move beyond such an understanding of ethics, that it must be universalizable and foundationalist. Instead, it suggests an ethics which is loosely fastened to local practices, and is understood to be historically *contingent*. However, a strictly non-universalized and non-foundationalist ethics is compromised on both of these counts. There is a will to universalization that cannot be denied in what the poststructuralist IR theorists aim to affirm, and it rests on the shifting and *contingent* grounds, but grounds, none the less, of the ontological possibility of radical autonomy in varied local practices.

The aim of a non-universalized ethics is compromised by a method that universalizes, and seeks universal application, of the claims which follow from its method. It universalizes power and violence in all attempts to secure grounds, whether they be abstract, transcendent moral claims on behalf of individuals, or claims from normative structures grounded in community practices. As a result, we – a universal 'we', one must assume – should celebrate difference and work to open space for alternative practices in world politics. Thus, the ethics suggested does not avoid universalism. However, what it does avoid is absolutism in its ethics. This ethics is not without foundations, since it works from the more weakly formulated grounds of historical and *contingent* practices of localities. Yet, what is significant, and distinguishes their ethics from that which follows from the cosmopolitans and communitarians discussed in part I, is that it understands that the ethical judgements which result from these *weak* foundations are necessarily qualified. It is a weaker or secondary ethics that is not seen to hold absolutely in a *strong* foundationalist sense. While remaining foundationalist to a degree, this ethics is a valuable contribution to normative IR theory, since the ethics that follows acknowledges its own contingency. However, what is left as a puzzle is whether these writers can maintain that they sufficiently avoid, or still see the need to avoid, a will to universalization which is deemed inconsistent with their methodological claims.

These writers might respond that this has been a difficulty obvious to them from the start. While Walker writes, as noted above, that universalism is the problem not the solution, he also writes that a major challenge of contemporary political life is that 'universalism has to be resisted and sought at the same time' (1988: 135).[9] It seems that a

[9] Also, as I wrote in n7, Connolly makes a similar point.

will to ethics cannot avoid universalization, but this raises the question: what kind of universalizability are we talking about, and what exactly are the dangers of oppression and exclusion in the universalization offered? I am not convinced that this question has been given sufficient self-conscious attention by Ashley, Walker and Connolly, since they have been focused largely on the task of illustrating the violence inherent in universalisms and sovereign notions and, in the process, creating space for poststructuralist readings of IR. However, recently, George (1995) has examined new efforts in poststructuralist IR theory, in particular the work of David Campbell, to argue that this approach does have something 'of "ethical significance" to say', and most importantly for the concern raised above, draws attention to the problem of universalizability for poststructuralists and the possibilities for a non-universalizable ethics. I will turn briefly to what George has to say about this question.

George writes that poststructuralists have a tough balancing act to perform. In offering an ethic of responsibility and articulating 'the art of the possible' in world politics, he finds that poststructuralist IR theorists must 'include some universalist sense of what is ethical behavior and what it is not, while avoiding the foundationalist, ahistorical absolutism characteristic of modernist universalism in general' (1995: 197). This is made evident when he outlines the position of Emmanuel Levinas, whose work is being used in the attempt to formulate a poststructuralist ethic of responsibility in IR.[10] Levinas reformulates modern subjectivity such that 'the identity of the ethical subject is constituted, not via its autonomy and independence from Otherness, but in its obligation to and responsibility for Others' by which we are all implicated; thus, ethical conduct depends upon 'the way in which humaneness and the self/Other relationship is understood and formulated' (George 1995: 210). George regards this position as philosophically problematic because it assumes a universalism that poststructuralists seek to avoid, raising the question of whether one can recognize universal claims from an anti-foundationalist position (1995: 211).[11] However, what redeems Levinas's position,

---

[10] See Campbell (1994) and the exchange between Warner (1996) and Campbell (1996) in *Millennium*.

[11] It should be noted that Campbell readily acknowledges 'an important moment of universality' in Levinas's work (1994: 461). However, since Campbell, unlike George, is not concerned explicitly to develop the problem of universalizability for poststructuralism, I focus here on George's discussion of this question.

to some extent, for George is the fact that it does not rely upon a *strong* or fixed foundationalist notion of an ahistorical subject, but instead is attentive to difference and particularity. According to George, what is important to keep foremost in our ethical considerations is Foucault's warning against speaking with fixed universal convictions. What George holds out hope for is that there *are* ways to articulate universal claims that, in taking this warning under advisement, do not control and oppress. He writes that such a poststructuralist ethic is committed to a democratic and emancipatory political agenda that seeks equalities of liberties and opportunities, but most importantly this ethic also entails 'the "permanent critique" of a universalist rationality such as this' (George 1995: 219–21). Thus, poststructuralist international ethics is moving towards a more self-conscious awareness of the universals it invokes and is working through ways to offer these universals that are sensitive to the dangers their position acknowledges to exist in such theorizing.

There is much that appeals to me in this ethics as George has outlined it. In particular, I am most struck by the way in which recent poststructuralist IR theory is attempting to think through what we understand by a universal claim. What follows from this is the potential reconceptualization of universals, such that we recognize that universals can and must be decoupled from absolutist or fixed assumptions, or else their very suggestion potentially excludes and controls. However, what remains unclear and potentially problematic is the *way in which* poststructuralists use the grounds or *weak* foundations they invoke. George writes that 'a post-modern ethics must be firmly and unequivocally located in the politico-normative terms of everyday life' (1995: 207). This resonates with the writings of Ashley, Walker and Connolly, which similarly point to local practices rather than abstract, ahistorical principles as the source and ground for ethical claims. What is unclear is what is intended by recourse to local practices, since to appeal to such a ground is compromised for these writers by their poststructuralist methodological assumptions, which see power and only limited possibilities of autonomy in the politico-normative structures of local practices.

This is a characteristic feature of the line of antifoundationalism which follows from poststructuralist, particularly Foucauldian, thought. Such thought problematizes the agency attributed to modernist subjectivities, and suggests an ideal of radical autonomy that understands social membership as having violent repercussions for the individual. Members are seen to be victims of the normative structures universalized within local practices. Thus, by the notion 'radical autonomy', I aim to suggest an illusive autonomy, available only to those divested of community and the power impositions its brings. Do these writers also subscribe to this trajectory within Foucauldian antifoundationalism? Connolly is cautious in his claims regarding the violence of social determinations and remains a democratic theorist, however radical. None the less, the tenor of his writings maintains a Foucauldian suspicion of social commitments and their normalizing tendencies.[12] The same can be said of Walker and Ashley, although Walker does on occasion argue that we cannot cynically go about reducing 'all normative claims to the legitimation of power' (Walker 1994: 265). However, it remains the case that neither Ashley, Connolly, nor Walker is particularly clear about this issue, and they make no effort to distance themselves from the 'radical autonomy' position that is a part of Foucauldian poststructuralism. Thus, it seems problematic that these writers would appeal to the everyday practice of local communities as the base of their theorizing, unless they are appealing to the practice itself and not the normative structures associated with it. Yet, to separate norm from practice is like separating ethics and politics; it is untenable within poststructuralist assumptions. Clearly, they begin here because it is the only place left to begin if one rejects ahistorical, absolute moral claims. However, they could appeal to the social traditions of local practices as a ground for ethics if they problematized the universalism within these normative structures in the way discussed above. Unfortunately, this is not raised as a question within post-structuralist IR theory.

I argue that this represents a difficulty for what kind of content this ethics has, because if they cannot appeal to the normative structures of community as a contextualized and shifting ground for ethical judgement, what criteria are left; and what exactly does beginning from these practices mean for these writers? I can only conjecture that the appeal to local practices is no more than an appeal to theorize in the world and the everyday situations it presents rather than to theorize abstractly; and 'local' is invoked to signify that these writers recognize that what happens in life, day in day out, is diverse and varied. It can be no more than this since their methodological assump-

---

[12] An example of this is in Connolly (1995: 88) where he distinguishes his counter-problematic from C. B. Macpherson's problematic for democratic theory.

tions rule out theorizing from the values shared within communities (unless the universals within them are qualified as I suggested above). So, what is the actual base of critique then?

Campbell, on the other hand, puts a different spin on beginning from our day to day practice, which potentially distances him from the 'radical autonomy' position that can result from Foucauldian poststructuralism. According to Campbell, what follows from a Levinasian position, with the help of Derrida, is a notion of 'radicalized interdependence': ethical conduct is a matter of 'how the interdependencies of our relations with Others are appreciated', such that 'what is transcendent is our embeddedness in a radically interdependent condition, where we are inescapably responsible to the Other' (Campbell 1996: 131 and 138). Such an ethics is generated from the philosophical implications of one overriding fact about our everyday experience: it is shaped by interdependence (Campbell 1996: 131). For Campbell, this interdependence is the most compelling aspect of a Levinasian-inspired ethics of responsibility because, in regard to conflicts such as the Balkan crisis, 'it maintains that there is no circumstance under which we could declare that it was not our concern' (1994: 462). Thus, the universal moment of this ethics has an absolute, sovereign quality as well, that we cannot escape this responsibility, no matter what the circumstances are; and, as a consequence, engagement with the other is ethically secured. The interdependence which connects our everyday experience is the ground for Campbell's ethics. While Campbell does not self-consciously acknowledge his own *weak* foundation, what his ground aims to establish are links or points of connection between persons – the many – which the radical autonomy position fails to do.[13] However, this ethics may still reflect an aspect of radical autonomy, since it is not located in normative structures that we share in local practices and regard as mutually constituting, but in the fact of our coexistence.

The lack of clarity in the relationship of Ashley, Connolly, and Walker (and to an extent Campbell) to the 'radical autonomy' position is a problem for the content of a poststructuralist ethics. Clearly, there is potential for the authority invested in social institutions and in

---

[13] Campbell's concern about the 'one-to-oneness' of Levinas's ethics is further evidence of his desire to illuminate ties of responsibility among persons (Campbell 1994: 464–68). However, I am not sure that Campbell satisfactorily makes clear how the leap from one-to-one relations of responsibility to one-to-the-many works: his nod to deconstruction does not fill this in for me.

sovereign ideas to do violence to individuals. Further, a poststructuralist ethics is useful for theorizing the relations of power that exist in the normative structures of community and absolute, sovereign notions or foundations generally. However, it is not as good at helping us think about the values that people, regardless, locate in communities and the shared value traditions which arise from them. To characterize such violence as ubiquitous is unworkable for considerations of ethics. This results in a negative politics of resistance and disengagement from societal constraints. Thus, the possibility of engagement in working towards a better global politics and better self/Other relationships is compromised, despite the transcendence of a 'radicalized interdependence', or of a cosmopolitan community of humankind that Walker posits in *One World, Many Worlds* (1988: 102), since the motivation behind the ethics of responsibility assumed is undermined by an ambiguous relation to the trajectory of 'radical autonomy' in their poststructuralist anti-method. Also, in not giving thought to the immediate loyalties people hold to local practices, the problems these loyalties present for the reach of the ethics these writers articulate are not sufficiently considered.

Concluding remarks

Having traced the difficulties in negotiating foundationalist claims in the impasse that is the cosmopolitan/communitarian debate at present, I find that it is important to pursue the avenues that antifoundationalist thought opens up for international ethics. This chapter is written out of the sense that normative IR theory should listen to the voices from the margins. The writings of Ashley, Walker, Connolly, Campbell and George shake the stasis of the debate, forcing valuable reconsiderations of the debate as a whole, and upon the two positions as well. Cosmopolitanism benefits from a poststructuralist understanding of its social, historical construction, and communitarianism benefits from the suggestion that the state cannot maintain itself as the only depository of communal identity and meaning for the individual. Most importantly, the debate as a whole benefits from an understanding of itself as an historically *contingent* modernist discourse. The source of the seemingly either/or choice within the debate stems from the modern era being marked by the rise of the abstracted individual as subject. The rise of subjectivity presents a dilemma for modern political practice; that is, how to reconcile this individual, who looks to herself as her own standard of truth, with the commitments and obligations of social membership. This is the historical condition that frames the debate and its core tension.

These poststructuralists problematize modernity and challenge modernist notions of rationality, autonomy, and foundational philosophy as historical constructions which silently assume sovereign status. Thus, the poststructuralist turn requires that we inquire into the ways in which the cosmopolitan/communitarian debate, and our consequent understanding of ethics, is framed by modernist, foundationalist assumptions. These writers suggest that the debate is misconceived as an either/or choice between unsustainable modernist dichotomies. As Walker writes, his concern is 'to destabilize seemingly opposed categories by showing how they are at once mutually constitutive and yet always in the process of dissolving into one another' (1993: 25). I agree with Walker's characterization of the task at hand. The cosmopolitan/communitarian debate sets up rigid ethical positions assumed to be mutually exclusive, yet the interplay of their differences does indicate a relationship that needs to be explored. However, that interplay cannot be effectively explored as long as the core foundational assumptions and the structural opposition they create linger.

Important questions remain as to whether the oppositions do indeed melt away and whether poststructuralist IR theorists cease playing the modernist, foundationalist justificatory game. With the incorporation of antifoundationalist approaches into normative IR theory, I find that a residue of this fundamental opposition rests in the *weak* foundations that antifoundationalists, concerned to articulate an ethics, cannot avoid. Regarding the normative position of poststructuralist IR theorists, it is evident that the subject of justice for these writers is the individual, and that their aim is the expansion of moral inclusion and individual autonomy in world politics.[14] Their concern with individual autonomy and its furthest possible extension represents the ontological convictions harboured within Foucauldian poststructuralism. However, what is unclear is the extent to which these writers endorse the 'radical autonomy' position that can result from Foucauldian thinking. This raises the question of whether or not poststructuralist antifoundationalism can adequately theorize the

---

[14] However, it should be noted that Campbell (1994: 461–62) is clear that he wants to undermine the preoccupation with individual autonomy and freedom in ethics.

value individuals find, not only in individual autonomy, but in community tradition and membership as well. This suggests that a residue of the opposition remains, since the ability to think about the interplay between the value of individual autonomy and social membership appears circumscribed in poststructuralism.

However, it is important to note that the degree of opposition which I find to remain is mitigated – that is, it is less fundamental, and this is why I call it a 'residue' of opposition – because there is a significant difference in the way *weak* foundations are employed by poststructuralists in IR. Their convictions are understood to be vulnerable, second-order claims subject to historical contingency. Since their ethical claims are *contingent* and not seen to hold absolutely, they are negotiable. Thus, the ethics that results is more flexible, wielding less power to exclude and oppress; and thus, it has more potential to shake the stasis of normative theorizing in IR. It also has the potential for opening new space for alternative ethical-political discourses and practices. Yet, as I said above, I still have a concern as to whether it can sufficiently theorize the value people find in community traditions. In the next chapter, I will examine another line of antifoundationalist thinking in IR which prioritizes the value traditions of communities as the place from which ethics must begin.

5 Neo-pragmatist antifoundationalism, ethics, and normative IR theory

This chapter examines a second line of antifoundationalist thought that follows from the philosophical tradition of American pragmatism. I will focus on the work of Richard Rorty to see what his antifoundationalism might yield in moving normative theory beyond the epistemological impasse of the cosmopolitan/communitarian debate. Rorty, although trained in analytical philosophy, rejected its foundationalism to construct a variant of American pragmatism that professes an anti-philosophy: a turn away from philosophy and its truth-seeking methods, towards politics and literature. Unlike the poststructuralists discussed in the last chapter, with the possible exception of William Connolly, Rorty is not generally regarded as an IR theorist. In his writings, he is not concerned to address issues of sovereignty and statehood, which are typically deemed central to IR and its theorisation. Thus, the introduction to this chapter suggests reasons why Rorty's writings *are* relevant to IR.

His discussion of each of four issues – liberalism, antifoundationalism, the implications of liberalism and antifoundationalism for human rights, and the call to extend our 'we' group – holds significance for IR theory. Moreover, together, their consideration has particular import for normative IR theory and its two ethical approaches for two reasons. First, Rorty has contributed to a debate within political theory between liberals and communitarians which, as has been discussed, resonates with the debate in IR theory. Secondly, through his discussion of an issue central to IR theory, human rights, we may enquire where a liberal, yet antifoundationalist, ethic might take normative IR theory. To begin, I want to briefly touch upon the four issues mentioned above, their relevance to IR theory, and their connection to Rorty's work.

144

Liberalism is a much-discussed topic within recent IR theory.[1] Since the events of 1989, the victory of liberalism and liberal democratic institutions has been discussed in tones ranging from the triumphal to the matter-of-fact. Francis Fukuyama's (1992) much-debated 'End of History' thesis draws the finishing line of history, placing liberalism as the political ideology first and last to cross the marker. Rorty writes in a similar vein, pointing to contemporary liberal society and sug-gesting a conceptual end of history; we in the West have perhaps had our last revolution of concepts within social and political thought (1989a: 63). Rorty too is a convinced liberal, yet what is key to Rorty's discussion of liberalism is captured by the way in which he contextua-lizes this revolution. It is limited to Western thought and does not suggest that the world requires no more political revolutions (Rorty 1989a: 63n). Rorty's utopian vision of liberalism and its ironic politics is far from conventional and not without controversy, but it is interesting to IR theory because of the way it contextualizes the good offered by liberalism.

A second theme in Rorty's work, antifoundationalism, is also relevant to IR theory. Richard Bernstein points out that antifounda-tionalism has been building steam in political and social theory for the last 150 years (Bernstein 1991: 288). IR has not been able to avoid its momentum. As Steve Smith writes, the debate between foundation-alism and antifoundationalism is 'the fundamental normative issue' in the discipline of IR (1992: 505). It is also the question which is behind the crisis of modern thought that Chris Brown (1994) identifies as a source of division among contemporary IR theorists. Rorty is a principal contributor to the momentum of antifoundationalism. For Rorty, our starting point should be the recognition that the 'link between truth and justifiability' is broken (1990a: 280). A closer look at Rorty's antifoundationalism could offer further insights into whether IR theory should take antifoundationalism seriously, what the reper-cussions might be if we do take it seriously, and how IR theory might then proceed.

Rorty espouses the two seemingly contradictory projects of anti-foundationalism and liberalism. It is the aim of his writing to persuade us of their compatibility. In a recent article, the implications of these two projects are played out in his discussion of the third issue mentioned above, human rights (Rorty 1993b). Human rights, a tenet

[1] For a recent sample of IR interest in liberalism, see Hovden and Keene (1995).

of liberal theory valued by Rorty and by the large number of us who participate in what Rorty understands to be a 'human rights culture', cannot be regarded as natural, universal or ahistorical. This represents an interesting turn on how human rights are generally discussed and how they can be defended in IR. It also provides us with a good case for examining the repercussions of such an antifoundationalist position in world politics. Ultimately, the conclusion that results from this piece on human rights is consistent with that drawn in *Contingency, Irony, and Solidarity (CIS)* and other articles: an ethic which calls for the extension of our 'we' group, those with whom we have sympathy. This fourth issue, the extension of 'we' feeling, is of particular import to normative IR theory as it is a sentiment which has no regard for boundaries, and thus has implications beyond state borders. Unfortunately, Rorty shows no interest in exploring the repercussions of this ethic for IR or its ethical approaches. It is left to IR theorists to evaluate.

It is important that the implications of Rorty's ethic for normative IR theory be developed in order to enquire further into the questions suggested at the end of the last chapter regarding the possibilities within antifoundationalism for moving beyond the present impasse. Those questions were: does such an approach retain the residue of oppositional positions in the normative IR debate; must we have at least *weak* foundations in order to offer inter-societal critique; and what is the nature of the universal implied in the ethics offered? Rorty can help us think through these questions and the stalemate of the cosmopolitan/communitarian debate. Once again it is evident, since it is true of Rorty too, that an antifoundationalist position does not inhibit the will or capacity to offer an ethic. This chapter proceeds in the first section by introducing Rorty's project. The second section of the chapter offers an analysis of Rorty's relation to the debate and its three central issues. The third section examines Rorty's discussion of human rights and evaluates the resulting ethic on its own merits and for its significance to normative IR theory.

Rorty, beastly foundationalists and the hope of liberal irony

A central theme throughout Rorty's work is his attack upon philosophy's wayward attempt to find generalizable theories and foundations. The most sustained attack can be found in *Philosophy and the*

Mirror of Nature (Rorty 1980). According to Rorty, philosophy aims to know a 'real' world, to tap into essences, particularly of the self, in order to divine truth. This search for neutral, ahistorical grounds for the justification of values and practices is the delusion of philosophy; truth is nothing more than belief justified through conversation and social practice (Rorty 1980: 170). For Rorty, it is language, as it is practised within cultures, that forms our understanding of ourselves and the world. Thus, truth is particular to time and place, absorbed from norms within the vocabulary of a society. What counts as knowledge changes as societal norms change. Rorty suggests that we should give up the definitional search for truth, rationality or knowledge. He maintains two reasons for doing so. First, philosophy's preoccupation with epistemology and universal truth is a form of repression that limits human possibilities. He writes that such philosophical inquiry could lead to the 'freezing over of culture', and thus, the 'dehumanization of human beings', by hampering human creative potential (Rorty 1980: 377). Secondly, in a more pragmatic vein, Rorty writes that philosophy is a diversion. He uses such words as 'distraction', 'inefficient' and 'unprofitable' to characterize philosophy in order to make the point that we should give up wanting something we cannot have, that for which philosophy has aimed for centuries: 'transcultural validity'(Rorty 1990b: 640).

As an alternative, Rorty offers his idea of an anti-philosophy which is articulated in terms of historical vocabularies, the languages that shape our comprehension of the world in which we live, rather than in terms of methods of justification. Rorty's anti-philosophy urges us to examine our vocabularies and the metaphors we use to represent our understanding, by asking questions that differ from the truth-seeking questions of conventional philosophy. We must aim to articulate new questions, new descriptions; that is, new metaphors. These would not seek to formulate general principles in their representations, but would try to work pragmatically to redescribe as many things as possible in different ways, until new vocabularies are created which will, in time, yield new forms of social practice. Intellectual and moral progress becomes 'a history of increasingly useful metaphors rather than of increasing understanding of how things really are' (Rorty 1989a: 9).[2]

---

[2] Rorty affirms the contention of Friedrich Nietzsche and Donald Davidson that this is a 'blind', evolutionary process.

According to Rorty, inquiry or critique begins from our 'we' group, our community. Since the linguistic practices of communities shape the beliefs of individuals, it is the community that defines the goods worthy of pursuit. Moral authority exists only within community, and there is no external means of justification. Inquiry is simply guided by coherence among the beliefs and value commitments of individuals. We must acknowledge that we can only begin from where we are. Thus, he writes, 'we must, in practice, privilege our own group, even though there can be no noncircular justification for doing so'(Rorty 1985b: 12). The 'we' with whom Rorty identifies are 'the liberal Rawlsian searchers for consensus'(1985b: 12).[3] This 'we' group begins with beliefs basic to liberal democratic society, loyalty to which, for Rorty, is 'morality enough'; it does not need ahistorical justification (1983a: 585). None the less, Rorty does see the need to say a few words in its defence within the here and now. This defence rests largely upon the ability of liberalism to cater to plurality.

Beliefs in freedom, toleration, and procedural justice constituted within liberal institutions are well suited to dealing with cultural diversity. As Rorty writes, there are 'practical advantages of liberal institutions in allowing individuals and cultures to get along together without intruding on each other's privacy, without meddling with each other's conceptions of the good'(1986b: 533). Yet, for Rorty, there is a hitch in liberalism, which requires a brief narrative encounter with Enlightenment tradition. As Rorty tells it, the Enlightenment tradition in which liberalism matured is two-sided, with both critical and foundational or rationalist elements (1989a: 56–7). The critical overtook the foundational, breaking down Enlightenment rationalism, yet, according to Rorty, rationalist elements remain. Rorty shares with the poststructuralists discussed in the last chapter the idea that we must rid ourselves of what remains of Enlightenment rationalism, but he does not share the belief of Michel Foucault and others that liberal democratic institutions, must go along with it. Rorty criticizes Foucault for not recognizing that contemporary liberal institutions produce better selves 'than the selves earlier societies created'(1989a: 63).[4] Actually, liberal society has in place what it needs for its own

---

[3] Rorty (1987) gives an account of eight theses shared by his 'we' group of social democrats.

[4] In an interview by Danny Postel, Rorty says that Foucault suggests nothing better, and Rorty is, in fact, 'inclined to think that his opposition to liberalism and reformism was merely a contingent French fashion' (Rorty 1989b: 201).

improvement (Rorty 1989a: 63).[5] The only impediments are the vestiges of Enlightenment rationalism. Its foundations limit the play of old and new vocabularies. The progress of liberal society is best served by irony; that is, metaphor and self-creation (Rorty 1989a: 44).

The most developed account of Rorty's notion of the ideal liberal society and the role of irony in constituting liberal utopia is to be found in *CIS*. An ideal liberal society has freedom as its purpose, takes truth to be whatever is the outcome of 'free and open encounters of present linguistic and other practices', and has as its hero the 'strong poet'(Rorty 1989a: 60–1). The strong poet is integral to the development of liberal utopia, as she is driven to set herself apart, that is, to speak metaphorically. Here, Rorty uses Donald Davidson's distinction between metaphorical and literal language. The literal is language which is familiar, comprehensible within the terms of old theories. Metaphorical language is unfamiliar, outside of the 'language game'. Thus, metaphorical language has no meaning nor any quality as true or false (Rorty 1989a: 17–18). Having no meaning, metaphor makes new vocabularies possible, serving two functions. It helps us relinquish the idea of 'language as a medium' relating subject and object. Secondly, it facilitates a larger project, undermining Enlightenment rationalism, by ridding ourselves of 'the traditional philosophical picture of what it is to be human' (Rorty 1989a: 19). Thus, metaphorical language is central to the vocabulary of the ideal liberal culture, and those who employ it to good effect are worthy of our admiration.

The model citizens of Rorty's liberal utopia are liberal ironists. Borrowing Judith Shklar's definition, Rorty says a liberal is someone who thinks 'cruelty is the worst thing we do'. An ironist is someone who 'faces up to the contingency of his or her own most central beliefs and desires' (Rorty 1989a: xv). The liberal ironist takes as one of these central, contingent desires the hope to lessen human suffering at the hands of other humans (Rorty 1989a: xv). This means extending our notion of 'we', as it is less likely that one will humiliate or give pain to those with whom one associates. Yet, the liberal ironist also holds as another groundless desire the will to self-creation or invention (Rorty 1989a: 64n). The two projects are 'ends in themselves' for the liberal

---

[5] Critics argue that Rorty has an unwarranted complacency towards liberalism: for examples, see Bernstein (1991: 230–92); Connolly (1983); Comay (1986); Fraser (1990). I remain unconvinced on this point. For an article that challenges those who charge him with liberal conservatism, see Moussa (1991).

ironist, who shares with Rorty a willingness to 'treat the demands of self-creation and of human solidarity as equally valid, yet forever incommensurable' (1989a: xv).

The liberal ironist is full of doubts, particularly about her 'final vocabulary': the circular way in which one's belief is justified. Aware of the contingency of language, culture, and self, she wonders whether she happened to find herself in the 'right' language or culture (Rorty 1989a: 75). Of course, there is no measure of rightness for the liberal ironist. Yet, this question leads the ironist to examine other vocabularies and their redescriptions, exploring and comparing alternative redescriptions with her own. As there is no criterion for judging vocabularies, all there can be is redescription followed by re-redescription in the hope of making 'the best selves for ourselves that we can'(Rorty 1989a: 80). It is literary criticism, not philosophy, that facilitates this continual redescription. However, not all citizens of the ideal liberal society will pursue this activity. Intellectuals will be the ironists, yet non-intellectuals will be fully aware of contingency and will be free of the 'why' questions of metaphysics (Rorty 1989a: 87). Although we all have the capacity to create metaphors, only ironists, particularly the heroic strong poets, make metaphor their obsession. Thus, the ideal liberal society works to 'make life easier' for these poets so they can 'make life harder for others only by words'(Rorty 1989a: 60–6). In challenging our vocabularies, ironists help us move towards the goals of liberal utopia by liberating us from the 'natural order of topics' imposed by Enlightenment rationalism, and by freeing us to make lives that are our own. Because we all benefit from their projects, ironists must be supported and encouraged.

Rorty anticipates the following challenge: might his antifoundationalism, and the ironists championing it, destroy the liberal institutions he values, which are generally founded upon notions of the self, the morality/prudence distinction, and progress? In response, Rorty argues that liberal institutions do not need metaphysical rhetoric to be stable. He points to the decline of religious faith, writing that it has not weakened liberal institutions, but has in fact strengthened them (Rorty 1989a: 85). Society is not bound by philosophy, but by common aspirations (Rorty 1989a: 86). Freedom is that shared hope, the social glue of liberal utopia. If we face our fear of contingency and quit the futile attempt of dodging it, the thought that community is ours and not nature's can contribute to a new sense of solidarity. Rorty posits solidarity as the link between the realms of irony and politics that are important to his project. Solidarity is that 'sense of other people and ourselves being "we" – we feel that what affects them affects us because we, to some extent, identify with them' (Rorty 1989b: 202).

None the less, a public/private split is centrally placed by Rorty to bear the strains which accompany the benefits of irony to liberal society. The historicist language of non-intellectuals in liberal culture is not politically dangerous, but Rorty concedes that irony within the public sphere, the political domain, can be. Rorty writes that he cannot conceive of a culture socializing its youth to question their socialization: '[i]rony seems an inherently private matter'(1989a: 87). Rorty sees that, by separating private irony from public political concerns, a liberal polity can accommodate self-creation as well as human solidarity, both of which are practical tools. Yet, what is intended to be a methodological support for his project turns out to be its weakest link. Of the numerous criticisms levelled at Rorty, I find criticisms of his public/private split to be the most damaging.[6] I will return to this in the concluding section, where I will argue that with the public/private distinction, Rorty's project is neither coherent nor desirable. Without this distinction, however, his project is recoverable and holds possibilities for mitigating the impasse of normative IR theory.

The liberal ironist and the cosmopolitan/ communitarian debate

Rorty does not directly address the cosmopolitan/communitarian debate within normative IR theory, but he does offer commentary on its counterpart in political theory. In particular, in his article 'The Priority of Democracy to Philosophy', Rorty seeks to defend John Rawls against his communitarian critics (Rorty 1990a). Drawing upon this article and other writings, I will offer an account of what Rorty contributes to the debate in normative IR theory.

A concept of the self

In line with his antifoundationalism, Rorty argues that there can be no objective notion of what it is to be human. The self is created. The self

---

[6] For a selection of literature critical of the public/private split in Rorty, see Bernstein (1991: 274–7, 286–7); Fraser (1990); Guignon and Hiley (1990); and Weislogel (1990).

and its nature are not out there waiting to be found, existing independently of social practice. The self is no more than a 'centreless web of historically conditioned beliefs and desires'(Rorty 1990a: 291), 'constantly reweaving itself . . . not by reference to general criteria, but in the hit and miss way' of cells reacting to their environment (Rorty 1983a: 586). Historical circumstance shapes the self, and any number of arbitrary things can form identity. A self is a 'contingent web to those with similar tastes and similar identities'(Rorty 1990a: 292). Thus, Rorty's position is similar to that of the communitarians, who understand the concept of the self to be shaped within the historicity of the social matrix.[7]

Although Rorty shares with communitarians the belief that selves are shaped rather than discovered, he sets himself apart from the communitarians by attributing to them a presupposition that societies are founded upon a concept of the self, and that liberal theory holds an incorrect concept of the self (1990a: 282). This raises the question of whether liberal society requires justification, which, for Rorty, is a rather modernist, philosophical request. He writes that no idea of the self can serve as a foundation for liberalism, and there is little point in demanding such a theory. He suggests that should one need such a theory, his picture of the self as a 'centreless web' suffices, but the point is that talk of a self need 'rarely occur'(Rorty 1990a: 291). While Rorty may write that talk of the self is unnecessary to social science, it does make numerous appearances in his work, and not simply in reference to its obsolescence.

Always the pragmatist, Rorty suggests two benefits of understanding the self to be a 'centreless web'. As there is no intrinsic self, one benefit is that there can be no 'natural order of justification of beliefs'. Secondly, questions about whom we need to justify ourselves to are left to public, political deliberation (Rorty 1990a: 293). In connection with the benefits of such an understanding, Rorty also raises a practical point. He asks whether an historical understanding of the self makes a better fit with liberal democracy than does the Enlightenment rationalist conception. Again, it is written in the tone of an

---

[7] Communitarians are frequently criticised for failing to offer any account of the substance of the self's social construction, its critical features, or how it takes place. It is interesting to note that one can infer that Rorty would answer that there is no way to account for the social construction of the individual. Borrowing from Sigmund Freud, he writes that 'any seemingly random constellation of such things [sound of a word, color of a leaf, feel of skin] can set the tone of a life'(Rorty 1989a: 37).

option: 'if we *want*' to answer such a question, then the communitarians are correct to believe that their concept of the person works well with liberal democracy (Rorty 1990a: 283).

In voluntarily offering a concept of the self, in a 'take if you need it' fashion, Rorty maintains his anti-philosophy by refusing to impose a metaphysical ground for a concept of the person. None the less, there is a notion of the self on which Rorty's ideal liberal society is built: the liberal ironist. He attributes to the liberal ironist a will to freedom through self-creation, and the need for the solidarity of a 'we', which implants self-doubt. Thus, in his discussion of a liberal utopia, Rorty is led to draw attention to certain attributes of human nature that he deems integral to this project. Two points with significance for the cosmopolitan/communitarian debate and its epistemological impasse should be noted here. First, it is interesting that Rorty's antifoundationalism does not prevent him from suggesting a concept of the person, or from constructing a notion of an improved liberal society upon that understanding. The liberal ironist serves as a ground for his project, despite his protestations against foundationalism. Secondly, Rorty's concept of the person is one which bridges cosmopolitan and communitarian understandings. As noted above, his idea of the person as a 'centreless web' has affinities with the communitarian understanding of the social construction of the person. Yet, what is also evident, particularly in his discussion of the liberal ironist in *CIS*, is that he attributes to individuals the capacity and the will for their own self-making. He writes that, most importantly, the ironist wants to be free of 'the metaphysical urge' so that he can say that 'the last of his final vocabularies . . . really was wholly *his*'(Rorty 1989a: 97). Thus, for Rorty, persons are socially as well as personally chosen, indicating there is interplay between the two positions on this issue of the debate.

The moral standing of states

As noted above, Rorty offers no commentary on states or sovereignty, nor on the morality of states. None the less, he does acknowledge and discuss the dilemma which I take to be the crux of the debate on the issue: 'whether our self-description ought to be constructed around a relation to human nature or around a relation to a particular collection of human beings'(Rorty 1985b: 6–7). The way we describe ourselves is integral to the question of the moral status of states, since those self-descriptions suggest social forms appropriate to such an understanding. For the cosmopolitan, the autonomy of states and/or communities has no normative relevance, because our particular social attachments are not primary to the meaning we accord to our lives. However, the species as a whole is primary, and cosmopolitans claim that communities/states are an obstacle to this moral identification. By contrast, Rorty shares with the communitarians the idea that morality exists only in relation to a community. As discussed earlier, the only form of truth is that which results from social practice. It is the result of conversation which is free and open. Thus, the community is morally significant since it is the locus of moral authority, the site where truth is made. Rorty writes that irrationality in ethics 'is a matter of behaviour that leads one to abandon or be stripped of membership in some such community'(1983a: 586). He clearly prefers a narrative of one's relation to a community, not to humanity, as the way in which we describe ourselves and make sense of our lives (Rorty 1985b).

As it is the aim of the liberal ironist to diminish cruelty, Rorty shares a concern with cosmopolitans for human dignity. Cosmopolitans, such as the Kantians discussed by Rorty in 'Postmodernist Bourgeois Liberalism', have a belief in 'intrinsic human dignity, intrinsic human rights'. However, Rorty allies himself with the Hegelians, writing that human dignity is the product of communities, and that human rights can only be born of societal tradition (1983a: 583, 588). Rorty is careful to distinguish human solidarity from humanity. Solidarity is strongest as an expression of '"one of us", where "us" means something smaller and more local than the human race'(Rorty 1989a: 191). One's sensitivity to the pain of others is the substance of solidarity for Rorty, but this solidarity cannot extend to the whole of humanity. As Rorty cannot envision the world as a moral community on the basis of our common humanity, he denies the core assumption of cosmopolitanism. Yet, while denying a non-parochial, human solidarity, Rorty does share the cosmopolitan impulse to extend human solidarity as wide as possible. He writes that we are 'profoundly grateful to philosophers like Plato and Kant . . . because they prophesied cosmopolitan utopias'(Rorty 1993b: 119). Although they may have been wrong, they gave us something worthwhile for which to aim. Rorty sees solidarity as 'not discovered by reflection, but created'(1989a: xvi). Thus, with the help of liberal ironists, we can work, through literature, metaphor, and imagination, to increase our sensitivity to cruelty, thereby expanding our notion of 'we'.

Thus, Rorty has given thought to the central problem behind the moral standing of states issue: whether or not the community is morally significant to the identity of individuals. However, he offers no indications of the institutional repercussions of an expanding 'we'; that is, whether the state will remain or new institutional forms will arise. None the less, we can draw some tentative conclusions regarding Rorty's position on this issue of states. If the liberal democratic institutions we have are all that we need, as Rorty maintains, then we can infer that the state form in which those liberal democratic institutions are housed holds no moral concerns worthy of mention for Rorty.[8] He would concur with communitarians on two points: first, that moral relations can only be constructed within communities; and second, that the state has moral standing as long as it is the conclusion of free and open encounters within liberal culture concerning its status. If not, then the state's moral status is highly questionable. For Rorty, the cosmopolitan contention that humanity is the locus of moral relations is compromised by the fact that 'we' expansion has its limits, since identity as 'we' requires opposition. Yet, Rorty cannot necessarily be seen as lending weight to the communitarian position. His call for 'we' expansion has no regard for state boundaries. It is a 'we' that is built around any kind of a practice, metaphor, or reading that can construct the necessary sympathy, which is not limited to the 'we' formed around a state. Thus, this leaves him open to the idea of moral community beyond the institutional form of the state, although this community will never include the whole of humanity. In sum, Rorty is interested in the question of the scope of moral relations, but not necessarily the institutional form which that scope takes.[9] None the less, it can be argued that Rorty falls somewhere in between the two positions. He does not deny the moral standing a state could have, but he does deny the possibility of humanity as a community,

[8] Rorty briefly mentions work undertaken towards building a 'multicultural global utopia' (1992a: 593). I do not think that this undermines the inference regarding states that I have made here, since utopias by their nature are unattainable and, like solidarity among humanity, a 'multicultural global utopia' is a good goal, but, according to Rorty, is unrealizable. What *does* possibly undermine this inference is Rorty's 'luck of history' thesis that no vocabularies, cultures or institutions presently valued are guaranteed to be permanent. Thus, Rorty would not say that states are a permanent feature of world politics, nor that their moral status is invulnerable.

[9] This is one indication of the lack of political engagement on the part of Rorty to be discussed later in the chapter.

and thus its moral standing. However, he does not rule out the possibility of moral standing belonging to a community beyond the state. Rorty cannot easily be assigned to either of the poles on this issue, which raises the question of whether the two positions, as they are presented in the framework of the cosmopolitan/communitarian debate, confine the way we can think about the ethical possibilities of forms of community between the state and humanity.

Universal versus the particular

As one might suspect, Rorty does not opt to argue definitely and conclusively for either a universalist or particularist justification of knowledge claims, nor does he attempt to reconcile universal and particular epistemological justifications. Instead, he rejects all forms of epistemologically centred philosophy, forms which are replicated in the cosmopolitan/communitarian debate.

The critique of epistemologically centred philosophy and the call for its reconstruction are central themes in American pragmatism. Rorty devotes much attention to surveying past epistemological strategies with the intention to show that they lack any 'good purpose'. Centuries of speculation on universals, objectivity, truth, and the numerous dualisms which spin off from the mind-body problem have led us nowhere. Philosophy is in a rut of its own making. Rorty writes that the question raised for the pragmatist is not one of the 'necessary and sufficient conditions for a sentence being true, but precisely *whether* the practice which hopes to find a philo-sophical way of isolating the essence of truth has, in fact, paid off'(1982: xxix). For Rorty, the answer is no. Truth-seeking philosophy has not paid off, and what is required, according to Rorty, is a 'new intellectual tradition' which relinquishes epistemological claims and abandons the intellectual obstacles which philosophy has created for itself.

Is the cosmopolitan/communitarian debate a good candidate for a pragmatist interrogation? Does its impasse represent a real problem? Rorty does not directly address this question for the debate in IR theory, but he does interrogate its counterpart in political theory. In justifying claims regarding the self with reference to human nature (a universalist position), or to one's relation to a community (a particu-larist starting point), Rorty writes that one cannot 'choose between these alternatives by looking more deeply into the nature of knowledge, or of man, or of nature'(1985b: 7). This is the mistake of both Kantians and communitarians.

Kantians insist upon an 'ahistorical distinction between the demands of morality and those of prudence'(Rorty 1983a: 583). As there is no intrinsic self for Rorty, there is no noumenal, rational self laboured with the imperative to fight against his or her inclination and desire. Also, for Rorty, as goods can only be defined within particular, historical communities, there can be no ahistorical truth or moral law that is distinguishable from goods which are seen to be only instrumental in fulfilling one's desire. Thus, there can be no distinction between morality and prudence. Kantians search illusively for objectivity upon which to found their claims. Rorty labels 'objectivists' those who seek knowledge, wanting to distinguish true and false in correspondence with reality (1985b: 5). With the Hegelians and communitarians, Rorty agrees that there is 'no appeal beyond the relative merits of various actual or proposed communities to impartial criteria'(1983a: 583).

The Kantians are not the only ones accused by Rorty of demanding correspondence. As discussed above, Rorty writes that the communitarians posit a requirement of correspondence by saying that liberal institutions rest upon a false notion of the self. I do not take this to be a fair representation of the communitarian position. That which Rorty understands to be correspondence is not a correspondence with an external, fixed truth, but simply a requirement that notions of the self or anything else be coherent with community practice.[10] Rorty himself has a concern similar to that of the communitarians when he volunteers his agreement with the communitarian account of the self, that Enlightenment rationalism and rights talk is dead, and that the socially and historically constituted self is appropriate to liberal democratic societies (1990b: 640). None the less, it is correct to say that communitarians are also involved in epistemologically centred philosophy, as they are equally concerned to play the game of knowledge justification, albeit within the shifting, historical grounds of community.

Indeed, debates between liberals and communitarians, and cosmo-

---

[10] Rorty also attributes communitarians with the prediction that society cannot survive the end of ahistorical moral truth (1990a: 281). On the contrary, one liberal communitarian writer, Michael Walzer, often charged with relativism (as is Rorty), employs a particularist method to defend liberal institutions in his book *Spheres of Justice* (1983).

politans and communitarians, are subsumed in the kind of philosophy
Rorty attacks, at least in terms of seeking forms of *weak* foundations
for knowledge claims. It is also evident that neither the debate in
political theory nor in IR theory has had any success in confirming
one or the other position. The debates are without resolution, leaving
theorists either to seek reconciliations between the positions or to
make technical points about how the debate is misconceived. Rorty's
antifoundationalism offers a radical suggestion as to how the debate is
misconceived. Should we be compelled by the pragmatist argument
that, if epistemologically centred philosophy cannot definitively settle
disputes about claims to knowledge, then we should consider letting
such questions go? To proceed without epistemological starting points
is a frightening prospect. Relativism ensues. Without such grounds,
how are ethical theorists to begin social critique?

Rorty writes that he can offer no more convincing an argument
than to say that the intellectual tradition of philosophy 'is more
trouble than it is worth', and that what we have is simply a choice
between vocabularies: 'one about whether philosophy should try to
find natural starting points which are distinct from cultural traditions,
or whether all philosophy should do is compare and contrast cultural
traditions' (1982: xxxvii). Whether we should, with the pragmatist,
prefer the second vocabulary is a question of whether a post-
philosophical culture is imaginable and desirable. This means a willingness to see ourselves as never 'encountering reality', but only
encountering descriptions of reality chosen and made by us (Rorty
1982: xxxix). Rorty recognizes that the effect such a culture has in
repressing the urge of philosophy for final vocabularies is, indeed,
'morally humiliating', and, thus, is a good reason for denying the
possibility of such a culture (1982: xlii). It is humiliating because it
means that we have to acknowledge the circularity of our claims, and
see that the principles we profess are based on criteria we have made
ourselves. Rorty grants that this is a difficult image of ourselves to
take on board. Yet, it is less difficult when we understand that post-
philosophical culture does not mean the end of social criticism. It
only replaces the philosophical aim of finding truth with the pragmatist's aim of acquiring the intellectual habits which best assist us in
coping with the social worlds we make. This is the basis of a cultural
criticism which aims not to play the justificatory game of foundational
thinking.

I will reserve critical analysis of the ethics that results from Rorty's work for the third section of the chapter. I want to conclude the present section by examining what Rorty's writings contribute to the discussion of the universal versus the particular, and the framework of the debate and its impasse. Rorty demonstrates that relinquishing epistemologically centred philosophy does not result in relinquishing ethics and social critique. Rorty's recognition of the particularity of his claims – his ethnocentrism – does not mean that claims originating from a single community have no reach beyond that community. Rorty's idea of the expansion of 'we' feeling is possible, because he holds that neither cultures nor vocabularies are irreconcilable, making an absolute, universal rationality unnecessary for the possibility of an overlap of values across cultures (1985b: 9). Thus, claims can have legitimacy beyond particular communities, without recourse to epistemological foundations, through, for example, the shared understanding of a metaphor, which allows scope for enlarged moral inclusion. Therefore, in regard to the third issue of the debate, the universal versus the particular, Rorty illuminates the limitations of the cosmopolitan/communitarian framework. It forces an either/or choice between universal and particular epistemological claims that has yielded few solutions. Similarly, one can draw this conclusion for the other either/or positions of the first and second issues of the debate. There is an interplay or a range that can be invoked in thinking about these questions, as opposed to the stark dichotomous choices that the cosmopolitan/communitarian framework forces. Alternatively, Rorty directs our attention to the manner in which an antifoundationalist position *can* yield ethical claims, allowing for the possibility of claims being both particular and something wider, but how wide or universal we cannot be sure. While I am not prepared to suggest that Rorty's ethic, as it stands, is entirely compelling, his pragmatist approach suggests another way of liberating normative IR theory from the stranglehold of foundationalism and its search for universal, ahistorical, transcultural validity.

Ethics, liberal irony and international relations

Looking at Rorty's work against the backdrop of the cosmopolitan/communitarian debate demonstrates that antifoundationalism and the will to offer an ethics are not mutually exclusive; as Bernstein writes, Rorty is a 'passionate moralist' (1991: 265). In this section, I will give a brief account of Rorty's ethics and his admitted ethnocentrism, developing the implications of his ethical stance for IR theory by working through his recent piece concerning an issue central to IR theory: human rights.[11]

In 'Human Rights, Rationality, and Sentimentality' ('HRS') Rorty begins by explaining how we can turn away from the war in Bosnia. We project upon the Serbs an identity as non-human and animal-like. We separate ourselves from such 'borderline cases' of humanity, making human/animal, adult/children or male/non-male types of distinction (Rorty 1993b: 112–14). Rorty discusses the attempt by traditional philosophy to counter these sentiments by establishing that which is universally human. He then finishes the story by writing of the progress made in the twentieth century in gradually replacing essentialist questions with those of self-creation: 'what can we make of ourselves'(Rorty 1993b: 115)? Rorty claims that we have created in this century a 'human rights culture'.

Rorty borrows the term 'human rights culture' from Eduardo Rabossi who makes the argument that the search for foundations, or an understanding of human rights as existing naturally, is pointless (Rorty 1993b: 116). The post-Holocaust world has changed us, and shaped us into a human rights culture; we should simply welcome it. Rorty agrees with this characterization. Anticipating charges of cultural relativism, Rorty writes that the claim that human rights are morally superior does not have to be backed by universal human attributes (1993b: 116). Human rights need only cohere with our beliefs. For that reason, as long as a *sui generis* understanding of moral obligation based upon human nature is a part of our culture, the argument against human rights foundationalism will be difficult (Rorty 1993b: 122). Ever the pragmatist, Rorty offers that it is a 'question of efficiency'. The best argument for moving beyond human rights foundationalism is that we need to get on with the task of 'manipulating sentiments'(Rorty 1993b: 122). The human rights culture which we have owes 'nothing to increased moral knowledge,

---

[11] Rorty does invoke Cold War concerns as part of the eight theses shared by his 'we' group. He writes that, 'Soviet imperialism is indeed a threat', and there probably will be 'a steady extension of Moscow's empire throughout the Southern Hemisphere'(1990b: 566). In terms of evaluating what Rorty has to offer IR theory, I do not think that these comments hold much interest. They are indicative of an outmoded liberal rhetoric that can be given the benefit of post-Cold War doubt. It may be that Rorty's personal history strongly influences the strident tone he uses in these passages, as his parents were committed Troskyites who housed one of Trotsky's secretaries after Trotsky was assassinated in 1940 (Rorty 1992b).

and everything to hearing sad and sentimental stories'(Rorty 1993b: 118–9).

Rorty suggests the following necessary conditions towards expanding our human rights culture and making it more powerful. First, we must get on with the business of 'sentimental education', acquainting different people with each other 'so that they are less tempted to think of those different from themselves as only quasi-human'(Rorty 1993b: 122–3). Although Rorty does not develop the nature of the means to this education within 'HRS', it flows naturally from Rorty's project outlined in *CIS*; that is, that metaphor, literary criticism, and, as he briefly suggests in 'HRS', powerful media images, facilitate sentimental education. The goal of this education is the same as that in *CIS*, namely, to expand our 'we' reference, the 'people like us'(Rorty 1993b: 123). Secondly, part of sentimental education involves ridding ourselves of the condescension of traditional philosophy. We must stop labelling those without moral truth as bad people, and replace this practice with an understanding that the violators of human rights are deprived of two things: security in their conditions of life and sympathy bred by sentimental education (Rorty 1993b: 128). Finally, we must simply learn to trust that sentimentality is a strong enough glue to bond our human rights culture.

A question for Rorty's readers must be the following: is the ethnocentricity of liberal human rights culture anything more than self-aware domination without the pretty wrapping of moral universals? To answer such a question one would have to examine the nature of encounters between the 'we' of a human rights culture and outsiders. Rorty gives us little indication of their nature in 'HRS', but there are indications in his earlier work. Against the charge of moral irresponsibility for being unable to 'answer Hitler' (that is, prove Hitler wrong), Rorty offers an alternative account of how he might set about converting a Nazi. It would be nothing more than the attempt to show him the contrast of life in free societies, 'how nice things can be'. Even so, one cannot necessarily refute a 'bully'; 'argumentative standoff' is always possible (Rorty 1990b: 636–7). It is terribly unsatisfactory that this is all that a free and open encounter can sometimes yield. Yet, for Rorty, it is better than having universals against Fascists and having them 'turn in our hands and bash all of the genial tolerance out of our own heads' (1991a: 43). Expanding 'we' consciousness is about looking into the detail of lives which are 'marginal' to our own, and examining their fit with us (Rorty 1989b:

202–3). Thus, in answer to the above question, Rorty's account of an expanding 'we' is a matter of consensus rather than power or domination.

Rorty writes that the 'phenomenon' of a human rights culture may just be a 'blip' in human history. He is unwilling to make any suggestions regarding the permanence of liberal democratic culture. We can hope that contingency will work in favour of our valued practices, but Rorty sees no sure way to move from the 'actual world' to our idealized 'theoretically possible ones' (1989a: 182). Nevertheless, there is room for hope. As mentioned above, for Rorty, cultures are not irreconcilable. There is enough overlap that conversation can take place. As long as that conversation is possible, Rorty's 'ideal world order' is possible, as an 'intricately textured collage of private narcissism and public pragmatism'(1986: 533–4).

Is this 'ideal world order' coherent or desirable? As it stands, with the public/private distinction in place, I want to argue it is neither coherent nor desirable. Rorty replaces the morality/prudence distinction, which he criticizes Kantians for using to 'buttress' liberal institutions, with an equally artificial private/public split. He has replaced one dichotomy with another, and uses it as a methodological prop to bolster his ideal liberal democratic society, now that the floodgates of antifoundationalism are down.[12] That irony and solidarity can not only coexist, but, indeed, together can improve liberal society, rests, for Rorty, upon his defence of a public/private split. Rorty writes that we should give up trying to reconcile the private and public in theory and recognize they can both exist, remaining separate in practice (1989a: xv). He anticipates the objection that irony and liberalism are unsuited to a degree that the private/public split cannot overcome, and responds that the demand for coherence is an essentialist, rationalist requirement (Rorty 1989a: 85–9). The 'why' should irony 'be this and be able to do that' kind of questions in regard to liberal institutions are the ones for which we should stop expecting answers.

---

[12] It should be noted here (however, it is discussed further in chapter 6) that, while Rorty adopts pragmatism as his general framework for philosophical thinking, he does not endorse Dewey's claim to offer a method for a reconstructed, non-epistemological philosophy. Thus, he would not agree that his use of the public/ private split serves as a methodological tool (Rorty 1991b: 63–77). None the less, I would argue that Rorty *does* offer such a method, however qualified, in his suggestions regarding how new metaphors are created, and in his use of the public/private split to support the project of the liberal ironist.

It is asking 'ironist philosophy to do a job which it cannot do, and which it defines itself as unable to do', that is, to offer non-circular justification (Rorty 1989a: 94). Different vocabularies can coexist within communities, as well as within the same person.

Even if we grant that irony and liberalism can coexist in practice, the idea that they can remain separate can only be imagined through the words of Rorty on the page. Rorty writes of the morality/ prudence distinction as an appeal to 'two parts of the network that is the self – parts separated by blurry and constantly shifting boundaries' (1983a: 587). Why should those boundaries not be equally blurry for the private/public split? This split, too, suggests divisions within the self between one's ends (one's private concerns, particularly irony, which can be harmful to the public), and one's means (a detached public self separate from one's ends) operating on practical, seemingly mundane public considerations.[13] It suggests there is a Rawlsian original chooser in a part of all of us, a chooser rejected by Rorty in an earlier article, 'Postmodernist Bourgeois Liberalism' (1983a: 585). This public/private split required of the self is sure to be blurred and shifting in the face of the contingency Rorty posits.

My second objection asks how we are to be compelled by this distinction when Rorty himself appears to blur the line. He writes that progress, whether poetic, philosophical or political, 'results from the accidental coincidence of a private obsession with a public need' (Rorty 1989a: 37).[14] Coincidence suggests haphazardness, but the underlying point is that the private and public do interact, however randomly, for our benefit. Granted, Rorty does write that irony is not relevant to politics and can in fact be cruel and dangerous when operating within the public realm. Yet, he suggests that the benefits of private irony outweigh its harmful effects, benefits which, despite a private/public split, somehow filter down to public liberal institutions. In *CIS*, Rorty posits what I would call a 'trickle down effect': that the growth of poeticized culture can lead to increased solidarity,

---

[13] When asked in an interview why he would reassert the public/private distinction given his praise of Dewey's dismissal of such distinctions, Rorty responded that he does not see it as the kind of distinction Dewey wanted to overcome (Rorty 1989b: 202). I disagree. Dewey, in my view, is attempting to bring the private and public of liberalism closer together, since he sees the reconceptualization of individuality as a socially connected self to be necessary to the organic, participatory democracy he envisions. Dewey writes that his own definitions of the public and private are 'in no sense equivalent to the distinction between individual and social'(1927: 13).

[14] This is echoed in Rorty 1982: 158.

strengthening and enhancing liberal institutions.[15] The good of the ideal liberal society is in the hands of the liberal ironists; take care of them and liberal institutions will take care of themselves. The question is, how can Rorty put forward this position without blurring the separation of private and public? The coherence of this distinction is undermined by Rorty himself.

One may argue that I am placing too much emphasis on something which, after all, is offered as no more than a tool. My contention, however, is that when used as a tool, it has undesirable political repercussions. To be sure, Rorty talks of this split as a tool which is not an accurate representation of reality. Yet, he regards it as crucial to his defence of irony and solidarity (Rorty 1990b: 641). The public/private distinction is drawn in order to provide for the authenticity of social difference,[16] allowing space for genuine self-creation without public interference, as well as space for the public which is free from the interference of the private creator. Thus, the private/public distinction is not something which simply fades into the background. As a tool, it has a prominent role for Rorty. Its use is universalized within liberal culture to provide vital support for his project. While it is a universalism of another guise, methodological rather than epistemological, it has a political effect similar to those aspects of traditional philosophy which he labels as dehumanizing. It puts a natural order not necessarily on *what* we speak, but on *where* and *when* we can speak.

Also, a third objection, offered by feminist theorists, is that the private realm is not a realm of freedom for all. For women, such space represents a limit on *who* is actually able to speak.[17] Thus, a rather

---

[15] Nancy Fraser (1990) criticizes Rorty for holding the view that irony or radical theorizing is antithetical to politics. She argues that Rorty thereby leaves no place for radical theorizing in the political sphere, and, in effect, 'homogenizes' it. I am arguing that while Rorty sets up the public/private split for the reason Fraser states, he does not consistently maintain this position, and in fact, stakes progress on their intermingling. Consequently, radical theorizing is not barred from the public sphere. The improvement of liberal institutions requires as he writes, that private obsession meets with public need.

[16] I want to thank Chris Brown for this point about authenticity. Mario Moussa makes a similar point (1991: 308).

[17] For feminist critiques of Rorty's use of the public/private split, see Fraser (1990); Haber (1994). However, Rorty (1991b) argues that pragmatism *is* well-suited to assisting the agenda of feminism. Fritzman (1993) writes that since 'Feminism and Pragmatism', Rorty 'has obviated' most of the feminist critiques, particularly as he makes clear in this piece for the first time (I argue that it is evident in earlier work) that the public and private do meet. None the less, I maintain that as long as the

shallow form of authenticity results at considerable ethical cost. Using Rorty's own pragmatic approach, in which tools are offered 'experimentally', this tension suggests that the public/private split as a practical tool warrants reconsideration. Rorty also faces the criticism that his public/private split is elitist, closing off the possibility of critical thought except to those ironic intellectuals in their private space (Haber 1994: 52–56). Discarding the public/private split would make social criticism available to a wider audience and would end the pretence that Rorty's ideal liberal society is open to all, even foundationalists and non-intellectuals.[18]

As I see it, Rorty's project can stand without the private/public distinction, and without it, his project just might be desirable. After long and unsatisfactory struggles with the search for a transcultural foundation, there is something quite appealing about giving up the fight, examining the consequences, and seeing that we can still say what we want, with no worse effect. For example, by telling a non-liberal government that there are naturally existing universal human rights, we are no better off or more convincing than saying that, 'from the perspective of my liberal culture, your citizens are suffering at the hands of your government, and that is where I stand'. Indeed, by undermining the universal moral authority of our claims about human rights, we may even serve to enhance our powers of persuasion.

For Rorty, the key to the success of efforts to extend our human rights culture rests in demonstrating the potential power that its principles might hold within other cultures as well. This might mean pointing to tensions, or problematic situations internal to those practices outside of our human rights culture – perhaps tensions created by economic freedoms unaccompanied by political freedoms – and illustrating how extending certain human liberties can alleviate or mitigate that tension. I find Rorty's argument compelling that the degree to which this human rights culture can be found to be persuasive hangs on the humility with which it is presented. It is only as persuasive as its grounds are weak. That is, an important element of this process of persuasion is an assumption that any principle

methodological straw man of the public/private is left in place by Rorty, the feminist critique has force.

[18] The problem that remains in Rorty's work is what appears to be a split-level theory of agency. In some inexplicable manner, intellectuals are not socialised all the way down, as are non-intellectuals, and thus only intellectuals are capable of social criticism.

offered can be mistaken and is always subject to revision. This assumption of 'fallibilism', dear to pragmatists, means that conclusions offered as to how the extension of human liberties might mitigate certain tensions within another cultural practice are suggestions to be tried, to be experimented with, and not assumed to be instantly workable, or a permanent solution of any kind.

There is much in this antifoundationalist ethic of Rorty's that is useful to normative theorists of IR. However, Rorty's light regard for the political and his lack of interest in the material, institutional conditions for realizing ethical or cultural critique is problematic. Thus, like Richard Bernstein, I remain uneasy with the way in which Rorty seems to put discussion of the political on hold; that the question of those to whom we justify ourselves, to whom we should listen, and who has the power to enforce claims is left to reflective equilibrium[19] at the time these issues meet in public conversation (Bernstein 1991: 243). I think Rorty's light regard for the political is reflected in two ways that become issues for normative IR theory. First, it is reflected by the way in which Rorty offers the tool of the public/private split without fully acknowledging its political implications; and second, in the lack of development of the potential institutional implications of his expanding 'we' group.[20]

While there are political difficulties, it is still the case that there is much in Rorty's work for normative IR theory to explore, and from which it can benefit epistemologically. Most importantly, Rorty's antifoundationalism suggests that the impasse of normative IR theory is an impasse of its own making, which need not be in the way of normative theorizing in IR. International ethics can work free of foundational thinking and, should it choose to do so, it would facilitate thinking in terms of *ranges* rather than oppositions in regard to questions about persons, states and the scope of ethical claims. Moreover, while it may be alarming to work without a structure of universals or absolutes in

---

[19] Rorty invokes reflective equilibrium, a notion suggested by John Rawls, which describes a state reached when 'a person has weighed various proposed conceptions and he has either revised his judgements to accord with one of them or held fast to his initial convictions'(Rawls 1971: 48).

[20] On these points, it may be helpful to refer to Dewey. He was deeply engaged in the political and, perhaps, as a consequence: (1) in no way promoted a public/private split, and (2) discussed the implications of his moral concern for growth *via* the reconstruction of philosophy for the nation-state. However, Dewey represents no vast improvement when it comes to considerations of power. Indeed, it may be said that power is generally undertheorized within pragmatism.

international ethics, particularly in situations of power or crisis, there is none the less reason to believe that Rorty's unique take on the promotion of human rights, free of claims to their naturalness, may be the most workable. Granted, it requires time and a particular context that can afford the slow, plodding process of persuasion and argument, but in casting aside the arrogance of foundational thinking it may work to provide the strongest basis available for long-term efforts towards the expansion of moral inclusion.

CONCLUDING REMARKS TO PART II

Having examined this second line of antifoundationalist thinking in IR theory and its implications for the cosmopolitan/communitarian debate, it may be useful to offer points of comparison between the Rortyian and the poststructuralist variants of antifoundationalism discussed here, and draw some conclusions from the argument of part II of the book. To begin with their similarities: it is evident that both lines of antifoundationalism open up the parameters of ethical theory/practice in IR by problematizing the foundationalist thinking which sustains the structure of opposition in the cosmopolitan/communitarian debate. Thus, the potential for exploring interplay within the debate's three issues is enhanced. As to whether relinquishing foundations means relinquishing the will to an ethics, this is clearly not true of these two antifoundationalisms, since both are concerned to articulate the ethical significance of their respective projects. However, what is interesting about both antifoundationalisms is that neither fully relinquishes foundationalist thinking.

Both the poststructuralists and Rorty begin from the historically *contingent* ground or *weak* foundation of local or community practices. Granted, the *contingent* nature of these grounds for theorizing is read into the ethical claims which follow, but foundations (albeit, *weak* and contextualized) are appealed to none the less. While they are engaged in shining a spotlight on foundationalist epistemologies, they leave in the shadows the ontologies at work in their own methodological assumptions. It seems that a turn away from epistemologically centred thinking places the burden of standards for ethical judgement onto ontology. A concept of the person and thoughts about being, despite their protestations about modern subjectivities, fuel the ethical claims that follow from their starting points. An unacknowledged foundationalism remains in the ontologies at work in their projects.

The poststructuralists' Foucauldian understanding of radical autonomy and Rorty's 'liberal ironist' motivate an ethics which aims to realize human autonomy to the highest degree possible or imaginable. Ultimately, both antifoundationalisms have a cosmopolitan thrust, as the subject of justice is taken to be the individual. Does this undermine the possibility of interplay suggested above, since foundational thinking remains in place, and these antifoundationalist positions thus overlap with sides in the cosmopolitan/communitarian debate? Yes, to some extent this is the case, particularly if these writers do not acknowledge the foundational weight their ontologies are carrying. However, more openings are created by their increased awareness of the difficulties associated with foundationalist thinking, even if it is only focused upon epistemologies for the time being. Thus, the dichotomy foundationalism/antifoundationalism cannot be sustained, and we have a range of foundationalisms from which to choose. Relative differences are evident in the way that cosmopolitans, communitarians, postructuralists and Rortyians participate in the justificatory project of foundational thinking, with the result that normative IR theory benefits from trying to distance itself, as best it can within this range, from the *non-contingent* end of the spectrum of ways of defending ethical claims.

It appears that we cannot completely divest ourselves of recourse to some kind of grounds, however temporary, in order to be able to offer criteria for ethical judgement. Those engaged in normative IR theory cannot avoid being *weak* foundationalists of one sort or another. While the categories foundationalist and antifoundationalist turn out to be two extremes which do not quite fit the writers discussed, it is still fair to say that relative degrees do apply in distinguishing these writers. This involves the extent to which theorists engage in the foundationalist justificatory project and what they believe is at stake. The writers discussed in part I of the book are deeply engaged in the justificatory project. What is at stake for them is the possibility of ethical critique and considerations of justice in world politics. Because so much is at stake, there is the tendency to use foundations, which, to varying degrees, they admit are *weak*, in *strong* foundationalist ways. Returning to the anchor analogy, the ground in which the anchor for ethical theorizing in IR is held to rest is the shifting sand of historical, contingent practices. None the less, these writers proceed as if the ethical claims which follow are more or less absolute and *non-contingent*, as if anchored in firm, solid foundations.

On the other hand, the writers discussed in part II see themselves as being outside of the justificatory project, looking in. The stakes deemed so important by those participant in the cosmopolitan/communitarian debate are regarded as illusory, and thus futile, by the antifoundationalists. However, these writers cannot help but engage in the same enterprise, since they too want to offer criteria for ethical judgement, although in a dissimilar way. So they label the project they are participant in as something else, and, relatively speaking, it does warrant another name, although antifoundationalism is not quite it. Their project is distinguishable because they are aware that the ethical claims that follow from the grounds that they invoke are equally *contingent*. That is, the anchor from which ethical judgement can be made is as likely to shift and *will* shift with the sand in which it rests. The result is a second-order ethicality, different from what we normally understand by ethics.

The failure of these antifoundationalist theorists explicitly to acknowledge that we may not be able to rid ourselves completely of foundational thinking is interesting when compared with the acknowledgement that these writers *are* beginning to make regarding universalization. They view the will to universalization, as well as foundations, as generally accompanied by nasty side-effects, such as exclusion, oppression and violence. However, some degree of universalization cannot be avoided in offering an ethics and aiming for further moral inclusion of persons in world politics. Both are similar recognitions that, perhaps, we are not able to rid ourselves of recourse to some form of universalizations or foundations, however *weak* or loosely held. Yet, for some reason the question of foundations is not given the same kind of self-conscious attention by these writers,[21] even though the two issues are linked. Morality is traditionally understood to follow from foundationalist epistemological claims that are universal in scope and hold absolutely. Thus, these two questions need to be simultaneously interrogated for normative IR theory to move beyond its present stasis.

If we cannot avoid foundations or universals of some sort in thinking about international ethics, we need to be conscious of this in our theory/practice constructions, in order to think about how we might

---

[21] William Connolly is perhaps the one exception to this. See my note in chapter 4, where I discuss his recognition of the danger of his own 'sovereign' accounts or foundationalism.

proceed in ways that work to avoid the kind of normative impasses and oppressions which undermine ethical considerations in IR at present. This means divesting foundations and universals from the absolutism with which they are traditionally held. In part III of the book, I will offer a notion of ethics as pragmatic critique which is self-consciously aware of the range of foundationalisms within which ontologies and epistemologies are invoked in normative theorizing. It attempts to reconceptualize the traditional understanding of ethics as holding foundationally and universally, in the effort to move us beyond the present impasse of normative IR theory in a way that provides for moral inclusion and social reconstruction. As this ethic is one built on the pragmatic tradition it appears that I have taken sides regarding these two variants of antifoundationalism and no doubt this is true. First, I have chosen to develop a pragmatist line because this approach is one that has not been pursued in normative IR theory, and is at least deserving of similar attention to that which has been focused upon poststructuralist approaches in IR over the last ten years. Secondly, I believe that such a 'quasi-foundationalist' (if we cannot say antifoundationalist) approach has a better capacity to theorize the attachment persons have to the practices shared within communities.

Why? It may seem unlikely since Rorty, like the poststructuralists, is ultimately concerned with the individual and her autonomy, as his attention to the private sphere and the space for individual creativity demonstrates. Granted, it appears that Rorty's capacity to theorize the value of community is therefore circumscribed, and that a residue of the oppositional nature of the cosmopolitan/communitarian debate remains. However, where I do not see the possibility within poststructural approaches, I do at least see the possibility of illustrating the connections between individuals and community and the dynamics of their ethical relationships in Rorty, since he is prepared to recognize the value individuals find in community practices and the role of the normative structures of community, to the extent that he takes these as the starting point for ethical theorizing. Yet, his ultimate concern with individual autonomy and self-creation, such that a public/private split is required, means that we cannot rely on Rorty's neopragmatism alone. I will suggest in part III that a pragmatic approach that reconnects Rorty with themes in the classical pragmatist tradition – in particular, the work of John Dewey – can theorize the interplay between the value of individual autonomy and social memberships.

Part III   International ethics as pragmatic critique

6 International ethics as pragmatic critique: a pragmatic synthesis of the work of John Dewey and Richard Rorty

> Pragmatism solves no real problems. It only shows that supposed problems are not real problems.
>
> (Peirce 1958b: 25)

This book has been concerned with the present condition of stasis in normative IR theory: the positions taken in the cosmopolitan/communitarian debate on its three central issues – a concept of the self, the moral standing of states and the universal versus the particular – are assumed to be irreconcilable with no means available for reaching conclusions regarding an ethical theory of IR. As discussed in the introduction, one could see such an impasse to be a cause for concern, since without resolution, without some ground for deciding upon criteria, how else can normative judgements in IR be offered? On the other hand, another might suggest, as indeed Chris Brown does, that there is no point in being concerned, since we must accept and find satisfaction in the only thing that can result from such a debate: 'good conversation' (1992: 239). Here, I will suggest there is an alternative way of looking at this impasse, a pragmatist approach, which may hold the promise of pulling normative IR theory out of its epistemological quagmire.

Since pragmatism regards the search for universal foundations for knowledge to be a delusion and thus, a distraction, the pragmatist would take issue with the first response that some resolution to the question of justification within the debate be found. Centuries of such philosophical endeavour has proved unprofitable. Yet, the pragmatist would agree that some form of a conclusion must be reached, because she understands ethical theory to be a guide to human action. Indeed, she does find that conversation is important to the process of inquiry into human action. Thus, while the pragmatist would share with Brown the same scepticism about what conversation between cosmopolitans and communitarians on the question of justifying ethical principles of IR can yield, she would not reflect the same casualness about the condition of stasis on which the debate rests. Such a tension or impasse spurs the pragmatist to ask: is the problem it presents actual? As the above quote from C. S. Peirce suggests, pragmatism aims to reveal that that which presents itself as a problem may only have the appearance of a problem. I aim to demonstrate that normative IR theory would benefit from such a pragmatist interrogation.

The chapter begins with an analysis of the core tenets of a pragmatist approach and its implications for the debate in normative IR theory. This ultimately raises the question of which pragmatism, or more to the point, *whose* pragmatism should be our focus. The body of the chapter will compare and contrast the pragmatism of John Dewey and Richard Rorty with two concerns in mind: (1) to explore what elements in the two writers' approaches to pragmatism can best assist us in understanding the framework of the debate and its impasse, and (2) to critically evaluate the ethics that results from the pragmatism of the two writers and its relevance for normative IR theory. I will argue that neither Deweyan nor Rortyian pragmatism can stand alone to provide a workable alternative for international ethics. However, section two develops an idea for a pragmatist synthesis and the ethics that would result from it. Section three evaluates the promise this approach may hold for normative IR theory. I will suggest that a synthesis of the pragmatist approaches of Dewey and Rorty in the idea of international ethics as pragmatic critique can confront the impasse of the debate, and mitigate its fundamental opposition, by offering ethical critique that begins from particular commitments, strives towards a more thorough-going antifoundationalism, yet has the capacity for moral inclusion and universality, and is politically engaged with a concern for social reconstruction.

Pragmatist thinking and the cosmopolitan/ communitarian debate: Dewey and Rorty

Pragmatism is a tradition of thought generally associated with the writings of Peirce, William James, John Dewey and G. H. Mead. As Richard Bernstein is careful to point out, it is a tradition that consists of 'a *plurality* of conflicting narratives' (Bernstein 1995: 55). None the less, themes can be identified as generally representative of pragmatist thought. Bernstein lists five such themes which I will turn to briefly as an introduction to this tradition: antifoundationalism, fallibilism, critical communities, contingency and plurality (1991: 326–30). While one will not find the term antifoundationalism used within pragmatist writings, Bernstein contends that its central arguments are found in Peirce. According to Bernstein, Peirce challenges the idea that knowledge has foundations from which philosophy can begin, and that philosophy's searching will end in the certainty it seeks. Bernstein sees variations of this argument, as well as efforts to purge philosophy of its foundational tendencies, among all the pragmatist writers. The consequence of this position is fallibilism, which recognizes the situatedness of inquiry, and sees any belief, principle or claim that follows from it as having a provisional status, always open to further correction and critique. To acknowledge our fallibility and the limitations of our particular perspectives means that we must recognize the social character of the self and our reliance upon a community of inquirers – critical communities – in pursuing philosophical questions that we cannot hope to answer on our own. In their own ways, pragmatist writers try to demonstrate how individual consciousness (and the inquiry, beliefs, etc., which issue from it) is integrally linked with social practice. Pragmatists are also aware of the pervasiveness of contingency. Despite the best efforts of traditional philosophy to suppress it, pragmatists regard contingency to be inescapable, shaping our understanding of both experience and philosophy. For this reason, pragmatism turns its attention to how we respond to this constant of our existence through the development of habits. Finally, plurality is a theme which is interwoven with the other themes. Bernstein writes that the pluralist ethos of pragmatism recognizes that with fallibilism comes a responsibility to engage and not silence the plural perspectives and traditions that will always exist (1991: 336).

Although we continue to hear echoes of these themes in both Anglo-American and Continental philosophy today, pragmatism has been dormant for some time. By the end of World War II, the heyday of pragmatism had been eclipsed by analytic philosophy and the appeal of the rigorous and formal methods offered by logical positivism and logical empiricism. Language philosophy, also within analytic philosophy, developed as a less formal analysis of concepts. As Bernstein writes, both formal and informal analysis in analytic philosophy were characterized by a new faith in philosophy's ability to answer its age-old epistemological quandaries (1986: 4). Today this faith is again under attack. Richard Rorty has breathed life into pragmatism by taking up one of its central themes with a new tenacity: the critique of foundationalist philosophy and its aim to know a 'real' world. He has also named one of its central figures, John Dewey as his intellectual hero.[1] According to Rorty, the ghost of Dewey can be found throughout his writings.[2] This raises a question which this chapter will consider: if we pursue a pragmatist interrogation of the epistemological impasse of the cosmopolitan/communitarian debate, and examine its consequences for an ethical theory of IR, can we take both Rorty's and Dewey's treatments of these questions to be the same? To whom do we turn? There are other reasons for singling out Dewey among the pragmatists for attention besides the fact that Rorty thinks we should. Since this book is evaluating an ethical debate, Dewey is important, because as H. S. Thayer writes, Dewey is the first to state and defend a pragmatic theory of ethics (Thayer 1981: 383). Also, as I am concerned with an ethical debate in IR to do with the moral relevance of states, Dewey is significant because he alone is interested in considering the moral and empirical status of the nation-state. This comes out in his discussion of the Great Community, which will be discussed in chapter 8. However, for now, we must come back to the question: to whom do we turn?

Rorty finds no significant differences between himself and Dewey. He writes that his position only slightly diverges in the way he offers 'a somewhat different account of the relations of natural science to the rest of culture, and in stating the problematic of representationalism and anti-representationalism in terms of words and sentences rather than in terms of ideas and experiences' (Rorty 1991b: 16–17). Rorty sees himself as doing no more than adapting Dewey's thought for a new team accustomed to a different intellectual playing field – the philosophy of language. In this respect, his work is often referred to as neo-pragmatism, suggesting that he has taken on board much of the tradition, yet with some re-working for the purposes of incorporating

---

[1] Rorty's most sustained attack on foundationalist philosophy is found in *Philosophy and the Mirror of Nature* (1980). In this book he names Dewey, Martin Heidegger and Ludwig Wittgenstein as his intellectual heroes, but later Rorty (1991b: 16) amends this, writing that, in the decade since, Dewey 'gradually eclipsed Wittgenstein and Heidegger'.

[2] Rorty writes that, 'whenever I thought I had found something general and useful to say, it sounded like an echo of something I had once read. When I tried to run it down, I was constantly led back to Dewey' (Rorty 1985a: 39).

recent developments in philosophical thinking.[3] Yet, he is accused by Dewey scholars of serious misreadings of Dewey's work and its intent (Edel 1985; Sleeper 1985).[4] I do not propose here to take as my task a critical evaluation of the substance of this charge. None the less, there is a need to acknowledge differences in their positions on two issues – the role left for philosophy and the question of method – since both are important in assessing what we might understand by a pragmatist approach and what its interrogation of the cosmopolitan/communitarian debate could offer. I aim to demonstrate that while both writers arrive at similar and interrelated ethical positions regarding growth and a notion of an expanding 'we', their differences on the role of philosophy and method have implications for the relationship of each writer to the political and how an ethics of IR might be pursued.

Dewey: a role for philosophy and pragmatist method

Dewey's work contains a strong attack on the will to fixity or absolutes; that is, ahistorical, universal knowledge as the end-goal of philosophy. He does so by tracing through the history of philosophy to examine what, if any, benefit has yielded from its epistemological orientation. In *Reconstruction in Philosophy*, Dewey tells a story of the origins of philosophy resting not in 'intellectual material', but in 'social and emotional material'. Philosophy emerges not from judgements about a suggestion's congruence with fact, but from its 'emotional congeniality': how it plays with the 'dramatic tale' of one's life. From this kind of representation – the signs and symbols of hopes and fears, of poetry and drama, not science – philosophy proceeds to pass through two more stages: first, the consolidation of stories and legends to constitute a social tradition; and second, the process of confirming that tradition with authority through appeals to reason and logic. Because that tradition was once accepted on the basis of feeling and sentiment, it relies all the more upon making much of reason and proof. Dewey writes that to see the origins of philosophy in this light radically changes the way we understand traditional

---

[3] For an account that notes differences between Rorty and the pragmatists, but finds that Rorty broadly captures the spirit of pragmatism, see Brodsky (1982).

[4] In a response to Sleeper and Edel, Rorty (1985a: 39) admits, with more modesty than seems warranted, to being 'relatively unlearned' in the works of Dewey and pragmatism generally, yet he feels compelled to make references to pragmatism to 'acknowledge my own lack of originality'.

philosophy. Its quest for certainty *via* epistemological appeals is not actually about getting reality right. It is about offering up an intellectual attachment to a social purpose or tradition. The clash of opinions about the real is really a dispute about social purposes. Thus, epistemological inquiry into the mind/body problem or the relation of subject and object can tell us nothing. Epistemology is, as Dewey writes, a 'species of confirmed intellectual lockjaw' (1931: 51n).

Dewey sees that epistemology, and the formalism it encourages, are evidence of philosophy's withdrawal from engagement with the social problems of his day, especially the pace of change, the wider scope of change, and the deeper penetration of its effects. The desire of past philosophical systems to 'find something so fixed and certain as to provide a secure refuge', is their 'defect' (Dewey 1948: vi-vii). The question then arises: what is left for philosophy if not securing truth or knowledge? Dewey is aware that the controversies over epistemology and realism and idealism are so deeply embedded that to cast them off leaves philosophical thinking at a loss. None the less, he employs what he calls the pragmatic rule: 'in order to discover the meaning of an idea ask for its consequences' (Dewey 1948: 163), and argues that there are indeed beneficial consequences to dropping these questions. He writes that to be free of epistemological controversies would

> encourage philosophy to face the great social and moral defects and troubles from which humanity suffers, to concentrate its attention upon clearing up the causes and exact nature of these evils and upon developing a clear idea of better social possibilities; in short upon projecting an idea or an ideal which, instead of expressing the notion of some other world or some far-away unrealizable goal, would be used as a method of understanding and rectifying specific social ills. (Dewey 1948: 124)

Dewey had a clear idea of the task that remained for philosophy and the role it can play. Reconstruction in philosophy means that we accept that inquiry does not have Archimedean starting points, nor universal categories from which to theorize, and turn to the task 'of developing, of forming, of producing the intellectual instrumentalities which will progressively direct inquiry into the deeply and inclusively human – that is to say, moral – facts of the situation' (Dewey 1948: xxvii). Thus, the function of philosophy is to inquire into inquiry. Its role is to provide a general method of inquiry and critically evaluate its application and the judgements that result.

For Dewey, a crucial step in this process is to have an understanding of the intellectual crisis that he believed to exist at that time: the crisis of the incursion of science into everyday life, usurping traditional authority represented in religion and morality (1948: xxi–xxii, xxvii–xxviii). Radical change has taken place and shaken the metaphysical comfort of these old authorities because natural science, by the force of its own developments, had to abandon what philosophy had not yet let go: fixity. Philosophy, in its dismissal of this incursion as a 'technical matter', has failed to acknowledge that its universal is now actually 'process', and represents, 'the most revolutionary discovery yet made' (Dewey 1948: xiii). For Dewey, the methods of science, which led to this discovery and its acknowledgment, are not necessarily the province of science alone. In fact, he writes that scientific inquiry is immature because it has not moved beyond the physical world to take human affairs as its subject (Dewey 1948: xxviii). Science cannot be viewed in isolation from human affairs and institutions. As long as it is, it will have 'partial and exaggerated effects' and be 'set in opposition' to human interests (Dewey 1948: xxiv–xxv; Dewey 1929: 11). What natural science has to offer is a general method of inquiry that is applicable across disciplines, that is self-correcting, and oriented to invention and discovery, such that it affords a 'positive intellectual direction to man in developing the practical – that is, actually effective – morals which will utilise the resources now at our disposal' (Dewey 1948: xxxiii). Thus, the role left for a reconstructed philosophy is systematically to study the general method of inquiry suggested by natural science, scientific method, and its application to '*human* processes'.

Dewey's contribution to this effort of philosophy reconstructed is his theory of inquiry. Dewey's theory of inquiry is, as Joseph Margolis writes, the 'driving force' of his philosophical project (Margolis 1977: 129). It promotes and defends an understanding of scientific method as a general method of intelligence, which is practical and critical. There are three ideas central to the formulation of Dewey's theory of inquiry: experience, intelligence and situation. As Thayer writes, the significance of experience cannot be stressed enough as it provides 'both the materials and the methods of inquiry' (1952: 22). Experience as subject matter refers not simply to physical nature, but to the interaction of living things with their environment. Dewey has a dynamic understanding of experience as context, conditioned by organic processes, and with human experience, in particular, understood to be conditioned by biological processes as well as cultural influences. While Dewey does not equate experience with knowledge, he does equate experience with method (Smith 1992: 33–34). Experience yields method because, for reasons both biological and emotional, it is necessary that we make use of experience, note its functional constancies, and act upon it, refining the ways in which we draw from experience to cope with the world. In this regard, the method which arises from experience is the same as that of the experimental method of natural science according to Dewey, since it aims through critical thinking to make better and better use of experience. As Dewey writes, scientific method presents an understanding of experience that 'ceased to be empirical and became experimental' and with this 'something of radical importance occurred', because it suggests that '[w]e *use* our past experiences to construct new and better ones in the future. The very fact of experience thus includes the process by which it directs itself in its own betterment' (1948: 94–5). This instrumentalist view of experience and the method it yields is at the heart Dewey's theory of inquiry.

Dewey's notion of intelligence is also central. Dewey writes that intelligence should not be confused with reason, if by reason is meant the 'faculty for laying hold of ultimate truths' (1948: viii). He writes that reason as a faculty apart from experience is 'remote, uninteresting and uninmportant' (Dewey 1948: 95). Instead, intelligence begins with experience; it is practical, critical, and assumes fallibility. Dewey defines intelligence as:

> [c]oncrete suggestions arising from past experiences, developed and matured in the light of needs and deficiencies of the present, employed as aims and methods of specific reconstruction, and tested by success or failure in accomplishing this task of readjustment, suffice . . . Intelligence is not something possessed once and for all. It is in constant process of forming . . . an open-minded will to learn and courage in readjustment. (1948: 96–7)

Intelligence in action is inquiry. Dewey stresses the active character of intelligence, because the purpose of its scientific method is the 'transformation of existing experiences', which Dewey calls 'growth'. In *The Problems of Men*, Dewey writes that it is in this act of intentionally shaping and directing change, that the method of intelligence, scientific method, gains its ethical significance (1946: 248–9). The instrumental character of the method of intelligence has ethical meaning for Dewey, and this is why he believes there can be no separation of science from the social environment.

This brings us to the third central theme of Dewey's theory of inquiry, the idea of situation. It is the situation that ultimately initiates, defines and directs inquiry. Context is everything for Dewey. He writes, '[i]n actual experience there is never any such isolated singular object or event; *an* object or event is always a special part, a phase, or aspect, of an environing experienced world – a situation' (Dewey 1938: 67). Thus, a situation is a contextual whole, and unique by virtue of its 'pervasive quality'. Often the quality of a situation is marked by interderminancy, a sense of confusion. This is the spark to inquiry. For Dewey, an indeterminate situation means 'its constituents do not hang together' (1938: 105), and inquiry begins when such a situation is deemed problematic. The inquiry conducted is framed by the way in which the indeterminate situation is characterized as a problem, and it proceeds by suggesting hypotheses as to the possible consequences of plans offered as solutions to the indeterminate situation. At this stage, Dewey evokes imagination and the role it plays in projecting hypothetical outcomes, but stresses that imagination is constrained by the conditions of the situation and a solution's 'functional fitness' to the problem at hand (1938: 110). The success of an inquiry is judged by whether the plan of the action suggested by a hypothesis, and the execution of that plan (experiment), resolve the doubt raised by the indeterminate situation. Thus, inquiry reaches a settled conclusion when the indeterminate situation is made determinate: when it answers and transforms the problem that once existed. However, the solution reached is not regarded as truth, but as 'warranted assertability'. Warranted assertability is a recognition of fallibilism, that any belief or principle offered has an element of miscalculation, and thus, cannot be known with certainty to be true. Therefore, a determinate situation represents only a temporary resting place until inquiry is initiated once again.

With this understanding of experience, intelligence and situation and their relation to Dewey's theory of inquiry, what remains to be discussed, and what is most important for an understanding of pragmatist critique and its potential for normative IR theory, is Dewey's theory of value or valuation. His theory of valuation directly follows from his instrumentalism, since the act of transforming a situation is ethically significant, and the method of intelligence, inquiry, is evaluative. Moral judgement, like all judgement, arises from a problematic situation and is arrived at, like any other judgement, *via* the general method of intelligence. Similarly, the good of a moral judgement is represented by the determination of the problematic moral situation. How this differs from epistemologically centred ethical theory, represented in a debate like the cosmopolitan/communitarian debate, is that, instead of being preoccupied with discovering and defending a final end or good for the purposes of critique, the idea is that 'every moral situation is a unique situation having its own irreplaceable good' (Dewey 1948: 163). By challenging the notion of a single, final good, this idea does not succumb to the epistemological conflict that prevails in traditional philosophy. As Dewey writes, 'the primary significance of the unique and ultimately moral character of the concrete situation is to transfer the weight and burden of morality to intelligence . . . The practical meaning of a situation – that is the action needed to satisfy it – is not self-evident. It has to be searched for . . . This inquiry is intelligence' (1948: 163). An inquiry not only into inquiry itself, but also into the character of the ethical agent, is integral to finding a right course of action.

Because inquiry is a socially shared process within critical communities, it is evaluated by the level of responsibility with which the general method of intelligence is pursued by individuals. Dewey has a clear idea of the individual as an ethical agent. These characteristics, '[w]ide sympathy, keen sensitiveness, persistence in the face of the disagreeable, balance of interests', are the moral virtues of both individuals and inquiry (Dewey 1948: 164). Social criticism facilitates the self-realization of individuals, transforming them as ethical agents, and improves inquiry by moving towards these virtues, not because they are deemed to be fixed ends, but because they enable processes of growth and learning. Virtues such as these are, as Dewey writes, 'directions of change in the quality of experience. Growth itself is the only moral "end"' (1948: 177). Thus, ethical judgement for Dewey is a matter of direction, a movement towards 'perfecting, maturing, refining', life activities, affirming the continuity of experience, the 'aim of living' (1948: 177). Deweyan ethics is the pragmatic critique of method in inquiry as it leads to growth. This is the role left for philosophy: to take the method of intelligence as its subject matter and critically examine its social use. Thus, ethical critique in this pragmatic logic of inquiry into situations, with their own individualized goods, is not a matter of formal concepts or rules of morality, but of effective methods of intelligence (Dewey 1948: 170). Dewey writes that finding such methods 'can render personal choice more intelligent but it cannot take the place of personal decision, which must be made in every case of moral complexity'.[5] As so much rides on individual judgement in these indeterminate situations, this is why inquiry into inquiry is not enough. Dewey must have an account of the individual, her character and her motivations towards inquiry (Festenstein 1997: 27).

Although I find Dewey's idea of growth and ethics located in critique compelling, there are three aspects of his work which I find problematic in regard to suggesting a workable international ethics. First, what must be cautioned against in Dewey is his tendency to assume that the method he offers will go a long way towards securing social well-being. As Cornel West writes, Dewey overestimates the role that critical intelligence can play in 'dislodging and democratizing the entrenched economic and political powers that be' (West 1989: 102). Dewey is genuinely concerned and engaged in a project of social reconstruction and advocates a democratic ideal that he finds to be vital to the linked projects of reconstruction and critical inquiry, but he never suggests that the general method of intelligence – scientific method – can be the panacea to social and political ills. It can only provide temporary solutions to the indetermenancies that result from the need to harmonize diverse and conflicting interests in modern societies. However, it is not difficult to see how one might find that Dewey is offering critical intelligence as a panacea. Although there is in Dewey a 'radical participatory democratic ethos' (Bernstein 1995: 65), Dewey's work has been preoccupied to a much lesser extent with developing the issues he raises around the institutional and material requirements for the growth he advocates. On the other hand, the method of critical inquiry is treated systematically in his work and much, perhaps too much, is invested in its capacities for harmonization, to the neglect of some important material considerations about power and coercion in modern societies.

This focus on a theory of inquiry, and the democracy necessary to it, is motivated by a comprehensive, ethical account of the individual, which is the second source of concern I have with Dewey's work. Critical inquiry is the means by which individuals actively engage the best in themselves, their capacities for self-development and autonomy, thereby providing for their growth. The kind of harmonization and growth which concerns Dewey relies not only upon critical

[5] Dewey as quoted in Festenstein (1997: 27). My following discussion of Dewey's concept of the person draws primarily from Festenstein's excellent account.

inquiry, but upon an idea of the agents who employ it, agents who, according to Matthew Festenstein, are invested by Dewey with a 'naturalistic view of the self-realization of the individual in the community' (Festenstein 1997: 49). This view, Hegelian and teleological, finds the good of the individual to be at one with the community, such that the critical reflection required by inquiry into problematic situations prompts an awareness that 'growth involves becoming responsible, that is, responsive, to the needs and claims of others'.[6] There is a *strong* ontology at work here motivating Dewey's epistemological and political concerns. Its naturalism works to assure the standards for growth, the need for democratic exchange, and the possibility of diverse interests and ends being reconciled within society. My concern is that it is a foundationalism that is left unproblematized, and it may be no more compelling nor have any less deleterious effect than the kind of epistemological foundations which preoccupy Dewey's critical attention.

Thirdly, it is up for question whether or not Dewey successfully provides something other than a foundationalist epistemology in his reconstruction of traditional philosophy. Experience is one of many terms that Dewey aims to infuse with a sense of fallibilism in order to develop a new vocabulary of philosophy free from the epistemological ends of traditional philosophy (Thayer 1981: 173; Margolis 1977: 130). However, Thayer has his doubts about how successfully Dewey, in his theory of inquiry, purges the term experience of its epistemological trappings (Thayer 1981: 173).[7] It is true that Dewey uses, and uses often, the words 'empirical' and 'experience', and speaks of their 'objective' nature, but the key question is whether he likens the use of these terms to knowledge and its acquisition. Dewey writes that the apparatus of social science is not to be taken as knowledge, but instead as the 'intellectual means' for discovering the meaning and social import of phenomena (1927: 203). Yet, as John Smith writes, there are those passages in Dewey's discussion of the role of experience in science which bring the term 'perilously close to becoming identified with experiment' (Smith 1992: 34). There is clearly a cognitive/noncognitive tension in Dewey's use of experience, and this is reflected in the varied opinions as to whether or not Dewey is

---

[6] Dewey as quoted in Festenstein (1997: 55).
[7] However, he does acknowledge that Dewey's use of experience differs from British empiricists.

indeed offering something other than knowledge as the end of philosophical thinking.[8] This question mark over whether Dewey does or does not offer an epistemology raises doubts about how effectively we can interrogate the epistemological orientation of the cosmopolitan/communitarian debate from a Deweyan pragmatist position alone.

Rorty: pragmatism without method, without a particular role for philosophy

Rorty takes up, with an intensity not yet seen in pragmatism, Dewey's task of deconstructing the will to fixity or absolutes in traditional Philosophy.[9] Rorty too, tells a tale about the history of philosophy which concludes that its quest for certainty has proven unproductive. However, differences between the writers emerge when we ask: where does philosophy go from here? Dewey's answer is that philosophy should take as its material the general method of intelligence and critically examine its application to human activity and problematic social situations. Thus, philosophy has a role in assisting social reconstruction. Rorty, on the other hand, does not see any special role for philosophy in examining social problems, and objects to the idea of pragmatism offering a method for social inquiry. Where Dewey wants to reconstruct Philosophy, as Edel writes, Rorty wants to overcome it (Edel 1985: 22, 30). In *Consequences of Pragmatism*, Rorty says that what is needed is a new intellectual tradition, 'reached, if at all, by acts of making rather than of finding – by poetic rather than Philosophical achievement' (1982: xxx). Rorty says that questions such

---

[8] For a selection of writers who find a theory of knowledge in Dewey see: Edel (1985: 34–5), who argues that knowledge has 'a firm place in Dewey's pragmatism' because of his focus on learning; and Margolis (1977: 123, 128), who writes that Dewey offers a naturalized epistemology that arises from his epistemological realism regarding the nature of knowledge. However, there are those who disagree, and argue that Dewey does move away from the idea of knowledge as an end-goal. See Alexander (1993: 383–84), who would disagree with Edel that a focus on learning points to an orientation towards knowledge. Instead, he finds that Dewey replaces the end of knowledge with learning. It was 'the human capacity to learn rather than know which so impressed Dewey'; and West (1989: 86), who writes that for Dewey, philosophy is 'neither a form of knowledge nor a means to acquire knowledge'.

[9] I will adopt, for purposes of clarity, Rorty's use of capital 'P' to refer to traditional epistemologically centred philosophy, and lower case 'p' to refer to post-Philosophical philosophy.

as, 'what are philosophers for?' should not be asked; Philosophy is no more than an arbitrary division made for bureaucratic purposes, and its practitioners should not be looked to for 'heroic virtue' (1983b: 42–3). What is left is a role not for specialist philosophers, but for 'all-purpose intellectuals', 'humanists' who are 'specialists in seeing how things hung together', and who have 'no special "problems" to solve, nor any special "method" to apply' (Rorty 1982: xxxix).[10]

Rorty recognizes a central tension in Dewey's work which leads Dewey to suggest that philosophy does have particular problems to solve and a special method to apply. That tension is manifest in Dewey's attempt to reconcile historicism with naturalism; to take contingency seriously, and, at the same time, point to 'generic traits' of experience that provide a neutral framework, *a* method for inquiry. Rorty writes that Dewey was trying to find some mid-way position between 'a well-defined procedure . . . and a mere recommendation to be open-minded, undogmatic, critical and experimental' (Rorty 1986a: xiii). Rorty regards something like the latter position to be a 'therapeutic stance towards philosophy', whereas Dewey was concerned that it offers little more than platitudes for directing criticism or inquiry (Rorty 1982: 73; Rorty 1986a: xiii).[11] The problem, for Rorty, is not with Dewey's goal of criticism, but in his aim to offer a neutral method that would improve our critical thinking. Dewey's mistake was to believe 'that criticism of culture had to take the form of a redescription of "nature" or "experience" or both' (Rorty 1982: 85). It is a mistake in that one cannot, with consistency, suggest that there are 'generic traits' of experience and simultaneously renounce, as Dewey does, a 'transcendental account of the possibility of experience' (Rorty 1982: 77). Yet, Rorty finds this to be a trivial mistake. Dewey 'should

---

[10] Rorty goes on to write that these specialists would have no disciplinary standards or a collective self-image of a profession. Dewey would disagree on these points as well for the reason that although he did want a level playing field of the disciplines, and saw each as sharing a general method with none having special privilege among the others, he found that disciplines, none the less, have particular functions, and for that reason have standards appropriate to their functions and an identity in accordance with that function.

[11] For Rorty, this points to Dewey's will to offer something more systematic and constructive for philosophy: an empirical metaphysics represented in his work *Nature and Experience*. Rorty sees this work as an aberration from what he regards to be the theme which should win out in Dewey, his historicism. However, this fails to acknowledge the way in which the theory of inquiry, the attempt to offer general traits, runs throughout Dewey's work.

not be blamed if he occasionally came down with the disease he was trying to cure' (Rorty 1982: 85).

Rorty writes that what Dewey was good at was showing how Philosophical and religious ideas permeated American common sense. What is left for all-purpose intellectuals (in this case, those concerned about the pragmatic tradition in American philosophy), as Rorty sees it, is to see 'how the dregs of Deweyan thought – all that stuff about scientific method – have permeated the common sense of the American public of our own day and have themselves become a "cake of convention" which needs to be pierced' (1985a: 44).[12] Rorty sees that recent developments in the philosophies of science and language have shown that scientific method is an empty vessel, sterile for the purposes intended in its general social application. For Rorty, Thomas Kuhn has demonstrated that progress in science is not a matter of methodological improvement, but of better jargon for redescribing phenomena. Herein, for Rorty, lies the value of the recent concentration in analytic philosophy on language. By replacing an examination of experience with attention to language, a more radical break with Philosophy is made possible; and thus, analytic philosophy is better able to defend pragmatism's holistic and anti-foundational themes than Dewey or James. Ultimately, the linguistic turn helped us 'see though the notion of method' to find that what intellectuals have to 'contribute to moral and political change is not methodology but brilliant new redescriptions of what is going on' (Rorty 1985a: 41, 43).

This is the task Rorty sets for himself: redescription. As discussed in chapter 5, his focus is on the terms of historical vocabularies, rather than a method of intelligence based on 'generic traits' of experience. The new intellectual tradition Rorty espouses is a 'study of the comparative advantages and disadvantages of the various ways of talking which our race has invented. It looks, in short, much like what is sometimes called 'culture criticism' (Rorty 1982: xl). It asks us to examine our vocabularies and the metaphors we use to represent our understanding, by asking questions that differ from the truth-seeking questions of traditional philosophy. The questions are different in that behind them is a recognition that to acknowledge contingency means there is no device, neither foundationalism nor Deweyan naturalism, to avoid circularity in generating claims from inquiry. The principles

---

[12] He goes on to write that he believes the task stated above would be assisted by Habermasian and Foucauldian critiques of contemporary social science.

we profess are based on criteria that we have made ourselves. Dewey is reluctant to accept that this circularity could not be mitigated, that distance from social norms could not be achieved by a neutral, general method of intelligence and critique. However, for Rorty, there is no way around this circularity.[13] Yet, as discussed in chapter 5, this does not mean the end of social criticism according to Rorty. This is the neo-pragmatic basis of Rorty's idea of ethical critique: to articulate new descriptions and metaphors that work pragmatically – that is, they are increasingly useful – to redescribe and create new vocabularies, which eventually generate better forms of social practice. Metaphors, not method, are the focus of critique.

In addition to sharing Dewey's aim of finding better, more useful means of adapting and coping in our malleable social worlds, Rorty agrees that critique, synonymous with intelligence for Dewey, must be freed of the dualisms that truth-seeking Philosophy imposed and should adopt a fallibilist, experimental attitude. Thus, instead of speaking foundationally, we speak 'experimentally', opening critique up as a matter of 'offering concrete alternative suggestions' and trying them out as new tools for political practice (Rorty 1990b: 641, 635). For Rorty, these concrete suggestions are a product of one's vocabulary, which means his social criticism starts from the only place it can: Rorty's liberal democratic 'we'. Rorty willingly admits that this leads him down the path of ethnocentrism. Ethnocentrism is 'the recognition that no description of how things are . . . is going to free us of the contingency of having been acculturated as we were' (1991b: 13). Those 'solidarists' like himself who locate moral authority within the community are left with this predicament, either privilege our community or 'pretend an impossible tolerance for every other group' (Rorty 1985b: 12). Rorty's answer is that we should 'grasp the ethnocentric horn of this dilemma' (1985b: 12). He grants that liberalism has no ahistorical moral privilege, but he clearly thinks that some ethnocentrisms are better than others. As he writes in *CIS*, what takes the curse off the ethnocentrism of liberal democratic culture is that it is the ethnocentrism of a ' "we" which is dedicated to enlarging itself, to creating an ever larger and more variegated *ethnos*. It is the "we" of the people who have been brought up to distrust ethnocentrism' (Rorty 1989a: 198).

---

[13] However, I will argue later in the chapter that Rorty does offer a way of avoiding it: the public/private split.

Ethnocentrism does not put a halt to widening our moral commitments, to enlarging our vocabularies and thus, the space for individual creativity. As Rorty writes in *Objectivity, Relativism and Truth*, tensions within cultures 'make people listen to unfamiliar ideas' (1991b: 14). This is the only sense in which we can transcend our ethnocentrism, by adding to our old vocabularies over time, 'modifying them by playing them off against each other' with the result of adding 'new candidates for belief and desire, phrased in new vocabularies' (1991b: 14). Thus, Rorty's passion for new metaphors has as its motivation an ethic of enlargement, of individual growth through adding these new candidates for belief, and a notion of an expanding 'we' group. However, it is an ethic which needs both self-creation and the private space for individuals that the rules and procedural justice of liberal institutions afford. As discussed in chapter 5, for Rorty, it is an ethic which has its best hope in the conversation and practice of liberal democratic society.

Rorty says that Dewey was right to see 'pragmatism not as grounding, but as clearing the ground for, democratic politics' (1991b: 13). Clearly, there is much that Rorty's neo-pragmatism takes from Dewey, but as this section has argued, there are important differences. Rorty aims to divest Dewey's work of its foundationalism, captured in his appeal to the idea of naturalism and scientific method, so as to make pragmatism more radically contingent, interpretivist and linguistified. As discussed in part II of the book, such a move has its positive aspects for considerations of widening moral inclusion. However, it is not clear that Rorty himself successfully divests his own work of appeals to grounds. At this point, it is worth noting that Rorty's critique of Dewey's naturalism has an *epistemological* focus and that he does not take Dewey to task, similarly, for the residues of naturalism which remain in the socially-oriented individual which motivates his ethic of growth. This is particularly interesting when one considers that the link between individuality and society or solidarity, which is unproblematic for Dewey, is the central difficulty which preoccupies Rorty in *CIS*. However, it is perhaps more interesting because a residue of realism and, thus, foundationalism remains in Rorty's own ontological priorities, evident in the ethics which follows from his concept of the liberal ironist, albeit within a particular, historical context. Rorty's conviction about the normative significance of providing for the autonomy of this liberal ironist leads him to employ a methodological tool which works foundationally and, as Rorty acknowledges, is the key to whether his project stands or falls: the public/private split. For reasons developed in chapter 5, in particular the undesirable ethical-political repercussions of this public/private split, the apoliticism it can generate, and the foundational weight placed on Rorty's own concept of the person, I find that the promise the pragmatist approach may hold for ethical theory in IR cannot rest upon Rorty's neo-pragmatism alone.

The need for a pragmatist synthesis: the problem of authentic critique in Dewey and Rorty

I am led to ask: why does Rorty offer the public/private split, particularly as his intellectual hero never endorses a separation of public and private realms?[14] Has he not thought through the political repercussions of such a split; or has he done so, and deemed that the consequences for a liberal democratic society without this separation are indeed more undesirable? Also, regarding Dewey, we are led to ask: why does Dewey turn to a theory of inquiry into the nature of experience and pin it on a concept of the ethical individual, the naturalness of which is unconvincing, given the contingency of experience? Dewey was aware of the tension in this, and sought to mitigate it through his particular version of naturalism and instrumentalism, but why did he feel it necessary to insist upon certain generalizable constancies? I will argue here that these questions are answered for both writers by the concern each has for realizing the best possibilities available for authentic critique; that is, being able to appeal against what societal norms and conventions allow us to say. I will begin with Rorty, and then examine the same concern in Dewey.

Rorty's thinking which leads to the public/private split is complex. In order to get a handle on it, we must look towards the goal which it serves: the enhancement of human powers and autonomy. Richard Shusterman notes that both Rorty and Dewey share the ideal of self-development, and its aesthetic features, but their differences over where they find the locus of this fulfilment result in separate political agendas: Dewey is concerned with participatory democracy, while Rorty concentrates on the public/private split (Shusterman 1994: 397). Where Dewey finds that the individual's growth requires active political engagement and participation in the public sphere, Rorty,

---

[14] This point will be defended below in the second section.

according to Shusterman, finds that self-development is a private affair and requires the space that the public/private split affords for self-creation. Shusterman points to the way in which Rorty finds that the commonalities and standardizing procedures of social convention seriously restrict creativity and imagination. This is one reason why Rorty sees the need for separation and wraps the heroic ironic liberal in a blanket of private fulfilment. Shusterman also suggests Rorty's turn to the private is a product of different times, since later in the twentieth century, the possibility of self-development within communities seems too 'bland', yielding little fulfilment. Shusterman does not discuss it, but there is also Rorty's concern, mentioned in chapter 5, about the damage private irony could unleash on the public sphere were they not kept apart. However, I want to inquire further and suggest there is another reason.

Herein, as I see it, enters the complexity of Rorty's position on the public/private split. There is a tension in Rorty's work ignored by those consumed with criticizing his promotion of private fulfilment and his resultant lack of constructive, political engagement. These critics fail to acknowledge, as does Shusterman, a point made in chapter 5: Rorty understands progress, whether poetic, political or philosophical, to be the consequence of 'the accidental coincidence of a private obsession with a public need' (1989a: 37). Coincidence suggests haphazardness, but the underlying point is that private and public do meet and interact, however randomly, with the benefit of developing human powers. In *CIS*, Rorty describes what I labelled in chapter 5 as a 'trickle-down effect': the growth of poeticized culture leads to increased solidarity, strengthening and enhancing public, liberal institutions. Rorty himself blurs the distinction that he erects, because, ultimately, he substitutes another tension for Dewey's, a tension that is indicated by the contradictions represented in: (1) Rorty's request for the space for private creation, yet his expectation of certain public transgressions of that space for the sake of progress; and (2) in Rorty's protestations against method, even though his liberal utopia stands upon what I regard to be a methodological device that works foundationally, the public/private split, which facilitates the creation of new vocabularies and, thus, critique. To what can this be attributed?

While Rorty claims to have given up all forms of neutral starting points, whether epistemologically based or instrumentally naturalized, none the less, he is troubled by the same question that prompted

Dewey's attempt to find some middle ground between historicism and naturalism. Rorty and Dewey, in acknowledging contingency and taking historicism seriously, are both concerned with the question of whether authentic critique is indeed possible; how we are able to speak against the current of 'what society lets us say' (Peirce 1958a: 407). The tension in Rorty rests, as it does for Dewey, in the answer offered to this problem. Both understand that to accept this contingency means recognizing that philosophical thinking begins in the community and is guided by its fit with the norms of social practice. Contingency results in a turn to community. There is clearly evident in Rorty a sense that this is a good consequence. As Rorty writes, a renewed sense of community is what we gain for our loss of metaphysical comfort with the fall of *a priori* structures (1982: 166). Thus, Dewey and Rorty can theorize the value community and its normative practices can hold for individuals, which I deemed important in the conclusion to part II of the book. Yet, they both recognize the difficulty this presents in offering authentic social criticism, for how are we able to offer a critical stand against social custom, rules and norms from within that normative practice?

Dewey, according to Gary Brodsky, has a two-part answer (Brodsky 1982: 330–3). He writes that Dewey finds that the experimentalism of inquiry provides a measure of 'objectivity' in its procedures, which results in a distancing from social opinion. Secondly, Dewey's naturalism draws attention to patterns or constancies of experience that can be treated functionally and instrumentally in regard to the way in which they help individuals cope with their environment and recover dynamic equilibrium with it. While more value-oriented, this too strives for a level of abstraction that can stand against social belief and custom, providing for the possibility of critique, the practice of which facilitates individual self-development and autonomy.

As noted above, Rorty cannot countenance what he regards as the side of Dewey that turns to the empirical, to experience, and a method for inquiry into that experience, as the way of finding some measure of distance for social critique. Such a method stymies growth, because it makes presuppositions about relevant material or vocabularies (Rorty 1982: 152). So what else does Rorty have to turn to? How can authentic critique be provided for if not by ahistorical, universal foundations for knowledge, if not by some neutral method based on naturalized experience? For Rorty, the question, more pointedly, is *where* does he have to turn. Rorty's answer is the private sphere. Only the ironist or the intellectual who is the strong textualist he describes in *Consequences of Pragmatism* can find wisdom, can be creative, and develop moral imagination, but it is 'purchased at the price of separation from his fellow humans' (Rorty 1982: 158). Rorty recognizes that the isolation from human affairs with which this is bought is morally objectionable. It makes the public responsibility of private individuals at least questionable, if not doubtful. He writes that his pragmatism leaves him unable to dispose of this objection, because pragmatism has an identification with the problems of 'finite men', a sense of 'our common human lot', a preference, which involves, for him, a defence of 'the possibility of combining private fulfilment, self realization, with public morality, a concern for justice' (Rorty 1982: 158). This is Rorty's tension in regard to offering ethical critique: the question of how to bridge the self-fulfilment only afforded by private isolation with the morality constituted in the norms of social practice, allowing us the scope to offer metaphors for critique.

I will conclude this section by saying that the problem of being able to appeal against social convention remains very real for Dewey and Rorty. In a life's work on a theory of inquiry, Dewey's experimentalism, his naturalism, never broke from the idea that science cannot exist without the common sense of community, a frame of reference that he identifies with the customs and norms of community life, and oriented to practical concerns: situations both emotional and intellectual.[15] The liberation for individuals that science represents is in furnishing a level of abstraction in applying a method of intelligence to practical affairs. None the less, common sense and science remain 'functionally interdependent' and any authentic space free of social convention seems little more than a semantic contrivance. The same is true for Rorty. There will always be public/private interventions. Self-creation and fulfilment cannot be wholly separate from community and Rorty recognizes this, although he is puzzled as to how better to defend it other than through his contrivance of a public/private split. Therefore, neither Dewey's idea of a neutral method of intelligence, nor Rorty's promotion of the space for private creation, can be achieved. For both writers, this kind of authenticity represents an *ideal* that we must keep in focus in the process of pragmatic critique. Unfortunately, each insists upon adopting unworkable tools to fashion

---

[15] This is drawn from Thayer's reading of Dewey's piece, 'Common Sense and Science' in *The Logic of Pragmatism* (Thayer 1952: 40–49).

this ideal. I will argue in the next section that these tools are unnecessary, and should be dropped in a synthesis of Dewey and Rorty under the banner of pragmatic critique.

A pragmatic synthesis: the ethic that results from pragmatic critique

In the last section, I pointed to difficulties in confronting the impasse of ethical theory in IR with an understanding of pragmatism as standing upon the work of *either* Dewey *or* Rorty alone. However, in this section I will argue that an understanding of ethics as pragmatic critique, building upon the idea of a synthesis of Dewey and Rorty, could be promising in two respects: (1) in being as thoroughly anti-foundationalist as is possible and, thus, conscious of the need to interrogate the kind of foundationalism which leaves cosmopolitans and communitarians gripped in deadlock; and (2) in offering an ethic that is politically engaged and oriented to community, yet has a will to universalization through the growth of human capacities and the expansion of 'we' feeling.

Before beginning this section, I must address a possible objection: that a synthesis of the projects of a pre-linguistic turn writer like Dewey and a post-linguistic turn writer like Rorty is unworkable.[16] In response, I want to say the following. It is worth noting that Dewey's critique of epistemologically centred philosophy anticipates the linguistic turn, and that this is evident in the way in which Rorty picks up this theme in Dewey and runs with it. However, a real obstacle remains as to whether Dewey properly acknowledged relativism, since relativism is understood to be the consequence of the conclusion which follows from the linguistic turn: that all there is left is discourse. As mentioned above, Dewey resorts to his form of naturalism because he is well aware of the dangers his historicism presents for finding standards for social critique. Dewey recognized the threat of relativism, but found a naturalist mechanism which for him, undercut its potential consequences for critical inquiry. However, one might just as well ask how seriously Rorty, as a post-linguistic turn philosopher, takes the implication of relativism. In arguing as I have that Rorty has his own mechanisms for establishing ethical criteria in the face of

---

[16] I must thank Mervyn Frost for raising this issue as a possible objection to the proposed synthesis which follows.

historicism and contingency – his concept of the ironic liberal and his idea that ethnocentrisms are not necessarily incompatible and can be transcended – I find his acknowledgement of relativism to be limited. To my mind, this provides the opening for the possibility of the synthesis which follows.

Synthesis towards a more thorough-going antifoundationalism

It is evident from the analysis of antifoundationalism in part II and in this chapter that a will to offer an ethics circumscribes a really-existing antifoundationalism. However, for the purposes of moving normative IR theory beyond its present impasse and the dangers of moral exclusion that come with the territory of foundationalism, we must aim for as thorough-going an anti-foundationalism as possible, which is self-aware of the dangers of its own *weak* foundations, both ontological and epistemological, for ethical critique. I will begin with Dewey. What I find to be valuable in Dewey are generally speaking those aspects of pragmatism which I recounted in Bernstein: his critique of Philosophy as a foundational discipline, his fallibilism, his turn to community, his recognition of contingency and his pluralism. However, as I argue above, Dewey's tendency to see his idea of a general method of intelligence as the corrective to social problems, his concept of the ethical individual grounded in the naturalness of her social commitments, and his turn to the general constancies of experience as the measure for social critique are problematic for a rigorous critique of the foundationalism within the cosmopolitan/communitarian debate. This is why Rorty's critique of method in Dewey is a step in the right direction. Rorty writes that he does not find 'clear nor useful' the terms absolute or objective in regard to reality or scientific method, yet he sees that a Deweyan approach to social science and morality which 'emphasizes the utility of narratives and vocabularies rather than the objectivity of laws and theories' is useful (1982: 195).

Yet, there are two cautions that must be sounded about the value of Rorty's critique of Dewey on this score. The first was raised earlier: Rorty fails to interrogate the way in which Dewey's concept of the person works foundationally in his ethic of growth, and Rorty himself needs to be self-conscious of the methodological grounds he invokes to support his ontological priorities. Thus, the public/private split in his work must be brought to the surface and critically analysed. Secondly, I want to caution against going as far as Rorty in emphasizing the utility of vocabularies such that one ends up privileging poetry in an effort to replace the privileging of science and its method. It is Rorty's deep-seated distrust of method which blocks his ability to see that science and its method have a function which is unique and valuable and cannot be collapsed into a vocabulary or a kind of poetry. As Larry Hickman argues, for Dewey, science and art are different types of inquiries with different subject matters and different kinds of tools, each deserving of an internal privileging based on their particular function (Hickman 1993: 229). Hickman illustrates this insight with the contemporary example of how the social problem of poverty and homelessness, for example, is 'expressed' or made meaningful by the work of someone like the photographer Stephen Shames, but how the problem is 'stated' by more quantitative treatments like Kevin Phillips' *Politics of Rich and Poor* or in a study by *Scientific American* (Hickman 1993: 229). Both media stimulate critical intelligence in useful, although different, ways. Dewey is more open to a variety of avenues into critique and growth, where Rorty focuses upon language and poetry. While it seems correct, in light of Kuhn's work (1970), to question objectivity in science and the degree to which Dewey replicates this in his experimentalism, one must not conclude that science collapses into poetry or that the idea of a general method of intelligence precludes the possibility of plural methods, each with different functions that vary according to particular disciplines. However, if we take Rorty's critique of method as a cautionary note against, first, conferring neutrality upon experience, and using it as a measure for authentic critique; and second, seeing method, including his own, as a *strong* ground for social reconstruction and the growth of critical intelligence, then this is a valuable contribution towards a more thorough-going antifoundationalism that I see as necessary to the pragmatic synthesis I want to offer.[17]

---

[17] It might be added that Rorty's warnings against method could only be taken to be cautionary as he, himself, does not avoid suggesting a method. As Bernstein (1991: 262) writes, although Rorty puts 'method' in scare quotes he suggests a 'method' for how new patterns of linguistic behaviour arise. Also, as I note in chapter 5, the public/private split is a methodological device for defending his juxtaposition of liberalism and irony.

Synthesis towards a more politically engaged notion of ethics as pragmatic critique

What I find to be particularly valuable in Rorty is the new vigour he has given pragmatic thinking, first, by bringing to it the insights of recent developments in the philosophy of language; and secondly, in demonstrating its range *beyond* American philosophical culture by pointing to its overlap with recent trends in Continental philosophy. However, his critics are right to be concerned by the way in which Rorty puts off the political. His public/private split is a hindrance to the possibility of real political engagement – that is, the kind of situational problem-solving that pragmatism works towards – as well as being a problematic methodological prop. This is why Dewey is particularly important to the synthesis I advocate here. Dewey understands the process of individual fulfilment and self-development to be a product of social and political engagement. If we reject the naturalness of Dewey's formulation and replace it with the idea that it is a phenomenon that we recognize as having value for certain persons and, therefore, needs to be accommodated in our normative theorizing, then what we value in Dewey is that he never loses sight of the social construction of the self.

When Rorty is asked in an interview why he would assert a separation of public and private realms, given his praise of Dewey's dismissal of such dualisms, Rorty responds that he does not see it as the kind of distinction Dewey wanted to overcome (Rorty 1989b: 202). However, Dewey's writing clearly indicates that such a split is unthinkable for him, and that he did indeed aim to overcome just this kind of distinction. As mentioned above, a reconceptualization of individuality as a socially connected self was important to Dewey's thought on critical inquiry, social reconstruction, and the participatory democracy he envisioned.

In *Individualism Old and New* (1930), Dewey evaluates individualism as an historically conditioned way of thinking that arises out of assigning human essences and using these attributes as a ground to justify moral thinking about social institutions.[18] There, he concludes that no aspect of morality can legitimately be regarded as a conflict of the individual against society. In *Reconstruction in Philosophy*, Dewey

---

[18] A similar argument can be found in Dewey (1948: 44–5) in his discussion of the rise of contract theory.

writes that the moral situation in which a good is realized cannot be one of private appetites, but necessarily requires communication, sharing, and therefore is public and social (1948: 206). Dewey's objection to the kind of distinction between public and private that Rorty offers is most clearly stated in *The Public and Its Problems*. In this book, Dewey distinguishes between public and private for purposes of defining the private realm as the area in which one is directly involved with the consequences one experiences, and the public as the area in which indirect consequences are felt and require solutions (1927: 12). However, the definitions are offered not as a line of separation 'equivalent to the distinction between the individual and the social' (Dewey 1927: 13). Dewey intended that his definitions of public and private undo the work of a conception like Rorty's, which separates the individual and society. This is illustrated by Dewey's understanding that the state has a liberating role to play in contributing to the intellectual growth of individuals (1927: 72–3).[19]

Shusterman agrees that a pragmatist approach should oppose a separation of public and private, and also argues that we can 'split the difference' and locate a pragmatist position between Dewey and Rorty (Shusterman 1994: 404–5). Yet, he is not concerned to insist that within such a synthesis, Rorty should relinquish the public/private split, because he suggests that Rorty has an answer to the charge Dewey would put to him of privileging private ends. As mentioned above, Shusterman suggests that, for Rorty, his turn to the private is in part a recognition that the self-fulfilment which the public has to offer is quite 'bland', and that, in today's postmodern society, philosophy has little it can do to improve public means, but 'it can do much to realize private ends; so, pragmatically speaking, it makes better sense to use philosophy where it can be profitably used' (1994: 405). Shusterman thinks that Rorty is right on this score, so he does not suggest that we move away from Rorty's public/private separation, he simply suggests that a synthesis would mean that Rorty might acknowledge that smaller, more intimate communities could be meaningful and contribute to self-fulfilment.

I have two problems with Shusterman's argument. First, while the notion that Rorty turns to the private in recognition of the loss of a meaningful public warrants some consideration, I see it only as a

---

[19] It is interesting to note here that Dewey qualifies the liberation a state can offer by recognizing the violence it can do to individuals as well.

minor contributing factor. Instead, I think the more significant contributing factor as to why Rorty turns to the private is the tension I point to above regarding how one can speak against the current of what social convention allows. Secondly, his concentration on this factor leads Shusterman to regard Rorty's error to be the idea that one has nothing available but the private sphere, in the face of the public/private split. This fails to acknowledge that Rorty does not turn wholly to the private. Indeed, Rorty sees that the public and the private must interact for moral progress, but feels that the split, none the less, must be maintained to provide for the authenticity of social difference: space for genuine self-creation without public interference, and space for a public free from the interference of the private creator. However, this is a rather shallow form of authenticity, paid for at considerable ethical cost, not only according to Dewey (or contemporary feminist theorists)[20] but according to Rorty himself. Thus, while I want to build on Shusterman's suggestion that a synthesis is possible, I contend that it requires that we drop the public/private distinction, and force Rorty to think through the conditions and process involved in public and private interaction.

If a possibility can be suggested for how Rorty's ironic critique might proceed in liberal democracy without such a split, I believe a profitable synthesis of the pragmatism of Dewey and the neo-pragmatism of Rorty can be suggested. The separation of public and private realms, for Rorty, is a means to offer the most authentic space available for self-creation, to make new metaphors, and thus, critique possible. However, at the same time he allows that this separation is an ideal which is transgressed, to the benefit of public morality. Despite his protestations about method, the split serves as a methodological tool to defend and lend support to his juxtaposition of irony and liberal democratic institutions, but it is a tool he does not need. As discussed above, he believes that irony exercised within the political is dangerous. Is it, however, as dangerous as he suggests? The postmodernist writers he criticizes for trying to use irony for public purposes (Rorty 1982: 83; Rorty 1990b: 640; Rorty 1983a: 572) have not exactly sent tremors through the foundations of liberal democratic institutions. My contention is that irony in the public realm is not as destabilizing as Rorty suggests, as long as community membership is valued within liberal democratic society. I think this is the defence to

---

[20] This issue will be discussed further in chapter 7.

which Rorty could turn: to work free of this separation, and give up the assumption that public and private concerns can be separated. The two can be separated in some instances, and this is a useful goal, given the political aims of liberal societies, but ends cannot always be separated from means in public discourse; the line easily gets blurred. Alternatively, he could offer the following defence for irony and solidarity. As he writes, in evaluating a claim, without recourse to transcultural validity, we are left with the question of whether that claim can be made to cohere with a sufficient number of our beliefs (Rorty 1990b: 640). Critique and scepticism have long been a part of the liberal ethos. Oddly enough, Rorty is the last person who should be asking the 'how' or 'why' questions as to whether both vocabularies can exist simultaneously within liberal culture.

I think that Rorty's project can maintain itself and be coherent without this dichotomy. However, there remains the problem for Rorty of authentic critique. To turn to the defence suggested – to acknowledge that both irony and solidarity are presently a part of our public liberal culture, and work on this basis, testing the coherence of claims against that culture without recourse to any theoretical props or tools – would still leave Rorty with a problem: how are we able to take a position critical of social norms and convention from within that community practice? This is a legitimate worry on the part of both Rorty and Dewey. They are right to be concerned about the power invested in the normative practices of communities, and how approximations to authentic critique can be facilitated. This worry is not a dissimilar worry to that expressed by Left Hegelians, discussed in chapter 3, in reaction against what they found to be the conservative reformism in Hegelian method and immanent critique. Granted, like Hegel, neither Rorty nor Dewey think there is a standpoint outside of a cultural situation. However, in their search for a measure of authenticity, neither fully trusts Hegel's insight regarding the possibility that remains for critique in the face of contingency. Within immanent critique is the recognition that all human thought and experience is a product of a historical and cultural situation, and that although we cannot free ourselves from this situatedness, we can still theorize critically without denying this conditionedness. As Steven Smith writes, immanent critique seeks 'standards of rationality within existing systems of thought and forms of life' (1989: 10). However, Rorty writes that immanent critique 'is relatively ineffective', because, as Kuhn pointed out, 'anomalies within old paradigms can pile up indefinitely without providing much basis for criticism until a new option is offered' (Rorty 1993a: 96). In other words, what Rorty is saying is that the only way in which critique is genuinely made possible is to offer an alternative vision, metaphor, etc. outside of the normative framework of the community practice concerned. He invokes moral imagination as the key to authentic critique. However, Rorty, none the less, draws from Hegel's notion of immanent critique in the lead up to the articulation of new vocabularies and new alternative visions.

Above, I discussed Rorty's (1991b) account of how vocabularies change, and new vocabularies are created. He suggests that tensions within a community and its settled vocabulary lead persons to look for new metaphors and listen to their resonance with those tensions, resulting in the incorporation of useful, new metaphors and thus, generating an expanded, and new vocabulary. Similarly, Hegel points to the existence of tensions, or contradictions which stimulate the motor of critical inquiry, the negation of the negation. In the *Phenomenology of Spirit*, he writes:

> [w]hen consciousness feels this violence, its anxiety may well make it retreat from the truth, and strive to hold on to what it is in danger of losing. But it can find no peace. If it wishes to remain in a state of unthinking inertia, the thought troubles its thoughtlessness, and its own unrest disturbs its inertia. (Hegel 1977: 51)

I believe this describes well what Rorty understands to be the stimulus behind the search for new vocabularies, why persons are ultimately moved to stray from the comfort of unthinking acceptance of social custom. Contradictions arise, unleashing doubts that need to be transformed and settled. As long as this stimulus exists, critique is possible. Rorty writes, 'without tensions which make people listen to unfamiliar ideas in the hope of finding a means of overcoming those tensions' there is no hope of social critique, of expanding our vocabularies and thus, our moral commitments beyond our ethnocentrism (1991b: 14). Thus, the tensions that give rise to immanent critique are also those that motivate the imagining and the projecting of new vocabularies and alternative visions for radical, authentic critique. Here lies the potential for confronting the 'reform' versus 'radical' change opposition in Hegelian method and using it to what I see as its best effect. The tantalizingly brief Hegelian-inspired discussion of the growth of new metaphors and vocabularies in Rorty suggests that there can be interplay between the reformist and radical versions of Hegelian method. There are times when immanent critique may not be suffcent for the purposes of the problematic moral situation at hand. However, the tensions that give rise to it, and find immanent critique wanting, provide the stimulus for moral imagination to project alternative ethical possibilities. In Rorty's mind, the private sphere is required to give authentic space to the kind of self-creation which generates these alternative notions. In my mind, the public/private split is not only normatively undesirable, but it is artificial and unnecessary: artificial, because the tensions that motivate private creativity and moral imagination are inherently social, and thus, some trespassing of the private/public line is required; unnecessary, because moral imagination does not require its own private space since it has the capacity to *create its own space in thought*. This is the kind of pragmatic critique – free of the public/private split in Rorty and using both immanent critique and moral imagination – that I want to develop.

To conclude, this is how I believe a synthesis of Dewey and Rorty on the question of ethics as pragmatic critique should be shaped. Regarding Dewey, it is the ethic that results from his pragmatism that holds the most appeal for me. If, with Rorty's cautionary note, we think of Dewey as replacing the epistemological goal of philosophical and moral thinking that was knowledge, in particular knowledge of fixed ends, with that of learning and openness towards a plurality of ends, we have an ethic of growth. Growth requires an experimental attitude which looks to the new, or different, and employs imagination for the purpose of intellectualizing practice; that is, critical intelligence better facilitating the ways in which we cope, make meaningful, and adapt to our social worlds. Growth is a continual process of reconstruction. This does not simply imply creating better techniques of production *via* scientific method, although this is certainly a part of growth. It also requires creation of an aesthetic sort, generating new feelings, meanings and significances. Dewey sees the function of art as 'to break through the crust of conventionalized and routine consciousness' (1927: 183). It too facilitates a critical, experimental attitude necessary to growth. For Dewey, to improve this kind of intelligence, to be critical and apply that critique practically to social and political life, is an ethical responsibility. For this reason, Dewey is politically engaged and concerned with social reconstruction to improve participatory democracy, although his idea of growth cannot provide substantive content to that reconstruction. To do so would require attributing fixed ends to human associations, yet what he can and does offer are the preconditions for social reconstruction that he deems necessary: rigorous social critique.

With good effect, Rorty highlights and advocates Dewey's critique of epistemologically centred philosophy, the experimental attitude and turn to community that results from his fallibilism, and the importance of the aesthetic and the emotive. Despite his protestations against method, Rorty shares with Dewey the fundamental idea of a general method of critical intelligence, which employs imagination and experimental attitude to help us solve problematic situations. Rorty writes that Dewey's insight, after the recognition that epistemology does not help us solve problems, is to propose that what remains is experimentalism in moral theory, such that you 'need to keep running back and forth between principles and the results of applying principles' to difficult moral situations (Rorty 1991b: 68). In my estimation, Rorty's insight is to highlight the role imagination and the aesthetic plays in this process for Dewey. In pragmatic critique, to focus on the role of imagination and the aesthetic in inquiry draws attention to the way in which the idea of growth and its ethics of critique requires an engagement with that which is different – with otherness, with the new – in order to generate new solutions to old, problematic situations when immanent critique is found wanting. It results in the ethics of an expanding 'we', which listens to different metaphors and imagines and constructs a notion of their fit with ours for the purposes of social critique. It is this step, of highlighting the role of moral imagination and drawing attention to the idea of an expanding 'we' group implicit in Dewey's notion of growth, that is Rorty's most significant contribution to the pragmatic synthesis I suggest here.

Finally, it is important for this reconstructed pragmatist project to have an open awareness of the ontological priorities which motivate its ethics of growth.[21] So far, we have established that, in the face of having only *contingent* epistemological grounds upon which to construct standards for ethical critique, more justificatory weight is being borne by ontology. The attributes that both Dewey and Rorty attribute to being work foundationally in their ethical projects and this must be brought to the surface for critical examination. As I see it, to move away from epistemologically centred argument means that we have

---

[21] This point will be taken up and developed in chapter 8.

no other choice but to rely upon some kind of ontological commitment in order to provide for the possibility of critique. However, what must be kept in mind is that, for the same reasons as the difficulties which arose with epistemologies that employ either *strong* foundations or *weak* foundations *non-contingently*, ontologies too should be held *weakly* and *contingently*. The *weak* ontology which motivates pragmatic critique has at its base an idea of human flourishing which Dewey and Rorty share: to realize improved forms of human autonomy and self-development. As we have seen, there is a tension between the two writers as to how that idea of human flourishing is best realized – for Dewey, *via* social commitments; for Rorty, *via* private creativity – and I think it is important to the synthesis fashioned here that this tension remain, since both writers point to ideas of self-development that we recognize as holding value for persons. These two ideas of the means towards improved forms of human autonomy can and do coexist in liberal society. Indeed, I think that they might work together constructively, since between them they represent a range of self-understandings that are valued in liberal societies and therefore should, out of a concern for consent that an orientation towards autonomy suggests, be negotiated. Also, there is the potential that they may work together constructively because, interestingly, both require forms of expansion and moral inclusion for the growth each envisions. As a *weak* ontology, a *via media* of more or less socially oriented approaches to improved forms of human autonomy intends to suggest a hypothesis, advanced under the assumption of fallibilism, that this basis for an ethic of growth may be a value around which convergence may be facilitated if tried experimentally. I will now turn to what this pragmatic approach can offer international ethics.

International ethics as pragmatic critique

In this concluding section, I want to recap my understanding of the unique problematic of international ethics, and then turn to what I believe international ethics as pragmatic critique can yield. For centuries, moral philosophers have assumed that morality, by definition, must be universalizable and its ends ahistorical. The momentum of antifoundationalism and its recognition of contingency have meant that today, while one may not be an antifoundationalist, none the less, one finds that the idea that moral ends are fixed and ahistorical has loosened its hold. Goods are understood to be socially constructed on different cultural bases. While the pursuit of finding fixed, ahistorical ends is grinding to a halt, this book has demonstrated that what has not subsided is the appeal to *weak* foundations and some idea of universality or of increasing moral inclusion in offering an ethics. Above, in the second section of this chapter, I asked how pragmatic critique needs to proceed in a way that is self-conscious and critical of its own *weak* foundational premises. Now, I will turn to a discussion of how this notion of international ethics as pragmatic critique is fully self-conscious of its will to universalization and offers a reconceptualization of what it means to universalize in a way that is wary of the pitfalls that accompany a universalizable ethics. Altogether, this pragmatist approach to international ethics offers an alternative hope for international ethics represented in: (1) its critique of foundationalist, epistemologically centred philosophy, and movement towards as thorough-going an antifoundationalism as is possible; and (2) its notion that the universal principles of moral inclusion are not to be found, but are to be constructed or created by the powers of 'moral imagination', otherwise understood by Dewey as critical intelligence.

The fundamental intuition of pragmatism for the impasse of the cosmopolitan/communitarian debate is that its focus on grounding claims for international ethics, its epistemological quest, represents an obstacle that *need not* be in the way of an international ethics. Pragmatism surveys the history of epistemologically centred philosophy and demonstrates that foundations do not solve problems. Foundations represent no more than pretensions to resolve indeterminate moral situations. As the debate in normative IR theory attests, the search for foundations to ground ethical claims has yielded little more than a clarification of its core tension: how to balance the claims of both individuals and states or communities. No solution to the question of a universalizable international ethic looks set to appear over the horizon. However, the turn away from epistemologically centred philosophy represents a horizon of possibility for international ethics.

According to the pragmatist approach I have advocated here, foundations, and the dualisms which result, are limitations on the formulation of ethical principles. Epistemologically centred philosophy is backward-looking, checking the fit of an ethical claim with received and accepted moral principles, and constrained within the rules set by those principles. Most importantly for the recent acceptance of contingency in social life, it has no mechanisms for dealing with new, problematic moral situations which are sure to arise. It lacks the necessary flexibility, hemmed in by its recourse to arguments that work foundationally. Alternatively, the attempt to find a more thoroughgoing antifoundationalist ethics results in an idea of philosophical thinking as cultural criticism. Pragmatic critique employs an experimental attitude orientated to the new, and an intelligence free of the strictures of moral Reason, which makes use of the powers of imagination in response to the transformation of indeterminate situations. In this ongoing process of acting to give meaning or determinacy to change and the situations which result, a pragmatic approach recognizes that ends are constructed in the process and are as plural as the number of situations which arise. A pragmatic approach has the flexibility required to engage the new, the different, which is bound to surface in any encounter with international, moral situations.

Also, this approach is particularly well suited to confront the problem of universalizability in international ethics. By definition, an ethic is understood to be universalizable. Relinquishing the quest for certainty or grounds in ethical theory, does not mean the end of universalizability as a question for ethics. While IR antifoundationalists working in the tradition of French poststructuralism have only recently begun to think openly about whether or not their aim of a non-universalizable ethics is possible, Dewey's and Rorty's move away from epistemologically centred philosophy openly admits a concern with moral inclusion and the range or universalizability of its claims. The idea of growth, an expanding 'we' that motivates the pragmatist understanding of ethics as critique, aims to transcend the particularity of one's ethnocentrism. However, there is a legitimate concern about the idea of an expanding 'we', that suggests the need for a warning about totalizing narratives: the risk of suppressing difference and otherness with an imperialistic 'we'. However, this risk is mitigated in pragmatism by its assumption of fallibilism.

Fallibilism represents an interesting way of offering universals and the *weak* foundations on which they are based without the undercurrent of absolutes and fixity that is associated with a traditional philosophical understanding of a universal. Any opinion or principle offered assumes it has an element of error, and thus, is always subject to revision. There may be hope for a principle to have a range of applicability, a degree of universality beyond the context of the situation from which it arises, but that principle is offered in an

206

experimental fashion, as a tool to be tried, although assumed to be endlessly revisable. Thus, the assumption of continual revision in fallibilism means that any principle offered to test its range of applicability, and the possibility it affords for an expanding 'we' and growth, proposes an alternative way in which universals can be offered which does not risk hitting otherness over the head and into submission with the hammer of an absolute. Fallib 'ism enables us critically to engage otherness with less danger of suppressing its difference, since principles are extended provisionally and experimentally. Indeed, fallibilism requires not only that we turn to community to resolve problematic situations, it also requires that we encounter those not like us and engage in dialogue assessing any fit which may help us imagine and anticipate new determinations, expanding the range of possible conclusions. The way in which this assumption requires an openness to difference is further suggested by the use of imagination in the process of ethical critique.

International ethics as pragmatic critique is fashioned, created, and shaped by the notion of imagination in pragmatism. The scope of the dilemma international ethics faces regarding value pluralism, and the difficulties and consequent impasse of attempts to isolate foundations for shared principles of international ethics, makes it clear that any conception of international ethics is one that must be constructed rather than found. In this regard, I find the notion of 'moral imagination', which Thomas Alexander (1993) attributes to Dewey, to be particularly compelling as a concept that can facilitate, along with fallibilism, a conception of international ethics.[22] Alexander writes that what pragmatism offers moral theory is a turn away from the modernist idea of obeying universal laws, a rule-oriented approach, to a focus upon the importance of moral imagination in the process of ethical thought and behaviour. Imagination in pragmatism is 'manifest as the *growth* and the *continuity* of meaning' (Alexander 1993: 371). He sees that, for Dewey, imagination is 'temporally complex' linking past, present and future 'so that a continuous process of activity may unfold in the most meaningful and value-rich way possible' (Alexander 1993: 386). By exploring the possibilities of a situation, imagination works to extend the environment of response,

---

[22] In this book, I will adopt Alexander's use of the term 'moral imagination'. The term is also employed by Johnson (1993), not only in reference to Dewey's theory of imagination, but in developing a comprehensive theory of moral reasoning.

transforming and enlarging the present context to anticipate development and growth. It thus has 'the central ability to generate new
values', according to Alexander (1993: 387). Imagination is social
activity which aims to discover 'new, integrative values' when con-
fronted with competing values in problematic, moral situations. In
addition, by its understanding of fallibilism, Pragmatism sees this as
an on-going, continual process. Thus, Alexander defines 'moral
imagination' in Deweyan pragmatism as acquiring a 'sensitivity to the
developmental meanings of events, which define the significance of
situations in which we find ourselves and the values they possess'
(1993: 390). Most importantly for the sensitivity necessary to the value
pluralism an international ethics must confront, it requires 'an ability
to understand the way other people think and live, and the ideal of
discovering through cooperative action solutions to conflicts . . . the
meanings at issue in a given situation' (Alexander 1993: 390).

Alexander argues that, in *CIS*, Rorty gives the role of imagination a
dimension not found before in Anglo-American theory in writing that
solidarity is to be 'achieved not by inquiry, but imagination, the
imaginative ability to see strange people as fellow sufferers. Solidarity
is not discovered by reflection, but created.'[23] Alexander understands
that imagination is central to the Rortyian project, but finds that what
Rorty can offer the idea of moral imagination is limited by the fact
that Rorty's only concern for imagination is in helping to continue
conversation, and avoiding pain and humiliation. For Alexander,
imagination is not seen by Rorty to serve the determination of difficult
situations, to transform social problems. This is not the first time
Rorty has been charged with a lack of concern for social reconstruction.[24] Alexander, like other critics of Rorty, takes his argument to be
that private self-creation cannot be reconciled with public, moral duty
under any circumstances (Alexander 1993: 378). However, this is not
the case. By dropping the public/private split, as suggested above,
Rorty can no longer be seen to be constrained in taking on the
political, or engaging with the moral problems he clearly has a will to
do. His turn to metaphor, vocabularies and language is out of a moral
concern that these tools can better defend and improve liberal democratic institutions than Dewey's appeal to experience and method.

---

[23] Alexander quoting from Rorty (1989a: xvi).
[24] For a sample even from fellow pragmatists see West (1989: 192–209) and Bernstein
(1991: 238–49, 283– 6).

Alexander finds this shift to language 'radical, irrational', and unable to offer a way of explaining how moral imagination works, or is educated, because metaphors and the new are regarded to be meaningless until they become literal, and entrenched in fixed habits. Thus, Alexander attributes to Dewey a workable theory of moral imagination, since its understanding of imagination as continuity in the process of capacities growing meaningfully can suggest how moral imagination develops and requires social expression.

Whether Rorty attributes meaninglessness to metaphors or not is in itself meaningless. The point is that there is a continuity in the process of imaginative, critical engagement in Rorty as well, which provides for the development of moral imagination. This is the Hegelian, dialectical side of Rorty, which suggests that as long as a tension is present within a culture, and meaninglessness itself can serve as that tension, then the process of critique and imagining moral possibilities is stimulated. Rorty sees that this process must connect with the public. While he finds that the determination of tensions benefits most from private creativity and irony, ultimately he understands that private determinations have a social element as well. They originate from a social need or doubt; and ultimately, for reasons of justice, must meet that public need or doubt. Like Dewey, Rorty cannot specify how this process of growth occurs, as it would require attributions to a human essence or fixed social requirements. He can only lay down what he believes to be necessary to useful cultural critique and moral imagination. Yet, without recourse to the public/private split, he will have to say more about the public, political conditions of this process as well as the private. I find that Rorty's most significant contribution to this concept of moral imagination is his stress on the role of language, literature and poetry in light of developments in analytic philosophy. It is up for question how Dewey might have responded to Kuhn, whether he too would have chosen to exchange experience for language in his idea of inquiry/critique/imagination. None the less, Dewey did find that the arts work to enlarge the responses of imagination to problematic situations, and saw the role they have to play in helping the public find and reconstruct itself as significant (1927: 182–4). He would certainly endorse the use of metaphor in Rorty's projection of moral imagination.

To conclude, this is what I find a synthesis of the work of Dewey and Rorty, under the heading of pragmatic critique, has to offer international ethics. It endorses the aim of the debate between cosmopolitans and communitarians in normative IR theory to go beyond the *modus vivendi* of the present understanding of relations between states, to suggest shared principles for further moral inclusion. However, it argues that this debate is going about it the wrong way, in an epistemologically centred way, which attempts to settle these principles as foundational knowledge claims. The impasse it has reached in this endeavour is a problem of its own making, which diminishes when one works to relinquish epistemologically centred philosophy. However, approaches aware of this problem, like pragmatic critique, must be careful not to replicate similar difficulties in the way they wield ontological priorities within their ethical projects. With this caution, what is left for international ethics is the task of cultural criticism. This critique is cultural in the sense that critique can only begin from the social context in which it originates, sparked by awareness of a doubt, need or tension which is regarded as problematic within this cultural context or situation. The process of transforming this problematic situation, the action taken or the metaphors used, is ethical. Its ethical significance requires that the tools employed – intelligence and imagination *via* whatever range of linguistic or scientific applications – and the judgements made, are the subject matter of critique as well. Because of the fallibility assumed in this whole process, ethics as critique is never ending. It can draw conclusions, but those conclusions have a shelf-life, the date of which runs out when change and contingency unsettle and make doubtful the conclusions reached.

The discomfort of this uncertainty bred into any determinations reached can, at the same time, enable those who call themselves liberals in IR – those who respect cultural diversity – to have a critical voice regarding the practices of varied, plural groups. The fallibilism assumed within pragmatic critique opens up new ways in which universals can be offered by liberals, who might otherwise be reluctant to breach liberal tolerance. They are free of ahistorical absolutes; and thus, facilitate dialogical communication with others not like us to imagine possible links or a fit between what the other has to offer and one's own situation, in order to yield more useful ways of coping with our world. The will to transcend our ethnocentrism is a will to expand human capacities, requiring us to engage with that which is different, extending our understanding of 'we'. Thus, considerations of justice in world politics cannot be seen as problems to do with *either* individuals *or* states/communities. The structural opposition of the cosmopolitan/communitarian debate is undermined. The line between one or the other form of moral responsibility is continually blurred by this process: a process of moral inclusion which sees this kind of growth to be the ethical principle it promotes. Although the process of this growth cannot be substantively detailed, pragmatic critique does stress the elements necessary to its continuity, primary among which is moral imagination. Also assumed is a faith in the progress of human capacities, that we all seek better means of coping, and that we turn to each other in our communities and to those beyond our communities in that process of improving critical intelligence. Thus, there are no guarantees. Pragmatic critique will be messy, and is by no means *the* solution to the difficulties of ethical judgement in international practice. The following chapters will further examine the contours of pragmatic critique and its capacity for unlocking the stasis of normative theory through a study of feminist ethical/political concerns. The first, chapter 7, will focus upon the theoretical possibilities of pragmatic critique for extending moral inclusion to women in international practice. The next, chapter 8, will examine the political and institutional implications of this engagement with feminism for facilitating the idea of growth at the base of pragmatic critique.

7 Facilitating moral inclusion: feminism and pragmatic critique

Introduction

In the previous chapter, I argued that a synthesis of the projects of John Dewey and Richard Rorty in an understanding of international ethics as pragmatic critique can effectively interrogate the epistemological impasse of the cosmopolitan/communitarian debate. Further, pragmatic critique shares the debate's central concern, the 'how' questions of moral inclusion and social reconstruction of world politics, and can offer constructive suggestions towards those goals. Now, it is the aim of this chapter and the next to demonstrate the ways in which a notion of international ethics as pragmatic critique can indeed be sufficiently political, critical and imaginative to provide for moral inclusion and social reconstruction in international practice.

To facilitate moral inclusion and social reconstruction requires that an approach not only be able to accommodate, but actually to promote, demands for justice and equality of marginalized individuals and groups in world politics. One such challenge offered from the margins of international practice is issued by women. Here, then, I will examine pragmatic critique's capacity for extending moral inclusion by examining whether it can help to further feminist ethical/political concerns. I choose to look at possibilities for facilitating feminist agendas rather than other marginalized groups in world politics – say along ethnic or racial lines – for two reasons. First, the body of work by Cornel West, another prominent contemporary advocate of the pragmatist tradition, locates interesting opportunities within this approach for addressing societal oppression and division on the basis of race and ethnicity (1987; 1988; 1989; 1993a; 1993b; and 1994). Although he often raises the question of oppression on gender lines as well, this is not the primary focus of his interest in developing the analysis. However, gender issues represent a significant concern that also requires exploration in order to make a case for the contemporary relevance of the pragmatist tradition. Clearly, Richard Rorty shares this belief. Rorty has started down the path of inquiring into the fit of pragmatism with feminist agendas in two articles: 'Feminism and Pragmatism' (1991a), and 'Feminism, Ideology, and Deconstruction: A Pragmatist View' (1993a). Feminists are also beginning to think through the prospects of such an alliance.[1] Thus, a good base for further exploration is in place.

Secondly, I develop a feminist case in order to make a specific point regarding a curious lacuna in normative IR theory. The question of how to address the claims of marginalized religious and ethnic groups is widely discussed within this literature.[2] However, any considered discussion and development of feminist concerns is missing from its central ethical debate. I will argue that both the dichotomous way in which cosmopolitan and communitarian positions are maintained, and the epistemological impasse of their deliberations, hinder their ability to respond to feminist ethical/political concerns.

The first section of the chapter examines what it means to talk about feminist ethical/political concerns or feminist agendas in order to see how well pragmatic critique can address these issues. Here, I briefly discuss the difficulties for feminists in articulating what is a 'feminist' concern, problems sparked by debates within feminist practice and politics, as well as in social science more generally. The second section discusses the limited interest shown by cosmopolitans, communitarians and feminists in developing feminist interpretations of the present debate in normative IR theory, and asks why this

---

[1] Fraser (1990) first raised the prospect of a productive alliance between pragmatism and feminism in offering her 'recipe' for a 'democratic-socialist-feminist pragmatism'. Since the publication of this piece by Fraser and the publication of Rorty's 1990 Tanner Lecture 'Feminism and Pragmatism', a number of articles and two special issues have appeared exploring the links between the two approaches. For the special issues see: *Transactions of the Charles Peirce Society* (1991), and *Hypatia: A Journal of Feminist Philosophy* (1993). For other articles see: Seigfried (1991) and Miller (1992).

[2] The claims of individuals and religious and ethnic groups to alternative forms of representation in international organizations, and in particular, their claims to sovereignty is a topic of much debate in normative IR literature. For a good example, see the exchanges between Luban (1985) and Walzer (1985). Also see Walzer (1994b) in which he considers other ways of accommodating the claims of minority groups than the granting of sovereignty.

213

failure has arisen. The answer offered is that the framework of the cosmopolitan/communitarian debate circumscribes its ability to address issues important to feminist agendas. I argue in the third section that pragmatist critique is not similarly circumscribed, and suggest that it can be a good discursive partner for feminists, furthering the demands for a wider incorporation of feminist problematizations of political practice. However, I do note that the capacity of pragmatic critique to be a good strategic partner in dismantling structures of social inequality is in some doubt. I will leave it to the following chapter to address these kinds of political and institutional considerations.

Articulating feminist ethical/political concerns

While there are numerous varieties of feminism – liberal, Marxist, socialist, radical, lesbian, black, phenomenological, psychoanalytic, postmodern – offering competing ideas of the character of gender relations and the sources of power operating within these relations,[3] Elizabeth Frazer and Nicola Lacey write that shared core concerns can be identified: '[w]e consider it sensible to say that all feminists are concerned with the oppression, subordination and exploitation of women as women; they are committed to understanding the nature, form and history of women's oppression, and to making an effort to dismantle it' (1993: 7). Of course, this is not the only articulation of common concerns within feminism. However, I choose to examine their formulation for two reasons: first, it is the starting point for their critical analysis of the liberal/communitarian debate, from which I will draw parallels for the debate in normative IR theory; and secondly, it is a recent formulation which takes account of the momentum of critical debates about modernity and postmodernity in social science and the way in which feminist approaches, as well as those of liberals and communitarians, are located within these debates. Frazer and Lacey explicitly address the implications of these critiques for their above claim by pointing out that the above formulation begs several questions: (1) the implications of the term 'women as women'; (2) the place of 'understanding' or theory in practice; and (3) the unity of feminist politics and tradition (1993: 7–12). I want to

---

[3] For overviews of these feminisms, see Jagger (1983). For a good collection of writings representative of these perspectives, see Tuang and Tong (1995).

take each of these questions in turn and discuss their consideration in feminist literature, because each touches upon important issues that link debates about competing feminisms, about foundational and antifoundational epistemologies in the modernity/postmodernity controversies of social science, and about the 'how' of extending moral inclusion in intersocietal practice.

Concerning 'women as women', Frazer and Lacey write that there are two contentious aspects to consider. The first regards explanation. In trying to explain gender inequality and to discuss strategies for change, are we necessarily committed to one particular theory of gender (Frazer and Lacey 1993: 7–9)? They point to the considerable number of disagreements between the varieties of feminism regarding explanations of gender inequality and the means of struggle. However, what should be noted here is that they raise *only* the question of one or more explanatory theories of gender; that is, whether feminist politics can be compatible with just one theory of gender when competing theories exist. While they rightly acknowledge the problems presented in recognizing plural and diverse feminisms – which is in line with the move away from universalizing, absolutizing tendencies in recent critiques of modernist discourses – they ignore another consequence of that critique: the problematization of the task of explanation. Because Frazer and Lacey argue that what is shared within feminism is 'the project of researching and discovering explanations for women's oppression' (1993: 9), they do not consider a recent development in feminist literature which takes up this aspect of postmodernist critique concerning the consensus on explanation, and challenges whether we should even be searching for one or more causal factors of women's oppression.[4] According to Michèle Barrett and Anne Phillips, the 'consensus' on the need to ask the causal questions regarding the sources of women's oppression has 'broken up' (1992: 2–4). Thus, in looking at this first contentious aspect of the 'women as women' question, there is more at issue than the question begged by competing theories of explanation. Although many feminisms share the common starting point that Frazer and Lacey identify, it can be argued that consideration is needed of another question potentially begged in Frazer's and Lacey's formulation: the very goal of explanation.

[4] For a sample of this literature, see the following collections: Barrett and Phillips (1992); Butler and Scott (1992); and Nicholson (1990).

215

The second problematic aspect regarding usage of the term 'women as women' that Frazer and Lacey identify concerns whether the idea of a feminist politics, issue or agenda implies that all women have something in common. Here, they argue, the question of essentialism is raised: is it possible to point to an identity that is 'woman'; an identity formed either upon the basis of biology, or socially constructed as a homogenous grouping? Frazer and Lacey write that in feminist politics, universalizable notions of what it is to be a woman, feminine, etc. have been associated with the notion that feminism and its identity of 'women as women' is a theoretical construct which serves white, heterosexual, middle class women only. While the charges of racism, sexism, and elitism in an understanding of 'women as women' has not put a halt to essentialist claims regarding women, Nancy Fraser and Linda Nicholson write that 'there is a growing interest among feminists in modes of theorizing that are attentive to differences and to cultural and historical specificity' (1988: 100). Frazer and Lacey reflect this interest in suggesting that what is required is a theory of identity that acknowledges the varied and plural aspects of the social construction of persons. They write that in any society, 'the definitions and expectations of what it means to be a woman will vary greatly, by race, by class, by status, by generation' (Frazer and Lacey 1993: 10). However, they do not find that this acknowledgement amounts to the idea of 'women as women' being useless simply because it may have no unitary content. Frazer and Lacey write that few categories have such content, yet the point is that

> [t]his experience, of being treated or acting as a woman, is only a part of one's total experience but is an element of experience which has particular social and political consequences, and which is only possible given a particular kind of social and political context (one in which gender is a structure). The undoubted reality of this structure, processual and fluid as it may be is the basis for feminism. (1993: 11)

Consequently, they find that the problems for feminism associated with essentialism are exaggerated (Frazer and Lacey 1993: 132).

In large part, an awareness of such problems has developed out of feminist practice. The need to think about the diversity of women's experiences arises from the plural voices in feminist politics and literature, women of different races and ethnicities, of different sexual orientations, of those poor and less well-off, who all talk about the ways in which a singular identity as 'woman' can marginalize and even do violence to those living alternative expressions of that identity. In addition, feminist attention has been drawn to the difficult questions raised by essentialism by critiques of modernist theorizing in the social sciences, especially critiques of the modernist understanding of the subject as centred or stable. These critics interested in feminism find that the diversity of identifications as women, and the diversity of identifications women have apart from being women, signals a need to problematize the ways in which we continue to offer up singular, universal notions of identity, subjectivity or a category 'women as women'. We need critically to examine the power imbued in such notions. For these feminists, essentialist talk about a subject or identity is hugely problematic, particularly one drawn from a notion of shared experience, since that experience is subject to varied interpretations. As much as we can talk about a self, it is a self that is radically decentred and fragmented.[5]

As noted above, Frazer and Lacey do not assume unity within the identity of 'women as women', yet they see no problem in continuing to use the category in an essentialist manner. They are able to come to this conclusion in a way that postmodernist feminists cannot, because they draw upon an idea of experience held in common by all women as foundational evidence. The appeal to the 'reality' that is the 'experience' of a category within a 'gendered structure' is used authoritatively to explain and provide the grounds for a common identity, even though the diversity of experience within that identity is admitted. Frazer and Lacey's conclusion cannot be arrived at from a postmodernist perspective, because it relies upon concepts of experience, reality, category, identity and structure in a way that does not fully acknowledge their constructedness and the problems generated in their regulative, uncontested usage. Postmodernist feminists would suggest that what Frazer and Lacey only regard as potentially begged in this second aspect of the 'women as women' question is indeed actually begged in the course of the claim that the problem of essentialism for feminism is exaggerated.

Frazer and Lacey write that the second problematic question begged by their formulation of the core concerns of feminism is the place of understanding and theory (1993: 11). They regard theory to be implicit in practice, and see that feminism relies upon an understanding, an

---

[5] For example, see Barrett in Barrett and Phillips (1992: 201–19) and Butler in Butler and Scott (1992: 3–21). Neither writer is suggesting that we do away with a concept of the self, only that we inquire into the multiple and varied ways in which it is constructed.

awareness, of particular practices having to do with sex or gender. Finally, they write that the third question potentially begged is that of unity (Frazer and Lacey 1993: 11–12). They assume that women can share interests and positions, and can organize struggles on the basis of those common interests, yet this does not mean that there has been, and will always be, one feminist movement. On the contrary, there are many such movements. Frazer and Lacey do not develop the implications of these last two questions, and it is the case that they are, on the whole, less problematic within the prevailing mood of social science discourses. In regard to the second question, those participant in modernist and postmodernist debates who would not go as far as to relinquish foundations and the will to explanation, are in the main prepared to concede the shakiness of fact/value or theory/practice distinctions. To say that theory is intertwined with practice and practice with theory is less controversial than was once the case. To say that feminism requires an understanding of particular practices having a gender character is not problematic for postmodernists, as long as that character of gender is not closed or laid down essentially, but is left open.[6] The third question reflects, in its suggestion of many feminisms, the 'growing interest' identified by Fraser and Nicholson in a theoretical approach that properly addresses difference, plurality and historicity. The implication of the third question, left undeveloped by Frazer and Lacey, is that what must be thought through carefully are the ways in which we talk about common recognitions and interests in problematic issues or situations, yet are attentive to diversity in the generalizing practice that is theory.

It is interesting that Frazer and Lacey are trying to have it both ways. By this I mean, on the one hand, they applaud the interpretivism that has issued into social science with the critique of objective knowledge justification in modernist epistemologies. This is evident in their recognition of the blurring of the theory/practice divide and the social construction of persons, and their willingness to theorize plurality, diversity and particularity in women's experiences and interests. However, on the other hand, they want to hold on to a form

[6] Sylvester provides for this as a possibility within her notion of a 'postmodern feminism' as distinguished from a 'feminist postmodernism' which would deny knowledge of self or gender or knowledge itself. However, one might argue that she is taming postmodern scepticism to enable gender analysis; in effect, having her cake and eating it too. Thus, I refer to her in note 24 below. See Sylvester (1994: 52–63).

of modernist ontology in order to have some purchase on a notion of social reality. They see that in the absence of any idea of a social reality in which gender inequality exists and can be pointed to, all that is left is relativism; that is, there is no base from which ethical/political claims across vocabularies can be made on the behalf of women. Thus, they want to defend what they call a 'modified realism', with a degree of 'openness to the possibility of realism on the ontological level . . . with respect to social structure and social relations' (Frazer and Lacey 1993: 184). This 'modified realism' is reflected in their nod to explanation and experience in the discussion of the questions potentially begged in their idea of a common core within feminism, and evident in the problems raised above from a postmodernist perspective, the ontology of which is anti-realist.

Since the 1980s, feminism, in its efforts to articulate women's ethical/political concerns, has faced a variant of Robert Frost's choice in his poem 'The Road Not Taken':

> Two roads diverged in a wood, and I -
> I took the one less travelled by,
> And that has made all the difference.

For feminists, one road through the wood is to pursue critique by examining the material conditions of women's oppression. That means having recourse to notions of social reality, macro social structures and experience, which have authoritative explanatory power, and provide the grounds for a distinctive concern and political movement called feminism. The other path pursues feminist critique discursively, as it denies recourse to a universal reality untouched by social context and interpretation. It is the abuse of meaning, not material, in subordinating women that feminist critique should focus upon. Yet, this approach loses an objective reality, a structure of inequality upon which feminist ethical claims can be founded. After centuries of realist ontology and foundationalist epistemology, the latter is the road less travelled by. However, Frost's choice of the less travelled road, which does indeed make all the difference, is not an easy option for feminists. It is not only a personal choice, but one laden with a sense of ethical responsibility to women and their concerns. While realism and objectivism have a proven track record of being largely uncritical of gender practices, and, indeed, for sustaining gender practices, questions of how we might make claims against women's suffering and oppression if we travel all the way down the

interpretivist road, unable to point to the material, institutional conditions of such domination, is in many respects more disturbing for
feminists. Frazer and Lacey are two among a number of feminists
aiming to construct a third road or middle path to feminist critique,
paying attention to both material, structural analysis and discursive,
interpretive analysis in articulating feminist agendas.[7] However, as
Frazer and Lacey are a case in point, such attempts have not moved
far beyond the stage of preliminary exploration. They, as well as many
varieties of feminism today, are still feeling their way through what
Fraser and Nicholson have called 'the *theoretical* prerequisites of
dealing with diversity' (1988: 100). Having discussed the difficulties in
articulating feminist ethical/political concerns, I will now turn to the
concomitant difficulties of thinking through feminist agendas within a
cosmopolitan/communitarian framework.

Feminism and the cosmopolitan/communitarian debate

Why are feminist concerns marginalized in normative IR theory? Is
there a lack of political and theoretical commitment to gender issues
on the part of cosmopolitans and communitarians? Or, is it something
else, perhaps a difficulty in the framework of the debate as it stands?
And why have feminist theorists shown so little interest in criticizing
this silence? Once again, it may be helpful to draw comparisons with
liberals and communitarians in political theory. In that debate, both
liberals and communitarians exert little or no intellectual energy to
address feminist ethical/political concerns.[8] Only two writers,
Michael Walzer and Rorty, explicitly discuss feminist issues (Frazer
and Lacey 1993: 159–60). The protagonists in the normative IR debate
perform no better on this score, and perhaps worse. While Rorty's
foray into a topic of IR concern, human rights, does discuss ways in
which women are excluded from 'true humanity' (1993b: 114), Walzer's work in IR does not explicitly develop gender concerns, nor does

---

[7] For other feminist writers working to link both structural and discursive, interpretive
approaches, see Fraser (1989 and 1995b); Hekman (1990 and 1995); Lovibond (1983
and 1992); and Sylvester (1994).

[8] This claim does not refer to writers such as Mouffe (1993), Okin (1989), Pateman
(1988) or Phillips (1991), whom I regard as feminist theorists interested in this debate.
However, it is worth noting that they could conceivably be regarded as participants in
the debate who engage with feminist ethical/political concerns.

the work of other writers typically associated with the cosmopolitan/communitarian debate. However, once again, Andrew Linklater stands out among this group as an exception. Linklater does not systematically develop feminist ethical/political concerns in his work, but it is important to note that he is attentive to feminist critiques and regards them as having an important role to play in incorporating and refining sensitivity to difference within discourse ethics (1998: 93–96). None the less, for the cosmopolitan writers in general, the idea that moral inclusion should be extended to women, as it should be to all persons, is implicit in their understanding that individuals must be the subject of justice. For the communitarians, it is implicit in, for example, Mervyn Frost's work that the freedom of all within the practice of a state, and within international practice, is compromised by the unfreedom of women in such practices, just as it would be by the unfreedom of anyone else within those practices. As I cannot imagine that ethical IR theorists would deny the importance of gender in their shared aim of extending moral inclusion, I must assume that their failure to discuss gender in any significant way means that they see no difficulty in incorporating feminist concerns into their theoretical frameworks. However, I want to argue that there *are* problems in the framework of the debate itself that limit its capacity to address feminist ethical/political concerns. This may also provide some indication as to why feminists in IR have not taken an active interest in normative IR theory debates.[9] Since there is a considerable body of feminist literature that critically engages the debate between liberals and communitarians in political theory, my task will be assisted by a brief look at the arguments found there.[10]

Within this literature, there is agreement that structural difficulties exist in the assumptions of both liberals and communitarians that make it difficult to incorporate gender issues. In regard to liberalism, Frazer and Lacey contend that several value assumptions in this tradition are problematic from a feminist perspective: for example, its

[9] I can only point to two writers who explicitly discuss cosmopolitan and communitarian positions from a feminist perspective: Robinson (1996 and 1997) and Hutchings (1994). Granted, the cosmopolitan/communitarian debate is a recent formulation of the issues at stake in normative IR theory. None the less, it remains striking how little has been written in the way of feminist readings of this debate.

[10] This discussion draws largely from Frazer and Lacey (1993); Friedman (1993); and Hekman (1995). Additional critical, feminist literature on positions within this debate include: Mouffe (1993);Okin (1989); Pateman (1988); and Phillips (1991).

concepts of the person and of freedom; its emphasis on rationality, state neutrality and the priority of the right over the good; and its metaphor of contract and use of public/private distinctions (Frazer and Lacey 1993: 53– 74).[11] However, of these, feminists focus most of their critical attention on the first, upon liberalism's assumption of abstract individualism, from which all other value preferences flow (Frazer and Lacey 1993: 100; Friedman 1993: 231; and Hekman 1995: 50). This is the notion of the pre-social individual: transcendent, unified, unencumbered and non-embodied. According to Frazer and Lacey, such an understanding of the self inhibits the incorporation of gender concerns for several reasons: first, as the person is disembodied, liberalism is unable to address gender exploitation, since such exploitation is largely associated with the body; second, liberal individualism inhibits a capacity to think critically about social institutions and relations, such as gender, class or race; and finally, its individualism hinders new ways of accounting for society that incorporate important aspects of social stability, change and meaning in thinking about traditions (1993: 54). Susan Hekman and Marilyn Friedman stress that gender gets left out because the liberal concept of the person lacks any understanding of characteristics such as care, nurturance, connection or mutual interestedness, which are generally associated with women (Hekman 1995: 50 and Friedman 1993: 232). These conceptual difficulties in liberalism indicate to a number of feminists the need for an understanding of the person as socially connected and constituted rather than atomized.

Feminists recognize the obvious parallels with the communitarian critique of liberalism here. However, here too they find that assumptions within the communitarian position inhibit the incorporation of feminist ethical/political concerns. For Frazer and Lacey, what is most troubling from a feminist perspective is the conservatism inherent in communitarianism; that is, its inability to produce genuine political critique. They attribute this to two aspects of communitarianism. First, its 'thoroughgoing social constructivism' denies women effective agency to articulate critique, since persons are largely determined by social structures. Secondly, its commitment to public values or 'value communitarianism' means that it does not have the wherewithal to be critical of the communities that are the source of those values, and

---

[11] The writers stress that liberalism is clearly a diverse tradition, however, they find that these values are generally shared within the tradition.

there are no guarantees that the critical evaluation of tradition will be among those public values (Frazer and Lacey 1993: 137–42).[12] Similarly, Friedman argues that political critique is hindered within communitarianism. She provides a further illustration of the difficulties in this regard by making three points: first, that communitarianism assumes that the selves created by communities are good, offering no means for saying that some selves are better or worse than others; secondly, that it says nothing about the illegitimate moral claims that communities can make on their members; and finally, that it is uncritical of the communities they invoke as their models – families, neighbourhoods and nations – which are associations with social roles that contribute to women's subordination (Friedman 1993: 237–42).[13] These writers agree that, although there are lines of argument that feminists have in common with communitarians regarding the self as being socially constituted and values being generated out of communal attachments, to take an unmodified communitarianism as an ally of feminism in theory and practice would be a dangerous strategy (see Friedman 1993: 233).

Regarding the liberal/communitarian debate as a whole, Hekman draws three conclusions from a feminist perspective. The first regards epistemology and makes three points. To begin, women are bankrupt of a moral identity, having only a choice between the 'masculinist, disembodied subject of liberalism or the subordinated, determined subject' of the communitarians. Secondly, this unacceptable choice stems from its grounding in a dichotomizing modernist discourse; that is, it sets up misleading oppositions between two positions that are mutually dependent, the individual and community, with harmful repercussions for women. Finally, she argues that it is futile for

---

[12] Frazer and Lacey also point to questions ignored by communitarians as further evidence of difficulties within their framework. For example, membership and power: how do subordinate groups within communities gain power and what about power between communities and between self and society? They also mention problems in the communitarian social ontology regarding its account of critical consciousness, the subject and community, and finally, that the communitarians ask nothing about gender itself. All of these concerns resonate with the central problem stated above: how is effective critique from a feminist perspective possible in a communitarian framework.

[13] Hekman (1995: 56–58) is also concerned about the possibility of critique from a communitarian position, however, she is concerned to make a somewhat different point about how communitarianism does not provide effective critique of the liberal individualism that is the target of feminist concern.

feminists to argue within the epistemological framework of this debate, as its oppositional nature will remain intact. What is required is a 'move to a different epistemological space', that does not operate along the absolutist or foundationalist lines that dominate modernist moral thinking, even so far as to provide a subtext for those relativists made to feel they have to defend their positions (Hekman 1995: 60–61).[14] Hekman's second conclusion concerns what feminists see as a serious omission within this debate: the question of power. She finds this neglect is particularly dangerous on the part of communitarians, who draw references to a 'we' that operates as *the* moral discourse within community (Hekman 1995: 61).[15] Thirdly, she concludes that the aim of modernist moral thought to found universal moral principles means that 'particular constituents of moral subjectivity' are overlooked in the attempt to articulate concepts of the self that are universalizable, either by being personally chosen or by being constituted by a particular, yet singular, unitary entity called community.

After this introduction to feminist critiques of the liberal/communitarian debate, I will now compare and contrast the difficulties that feminists have located in this political theory debate with those I find in cosmopolitan and communitarian argument within normative IR theory. To begin, I must raise a point of difference between myself and two writers who have employed feminist critiques of this debate in political theory to highlight the limitations of the cosmopolitan/communitarian debate. Both Kimberly Hutchings and Fiona Robinson begin with an assumption about moral theory in IR that I do not share. They begin from the starting point that the predominant moral view in IR is that of a morality of states which is liberal. States have moral personality in ways quite like individuals in liberal thought, and similarly, this moral view in IR prioritizes abstractness, autonomy, impersonality and impartiality (Hutchings 1994: 24–5; Robinson 1996: 21; Robinson 1997: 116–18). The implication of this is that neither cosmopolitanism nor communitarianism, which they regard to be symptomatic of this moral point of view, is a satisfactory moral theory. For Robinson, this moral view concerns 'minimal principles surrounding notions of state sovereignty and noninterference' that may be too narrow to deal with the moral demands of global practice,

---

[14] On the third point, Hekman is addressing Friedman who wants to reformulate communitarianism to be better suited to feminist concerns. Like Hekman, Frazer and Lacey aim to move beyond both liberalism and communitarianism.

[15] Frazer and Lacey (1993: 100) make a similar point about the debate as a whole.

increasingly influenced by globalization (1996: 21). For Hutchings, the abstractness and impartiality of these moral theories means that women, who 'are even further removed than most men from the regulation of state policies', have virtually no place in international ethics debates (1994: 25). My disagreement is not with where Hutchings and Robinson end up – the conclusion that we must look beyond the cosmopolitan/communitarian debate to theories that *can* incorporate gender – but with their assumption that feminist critiques of liberal theory map on to cosmopolitans and communitarians in much the same way.

The moral point of view that they attribute to cosmopolitans and communitarians is one which I find normative IR theorists actually to be taking to task. That is not to say that this debate is not concerned with states, sovereignty and practical issues like noninterference, but it is to say that cosmopolitans and communitarians in fact want to *challenge* the idea of morality that generally results from such considerations in IR: the ethics of coexistence. This is another label for what Hutchings and Robinson refer to as IR's moral point of view. Terry Nardin (1983) articulates the ethics of coexistence position, which he associates with international society theorists, that all there can be in IR is practical, not purposive association. In contrast, as the Introduction noted, I understand cosmopolitans and communitarians to be inquiring into the foundations upon which international ethics can move beyond the mere *modus vivendi* of an ethics of coexistence towards relations of ethical commitment and responsibility and expanding moral inclusion.[16] Cosmopolitans seek this on the grounds of a moral community of mankind. Communitarians cannot see the possibility of community being extended to humanity, but seek other bases for improved moral relations between communities. I think it is important to begin with this distinction regarding our differences on the starting point attributable to cosmopolitans and communitarians, because it has implications for how one approaches feminist critique of this debate. Robinson (1997: 117) uses Nardin and Mapel (1992) to establish a connection between liberal values and moral thinking in

---

[16] By this I do not mean to suggest that ethical considerations beyond a *modus vivendi* are not possible from the context of the international society tradition. Clearly, as mentioned in note 3 of the Introduction, writers are working within this tradition to bring out and develop its more solidarist elements. See also Wheeler (1992); Dunne and Wheeler (1996); and Keene (1998). However, these are not, as yet, dominant understandings of the international society tradition.

IR, but what I aim to demonstrate below is that this reflects a limited understanding of the aims of normative IR theory and the movements of late within its central debate. At first glance, cosmopolitan and communtarian positions may appear vulnerable to most feminist charges against liberal rights-speak. However, neither cosmopolitanism nor communitarianism can simply be regarded as variants of liberalism that are generally subject to the same feminist critiques of that tradition. On further examination from the perspective of feminist ethical/political concerns, it is *less* on the bases of the above critiques suggested by Hutchings and Robinson that cosmopolitan and communitarian argument is found wanting, and *more* on the grounds of feminist critiques of modernist epistemologies (including that of liberalism) that normative IR theory can be seen as stymied.

I want to illustrate this point by using Brian Barry's characterization of the essence of liberalism as 'the vision of society as made up of independent, autonomous units who cooperate only when the terms of cooperation are such to make it further the ends of each of the parties' (1973: 166). This characterization of liberalism also serves as a good characterization of what Hutchings and Robinson understand as IR's moral point of view or the ethics of coexistence position. To begin, there is an ontological claim in this characterization of liberalism regarding a pre-social self, the 'independent and autonomous' unit. However, as suggested in part I of the book, there is only one cosmopolitan who maintains this understanding of an unencumbered self: Charles Beitz. In the main, cosmopolitanism has moved on to an understanding of the self as both personally chosen and socially constructed. Also, the book has argued that communitarians in IR work on a similar assumption of the self. Thus, feminist critiques of the liberal concept of the self in political theory do not hold in the same way for normative IR theory; in fact, the idea of the self that normative IR theory has *moved towards* is closer to the kind of balance feminists seek in an understanding of the self as socially embedded, yet not so much so as to deny agency.

Following from this ontological claim are assumptions about freedom, rationality and the nature of relations between the units. While a similar regard for rationality is evident among cosmopolitans, their understanding of freedom and the nature of relations among international actors is different from that of both liberal political theory and its manifestation in mainstream IR theory. The understanding of freedom that generally flows from a notion of the units being independent and autonomous is negative freedom. It is a freedom defined by rights which protect individuals from the illegitimate powers of the state in domestic polities and which make illegitimate the interference in the affairs of one state by other states in international politics. Cosmopolitans do share a concern for rights of resistance on the part of individuals in their arguments against the moral standing of states, however, they have an understanding of positive freedom as well. That is, cosmopolitans see a connection or relatedness among humans in their capacity for reason and moral judgement that places moral obligations between them. This leads to an alternative understanding of the nature of relations between the units, be they individuals or other international actors, as relations moving beyond conflict and cooperation regarding competing ends and interests, to relations which fulfil the rights and obligations owed to our fellow humans. As for communitarianism in normative IR theory, it too holds both negative and positive understandings of freedom: negative, in its claims for the territorial integrity and political sovereignty of states; and positive, in its understanding of persons as socially constituted and ultimately connected in sharing ethical traditions. This latter understanding of positive freedom, of persons finding self-realization in their relations with other persons, justifies for communitarians the claims for negative freedom in the realm of the international. However, communitarianism in IR does not translate into the idea of liberalism characterized above. States are *not* necessarily like individuals in liberal theory, meaning that relations between the independent units known as states provides at best the ethical minimum of cooperation and coexistence in balancing ends and interests. It is true that communitarians harbour more doubt than cosmopolitans about the possibility of locating universal principles of moral obligation that reach across communities. None the less, they seek grounds for ethical responsibility in IR. Walzer offers a notion of thin morality with universal scope, and Frost develops the idea of an international practice in which we all participate and are constituted.

Finally, there is also an epistemological claim in this understanding of liberalism: that its content works foundationally and has universal application in political practice. As the book has argued, normative IR theory is also based upon a foundationalist epistemology. Cosmopolitans and communitarians in normative IR theory share this with both liberals and communitarians in political theory. In my view, this is one of the most potent criticisms that feminists wield against liberalism which is applicable and relevant to normative IR theory. I will develop this point further below.

I want to clarify that while I do not agree that the feminist critiques of liberal political theory that Hutchings or Robinson choose to apply to cosmopolitanism and communitarianism are the most hard-hitting, I do want to argue that normative IR theory is subject to criticisms that overlap with the conclusions Hekman draws regarding the liberal/communitarian debate in political theory. In addition to the epistemological critique, another formidable criticism is that the question of power is not adequately addressed within normative IR theory. This does not mean that discussion of power is absent from the debate. Cosmopolitans are clearly concerned about the illegitimate power wielded by states and other international actors against individuals. While communitarians see the power of state authorities, in the main, to be legitimate within the community that is the state, they are, however, concerned about the abuse of power between states such that respect for these moral communities is violated. None the less, these writers are not interested in pursuing a line of inquiry which seeks to locate and identify structures of power that either materially or discursively regulate and control intersocietal practices. As discussed above, this is clearly a significant concern for feminists.

Of particular concern to the argument of this book is the point that the framework of the debate is epistemologically problematic for feminists. While, in normative IR theory, women are not offered as stark a choice between the pre-social liberal self and the determined communitarian self of political theory, they do confront a debate that maintains dichotomies, since the cosmopolitan/communitarian debate is caught up in a modernist discourse concerned to ground ethical claims foundationally. As a consequence, women get left out of ethical debate in IR because of the structure of opposition upon which this framework is based, and because of the epistemological impasse over how to justify ethical claims.

To illustrate the first point, I will begin with the fundamental claim of cosmopolitanism. There is a very basic difficulty that inhibits the incorporation of feminist ethical/political concerns in cosmopolitanism: it aims to articulate the idea of moral obligations among humankind founded in the understanding that all individuals are equal by virtue of their moral capacities. This presents a difficulty since feminism is expressly concerned with the subordination of one group in particular: women. For some feminists, this means that the standpoint of women should be privileged in order to correct gender inequalities (Frazer and Lacey 1993: 128). Generally speaking, cosmopolitanism cannot sanction the privileging of one subset of humanity over other subsets, although I would suspect that the 'wrongful exclusion' of women in the past may meet Linklater's condition of justification that, as he writes in *TPC*, is necessary to any exclusionary practices (1998: 90 and 101). However, increasingly feminists are refusing to privilege gender over other significant social relations, arguing that relations of subordination of all forms have much to learn and gain from each other in ameliorating their conditions. This position is more readily assimilated into cosmopolitanism, as there is the shared aim of building more just social relations for all people. None the less, these feminists, simply in order to distinguish themselves as feminists, cannot help but prioritize a subset of values with particular relevance to women, which remains problematic and requires justification according to cosmopolitanism's foundational premise. Consequently, women as a distinctive concern are made invisible in cosmopolitan thought.

The foundational premise of communitarianism holds that bases of ethical judgement arise from the traditional practices of community and bond members of that community in ethical relationships with one another. The incorporation of feminist ethical/political concerns within communitarianism is obstructed by this foundational premise because communitarians do not see gender as constitutive of a 'real' community as such. By 'real' community, I do not simply mean that we cannot point to a state or community made up exclusively of women. I mean that the kind of bonds built upon language, culture and tradition, significant enough to generate mutual interestedness and ethical principles in communities, cannot be constructed upon gender association, at least so far as communitarians are concerned. As Friedman writes, communitarians are unable to conceive of gender as a social relationship, much less as one that can constitute communities (1993: 236). As a result, communitarians also fail to theorize gender.

Therefore, cosmopolitanism and communitarianism are locked in an opposition that structurally has little capacity to theorize gender. In effect, this dichotomy of an either/or choice between the two positions offers feminists no choice. Yet, the absence of gender is compounded by another element of the debate: the debate is firmly planted in modernist, foundationalist epistemology. As the above discussion of the difficulty in articulating feminist ethical/political concerns demonstrates, feminists are divided over how to proceed: whether to attempt to point to a reality that can work foundationally to ground epistemological concerns, whether to abandon foundationalist argument altogether, or to find a middle path between the two. The jury is still out on this question for feminists. However, the important point is that *it is a question within feminism*, because feminist theory is open and attentive to the wider debates regarding modernity and post-modernity in the social sciences. Normative IR theory can be of no assistance to feminists if it proceeds as if the Pandora's box of questioning foundationalist epistemologies had never been opened. Thus, the cosmopolitan/communitarian debate cannot help feminists as they try to work through these kinds of questions. This may explain feminists' general lack of interest in normative IR theory. For writers like Hutchings and Robinson who *have* engaged with this literature, the difficulties I indicate in the structure of its opposition and its epistemology support their call for a move beyond the cosmopolitan/communitarian debate in normative IR theory.

Feminism and pragmatism: good partners?

There is a good base of literature upon which to draw in thinking about whether pragmatism can assist feminist agendas. Charlene Haddock Seigfried writes that she is 'convinced that pragmatist theory has resources for feminist theory untapped by other approaches and that feminism, in turn, can uniquely reinvigorate pragmatism' (1991: 2). Themes in pragmatism useful to feminism, according to Seigfried, include: the critique of positivism in scientific methodology; the linking of fact and value; emphasis upon the aesthetic in experience, locating domination in discourse; a focus on social, cultural and political issues over logical analysis; reorienting theory to practice; and turning away from epistemology to prioritize experience (1991: 5).[17] It is important to note here that Seigfried is

---

[17] It is interesting to compare and contrast the common features to feminism Seigfried (1991: 7) offers to those offered by Frazer and Lacey: (1) to identify and investigate the structures of women's oppression and to dismantle them, and (2) to develop analyses of women's experience that are not biased by gendered assumptions. Lost here is the emphasis on explanation, but shared is an understanding of structures of domination, the need to identify those structures, and the emphasis on experience. Below, I will be discussing how pragmatism can help feminists think through the ways we can usefully draw from experience.

referring more generally to what classical pragmatism has to offer feminism, rather than the neo-pragmatism of Rorty as such. This is evident in her reference to prioritizing experience rather than language in the turn away from epistemology. I will begin by making a few introductory remarks about what I think a pragmatism consistent with both Dewey and Rorty can offer feminism. Then I will turn to a discussion of Rorty's engagement with feminism and the responses of feminists to that work. There is much to recommend in Rorty's argument that pragmatism can assist feminist agendas, but again, elements which suggest the need for a pragmatist synthesis discussed in the last chapter, particularly his privileging of language, also hold problems for feminists in articulating their ethical/political concerns. The synthesis offered here in the notion of international ethics as pragmatic critique can facilitate the moral inclusion of women and issues of concern to them. Most importantly, this is because pragmatic critique can be of assistance in thinking through the dilemma feminists have today, regarding how to proceed when one wants recourse to ethical/political judgement to reconstruct social relations of inequality, while recognizing the force of critiques of foundational epistemology which once grounded that kind of judgement.

A pragmatism that blends the projects of Rorty and Dewey has many strengths that feminists can appreciate. In the main, these strengths follow from its critique of traditional philosophy and the tendencies in philosophy toward abstraction and absolutism. There are several aspects of this critique to consider. First, it challenges dichotomous thinking, and zeroes in on the same dichotomies feminists attack: subject/object, reason/emotion, theory/practice and fact/value. Secondly, it highlights the regulative and dominating force of philosophical concepts such as reason and objectivity, concepts which have regulated gender relations in particular. Third, and perhaps most significant for the recent debates in feminist theory discussed above, it relinquishes the absolutizing, foundationalist epistemology of traditional philosophy to think in ways that are alert to difference and to cultural and historical specificity, without losing its will to ethics and unity in expanding moral inclusion. While sharing this aim of a reconstructed understanding of philosophy, tensions within the pragmatism of Dewey and Rorty remain as to the 'how' of moving away from epistemologically centred thinking, just as they do for feminists now. The kind of difficulties faced within pragmatism on this score can be instructive for feminism (and vice versa, as will be discussed

231

below). I believe that the synthesis suggested here may be of particular interest to those feminists working to construct that 'third road' through the epistemological wood.

Rorty's feminism

To illustrate what a synthesis under the banner of international ethics as pragmatic critique can do to assist the moral inclusion of women in theory and practice, I will begin by examining the efforts of Rorty to make pragmatist overtures to feminists.[18] Rorty states that the central problem for feminists, as he understands Catherine MacKinnon to frame it, is that ' "a woman" is not yet the name of a way of being human – not yet the name of a moral identity, but, at most, the name of a disability' (Rorty 1991a: 234). According to Rorty, this is a sign that there is not enough space for moral deliberation because human possibilities are being closed down. For Rorty, to project 'unrealized possibilities' is to prophesize, but to do so requires that we stop positing a 'moral reality', measuring the degree to which such a reality is accurately perceived in making moral claims. What is needed is a redescription of this notion of moral progress such that new moral space can be created for women to articulate a moral identity (Rorty 1991a: 234). Pragmatism facilitates this by dropping 'the appearance-reality distinction in favour of a distinction between beliefs which serve some purposes and beliefs which serve other purposes – for example, the purposes of one group and those of another group' (Rorty 1991a: 234). The idea of an absolute, unchanging reality in realism and universalism restricts moral space, and can be wielded to label groups which try to alter the boundaries of that moral space as 'crazies' who aim to distort moral reality. Rorty understands feminists to be one such group labelled as the 'crazies'. He writes that unless one is prepared to resort to violent means, only prophecy – voices proposing undreamt of possibilities – can break the

---

[18] Fraser writes in 'From Irony to Prophecy to Politics: A Response to Richard Rorty', *Michigan Quarterly Review*, 30:2 (1991: 259), that she feels as though Rorty is addressing feminists 'as a suitor with a marriage proposal'. It certainly could be read that way; and to carry the metaphor further, one can also see how Rorty might have read that Fraser herself had been dropping hints that such a proposal would be found desirable by feminists when she writes with Nicholson (1990:100) that feminists want to find modes of theorizing that are attentive to difference and to historical, cultural specificity.

kind of moral retrenchment that feminists are fighting (Rorty 1991a: 235).

Deweyan pragmatism, 'linguistified', can accommodate the prophetic voices of feminists as well as offer them several dialectical advantages: (1) freeing them from the need for a general theory of oppression; (2) dropping the essentialism of universalist claims about the terms 'human being' and 'woman'; and (3) giving up endless debates about how to represent 'women's experience' accurately (Rorty 1991a: 238). What the pragmatist feminist does is *create*. Instead of describing or explaining women and their experiences more accurately or foundationally, the pragmatist feminist imagines women and their experiences by 'creating a language, a tradition and an identity' (Rorty 1991a: 238). Rorty hopes that feminists will take up this role and give up on ideas that 'the subordination of women is *intrinsically* abominable', or that ' "right" or "justice" or "humanity" which has always been on their side', makes their claims true; and indeed, Rorty feels encouraged in that he understands contemporary feminism to be moving this way (1991a: 237). However, Rorty wants to take up two objections that might be raised against a pragmatist feminism: (1) that it is inherently conservative and *status quo* oriented; and (2) that if you claim that women should be created rather than freed, then you must be saying that women do not fully exist (1991a: 238–9).

To make appeals to community practices such as language or tradition raises charges of conservatism, similar to the feminist critiques of communitarianism discussed above, because they undermine the potential for any kind of radical ethical/political critique. A pragmatist cannot begin from anything else but the practices of community, yet this does not mean that critique is circumscribed. It simply means that when such practices are in need of radical critique, as prophetic feminists suggest, critique takes 'the form of imagining a community whose linguistic and other practices are different from our own', with the result that we value liberation movements 'not for the accuracy of their diagnoses but for the imagination and courage of their proposals' (Rorty 1991a: 239). Rorty notes that many feminists see liberalism as a political movement incapable of praiseworthy imagination and courage; but while he recognizes the phenomenon of power begetting power that feminists point out, he does not see that liberalism, or pragmatism for that matter, is the right label for it (1991a: 240). He refers to Dewey, who regarded himself as a liberal and a pragmatist to illustrate this point. Rorty understands Dewey's political project to be about creating the kind of moral space that feminists require, and is indeed capable of doing so precisely because it gives up on appeals to reality and turns to imagination and creation (1991a: 242). He quotes from one of the few passages where Dewey discusses women which reads:

> [w]omen have as yet made little contribution to philosophy, but when women who are not mere students of other persons' philosophy set out to write it, we cannot conceive that it will be the same in viewpoint or tenor as that composed from the standpoint of the different masculine experience of things . . . As far as what is loosely called reality figures in philosophies, we may be sure that it signifies those selected aspects of the world which are chosen because they lend themselves to the support of men's judgement of the worthwhile life, and hence are most highly prized. In philosophy, 'reality' is a term of value or choice. (Dewey as quoted in Rorty 1991a: 241)

Rorty writes that, by virtue of Dewey's idea of the means-end continuum, he sees that Dewey would be led to add that 'in the process of selecting a reality', a person cannot choose his or her goals on the grounds of an irrefutable reality, but only through a process of 'courageous and imaginative experimentation' that works to 'make invidious comparisons between the actual present and a possible, if inchoate, future' (Rorty 1991a: 242). Rorty recognizes that giving up an appeal to reality is troubling, since it can yield 'plenty of assent-commanding descriptions'; however, the problem of realism and universalism is that their descriptions of reality cannot provide what feminists need: moral space to create a moral identity as women (1991a: 242).

In regard to the second possible objection – his suggestion that women are only now coming into existence – some feminists may want to argue that women have always existed, but they have simply been denied the ability to express the essence of that existence. Rorty responds that he understands feminists such as MacKinnon and Marilyn Frye to be saying that only now are women starting to find a moral identity as women. He finds that the newness in this is suggested by the fact that, not long ago, for women to suggest that they found moral identity in being women would be 'as weird as for a slave to say that he or she finds his or her moral identity in being a slave' (Rorty 1991a: 243). Moral identity for pragmatists is not a fixed, essential identity that persons have had for time immemorial, but instead is 'a matter of degree' which varies in different contexts of time and place. Thus, Rorty writes that pragmatists 'have to identify most of the wrongness of past male oppression with the suppression of past potentiality, rather than in its injustice to past actuality' (1991a: 244). So, what makes the task of expressing this potentiality easier? For Rorty, having a club or some such community is most important. He reads Frye as saying that individuals need a shared practice in order to 'achieve semantic authority, *even semantic authority over themselves*' (Rorty 1991a: 247). He agrees. What Rorty sees the contemporary feminist movement as doing is playing the same role as other clubs (Plato's academy, early Christians meeting in catacombs, Copernican colleges, etc.) which have issued in moral progress: to test 'new ways of speaking, and to gather the moral strength to go out and change the world' (1991a: 247). There are no guarantees, but 'with luck' the new languages formed in separatist groups will be assimilated into the language everyone speaks such that larger society is changed for it, having learned to incorporate the identities gays, blacks and women create for themselves (Rorty 1991a: 249). In conclusion, Rorty sums up his position regarding a pragmatist feminism as this: '[f]eminists who are also pragmatists will not see the formation of such a society as the removal of social constructs and the restoration of how things were meant to be. They will see it as the production of a better set of social constructs than the ones presently available' (Rorty 1991a: 250).

Feminists respond to Rorty

While Rorty anticipates criticism from feminists who do not share his idea of the trajectory of contemporary feminism, and he attempts to respond to those criticisms, there remain feminists who are unconvinced of pragmatism's appeal (Bickford 1993; Fraser 1990; Frazer and Lacey 1993: 144–8 and 156–62; Fritzman 1993; Hekman 1995: 155–7; Kaufman-Osborn 1993; Leland 1988; Lovibond 1992). While these writers have different points of emphasis in their critique of Rorty's pragmatist feminism, I want to suggest there are three central criticisms being made: (1) that Rorty is not sufficiently political; (2) that Rorty's discussion of a moral identity as women has difficulties; and (3) that power within community is not problematized.

Fraser raised the first criticism as a substantial concern with Rorty's work before he wrote 'Feminism and Pragmatism'. She argues that the public/private split in his work assigns radical theorizing to the private realm such that all that remains for the public, political realm is conformism and solidarity of the purest form. Thus, politics, in effect, is 'detheorized' (Fraser 1990: 314–15) However, in 'Feminism and Pragmatism', Fraser sees that private and public do meet for Rorty, that social cleavages in the public realm are recognized, and that redescription – Rorty's form of radical critique – is a tool available to 'oppositional political solidarities' (Fraser 1991: 261–2).[19] None the less, Fraser finds that Rorty is still not adequately political. She agrees with Rorty on the role of feminists in creating new moral identities, sees redescription as important to this and, thus, rejects realism and universalism. Yet, she wants to 'put a more sociological, institutional, collective spin on these ideas to divest his account of its individualistic, aestheticizing, and depoliticizing residues' (Fraser 1991: 263). Fraser is concerned that Rorty does not tell us enough about the 'how' of getting from 'Prophecy to Politics'. She wants more material analysis and attention to social structures of inequality than Rorty appears willing to give.[20] While Fraser is not very explicit about the materiality she demands, other critics are more explicit on this point, and suggest that what is required is something like Frazer and Lacey's call for a modified realism: an understanding of reality as interpretive, in order for politics to be possible. For these critics, Rorty remains insufficiently political because he allows for no material bases of discrimination or judgement in order to make political decisions. Thus, all that remains are power struggles among groups over semantic authority. These writers maintain that we must appeal to notions of reality, social structure and experience, however historical. Dorothy Leland writes that while there may be no ahistorical criterion of appeal for deciding social and political questions, there must be

---

[19] Fraser is attempting to make a 'two Rorties' argument here: that there is the 1980s pre-'Feminism and Pragmatism' Rorty, and a post-'Feminism and Pragmatism' Rorty. Thus, thinking about feminism has had a major impact upon his thought. In arguing, as I have in the book, that it is evident as far back as *Consequences of Pragmatism* that public and private do meet for Rorty, I, do not want to say that thinking about feminism has not had a major influence upon Rorty's thought. I only want to say that it has led him to draw out and illuminate, in a way he had not before, how he sees the process of radical critique unfolding in the public sphere. I am not necessarily convinced by Fraser's 'two Rorties' thesis.

[20] Rorty (1991a: 253, 15n) writes in response to Fraser and Nicholson (1988: 90) that he is 'less sure about the need for, and utility of, "social-theoretical analysis of large-scale inequalities" than are Fraser and Nicholson'.

more than 'the hubris of Rortyish ethnocentric appeals' (1988: 281). She feels that feminists are heading down the right path, working towards a 'critique which arises when oppressed persons begin to recognize the disparity between extant vocabularies and the *reality* of their lives.' (Leland 1988: 281, emphasis added). Sabina Lovibond writes that there is 'nothing in Rorty's historicist contentions about language that would justify his disdain for the intuitive contrast between appearance and reality' (1992: 65). The only problem with using terms like 'right' and 'reality' is when they are used regulatively (Lovibond 1992: 60). She finds that realism and universalism can be properly 'historicist' and 'humble' in their assumptions as long as notions of 'truth' and 'reality' reflect their 'everyday use' and 'how things are *irrespective of whether or not they are currently believed to be so*' (Lovibond 1992: 64–5). Timothy Kaufman-Osborn writes that, in contrast to Rorty, he maintains that a notion of 'experience' is indispensable to feminist politics (Kaufman-Osborn 1993: 125). He finds that discourse and experience cannot be conflated, yet argues that the relationship between the two is 'problematic' and 'paradox-ical' (Kaufman-Osborn 1993: 141). However, he concludes that 'think-ing always remains inadequate until re-fused within the questionable sea of experience', and the meaning of any emancipatory discourse is, in part, 'contingent on its dialectical relationship with non-discursive experience' (Kaufman-Osborn 1993: 141). In sum, these writers are troubled that Rorty is unable and unwilling to offer any assurances that feminist ethical/political concerns will enter into the political fray of the dominant discourse, that the new moral language feminists offer will not be just one more discourse, neither more nor less deserving, in a power struggle among discourses.

The second criticism is that there are difficulties in Rorty's discus-sion of a moral identity for women. There are two aspects to the critique here: the first makes a philosophical point, the other an empirical point. Lovibond implies that there is a form of essentialism creeping into Rorty's discussion of a moral identity for women. She writes that there is nothing 'inherently feminist in the attempt to build an "identity" around one's gender position' (Lovibond 1992: 73). Lovibond asks what is to guarantee that the identity which results outside of one's sexual subordination will be a common identity among women. She argues that, without male domination in place, women may find their 'femaleness' to be of little consequence to them among many other possible identities; and thus, any future moral identity will be one 'indeterminate in content' (Lovibond 1992: 74). She sees that Rorty may be trying to disturb the dominant discourse by his account of women finding and articulating a new identity. However, her difficulty is that this identity is 'a new *but still common* identity' (Lovibond 1992: 74). J.M. Fritzman is also concerned by essentialist tones in Rorty's talk of 'women as women', writing that it is fine to talk about women with diverse interests uniting as a political movement, but that such talk cannot be laced with ahistorical, essentialist notions of women's identity (Fritzman 1993: 122).[21] Fraser, on the other hand, sees that Rorty's account of creating an identity as women mitigates against any essentialist understanding of women (Fraser 1991: 265). Instead, she wants to make an historical argument that Rorty has the facts wrong, that women have spoken as women, and that there are traditions of female culture from which we can draw, such as the 'Victorian ideologies of "the cult of pure woman-hood"' (Fraser 1991: 264). The consequence of this she writes, is that 'we will need another way of characterizing the innovation of feminist movements' (Fraser 1991: 264). Further, Fraser adds that, in thinking about how to create this moral identity, difficult political questions arise as to '*which* new descriptions will count' and '*which* women will be empowered to impose their "semantic authority" on the rest of us' (1991: 264). This taps into the third critical concern to be discussed.

Finally, there is the general criticism that power wielded within community is never problematized by Rorty. This is closely connected to the feminist critique of communitarianism discussed above, that political critique is severely limited by the social constructivism and value communitarianism espoused by communitarians. While Rorty does not assume that the person is socially constructed in a determi-nistic sense (otherwise irony would not be possible), it can be argued that he holds on to a form of value communitarianism: that ethical commitments arise from the values and traditions of one's shared, collective practice. While 'Feminism and Pragmatism' is explicitly concerned to elaborate how radical political critique is made possible within community, a concern remains for feminists about power, the persons or structures capable of blocking the incorporation of this critique into political practice or discourse. As Susan Bickford writes,

---

[21] As a preface to these comments, Fritzman writes that Fraser is right to find that Rorty's discussion of the moral identity of women 'is suspect', thus implying that Fraser is charging Rorty of essentialism. I do not agree that this is Fraser's point, as I will discuss next.

the difficulty in Rorty's position is not with the possibility of change within discourses, 'but *who* gets to change them' (Bickford 1993: 106). Relatedly, she writes that, as community and the conversations which take place within a community require commonality from the very start, persons have to be 'like us' before they can participate; and even if conversation is about 'understanding others as "like us,"' it can require obscuring significant differences' (Bickford 1993: 106–7). Thus, questions of who gets to participate, in what capacity, with what limitations on expression, are all questions that ask, ultimately, about power; that is, who determines, and how, the dominant discourse that is the value tradition of a community.

The critical force of these three points must be acknowledged and answered in order to suggest that pragmatism can facilitate the moral inclusion of women in societal and intersocietal practices. I do not find that Rorty alone can sufficiently address these concerns. However, by bringing Dewey and his own version of a modified realism or instrumentalism, back into consideration, a synthesis of their positions could generate several interesting and compelling responses to the issues raised. Yet, I must say at the outset that such a synthesis in the notion of ethics as pragmatic critique will never be able to perform the role required by one of the authors discussed above: Leland's idea that feminism must work to 'identify masculine distortions' (1988: 280). For Rorty, to talk about distortions requires the idea of a non-discursive reality against which distortions can be measured and identified as such: an idea in which Rorty does not hold faith (1993b: 99). While we cannot say what Dewey would have made of the linguistic turn, whether he would have held that there could be material objects external to discourses, it can be said that he does not regard any concepts or social practices to be natural or absolute, a belief also suggested by a claim to distortion. It is interesting to note that none of these critics is willing to argue in response to Rorty that language and discursive power is of little or no significance to women, or that the task of women creating new moral vocabularies is not useful. They all recognize the value of these concerns to varying degrees. However, they do share the concern that pragmatism, as it is presented by Rorty, does not have the balance right. In particular, there is too much emphasis on the discursive. I will now consider these criticisms again, this time, to illustrate what a pragmatist synthesis of Rorty and Dewey can alternatively suggest.

Feminism and pragmatic critique

Can pragmatism be sufficiently political and critical? Is it willing to get its hands dirty in the materiality that is experience, which these critics deem necessary? Is it then capable of providing criteria of ethical/political judgement? To begin, pragmatism shares with feminism the notion that we must rethink theoretical concepts in terms of their usefulness to our day to day lives (Seigfried 1991: 2). Problematic moral situations are the subject matter of inquiry for Dewey, while Rorty is concerned with the tensions in theory and societal practice that motivate the creation of new vocabularies, and these begin from lived experience. However, Rorty and Dewey disagree as to how we theorize from experience. For Rorty, discourse goes all the way down, meaning that we cannot draw upon an understanding of experience or reality as neutral, providing an authoritative and legitimate base for critique. While Dewey shares the idea that reality is interpretive, interpreted by and for someone or some group, he maintains that there is an extent to which we can regard experience as a neutral point from which we can judge social practices. As discussed in the last chapter, Rorty categorically rejects Dewey's instrumentalism; but it cannot be taken for granted that pragmatism, with Rorty, is ready to drop all use of the concept of experience in evaluating problematic situations. This is indicated by the fact that there are a group of writers advocating a feminist pragmatism different from Rorty's: one that employs Dewey's attempts to reconceptualize what is generally understood by experience (Clark 1993; Gatens-Robinson 1991; Hart 1993; Leffers 1993; Rooney 1993). Dewey's reconstruction of experience as theory and value-laden, as well as transformative, works, as Marjorie Miller writes, to insist that 'all that is done and undergone – all that is experienced – is a ground for the radical critique of views of experience which relegate to the "merely subjective" or to the "purely psychological", all aspects of experience which have been ignored by the tradition but have been all too real to women' (1992: 448).

This debate in pragmatism over whether and how to draw upon concepts of experience, social reality and materiality is recognised by Fraser when she writes that her disagreement with Rorty 'is a disagreement within pragmatism' (Fraser 1991: 263).[22] However, what is not added by Fraser here is that the debate that she identifies in

---

[22] Although she does not specify what that disagreement is in her reply to Rorty, it is

pragmatism is one that feminists share.[23] It is a disagreement, as indicated above in section one, about the relationship of experience and discourse, and concerns what is lost and what is gained for ethical/political critique if feminists go fully down the interpretivist road. Feminists are also thinking about ways in which the concept of experience can be reconstructed, moving away from universalizing, absolutizing usages to make the concept more serviceable in light of recent social science debates. Thus, I believe that the debate within pragmatism regarding the role of experience in philosophical thinking can be instructive for feminists as well. The position that I take, as discussed in the previous chapter, is that ethics as pragmatic critique must pursue both material and discursive inquiry, but cautiously, with attention to the potential pitfalls that accompany either approach. This is facilitated by the assumption of fallibilism within pragmatic critique. Thus, I believe the pragmatic synthesis I offer will perhaps have the most resonance for those feminists attempting to construct that third alternative road. However, it is important to note, in considering the suitability of any approach to incorporating feminist ethical/political concerns, that few feminists appear willing to relinquish material, experience-based analysis of some form;[24] thus any approach with the aim of extending moral inclusion to women, must consider mechanisms to enable these kinds of discussions.

Feminists would want some indication of what kind of political judgement can be offered in a notion of ethics as pragmatic critique that pursues both discursive and material analysis. Before I offer a response, first, I want critically to analyze the assumption – implied by those critics of Rorty who are explicit about their material demands – that in order to be sufficiently political, one must have at the ready legitimating, material bases for discrimination, or otherwise power struggle, not politics, results. These writers want guarantees of critical political judgement. They want what Rorty denies: to have 'right' on their side. They demand foundations; but, as Rorty writes, and Dewey would agree, this demand only amounts to another form of power

evident when she writes elsewhere that her aim is to link both discursive and structural (objectivating) approaches. See Fraser (1995b: 294n and 1987).

[23] Fritzman makes a similar point regarding a few specific issues, but I want to make a more general point about the differences between feminists

[24] This is demonstrated by Sylvester's (1994) efforts as a postmodernist to enable material analysis in distinguishing feminist postmodernism from her own post-modern feminism as discussed above.

play (Rorty 1991a: 253–4, 21n). As a result, it is not any more political. Being political cannot be reduced to having unflappable justifications that command assent rather than coerce. Human social relations could never have been regarded as political by this definition. Rather, I regard being political to be more a matter of whether an approach engages with tough social questions, working to clarify the parameters of debate, rather than whether it provides authoritative answers to political questions.

This pragmatist synthesis is oriented towards working from the starting points of material and discursive manifestations of problematic situations in social relations, yet it will never attempt to offer ethical/political judgements which hold foundationally in a strong or absolute sense; nor can it offer suggestions as to what should be the content of ethical/political deliberations. That content can only be provided by the particular circumstances of the problematic situation and its experimental outcome. However, this approach does provide guideposts in such deliberations, the aim of growth, or of creating more meaningful, liveable worlds. As Dewey writes, for conclusions to be of value, as well as the philosophical thinking from which they are generated, they must be 'conclusions which when they are referred back to ordinary life-experiences and their predicaments, render them more significant, more luminous to us, and make our dealings with them more fruitful' (Dewey 1929: 7 as quoted in Miller 1992: 448). This pragmatist synthesis aims to assist the process of identifying, clarifying and facilitating the resolution of problematic moral situations. Thus, it does offer criteria of judgement, a method of critique, and has the capacity for reaching conclusions. However, the conclusions drawn, while they aim for universality, are assumed to be fallible.

In regard to the second criticism – that there are difficulties in Rorty's discussion of a moral identity for women – I believe Rorty's attempt to talk about a moral identity for women is deserving of a defence. Much of that defence is available within Rorty's work, although I will argue that the second, empirical aspect raised by Fraser requires this pragmatic synthesis to supplement the defence. To begin, I will address the first aspect of this charge, which concerns essentialism in Rorty's formulation of the question.

It is easy to see how such a concern is raised, since to talk about a moral identity for women overlaps the issue discussed in section one about whether we can or should talk essentially about 'women as women'. To be sure, Rorty advocates women creating for themselves a moral identity as women. However, attention must be drawn to the fact that he is talking about *creating* an identity as women. Thus, it cannot be said that he is suggesting something natural or ahistorical about this moral identity. None the less, one might claim that some notion of unity among women is being suggested by Rorty in pursuing such a moral identity. This cannot be denied, nor should it be. Indeed, feminists recognize that an understanding of unity as women is required in order to identify social problems as a feminist concern, and to organize political movements around feminist interests. The question for feminists, is how to proceed carefully in this understanding of unity to allow for plural and varied interpretations of feminist concerns and their incorporation into a feminist moral identity. Rorty appreciates this as a concern. To pursue a moral identity is not about defining women essentially, but it is about locating a site of feminist ethical critique by sorting out what exactly is a feminist ethical/political concern. Rorty too is seeking a form of unity in diversity.[25]

However, assistance from a notion of ethics as pragmatic critique is needed in addressing the second aspect of this criticism: Fraser's charge that Rorty gets the facts wrong. I say this because, for Rorty, to make a claim that women have found no moral identity worthy of the name in the past requires historical and material analysis as well as discursive analysis. As discussed in the last chapter, the process of identifying a problematic moral situation, in this case gender inequality, requires more than the interrogation of vocabularies and language alone. All sorts of intellectual approaches should be pursued: science, art, anthropology, history and literature, etc. Fraser is right to challenge him on this, whether or not you agree with her reading that there *are* valuable traditions of women's moral identity in the past.

The criticism that is most difficult to answer satisfactorily on behalf of Rorty, or Dewey for that matter, is the third claim that power is not adequately problematized in pragmatism. To understand the motivation behind the charge, one might consider Rorty's view that 'groups build their moral strength by achieving increasing semantic authority

---

[25] See Rorty's (1991a: 245) discussion of persons finding that the 'tensions between their alternative self-descriptions as, at worse, necessary elements in a harmonious variety in unity'.

over their members, thereby increasing the ability of those members to find their moral identities in their membership of such groups' (1991a: 247). There is much room for the abuse of power in the establishment of semantic authority in community. Yet, while Dewey and Rorty see that value traditions can only arise from community, the problems for critique that value communitarianism generates are a serious concern for both writers. This is the concern for authentic critique, discussed in the previous chapter, that leads to Rorty's public/private split and Dewey's instrumentalism. For this reason, I think the third critique does not quite ring true. None the less, it does have resonance for pragmatic critique.

It is not that power is not problematized within the work of Dewey and Rorty, but rather, that it is undertheorized. To take as the starting point of theory the tensions and doubts raised within social practice means that pragmatic critique is concerned to engage oppressive situations which give rise to such tensions. However, it has problems in effectively carrying out that concern. Rorty's emphasis on the discursive means that he does not see much need for the analysis of social structures, and other possible material determinants of oppressive conditions. While Dewey (1927) does raise the issue of structures of power and domination in social relations as a concern, he has perhaps too much faith in the method of critical inquiry to dismantle such structures. I think a synthesis of the two writers' approaches in the notion of international ethics as pragmatic critique has much to gain from an engagement with feminism, as this engagement highlights the need for pragmatism to work through power considerations in a more deliberate and sustained manner.

I want to suggest that in developing the approach of international ethics as pragmatic critique, an important starting point for further consideration of power is to think through this dilemma for antifoundationalist approaches articulated by Biddy Martin:

> do we have to make a choice between the human need and desire for community, and the understanding that we have (to an unknown extent) been constructed to be members of that community? Can we only perceive knowledge as contributing to human solidarity, at the cost of ignoring power dynamics, or understand power relations at the expense of rejecting the possibility of community?[26]

---

[26] This quote is Bickford's eloquent characterization of Martin's (1982) position. See Bickford (1993: 116).

This dilemma poses the question of whether there is something structural that blocks the productive analysis of both power and human solidarity of community in tandem, generating an opposition between positions which begin from community (which pragmatism does) and those which employ a Foucauldian position on power. Bickford adds that both are very important considerations for feminists who attempt to 'understand power relations and claim a community from which they can speak' (1993: 116). I think there are indications within pragmatic critique that this in fact *does not* have to be a choice. This is evident in pragmatism's starting point being the practices of community, yet holding a concern for genuine possibilities of critique in the face of the power of value communitarianism. What remains to be developed is how ethics as pragmatic critique should pursue consideration of both material and discursive power in a way that is thoroughly attentive to the question this dilemma raises. I will explore how moral imagination might be employed to this effect in the next chapter, where I examine the political and institutional implications of the conclusion drawn here.

To conclude, international ethics as pragmatic critique shares with feminism a concern for transforming oppressive relations, but gains from an engagement with feminism an awareness that it must pursue power considerations in a more sustained way. This shift in awareness in the pragmatic synthesis offered here is a good example of the way in which a tension recognized and made the subject of critical inquiry – that valuing community may compromise the problematization of power relations and vice versa – can transform a practice, altering it for the better. Indeed, this chapter as a whole – its identification of the difficulties in theorizing feminist ethical/political concerns generally, and more specifically, in normative IR theory – demonstrates the way in which pragmatic critique works. A doubt or indeterminacy is raised and identified as a problematic moral situation that must be looked into. Inquiry is not limited to the given frameworks but looks beyond them, initiating engagement with marginalized discourses and institutions, to explore possibilities for determinacy. If it does its job right, if it pursues this inquiry with sympathy, sensitiveness, balance of interests, and persists even when aspects of the inquiry are hard to face, then growth and moral inclusion are possible.

From moral imagination to international public spheres: the political and institutional implications of pragmatic critique

Introduction

To summarize the point at which chapter 7 concluded, there is a central dilemma or tension that pragmatic critique must address in order adequately to incorporate feminist ethical/political concerns. The problematic moral situation takes the following form: how might pragmatic critique proceed in a way that properly interrogates the discursive and material power structures of communities, enabling radical critique, such that reformism is not all we have available. This has implications not only for extending moral inclusion to women in international practice, but for the extent to which pragmatic critique generally is able to facilitate moral inclusion. Can this pragmatic synthesis rely upon its answer to the authentic critique problem: the projection of alternative discourses and practices through moral imagination? Can we assume that the tensions which set immanent critique rolling will be readily and always apparent, and that social contradictions will at times be so glaring that we will be motivated and able to seek their determination through metaphor and the transformation of social practice? This is where power considerations must come into play.

However, at the same time, there is an associated danger with pursuing avenues of authentic critique in this way: that is, whether this pragmatic approach can have anything to say about the possibilities for consensus around ethical criteria and how such convergence might be facilitated. Bringing power considerations to the fore means that it matters whether or not one finds criteria of ethical judgement by and for oneself, because, if one does not, such criteria are likely to be felt as an external imposition by the individual concerned, which could lead to the occurrence of further morally problematic situations in the future. Since many contemporary societies and groups are characterized by plurality and diversity, the obstacles to voluntary convergence around ethical/political priorities in face of this diversity are considerable (as we have already witnessed among women), and we are back to the central problem faced by normative IR theorists today: how can we avoid giving up in resignation the attempt to find criteria for expanding ethical consideration in intersocietal practice? The answer I will provide here is that pragmatic critique can appeal to discursive and institutional mechanisms with which to facilitate the creation of possibilities for critique and convergence, *but not of the kind nor to the extent* that many might wish, particularly those well accustomed to the assumptions of formal liberalism, who anticipate that such efforts are to be directed towards establishing universal rules and principles that yield legitimate, reliable conclusions.

In this chapter, I aim to provide a picture of the normative structure of pragmatic critique. I will do this through an exploration of the political and institutional responses with which this approach can address the dilemma posed by the ideal of authentic critique: how best to facilitate effective challenges to the established value traditions within a community. I will also look at the related difficulty of how pragmatic critique might have anything left to say about the possibilities for convergence around ethical criteria.

In order to do so, some preliminary steps are required, which preoccupy the first section of this chapter. Here, I will examine the nature of my 'quasi-antifoundationalism' and its contingently held epistemological and ontological orientations, in light of the problems raised above. By posing the question – what motivates pragmatic critique? – I will demonstrate that it is still positing ideas of what it is to be human, it is still working from these ideas as the basis of critique, and it is also isolating methods which provide a form of knowledge or learning when diligently pursued. However, I will claim that it is doing so with a difference, since it provides for the openness that its aim of growth requires. I will also argue that this same openness and its measure, the democratic ideal, and its mechanism, the use of moral imagination that is integral to critical intelligence, could provide interesting avenues into the dilemmas posed above.

The second and third sections further explore the mechanisms through which the motivation of pragmatic critique unfolds and will focus on the role moral imagination plays in working towards the democratic ideal held by this approach. I will argue that moral imagination is the key to thinking not only about the discursive and material power within communities that may circumscribe critique, but also about possibilities for convergence around ethical criteria. I will demonstrate how moral imagination furthers the possibilities of both ethical critique and convergence by thinking beyond the context of community and identity, generating new values and new practices that may provide alternative bases for either voluntary consent or authentic critique. The second section will ask how moral imagination and its use of metaphor can be employed to think about discursive power, and will briefly contrast this approach with Habermasian discourse ethics. In the third section, I will turn to a more lengthy discussion of the ways in which moral imagination can be employed to think about material power – the institutions which block effective critique of social practices – and how it provides for the creation of ethical convergence as well. I will draw upon Nancy Fraser's efforts at critique of actually existing democracy, which employ a form of moral imagination through reconstructing the concept of a public sphere, and multiplying public spheres. Further distinctions between the use of moral imagination and discourse ethics will be made evident, since Jürgen Habermas's concept of the public sphere is Fraser's starting point. Here, I attempt to offer further insight into how moral imagination works to facilitate moral inclusion and social reconstruction in IR, by evaluating its potential to project alternative institutional possibilities, international public spheres, which operate both beyond and below the state level in extending moral inclusion and improving democratic intersocietal arrangements.

The normative structure of pragmatic critique

If it is indeed right that we should be disconcerted by the epistemological blockages and ethical/political harm that can be caused by the impositions of *non-contingently* held foundational claims, then pragmatic critique must have a response to the question of what possibilities for convergence around an ethical position are left, particularly ones that provide what the ideal of authentic critique requires for really-existing moral inclusion, rather than inclusion by compulsion.[1] This means that we must look further into the motivations of pragmatic critique, its normative structure; we must ask what the motor is behind pragmatic critique, and whether it is compelling. How is it that persons come to see their ends as being intertwined with those of others, in order to be interested in seeking convergence on ethical principles? Why should anyone work voluntarily and cooperatively to generate conditions for the growth and self-development of others? Certainly, in order to provide for the possibility of internally reached consensus around criteria for ethical critique, persons so concerned must develop the will towards participation, social commitment and some form of a democratic ethos. However, why should they?

The motivations within pragmatic critique rest upon both a *weak* ontological position and the identification of problematic situations. Normatively, there is the weakly held ontological priority of growth, where growth is understood as a view that individuals flourish best by improving upon their potential for realizing their autonomy and possibilities for self-development. In order to set out this *weak* ontological vision and its relation to the resolution of problematic situations, it would be useful here to draw some careful distinctions between my understanding and the naturalistic teleology mentioned in chapter 6 which characterizes Dewey's position.

For Dewey, growth comes with an individual's recognition of the needs of others, in seeing that a life shared communally – and the wider the participation the better – is more full, providing something richer in terms of self-realization (as discussed in chapter 6). Dewey also sees this idea of growth to be enhanced by the resolution of problematic situations which affect individuals. Therefore, he argues that cooperative, intellectual activity directed at social indeterminancies is an ethical priority. According to Dewey, the need to resolve the problematic situations which face a group of individuals also serves as a motor for ethical engagement. However, social tensions only provide a *stimulus* for such activity. They may, as Dewey sees it, assist us in learning the benefit of social cooperation, but in no way direct us 'reliably' towards a consensual outcome. For Dewey, what does direct us confidently, if not reliably, towards the social cooperation necessary

---

[1] The response which follows in this section endeavours to address concerns raised by Festenstein (1997) with regard to those who are interested in reworking Dewey for political theoretical purposes today.

to convergence around criteria for assessing and resolving problematic situations is his teleology of human nature. In his early writings, this took the form of a Hegelian, naturalistic account of the way in which the individual's self-realization is ultimately connected to the will of the community and the good of others. However, later he saw the need to discover a less metaphysical and more sociological, or rather moral psychological, account. Nevertheless, his theory maintained a grounding in human drives, impulses and habits of action that demonstrate the naturalness of the individual's connection to society (Honneth 1997: 13–14; Dewey 1922: 278–332).

While this is intended by Dewey to provide a justification for his understanding of growth and the possibilities for convergence around the resolution of problematic situations, the difficulty it presents for those who wish to work from Dewey, as Matthew Festenstein rightly points out, is that this naturalist teleology may feel like an external imposition upon someone who has other, more varied, ideas of what self-realization might mean (Festenstein 1997: 58–62). What about the person who finds a great deal of gratification in meeting her own requirements for her fulfilment by remaining no more socially committed than she must to earn a living and have certain civil and political rights of non-interference, preoccupying herself in her free time with her books and CDs instead of actively participating in the collective enterprise of resolving problematic social tensions, particularly if she is causing no one else any harm?[2] This is exactly the question that Rorty is trying to address in *CIS*. Rorty asks what is left for ethical critique and politics, if this kind of natural and immediate connection between the individual and society is not available to us. As I have argued in this book, it is important that the kind of *strong* foundational convictions that are found in Dewey's concept of the person are put up for question. This is why I think the move that Rorty makes to examine the ethical/political consequences of not taking this connection between the individual and the solidarity of community for granted is important, since taking it for granted could be felt as a form of coercion against those who might want either to be left alone in their individual pursuits, or to work against the grain of what societal convention allows.

Therefore, we must turn to the *weak* ontology at the base of my

---

[2] I must thank Chris Brown for this particular formulation of an alternative view of human flourishing.

notion of pragmatic critique. What growth might be for individuals cannot be fixed beyond the simple idea of the virtues necessary to critical inquiry discussed in chapter 6; that is, '[w]ide sympathy, keen sensitiveness, persistence in the face of the disagreeable, balance of interests' (Dewey 1948: 164). By relinquishing Dewey's *strong* ontology, grounded in human nature, in favour of a weaker formulation that cannot rest assured of the connection of persons to commonly held identity or values, I think pragmatic critique can offer a more compelling account of growth. Because this account of growth has at its base an idea of human flourishing which sees the development of critical faculties as being central to human autonomy, but does so without narrowing too radically the range of ways this growth might be pursued, it may be seen as less of an external imposition by more individuals. For example, the idea of flourishing held by the woman who just wants space to read her books and listen to her CDs is not compromised, since this idea of growth does not always and necessarily have to come through political activity and participation, although others might attach great importance to participation. Growth is a product of reflection (Festenstein 1997: 54), or, as Dewey would say, critical intelligence, that is called into action when we face problematic situations. Not only can this kind of reflection be stimulated and pursued apart from the political sphere, say in cultural, professional, or economic spheres of social activity, but it can be pursued in ways that are more private than others. However, the virtues associated with it call for, at the minimum, a degree of social consideration through the requirements of sympathy and sensitivity. This is the sense in which this *weak* ontology is not so open as to lose all possibility of holding a normative edge.

This idea of growth and the *weak* ontology which motivates it are not compromised by the woman in the example above, since she considers whether or not her activity may be harming others. However, this idea of growth would not be able to accommodate an idea of human flourishing which describes an individual's autonomy in ways which hold no regard for the harm one's actions may cause others. This woman's idea of human flourishing represents the minimum level of social engagement and responsibility to others required by the virtues of inquiry guiding pragmatic critique. However, these virtues have a maximal level as well, a point at which critical inquiry stops and becomes something else.

There are occasions when the dialogue and perseverance required by the *more optimal aspects* of these virtues, which *are* actively oriented to social engagement and cooperative problem solving, hit a concrete wall and can go no further. Perhaps lives are being lost in a situation of humanitarian crisis and the luxury of time for gentle, persuasive dialogue and persistent inquiry is not to be had. This is the kind of critical occasion when military intervention may have to be considered as the best resolution to the problematic situation at hand. However, violence is not a resolution that pragmatic critique can settle upon. Even in circumstances such as this when the question of intervention may be less controversial, critical inquiry, the ethical imperative of pragmatic critique, has reached its limit. It can proceed no further because to do so would stretch the virtues of pragmatic inquiry beyond their bounds, those bounds being the need to find improved ways of coping through the kind of sympathy, sensitiveness and balance of interests required not only by its *weak* ontology, but by its methodology and its assumption of fallibilism. In denying absolutes, the fallibilism assumed within pragmatic critique cannot sanction violence and its own form of absoluteness: once a life is taken, it cannot be given back. There is no certainty upon which reasons for military intervention, even in less controversial cases, can rest. There are no assurances regarding outcomes that the ends will in fact justify the means or that violence will secure better ways of coping or a workable solution to the indeterminate situation at hand.[3] Therefore, the absoluteness assumed within a decision to use violence cannot be

---

[3] Here, pragmatic critique has the benefit of hindsight. Dewey's decision to support U.S. entry into World War I was the subject of much controversy among like-minded liberals who felt Dewey had abandoned his own notion of critical intelligence. However, Dewey's support was bred from the idea that force was a means that could be executed intelligently and settled in a way so as to ensure a worthy end: the democratic re-ordering of international politics. Alas, neither the Peace which he regarded as unjust, nor the League of Nations, constituted for Dewey the democratic re-ordering he envisioned. Ultimately, this led Dewey to reconsider his position on war as an adequate means for any kind of democratic or peaceful end, and he became a central figure in The Outlawry of War movement. Nevertheless, this too was a position he could not hold absolutely, since eventually, after writing several articles discouraging U.S. entry, Dewey supported American involvement in World War II. See Westbook (1991). I read this reluctance as a recognition on Dewey's part that his critics were right: critical intelligence and the ethics which requires its use cannot sanction force. However, always the realist – that is, one concerned about solutions that are workable – Dewey knew that U.S. entry in World War II was unavoidable. Pragmatic critique can recognize this as the required *instrumental*, rather than ethical, decision.

arrived at from the normative structure of pragmatic critique. The resolution which calls for violence to address a problematic situation is one that may have to be made in particular instances, but it is made by *other forms* of reasoning – instrumentality, punishment or retribution sanctioned by international law, etc. – and not by the ethics that is pragmatic critique.

Two objections may be raised at this point. The first is the challenge that if pragmatic critique cannot theorize the use of violence, then it does not have much to offer IR. The second is that if pragmatic critique cannot theorize when it may or may not be justifiable to use force for the purposes of intervention, then it is not of much use to international ethics. Of course, assumed within the first challenge is the idea that war and conflict are at the centre of the discipline and that there is little else left, particularly nothing which is significant, for which pragmatic critique may be proved relevant. To suggest that force or the threat of force makes up the better part of international practice is a claim that has met with numerable and forceful challenges not only by normative theorists. However, even those who recognise the significant role that the normative plays in international practice may expect that any approach to international ethics worth its salt must have something to say about the tough moral choices presented by questions of intervention in world politics. One response to those who possibly hold this expectation, is briefly suggested by Andrew Linklater: while rights to intervention 'remain a crucial question', they are none the less a secondary concern (1998: 103n). Linklater cannot place the demand for intervention before his conseption of ethics: his cosmopolitan principle. What is prior for Linklater is that the powerful act in ways that respect the rights of all affected to have a say in activities which affect them (1998: 103). While it is unlikely that this would be found satisfactory by those holding the above expectation, I am sympathetic to his response, since I too think that something else is morally prior to considerations of violent intervention: an ethics. I am not convinced that an ethics can provide justification for such intervention and certainly no generalizable principles or criteria. However, Linklater and I may differ on this point, because Linklater does not close off the idea that a dialogic ethic might have something to say about intervention once we have established that those who may do the intervening have ethical credentials established through their participation in a politics of discourse (1998: 103). I would agree with Linklater to the extent that forms of intervention other than military intervention were pursued.[4] However, to my mind, for an ethics to be able to sanction force it has to have *strong*, incontrovertible foundations which, as I have argued, are not available to us. Instrumental considerations or dictates of international law are better equipped by their particular character to provide compelling reasons for intervention. Something which calls itself an ethics may sanction or justify force, but it would be one that did not acknowledge the contingency of its claims, or if it did, it did not recognize the responsibilities this acknowledgement of contingency suggests if it is indeed oriented to expanding moral inclusion and consideration. Therefore, it would be an ethics that I could not find convincing.

Despite this detour into the concerns of an avid CD-listener/book-reader and those who want to talk about the justifiable use of violence in international practice, it may remain that the virtues of inquiry still appear vague and fuzzy. I am afraid that this is an occupational hazard that comes with the practice of pragmatic critique. Granted, there is a broad band of possible resolutions, criteria and conclusions that could be drawn between the minimal and optimal aspects to the virtues which guide critical inquiry. However, that is as it is meant to be. As discussed in chapter 6, each problematic situation is unique and its solution equally so, and requires as wide and open a berth to inquiry as possible to facilitate the creation of workable solutions around which convergence might be found.

However, it remains that pragmatic critique is positing both more and less ambitious ideas of a sense of responsibility to others in respectively, its optimal and minimal aspects to the virtues of critical inquiry which lead to growth. Of course for Dewey, this was grounded by his naturalist teleology. However, in pragmatic critique, this sense of responsibility is offered as a tool to be tried, and cannot be seen as a well-founded source of expectation with regard to the possibilities for the voluntary acceptance of principles of normative judgement in societies. Naturally, this *weak* ontology leaves pragmatic critique vulnerable to the charge that it cannot produce the commitments to participation and social engagement required for finding consensus, since the possibility of convergence around criteria which might resolve an indeterminate situation has to be seen as *contingent* if recourse to a *strong* ontology is denied. For many, this is unsatis-

---

[4] See Hoffman (1993) for ideas of alternative forms of intervention.

factory, and there are elaborate attempts, such as those of Habermas, to demonstrate the possibility of consensus in ideal circumstances, bound by the requirements of practical reason. However, what a concern with the ideal of authentic critique generates in my mind is the opinion that the risk of consensus on ethical criteria being merely *contingent* is preferable to the epistemological and ethical/political dangers that I find lurking in both *strong* and *weak* ontologies which are held *non-contingently*.

Therefore, vulnerability to this charge is a significant indicator that possibilities for the approximation of authentic critique are not being unjustifiably narrowed. However, at the same time, I think that it remains important that any approach which aims to provide some kind of content for an ethics, should suggest normative criteria that might guide intersocietal relations, and should isolate ways in which avenues for consensus around those criteria may be, if not discovered 'out there', at least generated, albeit *contingently*.

The normative structure of pragmatic critique does not rely upon its *weak* ontology alone. It is bolstered by the methodological point that the resolution of problematic situations is enhanced when inquiry is pursued as openly and inclusively as possible. Since social tensions of various kinds are endemic within modern societies, it remains that all of us as individuals, except for those who are able to live completely isolated lives unaffected by such tensions, will be faced with moments when reflection on these situations will be required of us. Whether or not this *weak* ontology of autonomy realized through growth is compelling in encouraging responsibility toward others, it remains that there are two intuitions within this methodological point which not only encourage social cooperation and moral inclusion, but give us some indication of what kind of institutions should be encouraged. The first intuition is that the quality of resolutions found is improved by the openness with which they are determined. They benefit not only from drawing upon intellectual and material resources immediately available within the community affected, but from the use of moral imagination, looking beyond the familiar to that which is different in seeking creative alternative possibilities. Therefore, it requires societies to be discursively and institutionally open to the extent that they tend not to be seriously threatened or destabilized by change. Full information and freedom of speech, opinion, inquiry and movement are also essential to this openness. Institutionally speaking, what this all amounts to is that democratic societies are best suited to the resolution of difficult social tensions. The second intuition is that more critical minds at work are better than one. The degree to which resolutions are likely to be found workable is directly related to the number of those of engaged in reflection on the indeterminate situation at hand. Thus, it follows that human flourishing is best enhanced, whether you accept Kantian, Hegelian, Deweyan, or Foucauldian arguments for human autonomy, by solving social tensions cooperatively with those affected by the consequences of these tensions. This is the best possibility for convergence around ethical principles that pragmatic critique can offer.

In sum, pragmatic critique, ontologically and methodologically, provides a stimulus to seek the resolution of commonly shared problems communally. However, while it provides a stimulus, there is no guarantee that it will proceed consensually. Starting from the values of community or our own ethnocentrism, as Rorty puts it, does not ensure convergence. Just because we begin 'from where we are' – that is, shared traditions – in working to solve problems, this only suggests a common starting place, not necessarily a commonly shared resolution or end point. Problem solving by pragmatic critique aims to be as open as possible, guided only by: (1) those virtues of inquiry that suggest a responsibility to others and, as such, lead to growth; and (2) the methodological intuitions that suggest the need for democratic institutions and social cooperation. These guideposts provide the normative structure of pragmatic critique and suggest, as a *measure* of social activity, a democratic ideal that seeks the widest possible moral/political inclusion of those affected by that activity. Also, pragmatic critique employs the *mechanism* of moral imagination to create possibilities for realizing that ideal through sympathetic, sensitive, persistent and balanced inquiry.

Moral imagination at work: discursive possibilities for expanding moral inclusion

Having set out the normative structure of pragmatic critique, I will now come back to address more directly the difficulty left at the conclusion of chapter 7: can pragmatic critique sufficiently engage power considerations, such that it is able to realistically provide for both the distance required by authentic critique and the possibility of convergence around community as well? A concern has been raised as to whether the tensions that give rise to immanent critique – that is, critique internal to shared value traditions – can be relied upon to break or satisfactorily undermine discursive and material power within communities. In this section and the next, I aim to demonstrate that moral imagination works both discursively and institutionally *via* the concept of 'public spheres' to suggest interesting ways of bringing additional resources to immanent critique and addressing the above difficulty.

For two reasons, I will not dwell on the discursive aspects of power to the same extent as the institutional possibilities of public spheres and the use of moral imagination. First, I believe that Rorty, with the possible exception of not satisfactorily problematizing the discursive power of the 'we', does discuss this issue quite well. However, it remains important for the purposes of its application to normative IR theory that I at least contrast it briefly with Habermasian discourse ethics, which is being used in interesting ways in normative IR theory at present (Linklater 1998; Proops 1996; Haacke 1996; Hoffman 1993). Secondly, I think it important to develop to the fullest extent possible in the space that remains the institutional ramifications of pragmatic critique. While recent work by Andrew Linklater on the post-Westphalian state (1996a, 1997) and by Mervyn Frost on global civil society (1999) provides something of an exception, normative IR theory has been so deeply engaged in its metatheoretical entrenchments that it has not properly engaged in thinking about the institutions necessary to the kinds of moral inclusion it envisions. Neither Linklater nor Frost has developed these ideas systematically as yet, and I cannot say that I will have the opportunity here to do anything more myself than illustrate where future work on pragmatic critique should be directed in regard to thinking about public spheres as alternative international institutional sites. However, I see that it is important to at least take initial steps in this direction in order to begin the process of moving normative IR theory towards more adequate treatments of institutional questions.

In picking up from Rorty's analysis of discursive transformations discussed in chapter 7, what remains for me to elaborate is the role I believe moral imagination can play in providing for the possibility of a critical stance against the semantic authority of community. As I see it, moral imagination serves four important functions in this regard: (1) it identifies the operative metaphors within a moral practice; (2) it evaluates which metaphors are dominant and the particular moral issues that follow from their dominance; (3) it focuses upon what gets excluded – the moral issues left out – due to metaphors being over-looked or not yet having been articulated, in order to create alternative possibilities and space for new meaning and identity; and (4) it facilitates learning and growth.[5]

For example, moral imagination can be employed by feminists to look at the metaphors, and narratives elaborated by those metaphors, which constitute moral tradition within a particular community.[6] Feminists can employ moral imagination to work out which meta-phors are deemed most valuable, and how those dominant metaphors set up some moral questions or issues as significant, and others (such as gender concerns) as less so. Since moral imagination finds that there is partiality in our selection and use of metaphors, it is always looking out for missed possibilities, and moral ideas that are compromised or ignored, such as women's moral identity, due to the overriding authority of (perhaps masculinist) traditions within a community. Moral imagination is motivated to explore not only within, but also beyond the bounds of communal practice to create alternative under-standings, to open up space for concepts, associations and identities that enhance and make more meaningful those which we currently possess. Finally, and most importantly in terms of dislodging entrenched and powerful discourses, moral imagination is the mech-anism by which we learn to incorporate feminist points of view into the value tradition of community, because it is *via* imagination that we think about what it would mean to apply new or different moral ideas to old ways of life, how we might go about this task, and what the consequences would be likely to be. Also, it enables the possibility of feminist moral inclusion in helping one to learn or create an associ-ation with others by putting oneself in the place of women and imagining their experiences and its fit with one's own.

Perhaps the most central difference between the use of moral imagination and discourse ethics is the particular way in which discourse ethics aims to be 'self-referential', to find its own moral criteria via 'an inbuilt communicative rationality' that is part and parcel of the everyday use of language (Haacke 1996: 265). Moral imagination does not trust that the resources that are available to us,

---

[5] This list of four important functions of moral imagination has some overlap with Johnson's eight points on what he calls the 'chief imaginative dimension of moral understanding': metaphor (1993: 193–98).

[6] Feminists who recommend the idea of imagination to promote feminist agendas include: Lovibond (1983); Held (1993); and Fraser (1991).

including those suggested by communicative rationality, will provide appropriate criteria internally which might still allow for both the possibility of authentic critique and as wide a consideration as possible of potential solutions to problematic situations. The central thrust behind the idea that moral imagination is vital to critical intelligence is precisely that it pushes the boundaries of what might be found internally as criteria for ethical judgement, creating important discursive space not only for opening the parameters of what people can say against the prevailing semantic order in communities, but for opening the range of possibilities available in resolving indeterminate situations by looking beyond the internal dynamics of one's own community.

From the point of view of Habermasian discourse ethics, one might respond by saying that the criterion of communicative rationality could not be more open, since it is universal – it is based on the reason assumed in the human exchange that is language – because it has no fixed end points and understands the use of reason to be fallible. With pragmatic critique it shares not only the idea that communication should be open-ended and its results regarded as fallible, but that in the face of the growth of technical rationality in modern societies, power should be a central concern and we must ensure that communication is free in order to provide for what I have labelled as the ideal of authentic critique. Perhaps most significantly for the purposes of comparison, the two approaches are guided by this principle: that the validity of norms or evaluative criteria is a product of whether those who are affected by those norms actually approve of them. Habermas formulates this as principle (D), the distinctive idea of discourse ethics that: '[o]nly those norms can claim to be valid that meet (or could meet) with the approval of all affected in their capacity *as participants in a practical discourse*' (1990: 66). The appeal of discourse ethics is purported to be that it outlines formal procedures as guidelines for discussion which ensure that if universal agreement by those involved is found, the norm discussed can be regarded as legitimate.

However, from the perspective of pragmatic critique, this procedural formality is a liability because rules cannot ensure either approximations of authentic critique or convergence around ethical criteria. In the first place, rules cannot ensure authentic critique because the formality and the incontrovertibleness with which they are put forward may be seen as an external imposition. This concern is not dissimilar from that which, as we saw in chapter 7, feminists express with regard to the formalistic and rationality-bound elements of liberalism. Secondly, convergence around ethical criteria cannot be guaranteed merely by positing the incontrovertibility of a rule, particularly if it is seen as an external imposition, because, as I have already pointed out, moral inclusion through coercion can potentially generate more social tensions and morally problematic situations in the future. An externally imposed *rule* can only sanction convergence if it is sustained by force, and this hardly constitutes a case of moral inclusion. For example, Habermas relies on universal pragmatics as the ground rule which not only justifies his separation of communicative action (motivated by the aim of reaching moral agreement and the focus of discourse ethics) from strategic action (consent to one's will arrived at by threat) (1984: section 3), but suggests why persons are, in the main, concerned to engage in communicative action. It states that one has to accept the guiding principle of discourse ethics (D) if one engages in rational argumentation, or else slip into a performative contradiction which denies one's own expectation to be allowed free and fair representation and consideration (Habermas 1990: 82–94). Such a rule, and Habermas's elaborate attempts to maintain it, are a form of Archimedean contrivance which from the perspective of pragmatic critique, artificially separates the individual from her interests and ends in fetishizing the ideal of the procedures themselves, despite Habermas's insistence that there is no discourse apart from interests. Indeed, such a contrivance is likely to be felt as an imposition, particularly if, as critics of Habermas suggest, it cannot be guaranteed that its procedures are not tainted by semantic structures of power that obstruct the ability of certain groups to participate.[7]

An interesting point of comparison and contrast which illustrates the kind of artificial separation called for in discourse ethics is that Habermas suggests the need for 'the *universal exchange of roles*' – what a pragmatist, G. H. Mead, has called 'ideal role taking' – which assists persons in complying with condition (U) that '*[a]ll* affected can accept the consequences and the side effects its *general* observance can be anticipated to have for the satisfaction of *everyone's* interests' (Habermas 1990: 65). This kind of role playing activity, as suggested above, is important to the growth and learning function of moral

[7] These criticisms will be discussed further in the following part of this section on moral imagination and institutional possibilities.

imagination, but it operates in a very different way. Where Habermas intends this role playing to facilitate impartiality of judgement through adopting the perspectives of others, moral imagination does not expect participants to divide themselves from their interests and ends as part of this exercise. Instead, maintaining an awareness of one's own ends is vital to finding workable solutions to problematic situations and thus, the purpose of the exercise is to imagine oneself in the role of another so as to compare the fit between that role and one's own life, to run back and forth between the two, looking for what might be learned from such an exchange. Admittedly, interests and aims have to be foregrounded for Habermas, but because his aim is consensus for the purposes of legitimation, my concern is that interests get lost in the procedures and the impartiality they assume leading to that consensus. Since pragmatic critique is concerned with possibilities for convergence for purposes of social cooperation and growth, this requires that interests are not only foregrounded, but referred to throughout the process of critical intelligence and moral imagination that is employed in the solving of problematic social tensions.

In sum, the irony is that Habermas resorts to outlining how universal agreement or consensus can be reached via the standards assumed within language because he shares the same concern as pragmatic critique: we cannot leave the formulations of genuinely open and morally inclusive normative criteria to what historical communities might provide internally. However, pragmatic critique would add that we cannot leave these standards to the procedural narrowness or potential impositions that discourse ethics suggests either. Moral imagination is required to project thought about such evaluative standards beyond the strictures of both community tradition and formal, rule-bound procedures.

Moral imagination at work: public spheres and the institutional possibilities for expanding moral inclusion

Now, I want to turn to how moral imagination might help us think about the material, institutional bases of power that prohibit effective critique and resistance to forms of community practices. As the feminist critique discussed in chapter 7 notes, many feminists are uneasy with relinquishing the material analysis of social structures of gender inequality. However, they recognize the difficulties in talking about neutral social forms, as many acknowledge the interpretive nature of experience. This difficulty is fuelled by the accepted need to represent plural and varied aspects of women's experience without universalizing in an absolutist way, on the behalf of one subset of women, the institutions and practices they in particular find necessary to redress gender inequalities in social structures. For some, this is taken as a cautionary note, which does not inhibit them from offering detailed discussion of the practices that require dismantling. None the less, there are few suggestions about alternative institutional orders to replace the democratic state form. There are others for whom this is more than a cautionary note, which instills a hesitancy on the part of feminists, as well as others who recognize the force of this issue presently debated in the social sciences, about whether we can even talk about 'structures' of inequality that affect everyone similarly; and for that matter, whether we can talk about what in fact requires dismantling, and what 'better', alternative institutions might be.

The bottom line for both of these positions is that there is no clear vision of an institutional order beyond the democratic state form. Feminists, like the protagonists of the cosmopolitan/communitarian debate, find the state to be both normatively relevant as well as capable of a good deal of violence. For feminists, the democratic state form perpetuates conditions of gender inequality, while at the same time it is the author of the welfare programmes from which women benefit.[8] So where do we go from here? While at present, there appears to be no better alternative, I want to suggest that we do not have to wait, nor should we wait, for clear, possibly existing alternatives to appear. Moral imagination can work to create them. Moral imagination and the fallibilism assumed of any conclusions drawn through the use of moral imagination, can help feminists, and others with a will to critique present institutional arrangements, to think beyond them to other institutional forms which might facilitate critical stances against our social practices and encourage a convergence of opinion around the need for alternative institutions.

An initial step in this direction, which shares features with the idea of moral imagination, is Nancy Fraser's reconstruction of the concept of the public sphere and her call for multiple public spheres as sites

---

[8] It is not the intention of this statement to ignore concerns that have been raised about problems for women associated with welfare. For example, see Fraser (1989: chapter 7), and Fraser and Gordon (1994).

of critique and resistance to unjust social practices. I will offer a synopsis of her position and suggest how her conception of intra- and inter-public relations within domestic politics might successfully be translated into global politics, in an effort to imagine possibilities for critique of state and interstate practices, as well as thinking beyond state practice. I will argue that what this use of moral imagination may indicate is that it is not necessarily the democratic ideal itself that needs replacing, but that the ways in which it is manifested need to be enhanced. One way suggested by the guiding democratic measure or ideal of pragmatic critique is to expand its setting in institutions not only below the state form, but in interstate practices as well, so as to provide individuals with the wherewithal to work cooperatively in controlling activities that transgress state boundaries which affect them. Also, to develop the comparison and contrast already begun between pragmatic critique and Habermasian discourse ethics, it is interesting that Fraser draws upon Habermas's conception of the public sphere as the starting point for her reconstruction. Dewey too has a concept of the public sphere and I will demonstrate below that his conception makes important contributions both to the intentions of her reconstruction of Habermas and my aim of extending to international practice the work that Fraser has completed to date.

Fraser begins with this proposition: something akin to Habermas's notion of the public sphere is 'indispensable' for understanding the limitations of late-capitalist democracy and for projecting alternative democratic forms (Fraser 1992: 111). This sphere is an arena for discourse among citizens and is an institution on its own, apart from the state. Thus, the public sphere has the capacity to be critical of the state. From this premise, however, she goes on to argue that, in order properly to theorize the problems inherent in 'actually existing democracy', some critical reworking of Habermas's bourgeois public sphere is necessary (Fraser 1992: 111). Fraser traces through a revisionist historiography which suggests that Habermas's bourgeois conception of the public sphere was not just an unrealized ideal, but 'a masculinist ideological notion that functioned to legitimate an emergent form of class rule'; one that signalled the 'shift from a repressive mode of domination to a hegemonic one, from rule based primarily on acquiescence to superior force to rule based primarily on consent supplemented with some measure of repression' (1992: 116–17). Fraser argues that this historiography does not necessarily close down the use of the concept of a public sphere for critical purposes, but it does require that we question four assumptions at the core of Habermas's *'bourgeois, masculinist* conception': (1) that the public sphere is open and accessible to all, such that social equality is not a requirement for political democracy; (2) 'that a single, comprehensive public sphere is always preferable to a nexus of multiple publics'; (3) that discourse in the public sphere must steer away from private issues, and be restricted to discussion of the common good; and (4) 'a functioning democratic public sphere requires a sharp separation between civil society and the state' (Fraser 1992: 117–18).

Fraser writes that it is assumed within the concept of the bourgeois public sphere that social inequality can be 'bracketed', such that the participants can 'speak to one another as if they were social and economics peers' (1992: 118–19). Revisionist historiography is pointed to once again to show that this is far from the case. Even with a formal, legal equality of persons in place, Fraser writes that there are 'informal impediments' that remain, such as the tendency for men to interrupt women (1992: 119). There is also the mistaken assumption of 'zero-degree culture', which is seen to provide for neutrality and a good atmosphere for intervention. Yet, Fraser argues that there are informal pressures which mitigate against this as well: for example, 'unequally valued cultural styles', an informal pressure that is exacerbated by the fact that subordinated groups generally lack the material means to gain effective and equal participation (1992: 120). The question this raises for Fraser is whether we can think of public spheres as capable of this bracketing function when 'these discursive arenas are situated in a larger social context that is pervaded by structural relations of domination and subordination' (1992: 120). Because she finds that what is at issue here is the autonomy of political institutions, that is, public spheres *vis-à-vis* the encompassing social context, she examines liberalism and its features. She argues that liberalism assumes that democracy is possible among social structures of inequality; and thus, for liberals, 'the problem of democracy becomes the problem of how to insulate political processes from what are considered to be nonpolitical or prepolitical processes, those characteristic, for example, of the economy, the family, and informal everyday life' (Fraser 1992: 121). Fraser concludes that it is not politically sufficient to bracket social inequality. Political democracy requires a sort of 'rough equality', and it is a task of critical theory to illuminate the ways in which social inequality taints interaction within public spheres.

From 'intra-public relations', Fraser turns next to a discussion of 'inter-public relations' in considering the second assumption mentioned above: Habermas's emphasis on the bourgeois conception as the one, singular public arena. Here, Fraser compares the merits of a single versus multiple publics in both stratified and egalitarian societies. By a stratified society, Fraser refers to those societies 'whose basic institutional framework generates unequal social groups in structural relations of dominance and subordination' (1992: 122). In such a society, she writes, the most pressing question is what best 'narrows the gap in participatory parity' (Fraser 1992: 122). For Fraser, the answer is multiple public spheres. The effects mentioned above – that a discursive public sphere cannot be insulated from inequality in the larger social structure, and that public spheres will tend to disadvantage subordinate groups who do not have the material means to fight against domination – will only be made worse under one overarching public sphere. Fraser argues that these effects can be mitigated with multiple public spheres, since there would be alternative sites for deliberation, sites where the dominators are not present and where those subordinate groups can voice their ethical/ political concerns. Fraser labels these alternative discursive sites, *subaltern counterpublics* (1992: 123).[9] Subaltern counterpublics have a dual character according to Fraser, serving in the first instance as a space for 'withdrawal and regroupment'; and in the second, as 'training grounds for agitational activities directed toward wider publics' (1992: 124).[10] Both aspects are important to wear down unequal participatory practices in stratified societies. In regard to egalitarian societies, Fraser defines these as multicultural societies, 'whose basic framework does not generate unequal social groups', and thus, as societies 'without classes and without gender or racial divisions of labour' (1992: 125). Fraser writes that the important point to take into consideration here regarding merits of single or multiple publics is that the public sphere is also an arena for acting upon a

---

[9] Fraser adds that she is not suggesting that all subaltern counterpublics are good, only that their expansion is a good because it widens the possibilities for critique.

[10] Fraser (1991: 265) charges Rorty with advocating a form of feminist separatism that is concerned only with 'inward-directedness as opposed to outward-looking political struggle'. Yet, I find that Rorty's call for feminist entrenchment *does* possess the dual character of subaltern groups Fraser identifies, since Rorty advocates that feminists, like other clubs in history, turn in on themselves to 'try out new ways of speaking, and to gather the moral strength to go out and change the world' (Rorty 1991a: 247).

social identity and expressing one's cultural associations. According to Fraser, because public spheres cannot be 'culturally neutral', to have one public sphere means having one dominant set of cultural norms. Thus, for egalitarian societies as well, Fraser concludes that multiple publics are preferable.

Against the third assumption, Fraser challenges that there is no set line of division as to what can be regarded as a public versus a private matter. What counts as a common concern 'will be decided precisely through discursive contestation' (Fraser 1992: 129). Fraser is concerned that we should critically examine the ways in which public and private are used, because they 'are not simply straightforward designations of societal spheres; they are cultural classifications and rhetorical labels', which can be employed to 'delegitmate some interests, views, and topics and to valorize others' (1992: 131). The fourth assumption has to do with whether or not a sharp separation of civil society and state is necessary to a functioning democratic public sphere. Fraser concentrates on the conception of civil society that 'means the nexus of nongovernmental or "secondary" associations that are neither economic nor administrative' (1992: 133). Since Habermas sees the public sphere as an association of private persons, this means that participants in the bourgeois public are not state officials, and as a result, their decisions cannot authorize the use of state power. It is this aspect of state and civil society separation that confers upon the opinions which issue from the public sphere 'an aura of independence, autonomy and legitimacy' (Fraser 1992: 133–4). The consequence of this, according to Fraser, is to encourage what she calls '*weak publics*, publics whose deliberative practice consists exclusively in opinion formation and does not also encompass decision making' (1992: 134). However, Fraser points to a change of monumental importance in the history of the public sphere: the advent of sovereign parliaments that act as a 'public sphere *within* the state', which she calls '*strong publics*' (1992: 134). Their deliberations involve both the formulation of public opinion as well as decision-making, thus blurring the separation of civil society and the state. For Fraser, strong publics represent 'a democratic advance', because public opinion has the capability to turn its views into decisions that have authoritative force (1992: 134–5). This raises questions about the proper relationship of weak and strong publics to each another, particularly that of the accountability of strong publics to weak publics. She writes that there is also the question of the possibility of multiplying strong publics, manifested as 'self-managing institutions' like workplaces, child-care centres or residential communities, which establish 'sites of direct or quasi-direct democracy' (Fraser 1992: 135). Fraser concludes that a separation of civil society and the state inhibits our ability 'to imagine the forms of self-management, interpublic coordination, and political accountability that are essential to a democratic and egalitarian society' (1992: 136).

It is clear that features of moral imagination are employed here by Fraser. She draws attention to dominant forms of discourse, examining which discourses are excluded, thinking of ways in which alternative discourses can be given a voice, and imagining the institutional requirements necessary to this, as well as imagining the proliferation and possible incorporation of these institutions. I agree with Fraser that an idea of the public sphere is crucial to the critique of actually existing democratic states, but I want to add that the concept is equally indispensable for critique of actually existing IR. Interestingly, Dewey's writing suggests as much. Dewey, like Habermas, was concerned by the 'eclipse of the public', since it is with the public that the best hope for the democratic ideal at the base of his idea of growth rests. His book, *The Public and its Problems*, gives several indications of ways in which the concept of the public sphere could usefully be extended to global politics. I want to bring Dewey back into the frame of discussion here, not only for drawing out the dimension for international critique that publics can serve, but also for his emphasis upon two points that Fraser does not develop: (1) the problem of self-awareness as a public, and (2) the problem of what might serve to link diverse publics.

Many, although not all, of Fraser's concerns about Habermas's public sphere are addressed by Dewey in a way that may be deemed more satisfactory. To discuss how Dewey stands in relation to the four assumptions examined by Fraser, I will begin with Dewey's definitions of public and private. Dewey sees the starting point for theory to be human acts and their consequences upon others. He understands consequences to be of two kinds: the kind that affect persons directly engaged, and the kind that affect those who are not immediately engaged (Dewey 1927: 12). From this follows his distinction between the public and private. The public is constituted when 'indirect consequences are recognized and there is effort to regulate them, something having the traits of a state comes into existence' (Dewey 1927: 12). When the consequences are confined to those involved in a transaction, then it is private. Thus, not unlike Habermas's definition of the public, Dewey is interested in identifying common areas of concern or connection in the understanding of publics as arenas of discourse and inquiry into those interests.

In regard to Fraser's first concern, that social inequality be problematized within publics, Dewey agrees. He finds that the condition for a democratically organized public does not yet exist. That condition is the freedom of social inquiry and publicity of its conclusions (Dewey 1927: 166). He writes, that 'removal of formal limitations is but a negative condition', and what is needed is a positive freedom in having the wherewithal for inquiry (Dewey 1927: 168). Fraser may still have a point of argument with Dewey, since one could argue that his analysis focuses more upon the intellectual, rather than the material conditions of this requirement. However, on the other hand, the requirement of social equality is contained in Dewey's conception. It is exactly because Dewey presupposes 'a just organising of the division of labor' as functionally necessary to his conception of the democratic public that Axel Honneth finds it to be particularly compelling and to represent an improvement over Habermas (Honneth 1997: 24–6). However, it would not be unfair to question this commitment in Dewey's work, given his limited treatment of the economic aspects of social inequality. None the less, it can be said that both Dewey and Fraser share a belief in the need for a critical look at the possibility of participatory parity within publics.

Like Fraser, Dewey also recognizes the existence of multiple publics. Indeed, he sees their proliferation as a feature of the technological age, an age which has 'multiplied, intensified and complicated the scope of the indirect consequences' (Dewey 1927: 126). However, Dewey, unlike Fraser, is not prepared to celebrate this as a positive step in redressing unequal relations between differently empowered groups, because he maintains that an overarching democratic public remains integral to this task. He sees this proliferation as potentially blocking the organization of such an overarching public, as it distorts our capacity to perceive the reach of indirect consequences.

Thirdly, Dewey does not hold that private matters should be insulated from public debate. Because an act is private does not mean it is not social: 'private acts may be socially valuable both by indirect consequences and by direct intention' (Dewey 1927: 14). Most importantly, he emphasizes, as does Fraser, that what is public and what is private is a matter of dispute, and the question of where to draw the line for purposes of private action and public management can only be 'discovered experimentally' (Dewey 1927: 64–5).

Regarding the fourth assumption, it is evident from the definition above that what Dewey understands by a public is that which Fraser defines as a strong public, consisting of officials having the capacity for decision making. Dewey shares the idea that the practical concerns around which publics are formed are better served by having agencies and official representatives to attend to these concerns. For Dewey, a state is an articulated public, so there is not a civil society/state separation. However, not all publics are states. Publics by Dewey's definition are also the kind of institutions that Fraser describes as self-managing institutions. In addition, Dewey has a conception of a weak public understood as associated activity, but sees that without representative officials it is a public unorganized and ineffectual. Finally, as will be developed below, Dewey shares Fraser's concern that we must think about the character of the relationships between these various kinds of publics.

Due to limitations of space in her article, Fraser's discussion tails off at the point that her argument leads to the questions: how are we to think about the relationships between multiple publics, and what arrangements ensure democratic accountability between the various kinds of publics? For Dewey, in his book *The Public and its Problems*, this is the stage at which his primary concerns are just being articulated. Dewey finds the elaborate network of indirect consequences to be a global network that links us all in a Great Society, immense and impersonal, lacking of any political organization. States, the actually existing political and legal forms, are *incapable* of dealing with transnational consequences, once invisible, now made visible by World War I.[11] He writes that the 'need is that non-political forces organize themselves to transform existing structures: that divided and troubled publics integrate' (Dewey 1927: 128–9). However, this requires an overarching awareness of *the* public, that he finds cannot become self-aware. Thus, it remains 'in eclipse', until 'the Great Society is converted into a Great Community' (Dewey 1927: 142). Here Dewey is taking the consideration of publics beyond the realm of the domestic polity that is the nation-state, to analysis at the level of the international. In so doing, interesting questions are raised about the

[11] Fraser (1992: 136) also raises the issue of global interdependence challenging the state form but does not develop it further.

critical potential of public spheres that are not developed by Fraser, particularly two aspects that are exacerbated at the level of the international. For example, she takes it for granted that publics will know themselves to be publics, and that they will proliferate. Thus, she does not consider the problems for self-awareness as a public, forces that might obfuscate recognition of common interests or ties. Secondly, as she is ultimately focused in this article on the good of multiple publics providing alternative sites of critique, she does not develop the question of what happens when those publics have to coordinate for social purposes. What enables them to work together? Fraser recognizes that there is a need for a more comprehensive arena for discussion of issues that affect all publics, but she is not able to take this point very far, other than a brief discussion of the possibility of intercultural communication.

For Dewey, this is an important point, since it is from this kind of overarching coordination that critique of actually existing democracy begins. I do not think Fraser would disagree. The proliferation of publics can be an important institutional development for expanding opportunities for critique in the stratified societies that constitute IR. However, we cannot lose sight of the fact that these publics are situated in a wider setting of international practice, a point similar to Fraser's with regard to publics being embedded in the single struc-tured setting of the domestic polity. Thus, in taking the consideration of publics to the international, as institutions of international ethical critique, what is required is not only consideration of the possibility of their proliferation, but also consideration of the 'how' of self-aware recognition and the provision of relationships of accountability and coordination in the setting of international practice. In order to do so, moral imagination must be employed to see what discourses and institutional practices have been trapped under layers of interstate relations, dominant for so long. Layers to be stripped might include: (1) the assumption of formal equality among states, in order to theorize the ways in which material and discursive inequality among state actors distorts democratic participatory parity in IR; (2) the assumption of states as sovereign, in order to theorize first, the roles of non-state actors as sites of international ethical critique, and secondly, the material and discursive possibilities for their democratic participation; and (3) the assumption that the state form is ahistorical, in order to consider the state's potential obsolescence so that new institutional forms might be imagined and constructed. In removing these layers of dominant discourse we are able to see inchoate groups and practices, clearly marginalized, yet generally lacking sufficient awareness and political organization to be strong publics internationally. From here, moral imagination must be employed to communicate the possibilities for their integration internally as well as externally in the setting of international practice.

Conclusion

There are several questions that remain which would require treatment in any future work that would aim to develop the institutional possibilities represented in the Deweyan concept of the public sphere. Awareness of the public hinges on the recognition of indirect consequences which affect us and are seen to require social cooperation, but how are we to know which consequences are so serious as to need controlling (Smiley 1990: 371)? Future work must address this and draw from its response to give some indication of how publics become institutionalized. It must inquire as to how public spheres could exercise power in international politics and when they should seek to exercise that power. Also it would need to examine how international public spheres would be internally regulated and made democratically accountable in the way that states are assumed to be in modern international politics.

Of course, Dewey recognized the insurmountable difficulties in establishing the kind of international coordination and accountability *among* multiple publics that I am suggesting could be an interesting way into better realizing the democratic ideal. While I too understand that these are certainly considerable, I see that what could take place *within* particular international public spheres is a good place to start, since they are particularly well suited institutionally for facilitating possibilities for both authentic critique and convergence around a democratic ethos. Their advantage in regard to authentic critique rests in the fact that publics are not held together solely by communal ties and do not rely on those ties to motivate social cooperation. Nor are they held together by an abstract communicative requirement, which may be seen as an external imposition. What brings them together and holds them together is the need for social cooperation, which is occasioned by the recognition of an intersocietal tension as a problem that must be addressed. Such tensions may arise, become entrenched and maintain international public spheres for a considerable length of

271

time; others may not engender or sustain international publics for long. However, those that do arise around particular transnational situations which are found problematic can encourage convergence around shared normative standards as well as possibilities for transformation of past intersocietal practice. They serve as sites where individuals can work out the specific concerns they share, find consensus on mechanisms for articulating those concerns, and press their concerns to better effect within wider arenas such as states or international and non-governmental organizations. The emergence of international public spheres is in many ways contingent. However, the prospects for the incorporation of marginalized groups in world politics and the possibilities for improving beyond the actually existing institutions of international practice provide compelling reasons for pursuing them further. This is one of the central tasks in which moral imagination is to be engaged. To *create* these relationships is the aim of international ethics as pragmatic critique.

To conclude this chapter, while modernist and postmodernist debates continue, while we are still unsure as to what we can legitimately identify as a feminist ethical/political concern, while we still are unclear about the relationship of discourse and experience, it is particularly important for feminists that we proceed with analysis of both the material (institutional and structural) as well as the discursive. This holds not only for feminists, but for all theorists oriented towards the goal of extending further moral inclusion in the present social sciences climate of epistemological uncertainty. Important ethical/political concerns hang in the balance. We cannot afford to wait for the meta-theoretical questions to be conclusively answered. Those answers may be unavailable. Nor can we wait for a credible vision of an alternative institutional order to appear before an emancipatory agenda can be kicked into gear. Nor do we have before us a chicken and egg question of which comes first: sorting out the meta-theoretical issues or working out which practices contribute to a credible institutional vision. The two questions can and should be pursued together, and can be, *via* moral imagination. Imagination can help us think beyond discursive and material conditions which limit us, by pushing the boundaries of those limitations in thought and examining what yields. In this respect, I believe international ethics as pragmatic critique can be a useful ally to feminists and normative theorists generally.

Conclusion

Wittingly or unwittingly, the construction of normative IR theory in terms of the cosmopolitan/communitarian debate has given primacy to epistemology, through its efforts to justify its ontological priorities and stake a claim that can rest solidly, providing an unshakeable international ethics in face of the diversity within international practice. In bolstering their ontologies with a contestable orientation to epistemologically centred argument, cosmopolitans and communitarians are creating obstacles that need not be in the way of normative theorizing in IR and as a result, are closing down the possibilities we may have for exploring the interplay between these positions. Also, until we recognize that there is no truth for these claims to be found 'out there', we will be needlessly diverting energies that are required for continual engagement with the ethical criteria that we propose, the interrogation of existing institutional arrangements, and the imagining of new institutional possibilities. Once a move is made to work as free of epistemologically centred argument as someone who wants to outline an ethical position is able, we are not left with the conclusion that normative standards are no longer available, only that we have to recognize their contingency and build upon what possibilities can then be created for the expansion of moral inclusion in international practice.

The first line of inquiry pursued in this book was to examine the nature and the extent of the impasse in normative IR theory, as it is presently discussed within the framework of the cosmopolitan/communitarian debate. Using the formulation of three central issues to analyse points of difference in the debate – a concept of the person, the moral standing of states, and the universal versus the particular – it was argued in part I that, while possibilities for accommodation on

273

each of these issues are evident, a structural opposition remains regarding how to justify ethical claims in IR. Should individuals on the basis of their equal capacities for moral judgement and autonomy be the focus of considerations of justice; or should states, as institutions which allow for the self-actualization of persons in a mutually constitutive practice, be at the centre of ethical considerations in IR?

Having established that there is indeed an impasse and having determined its epistemological nature, a second line of inquiry followed, as to whether normative IR theory was in fact addressing the most pressing questions facing it. Here, I asked what an engagement with antifoundationalist approaches might suggest. An examination of two lines of antifoundationalist thinking in political and normative IR theory in part II concluded that both antifoundationalisms open up the parameters of ethical theorizing in IR, in their efforts to illuminate the dangers of exclusion and oppression in the kind of foundationalism that generates the oppositions within the cosmopolitan/communitarian debate. It was established that with the critique of foundationalist epistemologies that has been unleashed in the social sciences, a central issue that normative IR theory must face is what kind of ethical claims it can now make and how it should proceed. Unfortunately, neither of the antifoundationalist approaches discussed in part II fully problematizes its own recourse to weak foundations in the kind of ethics that results from its project.

Part III began the third line of inquiry, which proposed a notion of international ethics as pragmatic critique which works towards as thoroughgoing an antifoundationalism as is possible, yet is politically engaged with concerns for expanding moral inclusion and social reconstruction. An examination of the capacity of such an ethics to extend moral inclusion – in particular, to a feminist ethical/political agenda – suggested that the pragmatic synthesis offered here is prepared to get stuck into difficult ethical questions, but without recourse to absolutizing possibilities for convergence, and with an eye to both the discursive and the material aspects of power that may block effective ethical critique.

In closing the book, I would like to offer some final thoughts about the relationship of the notion of ethics as pragmatic critique to the ethical projects of the writers discussed in the book. We all share a basic impulse that motivates the projects we pursue. It is the same impulse, as I see it, that places us all – foundationalists and antifoundationalists alike – under the umbrella of normative IR theory: a concern to suggest shared principles for extending moral obligations, and thus moral inclusion, that reaches beyond a *modus vivendi* understanding of interpersonal and intersocietal relations in world politics. This motivation arises from a shared commitment among these writers, albeit with different weights attributed to personally and socially chosen aspects of selfhood, to enhance human autonomy. In regard to this aim, the cosmopolitanism of Charles Beitz and Thomas Pogge is significant not only for the attention it focuses upon a fair distribution of liberties among persons, but also for arguing that issues concerning the just distribution of opportunities and resources are important questions of international ethics. Michael Walzer's idea of a minimum morality is an important communitarian effort in establishing possibilities for shared universal moral principles across plural and diverse ethical practices. Andrew Linklater and Mervyn Frost, from their respective cosmopolitan and communitarian positions, focus upon what has been a crucial problem in articulating shared principles for ethical critique in world politics and work to solve that problem: the tension over the base for critique and the subject of justice, individuals or states.

All are significant contributions to normative IR theory, yet from the perspective of international ethics as pragmatic critique, each has problems. To begin, pragmatic critique shares with Beitz and Pogge a concern for international distributive justice, however, not only is this concern compromised by their use of weak-foundationalist argument non-contingently, but it is also limited by their reluctance to contemplate any possible moral significance to more local or particular ethical relations based on community or the links between these relations and wider human relations. Pragmatic critique has much in common with Walzer, in terms of starting from the traditions of community practice as the ground for ethical critique, yet seeking possibilities for extended moral inclusion in principles which reach beyond particular communities. However, where Walzer understands those principles to be given, pragmatic critique understands that those principles must be created and that we must work hard to be aware of the particular values reflected, or at times dominant, in the universals offered.

Frost and Linklater share with pragmatic critique the aim of showing that the problem of the core tension within normative IR theory is indeed not a problem. None of us quite manages to do so, nor will we, for as long as weak foundations are invoked for ethical theorizing in IR, some residue of this core tension will remain. Yet, as the book has demonstrated, pragmatic critique offers insights into the interplay between the value of individual autonomy and the value of community membership in a way that the knowledge-stakes of the foundationalist projects in which Frost and Linklater work cannot. Also pragmatic critique suggests a way in which Hegelian method can best be used, now that the ghost of truth/knowledge has been given up, such that a trade-off or opposition between 'reform' versus 'radical change' appropriations of Hegel does not have to result. It begins with the acknowledgement that the social tensions which give rise to immanent critique may not be sufficient for initiating anything more than reform in some instances. Perhaps nothing more is required and this is how inquiry is temporarily concluded. However, the same tensions may suggest the need for moral imagination to play an important supplementary role to immanent critique by projecting possibilities for radical change that may only be available through an engagement with that which is other or different, outside of our immediate resources of value. Normative theorizing in IR cannot necessarily rely on immanent critique as Frost and Linklater would have it.

Finally, there is much that pragmatic critique has in common with poststructuralist antifoundationalism: the critique of epistemologically centred thought, a will to wider moral inclusion and social reconstruction, and a recognition of the need to create a democratic and pluralist ethos. Also, both R. B. J. Walker and William Connolly invoke the power of imagination in projecting alternative ethical/ political practices, and there are many similarities between Walker's discussion of the role of critical social movements in *One World, Many Worlds* (1988) and my discussion of the alternative world politics enabled by 'publics' in chapter 8. However, a pointed challenge from this perspective to pragmatist approaches suggests a dividing line.

Chantal Mouffe writes that the 'consensus approach' of Rorty does not grasp the nature of democratic politics, since it 'requires coming to terms with the dimension of antagonism that is present in social relations' (Mouffe 1996: 8). Mouffe does acknowledge, along with pragmatists, that consensus is necessary and that the creation of a democratic ethos is needed to 'secure allegiance and adhesion' to democratic principles (1996: 5). Yet, although there is this acknowledgement, the focus of Mouffe and others who share her poststructuralist perspective, Derrideans and Foucauldians alike, is centered in the main upon the power relations that constitute the public realm, suggesting the need for this antagonistic dimension. For Mouffe, Rorty eliminates the political, these forces of antagonism in democratic politics, through a public/private split which provides for the possibility of consensus within the public realm (Mouffe 1996: 8–9). However, as I see it, pragmatic approaches do not have to be incapacitated in this way. By dropping the public/private split in Rorty and facing the need to think more comprehensively about the power considerations already present in pragmatism's concern to provide for the possibilities of authentic critique, international ethics as pragmatic critique is better placed to theorize this aspect of democratic politics. However, the challenge that I want make in return to poststructuralists is that they too have a similar responsibility to take up consideration of the same dilemma that brought pragmatic critique to this place: whether consideration of power relations, on the one hand, and the understanding of community and its normative structures as being valued, on the other, can be theorized together. I do not see that poststructuralists are necessarily incapacitated in this regard, but their energies have not been directed towards thinking about how either the value we place in community or the 'adherence' or 'consensus' also necessary to democratic politics may be theorized from their approach. The concerns of normative IR theory would benefit from a cooperative antifoundationalist engagement with this question.

However, I think the most clear summary I can provide for the position outlined here in terms of its relation to other projects discussed in the book is to come back and look once again at the project of the critical foil whom I identified in the introduction, Linklater. To begin, there are many points of convergence in our projects. We share a concept of the person which values autonomy and sees as necessary to that autonomy the wherewithal to participate in shaping the contexts which affect and are important to the individual concerned. For this reason, among others, we share a commitment to democratic institutions which allow for the possibility of communities of practical deliberation among persons. The possibility for this kind of deliberation is key because of two features of modern society that are a concern for both of us as normative theorists. The first is that the *diversity and plurality* which characterize modernity must be properly acknowledged. In the face of this diversity, we share the idea that we can only begin 'from where we are' in finding some basis for critique of intersocietal relations. With this recognition and from the basis of our orientation to human autonomy, we share the idea that any criteria found can only 'prove workable', to put it in my terms, or 'legitimate' to put it in Linklater's, if they are derived consensually through deliberation among those affected. The second feature of modern societies which concerns us is the feature Linklater describes as 'transnational harm', or what Dewey describes as the worrying effects of the unrecognized, indirect consequences of transnational activity. This concern too arises from our particular ontological proclivities, that it is necessary to the full individuality and freedom of persons that they have a say in regard to outcomes, decisions, phenomena which affect them.

Because of the number of similarities here, it is important to clarify the differences between our positions, the 'whys' of these differences and their significance. The most basic difference is that Linklater is pursuing a foundationalist basis for the ontological claims we share and I am aiming for what I would call a 'quasi-antifoundationalist' position. This is a difference, as the introduction suggested, that leads to the need I see for tracing through that which distinguishes cosmopolitans and communitarians, and why Linklater is less convinced of this need. While Linklater recognizes that foundations today have to be formulated *weakly* and he agrees that *weak* foundations open up possibilities for finding overlap in divergent positions, I have suggested that what must also be acknowledged is the possibility that a significant obstacle may remain in seeking convergence when one holds a *weak* foundation *non-contingently*; that is, when one assumes it is not up for question that all human beings are morally equal and should be treated universally as ends. This kind of *weak* but *non-contingent* foundationalism creates difficulties which have methodological and political repercussions.

The methodological difficulties are related to assumptions within Habermasian discourse ethics discussed in chapter 8. The extent to which Linklater may share these difficulties was discussed in chapter 3. However, here, I want to pick up again the political difficulty that I raised in chapter 3 in order to draw attention to what pragmatic critique has to offer. That political difficulty identified was: if the foundational claim for the unfinished project of modernity is indeed contestable, how can the logic of human autonomy, or as Linklater puts it – the full extension of citizenship rights – be promoted? If Linklater takes seriously his idea that all we can lay claim to is a thin notion of progress, then we cannot count on the paradox of the state to create and mould wider universalities of discourse which are capable of transforming our notions of responsibility to persons in intersocietal practice. As I see it, a wider conception of the institutions of international political practice than these state-based discourses, albeit radically changed state-based discourses, must be actively theorized by Linklater. International public spheres, as discussed in chapter 8, can fulfil that wider conception of international institutional practice and may facilitate not only the creation of connection, convergence and social cooperation among persons, but also the kind of agonistic politics and possibilities for at least approximating authentic critique which concern poststructuralists and feminists. Pragmatic critique sees oppositional politics, politics that for a time is not linked to the state or the economy, to be crucial to enlarging the possibilities for imaginative solutions to pressing social tensions and to providing possibilities for convergence around a democratic ethos. Indeed, I see that international public spheres are necessary to social interaction within the post-Westphalian state Linklater envisions.

In sum, I argue that a wider conception of international political practice on the basis of more *contingently* held foundations is key to the transformations we would both like to see transpire. While Linklater and I share the idea that the contradictions and social tensions of modern society are the stimulus to seeking convergence, I want to stress that we cannot be confident of a singular logic emerging from those contradictions which is capable of revealing the possibilities for value consensus. In my mind, to read into these contradictions such a singular logic presents possibilities for epistemological gridlock and nasty political repercussions, since such a logic may be felt by some as an external imposition that compromises their own ideas of human flourishing. Instead, pragmatic critique begins with the assumption that there is no such 'reliable' motor. Yes, the identification of problematic situations is a motor for ethical engagement, but it provides only a stimulus for such activity and in no way directs it 'reliably' towards a consensual outcome. Behind this engagement with problematic situations is a weakly held ontological priority of growth, where growth is understood as a view that individuals flourish by improving upon possibilities of expressing their freedom and autonomy in cooperation with others. While one cannot cling to this ontological priority in any strong sense, critical intelligence and its use of moral imagination can create possibilities for consensus around a democratic ethos through its discursive and institutional aspects. In particular, the benefit gained by this orientation to the contingent nature of the possibility of convergence is this: by not counting on 'reliable' motors, or logics of modernity, it is forced to look beyond the dynamics of the transformation of the state which may or may not be taking place to wider ideas of intersocietal political practice and their transformative potential.

To conclude, by evaluating the impasse of the cosmopolitan/ communitarian debate, I have situated it within a larger debate in the social sciences about modernist, foundationalist epistemologies and also demonstrated its relation to a parallel debate in political theory between liberals and communitarians. Normative IR theory already possesses an advantage lacking in other subfields of the discipline: it draws from many fields within the social sciences. Yet, oddly enough, those participant in the cosmopolitan/communitarian debate have not applied enough thought to the epistemological nature of their own debate and the debate's connection to what is going on in the social sciences generally. This book has argued that normative IR theorists must face the questions feminists and others have been facing about how theory should proceed now that the questioning of foundationalist epistemologies has been unleashed. Normative IR theory must recognize and confront the epistemological nature of its current impasse. It has also been the aim of this book not only to discuss what needs to be done, but to make a constructive attempt at doing it: to reconceptualize the way in which universals based on *weak* foundations might be offered, through the assumption of fallibilism, and to suggest how moral inclusion might be extended through moral imagination applied to both discursive and material possibilities. This is my hope for what international ethics as pragmatic critique might achieve.

References

Alexander, Thomas (1993), 'John Dewey and the Moral Imagination: Beyond Putnam and Rorty toward a Postmodern Ethics', *Transactions of the C. S. Peirce Society* 29: 369–400.

Allen, Jonathan (1992), 'Liberals, Communitarians and Political Theory', *South African Journal of Philosophy* 11: 77–90.

Arneson, Richard (1989), 'Symposium on Rawlsian Theory of Justice: Recent Developments, Introduction', *Ethics* 99: 695–710.

Ashley, Richard (1987), 'The Geopolitics of Geopolitical Space: Toward a Critical Social Theory of International Politics', *Alternatives: Social Transformations and Humane Governance* 12: 403–34.

(1988), 'Untying the Sovereign State: A Double Reading of the Anarchy Problematique', *Millennium: Journal of International Studies* 17: 227–62.

(1988), 'Living on Borderlines: Man, Poststructuralism and War', in Der Derian and Shapiro (eds.), pp. 259–321.

Ashley, Richard and Walker, R. B. J. (1990), 'Reading Dissidence/Writing the Discipline: Crisis and the Question of Sovereignty in International Studies', *International Studies Quarterly* 34: 367–416.

Barrett, Michèle (1992), 'Words and Things: Materialism and Method in Contemporary Feminist Analysis' in Barrett and Phillips (eds.), pp. 201–19.

Barrett, Michèle and Phillips, Anne (eds.) (1992), *Destabilizing Theory: Contemporary Feminist Debates*, Cambridge: Polity Press.

Barry, Brian (1973), *The Liberal Theory of Justice*, Oxford: Clarendon Press.

(1989), *Democracy, Power and Justice: Essays in Political Theory*, Oxford: Clarendon Press.

Beitz, Charles (1979), *Political Theory and International Relations*, Princeton University Press.

(1983), 'Cosmopolitan Ideals and National Sentiment', *Journal of Philosophy* 80: 591–601.

Bell, Daniel (1993), *Communitarianism and its Critics*, Oxford: Clarendon Press.

Bellamy, Richard (1992), *Liberalism and Modern Society*, Cambridge: Polity Press.

Bernstein, Richard (1976), *The Restructuring of Social and Political Theory*, University of Pennsylvania Press.

(1986), *Philosophical Profiles: Essays in a Pragmatic Mode*, Cambridge: Polity Press.

(1991), *The New Constellation: The Ethical-Political Horizons of Modernity/ Postmodernity*, Cambridge: Polity Press.

(1995), 'American Pragmatism: The Conflict of Narratives', in Saatkamp (ed.), *Rorty and Pragmatism*, Vanderbilt University Press, pp. 54–67.

Bickford, Susan (1993), 'Why we Listen to Lunatics: Antifoundational Theories and Feminist Politics', *Hypatia: A Journal of Feminist Philosophy* 8: 104–23.

Brodsky, Garry (1982), 'Rorty's Interpretation of Pragmatism', *Transactions of the C. S. Peirce Society* 18: 311–37.

Brown, Chris (1992), *International Relations Theory: New Normative Approaches*, Columbia University Press.

(1994), ' "Turtles All the Way Down": Anti-Foundationalism, Critical Theory and International Relations', *Millennium: Journal of International Studies* 23: 213–38.

Bull, Hedley (1966), 'The Grotian Conception of International Society', in Butterfield and Wight (eds.), *Diplomatic Investigations: Essays on International Politics*, London: George Allen and Unwin, pp. 51–73.

(1977), *The Anarchical Society: A Study of Order in World Politics*, London: Macmillan.

(1984), 'Justice in International Relations: The Hagey Lectures', University of Waterloo.

Bull, Hedley and Watson, Adam (eds.) (1984), *The Expansion of International Society*, Oxford: Clarendon Press.

Butler, Judith (1992), 'Contingent Foundations: Feminism and the Question of "Postmodernism" ', in Butler and Scott (eds.), pp. 3–21.

Butler, Judith and Scott, Joan (eds.) (1992), *Feminists Theorize the Political*, London: Routledge.

Campbell, David (1992), *Writing Security: United States Foreign Policy and the Politics of Identity*, Manchester University Press.

(1993), *Politics Without Principle: Sovereignty, Ethics, and the Narratives of the Gulf War*, Boulder, CO: Lynne Rienner.

(1994), 'The Deterritorilization of Responsibility: Levinas, Derrida, and Ethics After the End of Philosophy', *Alternatives: Social Transformation and Humane Governance* 19: 455–84.

(1996), 'The Politics of Radical Interdependence: A Rejoinder to Daniel Warner', *Millennium: Journal of International Studies* 25: 129–41.

Campbell, David and Dillon, Michael (eds.) (1993), *The Political Subject of Violence*, Manchester University Press.

Caney, Simon (1992), 'Liberalism and Communitarianism: A Misconceived Debate', *Political Studies* 40: 273–89.

Carens, Joseph (1995), 'Complex Justice, Cultural Difference, and Political

Community', in Miller and Walzer (eds.), *Pluralism, Justice and Equality,* Oxford University Press, pp. 45–66.

Charvet, John (1998), 'International Society from a Contractarian Perspective', in Terry Nardin (ed.), *International Society: Diverse Ethical Perspectives,* Princeton University Press, pp. 114– 131.

Clark, Ann (1993), 'The Quest for Certainty in Feminist Thought', *Hypatia* 8: 84–93.

Cochran, Molly (1995), 'Cosmopolitanism and Communitarianism in a Post-Cold War World', in Macmillan and Andrew Linklater (eds.), *Boundaries in Question: New Directions in International Relations,* London: Pinter Press, pp. 40–53.

Comay, Rebecca (1986), 'Interrupting the Conversation: Notes on Rorty', *Telos* 19: 119–30.

Connolly, William (1983), 'On Richard Rorty: Two Views', *Raritan* 2: 124–35.

(1991), *Identity/Difference: Democratic Negotiations of Political Paradox,* Cornell University Press.

(1995), *The Ethos of Pluralization,* University of Minnesota Press.

Danielson, Peter (1973), 'Theories, Intuitions and the Problem of World-Wide Distributive Justice', *Philosophy of the Social Sciences* 3: 331–40.

Der Derian, James (1987), *On Diplomacy: A Genealogy of Western Estrangement,* Oxford: Blackwell.

(1992), *Antidiplomacy: Spies, Terror, Speed and War,* Oxford: Blackwell.

Der Derian, James and Shapiro, Michael (eds.) (1989), *International/Intertextual Relations: Postmodern Readings of World Politics,* Lexington: Lexington Books.

Dewey, John (1922), *Human Nature and Conduct,* New York: Random House.

(1927), *The Public and its Problems,* London: Swallow Press.

(1929), *Experience and Nature,* London: George Allen and Unwin.

(1930), *Individualism, Old and New,* New York: Minton, Balch and Company.

(1931), 'The Practical Character of Reality' in Dewey, *Philosophy and Civilization,* New York: G. M. Putnam and Sons, pp. 36–55.

(1938), Logic: *The Theory of Inquiry,* New York: Henry Holt and Company.

(1946), *The Problems of Men,* London: Philosophical Library.

(1948), *Reconstruction in Philosophy,* Boston: Beacon Press.

Doppelt, Gerald (1979), 'Walzer's Theory of Morality in International Relations', *Philosophy and Public Affairs* 8: 3–26.

Dunne, Timothy and Wheeler, N. J. (eds.) (1996), 'Hedley Bull's Pluralism of the Intellect and Solidarism of the Will', *International Affairs* 71: 91–107.

Edel, Abraham (1985), 'A Missing Dimension in Rorty's Use of Pragmatism', *Transactions of the C. S. Peirce Society* 21: 21–38.

Festenstein, Matthew (1997), *Pragmatism and Political Theory,* Cambridge: Polity Press.

Foucault, Michel (1970), *The Order of Things: An Archaeology of the Human Sciences,* London: Routledge.

(1984), 'What is Enlightenment?' in Paul Rabinow (ed.), *The Foucault Reader*, London: Pantheon Press.

Fraser, Nancy (1987), 'On the Political and the Symbolic: Against the Metaphysics of Textuality', *Enclitic* 9: 100–14.

(1989), *Unruly Practices: Power, Discourse and Gender in Contemporary Social Theory*, Cambridge: Polity Press.

(1990), 'Solidarity or Singularity? Richard Rorty Between Romanticism and Technocracy;, in Malachowski (ed.), *Reading Rorty*, Oxford: Basil Blackwell, pp. 303–21.

(1991), 'From Irony to Prophecy to Politics: A Response to Richard Rorty', *Michigan Quarterly Review* 30: 259–66.

(1992), 'Rethinking the Public Sphere: A Contribution to the Critique of Actually Existing Democracy', in Calhoun (ed.), *Habermas and the Public Sphere*, Cambridge, Mass.: MIT Press, pp. 109–42.

(1995a), 'False Antitheses', and 'Pragmatism, Feminism and the Linguistic Turn' in Benhabib, Butler, *et al.*, *Feminist Contentions: A Philosophical Exchange*, London: Routledge, pp. 59–74 and 157–71.

(1995b), 'What's Critical about Critical Theory?: The Case of Habermas and Gender', in Tuana and Tong (eds.), *Feminism and Philosophy: Essential Readings in Theory, Reinterpretation, and Application*, Boulder, CO: Westview Press, pp. 272–98.

Fraser, Nancy and Gordon, Linda (1994), 'A Genealogy of *Dependency*: Tracing a Keyword of the U.S. Welfare State', *Signs: a Journal of Women in Culture and Society* 19: 309–36.

Fraser, Nancy and Nicholson, Linda (1988), 'Social Criticism without Philosophy: An Encounter between Feminism and Postmodernism' in Ross (ed.), *Universal Abandon: The Politics of Postmodernism*, University of Edinburgh Press, pp. 83–104.

Frazer, Elizabeth and Lacey, Nicola (1993), *The Politics of Community: A Feminist Critique of the Liberal-Communitarian Debate*, New York: Harvester/ Wheatsheaf.

Friedman, Marilyn (1993), *What are Friends For? Feminist Perspectives on Personal Relationships and Moral Theory*, Cornell University Press.

Fritzman, J. M. (1993), 'Thinking with Fraser about Rorty, Feminism, and Pragmatism', *Praxis International* 13: 113–25.

Frost, Mervyn (1986), *Towards a Normative Theory of International Relations* Cambridge University Press.

(1986), 'What is to be Done about the Condition of States?' in Navari (ed.), *The Condition of States*, Milton Keynes: Open University Press, pp. 183–96.

(1993), 'Towards a Resolution of the Debate Between Liberals and Communitarians', paper for the *British International Studies Association Annual Meeting*, Warwick.

(1994a), 'Constituting a New World Order: What States, Whose Will, What Territory?', *Paradigms: The Kent Journal of International Relations* 8: 13–22.

(1994b), 'Transformation? The Non-Intervention Norm and International

Society', paper for the 11 June, Ford Foundation *Workshop on Humanitarian Intervention and International Society*, London.

(1996), *Ethics in International Relations: A Constitutive Theory* Cambridge University Press.

(1999) forthcoming, 'Global Civil Society', in Hovden and Keene (eds.), *The Globalisation of Liberalism?*, London: Macmillan.

Fukuyama, Francis (1992), *The End of History and the Last Man*, London: Free Press.

Galston, William (1982), 'Moral Personality and Liberal Theory: John Rawls's Dewey Lectures', *Political Theory* 10: 492–520.

(1989), 'Community, Democracy and Philosophy: The Political Thought of Michael Walzer', *Political Theory* 17: 119–30.

Gatens-Robinson, Eugenie (1991), 'Dewey and the Feminist Successor Science Project', *Transactions of the C. S. Peirce Society* 27: 416–433.

George, Jim (1993), 'Of Incarnation and Closure: Neo-Realism and the New/ Old World Orders', *Millennium: Journal of International Studies* 22: 197–234.

(1994), *Discourses of Global Politics: A Critical (Re)Introduction to International Relations*, Boulder, CO: Lynne Rienner.

(1995), 'Realist "Ethics", International Relations, and Post-modernism: Thinking Beyond the Egoism-Anarchy Thematic', *Millennium: Journal of International Studies* 24: 195–223.

Gong, G. W. (1984), *The Standard of 'Civilization' in International Society*, Oxford: Clarendon Press.

Guignon, Charles and Hiley, David (1990), 'Biting the Bullet: Rorty on Private and Public Morality', in Malachowski (ed.), *Reading Rorty*, Oxford: Blackwell, pp. 339–64.

Haacke, Jürgen (1996), 'Theory and Practice in International Relations: Habermas, Self-Reflection, Rational Argumentation', *Millennium: Journal of International Studies* 25: 255–289.

Haber, Honi (1994), *Beyond Postmodern Politics*, London: Routledge.

Habermas, Jürgen (1984), *The Theory of Communicative Action, Volume 1: Reason and Rationalization of Society*, Boston: Beacon Press.

(1990), *Moral Consciousness and Communicative Action*, Oxford: Polity Press.

Hampton, Jean (1989), 'Should Political Philosophy Be Done Without Metaphysics?', *Ethics* 99: 791–814.

Hart, Caroll Guen (1993), 'John Dewey's *Logic* and the Dream of a Common Language', *Hypatia: A Journal of Feminist Philosophy* 8: 190–214.

Hardimon, Michael (1994), *Hegel's Social Philosophy: The Project of Reconciliation*, Cambridge University Press.

Hekman, Susan (1990), *Gender and Knowledge: Elements of a Postmodern Feminism*, Cambridge: Polity Press.

(1995), *Moral Voices, Moral Selves: Carol Gilligan and Feminist Moral Theory*, Cambridge: Polity Press.

Hegel, G. W. F. (1967), *Philosophy of Right*, trans. T. M. Knox, Oxford University Press.

(1977), *The Phenomenology of Spirit*, trans. A. V. Miller, Oxford University Press.

Held, Virginia (1993), *Feminist Morality: Transforming Culture, Society, and Politics*, Chicago University Press.

Hickman, Larry (1993), 'Liberal Irony and Social Reform', in Stuhr (ed.), *Philosophy and the Reconstruction of Culture: Pragmatic Essays after Dewey*, New York: SUNY Press, pp. 223–39.

Hoffman, Mark (1985), 'Normative Approaches', in Light and Groom (eds.), *International Relations: A Handbook of Current Theory*, London: Pinter Press, pp. 27–45.

(1993), 'Agency, Identity and Intervention' in Forbes and Hoffman (eds.), *Political Theory, International Relations and the Ethics of Intervention*, London: Macmillan, pp. 194–211.

Hollis, Martin and Smith, Steve (1991), *Explaining and Understanding International Relations*, Oxford: Clarendon Press.

Honneth, Axel (1997), 'Democracy as Reflexive Cooperation: John Dewey and Democratic Theory Today', unpublished manuscript from his Hannah Arendt Memorial Lecture at the University of Southampton, 12 June.

Hovden, Eivind and Keene, Edward (eds.) (1995), 'The Globalisation of Liberalism?', Special Issue of *Millennium: Journal of International Studies* 24:3.

Hutchings, Kimberly (1994), 'Borderline Ethics: Feminist Morality and International Relations', *Paradigms: Kent Journal of International Relations* 8: 23–35.

Ikenberry, G. I. and Kupchan, C. A. (1990), 'Socialization and Hegemonic Power', *International Organization* 44: 283–317.

Jagger, Alison (1983), *Feminist Politics and Human Nature*, Harvester Press.

Johnson, Mairi and Maiguashca, Bice (eds.) (1994), 'Social Movements and World Politics', Special Issue of *Millennium: Journal of International Studies*, 23:3.

Johnson, Mark (1993), *Moral Imagination: Implications of Cognitive Science for Ethics*, Chicago: University of Chicago Press.

Kaufman-Osborn, Timothy (1993), 'Teasing Feminist Sense from Experience', *Hypatia: A Journal of Feminist Philosophy* 8: 124–44.

Keene, Edward (1998), *The Colonising Ethic and Modern International Society: A Reconstruction of the Grotian Tradition of International Theory*, PhD thesis, University of London.

Kolakowski, Leszek (1978), *Main Currents of Marxism: Its Rise, Growth and Dissolution, Vol.I*, trans. P. S. Falla, Oxford: Clarendon Press.

Kukathas, Chandran and Pettit, Philip (1990), *Rawls: A Theory of Justice and its Critics*, Cambridge: Polity Press.

Kymlica, Will (1995), *Multicultural Citizenship: A Liberal Theory of Rights*, Oxford: Clarendon Press.

Leffers, M. Regina (1993), 'Pragmatists Jane Addams and John Dewey Inform the Ethic of Care', *Hypatia: A Journal of Feminist Philosophy* 8: 64–77.

Leland, Dorothy (1988), 'Rorty on the Moral Concern of Philosophy: A Critique from a Feminist Point of View', *Praxis International* 8: 273–83.

Linklater, Andrew (1990a), *Beyond Realism and Marxism*, London: Macmillan.

(1990b) (2nd edn), *Men and Citizens in the Theory of International Relations*, London: Macmillan.

(1990c), 'The Problem of Community in International Relations' *Alternatives: Social Transformation and Humane Governance* 15: 135–53.

(1992a), 'The Question of the Next Stage in International Relations Theory: A Critical Theoretical Point of View', *Millennium: Journal of International Studies* 21: 77– 98.

(1992b), 'What is a Good International Citizen?', in Keal (ed.), *Ethics and Foreign Policy*, London: Allen and Unwin, pp. 21–43.

(1996a), 'The Achievements of Critical Theory' in Smith, Booth and Zalewski (eds.), *International Theory: Positivism and Beyond*, Cambridge University Press, pp. 279–98.

(1996b), 'Citizenship and Sovereignty in the Post-Westphalian State', *European Journal of International Relations* 2: 77–103.

(1996c), 'Community', in Danchev (ed.), *Fin de Siecle: The Meaning of the Twentieth Century*, London: I. B. Tauris, pp. 177–97.

(1996d), 'Hegel, the State and International Relations', in Clark and Neumann (eds.), *Classical Theories of International Relations*, London: Macmillan, pp. 193–209.

(1998), *The Transformation of Political Community*, Cambridge: Polity Press.

Lovibond, Sabina (1983), *Realism and Imagination in Ethics*, Oxford: Basil Blackwell.

(1992), 'Feminism and Pragmatism: A Reply to Richard Rorty', *New Left Review* 193: 56–74.

Luban, David (1985), 'Just War and Human Rights' and 'The Romance of the Nation-State', in Beitz *et al.* (eds.), *International Ethics*, Princeton, NJ: Princeton University Press, pp. 195–216 and 238– 243.

MacIntyre, Alasdair (1981), *After Virtue*, London: Duckworth Press.

(1988), *Whose Justice? Which Rationality?*, London: Duckworth Press.

Margolis, Joseph (1977), 'The Relevance of Dewey's Epistemology' in Cahn (ed.), *New Studies in the Philosophy of John Dewey*, The University Press of New England, pp. 117–48.

Martin, Biddy (1982), 'Feminism, Criticism and Foucault', *New German Critique*, 27: 3–30.

Miller, David (1988), 'The Ethical Significance of Nationality', *Ethics* 98: 647–62.

(1994), 'The Nation-State: a Modest Defence', in Brown (ed.), *Political Restructuring in Europe: Ethical Perspectives*, London: Routledge, pp. 137–62.

Miller, Marjorie C. (1992), 'Feminism and Pragmatism: On the Arrival of a "Ministry of Disturbance; a Regulated Source of Annoyance; a Destroyer of Routine; an Underminer of Complacency"', *The Monist* 75: 445–57.

Morganthau, Hans (1954) (2nd ed.), *Politics Among Nations: The Struggle for Power and Peace*, New York: Alfred Knopf.

Mouffe, Chantal (1993), *The Return of the Political*, London: Verso.

(1996), 'Deconstruction, Pragmatism and the Politics of Democracy' in Mouffe (ed.), *Deconstruction and Pragmatism*, London: Routledge, pp. 1–12.

Moussa, Mario (1991), 'Misunderstanding the Democratic "We": Richard Rorty's Liberalism and the Radical Urge for a Philosophical Foundation', *Philosophy and Social Criticism* 17: 297–312.

Mulhall, Stephen and Swift, Adam (1992), *Liberals and Communitarians*, Oxford: Blackwell.

Murray, Alastair (1996), 'The Moral Politics of Hans Morganthau', *The Review of Politics* 58: 81–107.

Nardin, Terry (1983), *Law, Morality, and the Relations of States*, Princeton, NJ: Princeton University Press.

Neal, Patrick and Paris, David (1990), 'Liberalism and the Communitarian Critique: A Guide for the Perplexed', *Canadian Journal of Political Science* 23: 419–39.

Neufeld, Mark (1995), *The Restructuring of International Relations Theory*, Cambridge: Cambridge University Press.

Nicholson, Linda (1990), *Feminism/Postmodernism*, London: Routledge.

Okin, Susan Moller (1989), *Justice, Gender and the Family*, New York: Basic Books.

O'Neill, Onora (1986), *Faces of Hunger: An Essay on Poverty, Justice and Development*, London: Allen and Unwin.

(1990), 'Justice, Gender and International Boundaries', *British Journal of Political Science* 20: 439–59.

(1994), 'Justice and Boundaries' in Brown (ed.), *Political Restructuring in Europe: Ethical Perspectives*, London: Routledge, pp. 69–88.

Pateman, Carole (1988), *The Sexual Contract*, Cambridge: Polity Press.

Peirce, C. S. (1958a), *The Collected Papers of Charles Sanders Peirce, Vol. 5*, A. W. Burkes (ed.), Cambridge, MA: Harvard University Press.

(1958b), *The Collected Papers of Charles Sanders Peirce, Vol. 8*, A. W. Burkes (ed.), Cambridge, MA: Harvard University Press.

Phillips, Anne (1991), *Engendering Democracy*, Cambridge: Polity Press.

Pogge, Thomas (1989), *Realizing Rawls*, Cornell: Cornell University Press.

Proops, Anya (1996), 'Habermas, Discourse Ethics and Liberal International Society', University of London, Ph. D. Thesis.

Raphael, D. D. (1970), *Problems of Political Philosophy*, London: Macmillan.

Rawls, John (1971), *A Theory of Justice*, London: Belknap Press.

(1980), 'Kantian Constructivism in Moral Theory', *Journal of Philosophy*, 77: 515–72.

(1987), 'The Idea of an Overlapping Consensus', *Oxford Journal of Legal Studies* 7: 1–25.

(1989), 'The Domain of the Political and Overlapping Consensus', *New York University Law Review* 64: 233–55.

(1993a), 'The Law of the Peoples', in Shute and Hurley, (eds.), *On Human Rights*, New York: Basic Books, pp. 41–82.

(1993b), *Political Liberalism*, New York: Columbia University Press.

Rengger, N. J. (1992), 'A City Which Sustains all Things? Communitarianism and International Society', *Millennium: Journal of International Studies* 21: 353–70.

(1995), *Political Theory, Modernity and Post-Modernity: Beyond Enlightenment and Critique*, Oxford: Blackwell.

Robinson, Fiona (1996), 'Rethinking Ethics in an Era of Globalization', *Sussex Papers in International Relations*, No. 2, International Relations and Politics Subject Group.

(1997), 'Globalizing Care: Ethics, Feminist Theory, and International Relations', *Alternatives* 22: 113–133.

Rooney, Phyllis (1993), 'Feminist-Pragmatist Revisionings of Reason, Knowledge and Philosophy', *Hypatia: A Journal of Feminist Philosophy* 8: 15–37.

Rorty, Richard (1980), *Philosophy and the Mirror of Nature*, Oxford: Basil Blackwell.

(1982), *Consequences of Pragmatism*, University of Minnesota Press.

(1983a), 'Postmodernist Bourgeois Liberalism', *Journal of Philosophy* 80: 583–89.

(1983b), 'What are Philosophers For?' *Center Magazine* Sept/Oct: 40–51.

(1985a), 'Comments on Sleeper and Edel', *Transactions of the C. S. Peirce Society* 21: 39–48.

(1985b), 'Solidarity or Objectivity?', in Rajchman and West (eds.), *Post-Analytic Philosophy*, New York: Columbia University Press, pp. 3–19.

(1986a), 'Introduction', in Boydston (ed.), *John Dewey: The Later Works, 1925– (1953), Vol. 8: 1933*, Southern Illinois University Press, pp. ix–xviii.

(1986b), 'On Ethnocentrism: A Reply to Clifford Geertz', *Michigan Quarterly Review* 25: 525–34.

(1987), 'Thugs and Theorists: A Reply to Bernstein', *Political Theory* 15: 564–80.

(1989a), *Contingency, Irony, and Solidarity*, Cambridge: Cambridge University Press.

(1989b), Interview by Danny Postel, 'A Post-Philosophical Politics?', *Philosophy and Social Criticism* 15: 199–204.

(1990a), 'The Priority of Democracy to Philosophy', in Malachowski (ed.), *Reading Rorty*, Oxford: Basil Blackwell, pp. 279–302.

(1990b), 'Truth and Freedom: A Reply to Thomas McCarthy', *Critical Inquiry* 16: 633–43.

(1991a), 'Feminism and Pragmatism', *Michigan Quarterly Review* 30: 231–58.

(1991b), *Objectivity, Relativism, and Truth: Philosophical Papers, Volume I*, Cambridge: Cambridge University Press.

(1992a), 'A Pragmatist View of Rationality and Cultural Difference' *Philosophy East and West* 42: 581–96.

(1992b), 'Trotsky and the Wild Orchids', *Common Knowledge* 1: 140–53.

(1993a), 'Feminism, Ideology, and Deconstruction: A Pragmatist View' *Hypatia: A Journal of Feminist Philosophy* 8: 96–103.

(1993b), 'Human Rights, Rationality, and Sentimentality', in Shute and Hurley (eds.), *On Human Rights: The Oxford Amnesty Lectures*, New York: Basic Books, pp. 112–34.

References

Rosenberg, Justin. (1994), 'The International Imagination: IR Theory and Classic Social Analysis.' *Millennium: Journal of International Studies* 23:1, 85–108.

Rosenblum, Nancy (1984), 'Moral Membership in a Postliberal State', *World Politics* 36: 581–96.

Sandel, Michael (1982), *Liberalism and the Limits of Justice*, Cambridge: Cambridge University Press.

Sayers, Sean (1987), 'The Actual and the Rational', Lamb (ed.), *Hegel and Modern Philosophy*, London: Croom Helm, pp. 143–60.

Seigfried, Charlene Haddock (1991), 'Where Are All the Pragmatist Feminists?', *Hypatia: A Journal of Feminist Philosophy* 6: 1–19.

Shapiro, Michael (1992), *Reading the Post-Modern Polity*, Minneapolis, MN: University of Minnesota Press.

Shusterman, Richard (1994), 'Pragmatism and Liberalism Between Dewey and Rorty', *Political Theory* 22: 391–413.

Sleeper, R. W. (1985), 'Rorty's Pragmatism: Afloat in Neurath's Boat', *Transactions of the C. S. Peirce Society* 21: 9–20.

Smiley, Marion (1990), 'Pragmatic Inquiry and Social Conflict: A Critical Reconstruction of Dewey's Model of Democracy', *Praxis* 9: 365–80.

Smith, John (1992), *America's Philosophical Vision*, Chicago: University of Chicago Press.

Smith, Steve (1992), 'The Forty Years Detour: The Resurgence of Normative Theory in International Relations, *Millennium: Journal of International Studies* 21: 489–506.

Smith, Steven (1989), *Hegel's Critique of Liberalism: Rights in Context*, Chicago: University of Chicago Press.

Sylvester, Christine (1994), *Feminist Theory and International Relations in a Postmodern Era*, Cambridge: Cambridge University Press.

Tamir, Yael (1993), *Liberal Nationalism*, Princeton: Princeton University Press.

Taylor, Charles (1985a), 'The Nature and the Scope of Distributive Justice', *Philosophy and the Human Sciences: Philosophical Papers, Vol. II*, Cambridge: Cambridge University Press, pp. 289–317.

(1985b), 'Self-Interpreting Animals', *Human Agency and Language: Philosophical Papers, Vol. I*, Cambridge: Cambridge University Press, pp. 45–76.

(1990), *Sources of the Self*, Cambridge, MA: Harvard University Press.

Thayer, H. S. (1952), *The Logic of Pragmatism*, London: Routledge and Kegan Paul.

(1981), *Meaning and Action: a Critical History of Pragmatism*, Hackett.

Thompson, Janna (1992), *Justice and World Order: A Philosophical Inquiry*, London: Routledge.

Toews, J. E. (1980), *Hegelianism: The Path Towards Dialectical Humanism: 1805–1841*, Cambridge: Cambridge University Press.

Tong, Rosemarie (1989), *Feminist Thought*, Westview.

Tuang, Nancy and Tong, Rosemarie (eds.) (1995), *Feminism and Philosophy: Essential Readings in Theory, Reinterpretation and Application*, Boulder, CO: Westview.

Vincent, R. J. (1986), *Human Rights and International Relations*, Cambridge: Cambridge University Press.

Walker, R. B. J. (1988), *One World, Many Worlds: Struggles for a Just World Peace*, Boulder, CO: Lynne Rienner.

(1993), *Inside/Outside: International Relations as Political Theory*, Cambridge: Cambridge University Press.

(1994), 'Norms in a Teacup: Surveying the "New Normative Approaches"', *Mershon International Studies Review*, 38: 265–70.

Walzer, Michael (1977), *Just and Unjust Wars*, New York: Basic Books.

(1981), 'Philosophy and Democracy', *Political Theory* 9: 379–99.

(1983a), 'Objectivity and Social Meaning', in Nussbaum and Sen (eds.), *The Quality of Life*, Oxford: Clarendon Press, pp. 165–84.

(1983b), *Spheres of Justice*, New York: Basic Books.

(1984), 'Liberalism and the Art of Separation', *Political Theory* 12: 315–30.

(1985), 'The Moral Standing of States', in Beitz et. al. (eds.), *International Ethics*, Princeton University Press, pp. 217–37.

(1987), *Interpretation and SocialCriticism*, Cambridge, MA: Harvard University Press.

(1988), *The Company of Critics*, New York: Basic Books.

(1990a), 'The Communtiarian Critique of Liberalism', *Political Theory*, 18: 6–23.

(1990b), 'Nation and Universe', *The Tanner Lectures on Human Values XI*, Utah: Utah University Press, pp. 507–56.

(1994a), 'Multiculturalism and Individualism', *Dissent*, 41: 185–91.

(1994b), *Thick and Thin: Moral Argument at Home and Abroad*, New York: University of Notre Dame Press.

Warner, Daniel (1996), 'Levinas, Buber and the Concept of Otherness in International Relations: A Reply to David Campbell', *Millennium: Journal of Internaitonal Studies* 25: 111–28.

Wasserstrom, Richard (1978), 'Book Review: *Just and Unjust Wars*', *Harvard Law Review* 92: 536–45.

Weber, Cynthia (1995), *Simulating Sovereignty: Intervention, the State and Symbolic Exchange*, Cambridge: Cambridge University Press.

Weislogel, Eric (1990), 'The Irony of Richard Rorty and the Question of Political Judgement', *Philosophy Today* 34: 303–11.

West, Cornel (1987), 'Race and Social Theory: Towards a Genealogical Materialist Analysis' in Davies *et.al.* (eds.), *American Left Year Book 2*, London: Verso, pp. 74–90.

(1988), *Prophetic Fragments*, Africa World Press.

(1989), *The American Evasion of Philosophy: A Genealogy of Pragmatism*, University of Wisconsin Press.

(1993a), *Beyond Ethnocentrism and Multiculturalism*, London: Courage Press.

(1993b), *Race Matters*, Boston, MA: Beacon Press.

(1994), *Keeping Faith*, London: Routledge.

References

Westbook, Robert (1991) *John Dewey and American Democracy*, Ithaca, NY: Cornell University Press.

Wheeler, N. J. (1992), 'Pluralist and Solidarist Conceptions of International Society: Bull and Vincent on Humanitarian Intervention', *Millennium: Journal of International Studies* 21: 463–87.

Wight, Martin (1966), 'Why is There No International Theory?', in Butterfield and Wight (eds.), *Diplomatic Investigations: Essays on International Politics*, London: George Allen and Unwin, pp. 17–34.

292

Index

Alexander, Thomas, 207–09, 207n.22
American pragmatism, 118, 144, 156, 174
anarchy problematique, 124, 126
anchor analogy, 15, 49–50, 75, 106–07, 110,
 114, 168–69
antifoundationalism, 196, 121–43, 144–67,
 167–70, 174, 175, 195, 196, 205, 274,
 276
 Foucauldian, 139, 168
 quasi, 247
Ashley, Richard, 121–43, 123n.3
authentic critique, 190, 192, 196, 200, 201,
 244, 246, 247, 255, 256, 255–60, 271,
 277

Barrett, Michèle and Phillips, Anne, 215,
 215n.4, 217n.5
Barry, Brian, 22n.1, 40, 226
Beitz, Charles, 21–51, 54, 79n.3, 85n.6, 226,
 275
Bellamy, Richard, 29, 29n.8
Bernstein, Richard, 145, 149n.5, 151n.6,
 159, 166, 174–75, 183, 195, 196n.17,
 208n.24
Bickford, Susan, 235, 238–39, 244n.26, 245
Brodsky, Gary, 192
Brown, Chris, 7–8, 13, 78, 87, 106n.16, 145,
 164n.16, 173–74, 250n.2
Bull, Hedley, 2n.3

Campbell, David, 137, 137n.10, 137n.11,
 140, 141, 142n.14
Caney, Simon, 10
Carens, Joseph, 54
citizenship, 91, 93, 95, 99, 112, 115, 278
communitarianism, 47, 49, 52–77, 128,
 129, 130, 131, 136, 152, 152n.7, 154,
 155, 157, 168, 194, 210, 213, 221,

222–23, 223n.12, 223n.13, 224, 225,
 226, 227, 228, 229, 233, 238, 273,
 275
 communitarian critique in political
 theory, 9, 28–29, 30, 33–34, 81,
 222–24
 nation-based, 53
 state-based, two kinds of, 53, 86:
 ethical, 53, 86; instrumentalist, 53,
 59–62, 86
concept of the person, 11, 45, 46–47,
 55–59, 66, 74, 80–85, 128–29, 151–53,
 167, 183n.5, 189–90
Connolly, William, 121–43, 123n.3, 149n.5,
 169n.21, 276
contract theory, 197n.18, 222
cosmopolitan/communitarian debate
 definition, 7–8
 and feminism, 220–30
 and the liberal/communitarian debate,
 10–11, 12, 13n.8, 227
 three central issues, 11–13, 46–50, 118,
 122, 146, 167, 173, 273
cosmpolitanism, 21–51, 52–53, 54, 56, 59,
 60n.2, 75, 84n.6, 88, 92, 94, 128, 129,
 130, 136, 154, 155, 168, 194, 210, 213,
 221, 225, 226, 227, 228, 229, 273, 275
 thick, 16, 96, 111
 thin, 14, 16, 96–97, 111
critical inquiry, 183–84, 194, 197, 201, 244,
 245, 251, 252, 254
critical intelligence, 183, 196, 202, 205, 211,
 251, 252n.3, 259, 279

Davidson, Donald, 147n.2, 149
democratic ideal, 247–48, 255, 262, 267,
 271
Derrida, Jacques, 121

Dewey, John, 162n.12, 166n.20, 170, 173–211, 212, 231, 233–34, 239, 240–45, 249–56, 267–72
discourse ethics
    of Habermas, 114n.9, 248, 259–62, 263–67, 278
    of Linklater, 91

epistemologically centred philosophy, 15, 18, 156, 157, 158, 159, 182, 185n.9, 194, 203, 205, 206, 210, 231, 273
epistemology, 15, 17, 51, 95n.8, 110, 113–14, 118, 134, 147, 178, 184–5, 185n.8, 189, 203, 215, 218–19, 223–24, 226, 227, 229–30, 231, 273, 274, 280
    weak foundationalist, 15–16, 75, 110, 114, 115, 118, 16, 138, 140, 143, 169, 195, 205, 206
    strong foundationalist, 15–16, 49, 51, 75, 107–08, 110, 118, 134, 136, 138, 168
ethics of coexistence, 2, 225, 226
ethics of marginal conduct, 133–34

fallibilism, 166, 203, 204, 206–07, 208, 210, 241, 252, 263, 280
feminism, 96, 212–45, 258, 262, 272
    postmodern, 217, 219
Festenstein, Matthew, 183, 183n.5, 184, 249n.1, 250, 251
Foucault, Michel, 96, 121, 123, 132, 138, 148, 148n.4, 187n.12
foundationalism, 15, 130, 144, 145, 153, 159, 167–68, 169n.21, 170, 184, 187, 189, 194, 195, 274, 278
    of human rights, 160–61
    see also epistemologically centred philosophy
Fraser, Nancy, 149n.5, 151n.6, 164n.15, 164n.17, 213n.1, 220n.7, 232n.18, 235, 236n.19, 236, 238, 238n.21, 240–41, 242, 243, 248, 258n.6, 262n.8, 262–70
Frazer, Elizabeth and Lacey, Nicola, 214–20, 221n.10, 221–24, 230n.17, 235, 236
Friedman, Marilyn, 222, 223, 224n.14, 229
Fritzman, T. M., 238, 241n.23
Frost, Mervyn, 4–5, 6, 7, 53, 78–117, 194n.16, 221, 227, 257, 275, 276
Frye, Marilyn, 234, 235
Fukuyama, Francis, 145

George, Jim, 127, 137–38, 137n.11, 141
growth, 177, 180, 182, 183–84, 189, 190, 191, 192, 194, 195, 196, 198, 202, 206, 207, 242, 245, 249, 250, 251, 255, 279

Haber, Honi, 164n.17
Habermas, Jürgen, 96, 114, 187n.12, 248, 255, 259, 260, 261, 262–66, 267
Hegel, G. F. W., 8, 15, 80, 82, 82n.4, 84, 85, 92, 94, 97, 98, 101, 103, 103n.13, 105–07, 108, 110, 110n.18, 113, 200, 201, 276
Hegelian method, 79, 85, 97–107, 107–08, 117, 200, 201–02, 209, 276
    critique of Kant, 95
    Hegelian concept of the person, 84, 84n.7, 85, 184, 250
    Right/Left split, 98–99, 98n.9, 102, 102n.11, 106, 106n.16, 113, 200
Hekman, Susan, 220n.7, 221n.10, 222, 223n.13, 223–24, 224n.14, 228, 235
Hickman, Larry, 196
Honneth, Axel, 268
human rights, 146, 160–67
    human rights culture, 160, 161, 162, 165
Hutchings, Kimberly, 221n.9, 224–30

immanent critique, 200–01, 202, 257, 276
international society, 2
intervention, 68–69, 252–54

Kant, Immanuel, 8, 15, 21–51, 95
    categorical imperative, 15, 95
Kantian conundrum, 39, 40, 50
Kaufman-Osborn, Timothy, 235, 237
Kuhn, Thomas, 187, 196, 200, 209
Kukathas, Chandran and Pettit, Philip, 23, 29–30, 34, 37, 44, 46

Leland, Dorothy, 235, 236–37, 239
Levinas, Emmanuel, 137, 137n.11, 140n.13, 140
liberal/communitarian debate, 8–10, 22, 28, 52, 53, 57, 61n.3, 74, 80, 128, 144, 151–59, 227–28, 280
    feminist interpretation of, 221–24
liberal irony, 149–51, 153, 164, 168, 189, 195
liberalism, 144, 145, 148, 148n.4, 149n.5, 162, 222, 222n.11, 264
Linklater, Andrew, 2n.3, 3–4, 5–6, 7, 14, 15, 16, 78–117, 221, 253, 257, 275, 276, 277–79
Lovibond, Sabina, 220n.7, 235, 237–38, 258n.6

MacKinnon, Catherine, 232, 234
Margolis, Joseph, 179, 184, 185n.8
Martin, Biddy, 244, 244n.26
Marx, Karl, 8, 82, 116

moral imagination, 201, 202, 207–09, 211, 245, 247–48, 256, 257, 258, 260, 261, 262, 266, 271, 276, 279, 280
moral inclusion, 4, 7, 24, 90–91, 103, 116, 142, 169, 170, 174, 189, 204, 206, 211, 212, 215, 221, 225, 231, 232, 245, 246, 248, 254–55, 256, 258, 272, 273, 275, 280
moral maximalism, 65–66, 69, 70, 72
moral minimalism, 65–73, 75, 78, 275
moral standing of states, 12, 14, 47–48, 59–62, 66, 74–5, 86–94, 120–30, 153–56, 227, 273
Morganthau, Hans, 1–2
Mouffe, Chantal, 220n.8, 221n.10, 276–77
Moussa, Mario, 164n.16
Mulhall, Stephen and Swift, Adam, 9, 29, 29n.8, 37, 38, 39

Nardin, Terry, 2n.3, 225
neo-pragmatism, 144–70, 176, 189, 199, 231
Nietzsche, Friedrich, 132, 147n.2

Okin, Susan Moller, 220n.8, 221n.10
ontology, 14, 17–18, 123, 128–29, 133, 134, 136, 142, 167–68, 170, 189, 195, 203, 210, 219, 223n.12, 226
strong, 184, 255
weak, 195, 204, 249, 250–52, 255

Pateman, Carole, 220n.8, 221n.10
Peirce, C. S., 173, 174, 192
Phillips, Anne, 220n.8, 221n.10
Pogge, Thomas, 21–51, 54, 79n.3, 84n.6, 275
poststructuralism, 118, 121–43, 167–70, 206, 276, 277
pragmatic critique, 170, 174, 182, 193–94, 202, 204–11, 212–14, 231, 232, 239, 240–45, 246–56, 261, 272, 274–80
private sphere, 170, 189, 191, 192–93, 198, 199, 202, 209, 236, 265, 267–68
public/private split, 151, 162–65, 166n.20,

170, 188n.13, 190, 191, 193, 195, 196n.17, 197, 198, 199, 200, 208, 209, 222, 236, 244, 277
public sphere, 151, 190, 191, 198, 199, 209, 236, 236n.19, 248, 256, 262–66, 267–68, 269, 271, 277
international, 248, 269–72, 279

Rabossi, Edwardo, 160
radical autonomy, 138–39, 140, 142, 168
Rawls, John, 9, 21–51, 79n.3, 100, 166n.19
reflective equilibrium, 100, 166, 166n.19
relativism, 64, 131, 157n.10, 158, 194–95, 219
cultural, 160
Robinson, Fiona, 221n.9, 224–30
Rorty, Richard, 144–70, 173–211, 212, 213, 220, 231, 232n.18, 232–35, 235–39, 240–45, 250, 255, 256, 257, 265n.10, 277

scientific method, 183, 187, 195
Seigfried, Charlene Haddock, 230–31, 240
Shklar, Judith, 149
Shusterman, Richard, 190–91, 198–99
Smith, John, 184
Smith, Steve, 145
Smith, Steven, 200
Sylvester, Christine, 220n.7, 241n.24

Thayer, H. S., 176, 179, 184
Thompson, Janna, 8, 13, 53, 78

universal versus particular, 12–13, 48–50, 62–66, 73, 75–76, 94–97, 130–31, 156–59, 273

Vincent, R. J., 2n.3

Walker, R. B. J., 121–43, 123n.3, 276
Walzer, Michael, 8, 9, 52–77, 79n.3, 86, 157n.10, 213n.2, 220, 227, 275
Warner, Daniel, 137n.10
West, Cornel, 183, 184n.8, 208n.24, 212

CAMBRIDGE STUDIES IN INTERNATIONAL RELATIONS

56 *N. Piers Ludlow*
Dealing with Britain
The Six and the first UK application to the EEC

55 *Andreas Hasenclever, Peter Mayer and Volker Rittberger*
Theories of international regimes

54 *Miranda A. Schreurs and Elizabeth C. Economy (eds.)*
The internationalization of environmental protection

53 *James N. Rosenau*
Along the domestic–foreign frontier
Exploring governance in a turbulent world

52 *John M. Hobson*
The wealth of states
A comparative sociology of international economic and political change

51 *Kalevi J. Holsti*
The state, war, and the state of war

50 *Christopher Clapham*
Africa and the international system
The politics of state survival

49 *Susan Strange*
The retreat of the state
The diffusion of power in the world economy

48 *William I. Robinson*
Promoting polyarchy
Globalization, US intervention, and hegemony

47 *Rober Spegele*
Political realism in international theory

46 *Thomas J. Biersteker and Cynthia Weber (eds.)*
State sovereignty as social construct

45 *Mervyn Frost*
Ethics in international relations
A constitutive theory

44 *Mark W. Zacher with Brent A. Sutton*
    Governing global networks
    International regimes for transportation and communications

43 *Mark Neufeld*
    The restructuring of international relations theory

42 *Thomas Risse-Kappen (ed.)*
    Bringing transnational relations back in
    Non-state actors, domestic structures and international
    institutions

41 *Hayward R. Alker*
    Rediscoveries and reformulations
    Humanistic methodologies for international studies

40 *Robert W. Cox with Timothy J. Sinclair*
    Approaches to world order

39 *Jens Bartelson*
    A genealogy of sovereignty

38 *Mark Rupert*
    Producing hegemony
    The politics of mass production and American global power

37 *Cynthia Weber*
    Simulating sovereignty
    Intervention, the state and symbolic exchange

36 *Gary Goertz*
    Contexts of international politics

35 *James L. Richardson*
    Crisis diplomacy
    The Great Powers since the mid-nineteenth century

34 *Bradley S. Klein*
    Strategic studies and world order
    The global politics of deterrence

33 *T. V. Paul*
    Asymmetric conflicts: war initiation by weaker powers

32 *Christine Sylvester*
    Feminist theory and international relations in a postmodern era

31 *Peter J. Schraeder*
    US foreign policy toward Africa
    Incrementalism, crisis and change

30 *Graham Spinardi*
    From Polaris to Trident: the development of US Fleet Ballistic Missile technology

29 *David A. Welch*
    Justice and the genesis of war

28 *Russell J. Leng*
    Interstate crisis behavior, 1816–1980: realism versus reciprocity

27 *John A. Vasquez*
    The war puzzle

26 *Stephen Gill (ed.)*
    Gramsci, historical materialism and international relations

25 *Mike Bowker and Robin Brown (eds.)*
    From Cold War to collapse: theory and world politics in the 1980s

24 *R. B. J. Walker*
    Inside/outside: international relations as political theory

23 *Edward Reiss*
    The Strategic Defence Initiative

22 *Keith Krause*
    Arms and the state: patterns of military production and trade

21 *Roger Buckley*
    US–Japan alliance diplomacy 1945–1990

20 *James N. Rosenau and Ernst-Otto Czempiel (eds.)*
    Governance without government: order and change in world politics

19 *Michael Nicholson*
    Rationality and the analysis of international conflict

18 *John Stopford and Susan Strange*
    Rival states, rival firms
    Competition for world market shares

17 *Terry Nardin and David R. Mapel (eds.)*
    Traditions of international ethics

16 *Charles F. Doran*
    Systems in crisis
    New imperatives of high politics at century's end

15 *Deon Geldenhuys*
    Isolated states: a comparative analysis

14 *Kalevi J. Holsti*
    Peace and war: armed conflicts and international order 1648–1989

13   *Saki Dockrill*
      Britain's policy for West German rearmament 1950–1955

12   *Robert H. Jackson*
      Quasi-states: sovereignty, international relations and the Third World

11   *James Barber and John Barratt*
      South Africa's foreign policy
      The search for status and security 1945–1988

10   *James Mayall*
      Nationalism and international society

 9   *William Bloom*
      Personal identity, national identity and international relations

 8   *Zeev Maoz*
      National choices and international processes

 7   *Ian Clark*
      The hierarchy of states
      Reform and resistance in the international order

 6   *Hidemi Suganami*
      The domestic analogy and world order proposals

 5   *Stephen Gill*
      American hegemony and the Trilateral Commission

 4   *Michael C. Pugh*
      The ANZUS crisis, nuclear visiting and deterrence

 3   *Michael Nicholson*
      Formal theories in international relations

 2   *Friedrich V. Kratochwil*
      Rules, norms, and decisions
      On the conditions of practical and legal reasoning in international relations and domestic affairs

 1   *Myles L. C. Robertson*
      Soviet policy towards Japan
      An analysis of trends in the 1970s and 1980s